LSTC: DECADE OF DECISION

A HISTORY OF THE MERGER OF THE LUTHERAN SCHOOL OF THEOLOGY AT CHICAGO WITH SPECIAL EMPHASIS ON THE DECADE 1958-1968

Harold Clayton Skillrud

Lutheran School of Theology at Chicago
Chicago, Illinois
1969

McKnight and McKnight
Bloomington, Illinois

Copyright © 1969
by Harold Clayton Skillrud

Library of Congress Catalog Number: 78-94887

Skillrud, Harold Clayton
    LSTC: Decade of Decision A History of the Lutheran School of Theology at
    Chicago with Special Emphasis On the Decade 1958-68
Bloomington, Illinois Lutheran School of Theology at Chicago 1969

7-4-69

IN APPRECIATION
TO
AID ASSOCIATION FOR LUTHERANS
APPLETON, WISCONSIN
WHOSE INTEREST AND GENEROSITY
MADE POSSIBLE THE PUBLICATION AND
DISTRIBUTION OF THIS VOLUME

To my wife, Lois,
and Dr. and Mrs. C.W. Sorensen
this volume is gratefully dedicated

TABLE OF CONTENTS

PREFACE

This is a history of the development of the Lutheran School of Theology at Chicago. It is the author's contention that the decision to locate this school in a university-urban setting was informed by an educational ideal transmitted to America by the Lutherans who founded seminaries in their new homeland during the last century. Accustomed to a university oriented theological education in their European homelands, these pioneers were concerned that theology continue to be related to all other academic disciplines and relevant to all facets of culture and society. This is evident in the approach to theological education in these young American Lutheran seminaries. However, the educational ideal was never fully achieved by seminaries located on the campuses of church liberal arts colleges or on isolated sites away from other academic institutions.

That which could not be achieved, solely as the result of this educational ideal, became possible because of economic and practical considerations. The merger of four Lutheran bodies to form the Lutheran Church in America in 1962, placed seven theological seminaries in the greater midwest area under the control of one Church. All could not successfully compete for students, faculty, and funds on a territory so limited. Anticipating this, four of these seminaries voluntarily entered into merger negotiations which eventuated in the formation of the Lutheran School of Theology at Chicago in September, 1962. A fifth school participated in the merger at a later date. The other two schools continued their separate existences.

The seminary merger provided the opportunity for a relocation to a new campus. That a site was chosen immediately adjacent to a great university in the heart of an urban area was due to the educational ideal which had informed Lutheran theological education in America for the past century, combined with the resources made available through merger. Both were essential to the task. Without either it could not have been achieved.

This volume traces this educational ideal and its influence upon the development of the Lutheran School of Theology at Chicago and its predecessor schools.

Harold C. Skillrud
Bloomington, Illinois
December 1968

ACKNOWLEDGEMENTS

The writer acknowledges with appreciation the vast number of persons who have contributed to this historical study. The opportunity to participate in the development of a recent portion of this history came to the writer as the result of being elected to a term on the Board of Directors of the former Augustana Theological Seminary, and two terms on the Board of Directors of the Lutheran School of Theology at Chicago; gratitude is hereby expressed to the Church for the privilege of being elected to this service. Freedom from parish responsibilities to serve on these boards and to attend summer school, and the granting of a leave of absence to write this thesis were the generous contributions of the writer's congregation, St. John's Lutheran Church of Bloomington, Illinois. The additional duties assumed during this time by Rev. Donald H. Fagerberg, Assistant Pastor of St. John's, is gratefully acknowledged. To the members of Moses Montefiore Temple of Bloomington, Illinois, the writer expresses thanks for the use of a study room which provided the necessary quiet and freedom from interruption during the research and writing of the manuscript.

The writer is indebted to the faculty and staff of the Lutheran School of Theology, especially former Dean of Graduate Studies, Dr. Johannes Knudsen, and his advisor, Dr. G. Everett Arden, Acting Director of Graduate Studies and Professor of Church History, whose guidance and counsel have been invaluable. The complete cooperation of the LSTC Library and Archives Staff was granted, and grateful acknowledgment is here tendered to Rev. Joel W. Lundeen, Director of Library.

Since most of this study is concerned with the decade 1958-68, the writer has depended upon many of those who were involved in this history for their recollection and interpretation of these events. To the following who wrote letters supplying such information the writer conveys his appreciation: Dr. O. V. Anderson, Dr. G. Everett Arden, Dr. Arthur O. Arnold, Dr. E. Theodore Bachmann, Rev. William J. Boldt, Dr. Jerald Brauer, Dr. Theodore Conrad, Dr. Earl Erb, Rev. Donald Flatt, Dr. Gerhard Gieschen, Rev. Lyman Grimes, Dr. Donald Heiges, Dr. Stewart Herman, Mr. James M. Kating, Rev. Axel Kildegaard, Dr. Lawrence A. Kimpton, Dr. Johannes Knudsen, Dr. Walter Kukkonen, Dr. L. Dale Lund, Rev. Joel Lundeen, Dr. Frank Madsen, Dr. Theodore E. Matson, Dr. Robert Mortvedt, Rev. Russell Olson, Dr. John Rilling, Rev. Walter E. Rowoldt, Dr. E. Rudolph Walborn, Dr. Granger Westberg, Dr. Walter Wick, and Mr. Frank Zimmerman. The writer is especially grateful to the following who granted personal interviews: Dr. O. V. Anderson, Dr. G. Everett Arden, Dr. Arthur O. Arnold, Dr. E. Theodore Bachmann, Dr. Jerald Brauer, Dr. Theodore Conrad, Rev. Donald Elder, Dr. Robert Fischer, Rev. Donald Flatt, Dr. Donald Heiges, Dr. Arlan Helgeson, Dr. Stewart Herman, Dr. T. A. Kantonen, Rev. Axel Kildegaard, Dr. Johannes Knudsen, Dr. Walter Kukkonen, Dr. L. Dale Lund, Rev. Joel Lundeen, Dr. Theodore E. Matson, Rev. Russell Olson, Dr. W. Carl

Satre, Dr. Joseph Sittler, Dr. Armin G. Weng (deceased), Dr. Granger Westberg, Dr. Walter Wick, Dr. Clemens H. Zeidler, and Mr. Frank Zimmerman.

It was Dr. C. W. Sorensen, then Dean of the Graduate School at Illinois State University and valued member of the writer's parish, currently President of Augustana College, Rock Island, Illinois, and his wife whose encouragement led their pastor to pursue graduate studies, and thus deserve credit for providing the impetus that led to this work.

Above all, the writer expresses sincere appreciation to his wife and children whose willing understanding permitted their husband and father to take on these extra opportunities.

LIST OF TABLES

LIST OF FIGURES

LIST OF PLATES

Chapter I

INTRODUCTION

The Lutheran School of Theology at Chicago is one of nine theological seminaries of the Lutheran Church in America. Its primary object—"To prepare men for the Gospel ministry, especially in the Lutheran Church"[1]—unites it in purpose with all of the other eight schools.

Its many distinctive qualities, born of merger and relocation,[2] set it apart as unique among LCA seminaries:

1. It is the largest LCA seminary. Its 1967-68 B.D. student body of 242[3] far exceeds the average LCA seminary enrollment of 100 and is almost double the size of the student body of the next largest school.[4] Likewise the size of its full-time faculty and administration, numbering thirty-three in the 1967-68 school year, and its new campus, valued at $8,500,000 are unexcelled among LCA seminaries.

2. It is supported by the largest constituency. Nine synods of the Lutheran Church in America—Central States, Illinois, Indiana-Kentucky, Iowa, Michigan, Nebraska, Rocky Mountain, Texas-Louisiana, and Wisconsin-Upper Michigan—with a combined membership of over 500,000 active confirmed members own and support this school.[5]

3. In addition to its being the only LCA seminary produced by a consolidation of seminaries, LSTC alone embraces the theological traditions of all four Lutheran bodies which united in 1962 to form the Lutheran Church in America.[6]

---

[1]*LSTC Constitution*, Article I, Section 3, Paragraph a.

[2]The Lutheran School of Theology at Chicago is the fruit of the merger of four seminaries in 1962, and a fifth in 1967, and a relocation to its present campus adjacent to the University of Chicago in 1967, *Infra* Chapters IV, V, VI, and X.

[3]*LSTC Catalog*, 1968-69, pp. 95-105.

[4]*LCA 1968 Yearbook*, pp. 346-348.

[5]For a comparative study of the size of constituency supporting the other eight seminaries see *LCA Bulletin of Reports*, 1968, p. 497.

[6]Augustana Theological Seminary of the Augustana Lutheran Church, Central Lutheran Theological Seminary and Chicago Lutheran Theological Seminary of the United Lutheran Church in America, Grand View Theological Seminary of the American Evangelical Lutheran Church, and Suomi Theological Seminary of the Finnish Evangelical Lutheran Church of America—Suomi Synod.

4. Though some of the other seminaries possess elements of LSTC's extra-B.D. program, this seminary alone embraces all four of these academic programs: Bachelor of Divinity, Graduate Studies, the School of Missions, and Continuing Education.[7]

5. Most significantly, LSTC alone of the LCA seminaries possesses the twin benefits of being located adjacent to a major university campus, the University of Chicago, and in the heart of a major urban center, the city of Chicago.

These distinctive qualities were made possible only because of the unification of seminaries and the relocation to a new campus. The will to consolidate and relocate was made possible by the merger of the four Lutheran bodies which formed the Lutheran Church in America. The desire, however, for this kind of seminary in this kind of university—urban setting was present as long as a century ago in the minds of many who founded and fostered these five seminaries. It grew out of an educational ideal which these founding fathers brought with them from Germany and Scandinavia. This ideal, described by Dr. G. Everett Arden in its application to Swedish pioneers, could likewise be applied to the Germans, Danes, and Finns who founded these American seminaries:

> That ideal involved a conception of the Christian ministry, and indeed, of Christian life, which would take into account and be informed by the total culture of a people. It was an educational ideal which would escape the temptation, so often seen on the American frontier, of isolating religion from the total context of human existence so that it became a concern apart from the realities and perplexities of the everyday, the commonplace and the banal. It was an ideal of education which envisaged an awareness of life's wholeness in order to structure that wholeness with the redemptive power of the gospel of Jesus Christ.[8]

Historical circumstances, associated with an immigrant Church, militated against its fulfillment in the beginning. The pioneer fathers, with their paucity of funds, leadership, and church structure, simply could not reproduce in America in their generation the kind of theological school in a university-urban setting to which they were accustomed in Europe, despite their dreams and ambitions. Later generations, yet possessing the ideal and finally also possessing the economic and ecclesiastical means to achieve the goal, were content, in the main, to retain the status quo of their inheritance. A narrow parochialism—fostered by ethnic and theological isolation, ecclesiastical and regional distinctiveness, and an over-arching concern for institutional self-preservation—frustrated every effort on the part of those church leaders who had kept this ideal alive and sought to fulfill it. Only a pending union of four Lutheran bodies, which would place four

---

[7]*LSTC Catalog*, 1968-69, pp. 10-37.
[8]G. Everett Arden, *The School of the Prophets* (Rock Island, Ill.: Augustana Book Concern, 1960), p. x.

seminaries in the competitive setting of occupying the same geographic territory, was an adequate impetus to achieve this goal.

This paper will trace this educational ideal as it manifested itself in the thinking of the founding fathers of these seminaries, the numerous, unsuccessful attempts to implement this ideal as the churches grew and developed, and finally the successful efforts of the Inter-Seminary Committee which, under the pressure of pending Church merger, grappled with the problems of consolidation and relocation during the years 1958 to 1962, and eventually produced the Lutheran School of Theology at Chicago. Further, this paper will trace the developments which followed this decision, including the purchase of land; the building and funding of the new campus; the sale of the old campuses; the merger with Central Lutheran Theological Seminary of Fremont, Nebraska; the building of an administration, faculty, and student body; and the development of the academic program.

SOURCES

The major area of concentration in this paper is the decade 1958-1968. During this decade the Inter-Seminary Committee did its significant work, Suomi Seminary and Grand View Seminary relocated to the campus of Chicago Lutheran Seminary at Maywood, the Lutheran School of Theology officially came into being, the initial Board of Directors of LSTC was elected, and the new campus and program were built.

During seven of these ten years the writer was a member of the boards making and implementing these decisions. Elected to the Board of Directors of Augustana Theological Seminary at the 1961 Synod of the Augustana Lutheran Church,[9] he was elected by the board in October of that year to be one of seven Augustana representatives on the new interim board of the proposed Lutheran School of Theology at Chicago.[10] As a member of this interim board he attended the three final meetings of the Inter-Seminary Committee held November 7, 1961, January 29, 1962, and March 26, 1962. When the members of the interim Board of Directors of LSTC met February 23, 1962, to organize officially and elect officers, he was elected Chairman of the Board,[11] a position to which he was re-elected each Fall from 1962 through 1968. As Chairman, he has attended all meetings of the Board of Directors and of the Executive Committee, most meetings of the Standing Committees and special committees, including the committee which worked out merger arrangements with Central Seminary, from 1962 to 1968. In addition to calling upon his personal recollection of events during this seven year period, the writer has made a

[9]*Augustana Lutheran Church Minutes*, 1961, p. 531.
[10]Augustana Theological Seminary, *Board of Directors Minutes*, October 6-7, 1961, p. 2.
[11]Lutheran School of Theology at Chicago, *Board of Directors Minutes*, February 23, 1962, p. 2.

detailed study of the various sets of minutes of the Inter-Seminary Committee, the LSTC Board of Directors and Executive Committee, the faculty of LSTC and its predecessor schools, supporting synods and church bodies of LSTC and their predecessor schools, and the Joint Commission on Lutheran Unity. In addition he has had personal interviews and extensive correspondence with numerous persons who played major roles in this history.[12]

In reviewing the period prior to this decade, the writer has relied heavily upon minutes of boards of directors and faculties of the united seminaries and their supporting churches and synods, major works dealing with the predecessor seminaries and church bodies,[13] journals and catalogs published by the seminaries, and personal interviews and correspondence.

---

[12]See Acknowledgments, pp. viii, ix, for names of persons.

[13]Augustana Seminary: G. Everett Arden, *The School of the Prophets* and *Augustana Heritage*.

Central Seminary: Thomas D. Rinde, *After Seventy-Four Years*.

Chicago Lutheran Seminary: G. H. Gerberding, *Life and Letters of W. A. Passavant, D.D.*, and *Reminiscent Reflections*; Joel W. Lundeen, *History of the Library of the Chicago Lutheran Theological Seminary of Maywood, Illinois* (unpublished Master's dissertation); S. E. Ochsenford, *Documentary History of the General Council*; Marjory R. Weng, *Passavant's Vision*.

Grand View Seminary: Enok Mortensen, *The Danish Lutheran Church in America*.

Suomi Seminary: Henry R. Kangas, *Blades, Ears, and Corn—Suomi Synod, 1890-1962* (unpublished history of the Suomi Synod).

Chapter II

THE UNIVERSITY–URBAN SETTING

BLEST AND DEDICATE

INVITATION TO DEDICATION

The Board of Directors, Administration and Faculty
request the honour of your presence
at the Dedication of
the Lutheran School of Theology at Chicago

Sunday, the twenty-second of October
Nineteen hundred and sixty-seven
at three-thirty o'clock
in Rockefeller Chapel
of the
University of Chicago
Woodlawn Avenue at 59th Street
Chicago, Illinois

PLATE I

On October 22, 1967—four hundred fifty years after the Lutheran Reformation had begun in the courts of Wittenberg University in Saxony—Lutherans in America were dedicating a new seminary, the first on the campus of a distinguished university, in the heart of a major city. Lutheran theological education, fostered in the context of the university-urban setting throughout Europe, had come at long last to the same setting in America.

Throngs converged on the campus of the University of Chicago to witness the historic spectacle. When the carillon recital, featuring the music of Johann Sebastian Bach, began forty-five minutes before the Service of Dedication in Rockefeller Chapel, two thousand persons had already occupied every available space in the massive nave. Several hundreds more stood outside on the chapel grounds to observe the pageantry of the processional—crucifer, torch bearers, banner bearers, followed by church leaders and representatives of eighty colleges, universities, theological seminaries, and learned societies.[1] Additional hundreds remained at the campus site lining 55th Street from University Avenue to Greenwood Avenue waiting for the Rite of Dedication which would take place at the main entrance after the chapel service. Other hundreds of thousands who could not attend had listened in their home churches to a recording which contained greetings by Rev. Dr. Jerald Brauer, President of the Board of Theological Education of the Lutheran Church in America and Dean of the Divinity School of the University of Chicago, Rev. Dr. Franklin Clark Fry, President of the Lutheran Church in America, and Rev. Dr. Stewart W. Herman, President of the Lutheran School of Theology at Chicago. The record had been distributed earlier to the one thousand five hundred congregations of the nine supporting synods. Hundreds of thousands more had seen pictures and read accounts of the new seminary on the LCA bulletin cover for the day or in the October 11, 1967, issue of the *Lutheran*, while millions of others read of the event in daily newspapers in Chicago and throughout the country. The eyes of the nation focused on the Lutheran School of Theology at Chicago on the Day of Dedication, October 22, 1967.

At the Service of Dedication, the Rockefeller Chapel congregation united in Vespers conducted by Rev. John W. Arthur, seminary chaplain, and Rev. Harold C. Skillrud, board chairman. In a dramatic narrative, composed for the occasion by Rev. Dr. G. Everett Arden of the seminary faculty, the seminary's history was unfolded. While colorful banners, representing the five seminaries which merged to form the Lutheran School of Theology at Chicago, were placed in the chancel, professors from each of these traditions read historical sketches depicting the various theological heritages.[2] Representing Augustana was Dr. Arden; Maywood, Rev. Dr. H. Grady Davis; Central, Rev. Dr. Richard R. Syre; Grand View, Rev. Dr. Johannes H. V. Knudsen; and Suomi, Rev. Dr. Walter J. Kukkonen. Following a festive rendition of "A Mighty Fortress Is Our God,"

---

[1]Participants are named in the *Service of Dedication* program folder, pp. 11-18. See Appendix I.
[2]*Ibid.*, pp. 3-4.

sung alternately by the congregation and a massed choir, accompanied by both chapel organs and a brass ensemble, President Fry addressed the large assembly.[3] Taking note of the several theological traditions represented by the seminaries which merged to form the new school, Dr. Fry identified LSTC as "a living parable of that segment of the Christian church [which is] represented by the Lutheran Church [in America] with its diversity of origins and cultural identities coming together in an emerging single heritage."[4] He then focused on the urban setting of the school and observed, "Even the location of the new edifice in itself is a picture of the stance of the church. There is not the slightest suggestion of recoil or withdrawal."[5] As he spoke of LSTC's location near a university campus training personnel for the serving professions, President Fry asserted, "This means that the Christian in society must above all be humanitarian to the highest extent, with one additional power, and that is the knowledge and sense of what man needs in the inmost core of his being in order to love himself, to carry his head erect, and to find the love in himself worthy of bestowing upon his brother man."[6] Dr. Fry concluded his address with the expressed hope that the style of living stamped as an indelible imprint on all students in this new seminary would subsequently "spread into the congregations they will serve and will more and more be the mark of authentic Christianity that is needed in the days to come."[7]

At the conclusion of the service, participants and congregation, joined now by those who had not previously found room in the crowded chapel, proceeded up University Avenue to the seminary campus. The warm October sun illuminated the neighborhood where LSTC had come to carry on its work of theological education and carry out its mission as an institution of the church. Music from the carillon tower echoed about the majestic buildings of the university campus. The procession moved past the Oriental Institute, a limitless resource for the Biblical Department and the School of Missions of the new seminary. Within view were the Divinity School of the University of Chicago, Chicago Theological Seminary, and the Disciples House, while one block away was Meadville Seminary—all theological schools offering opportunity for lively dialog. Next came the site for the new multi-million dollar library of the university, soon to be under construction, within one block of the seminary campus. At the southeast corner of 55th Street and University Avenue, directly across the street from LSTC, the new Augustana Lutheran Church was under construction. As the processional turned the corner to walk the final block to the dedication site, viewers could see the Child Care Center opposite the seminary, one of many social and community agencies to which students would be related in their training and experience while readying themselves for the

---

[3]The entire address is recorded on tape and is on file in the LSTC Archives.
[4]*Hyde Park Herald* (Chicago), October 25, 1957, p. 1.
[5]Lutheran School of Theology at Chicago, *News Release*, October 22, 1967, p.2
[6]*Ibid.*, p. 3.
[7]*Illinois Lutheran* (Illinois Synod-LCA), November, 1967, p. 1.

multiplicity of ministries in the modern church. And finally, surrounding the campus on all sides were the endless rows of apartment buildings, the urban dwellers who would soon become more conscious of the seminary's presence and ministry and who represented the kind of people to whom most of the future pastors trained here would minister. Overhead modern jets streaked to Midway and O'Hare Airports, blocks away busy expressways and skyways carried the endless streams of traffic, and minutes away to the north was the Chicago loop. Into this university-urban setting had come the Lutheran School of Theology at Chicago.

The throngs now converged upon the Southwest Entrance of the seminary building for the brief Rite of Dedication. Rev. Dr. L. Dale Lund, then Dean of Faculty, conducted the responsive readings. The key to the new building was passed by Mr. James McHugh, President of the James McHugh Construction Company, general contractor, to Mr. Wilmont Vickrey, of Perkins and Will Partnership, architects, who turned it over to Rev. Dr. Robert J. Marshall, then President of the Illinois Synod-LCA and Chairman of the Building Committee, who placed it in the hand of the President Herman; he prayed:

> Almighty God, look with favor, we beseech thee, upon this building which has been erected to thy glory and for the use of thy people, and be thou pleased to grace it with thy presence, and accept it of our hands. Amen.[8]

The official act of dedication followed as President Fry declared:

> And now blest and dedicate be this Lutheran School of Theology, to the glory of Almighty God, and to the service of his Holy Church: In the Name of the Father, and of the Son, and of the Holy Ghost. Amen.[9]

The President of the Church had lived to see the fulfillment of a dream wistfully expressed almost a decade earlier:

> Wouldn't it be a wonderful thing if the church which follows the ULCA would be equipped with one or two seminaries (allowing for a reasonable geographical distribution of others) deserving recognition among the top-ranking theological institutions on this continent—in size of faculty and student body, caliber and variety of teaching, scholarly production, and facilities? Frankly that is not possible in our present diffuse pattern. Who will take the lead, leaving behind all rivalry and pride of history, in a spirit of dedication to the radiant future that we believe that God is eager to bestow on the church of our sons and grandsons?[10]

The Lutheran School of Theology had taken the lead. Lutheran theological education was near the university campus and in the heart of the city. A

[8]*Service of Dedication*, p. 9.
[9]*Ibid.*
[10]*Desk Letter* (ULCA), September, 1958, pp. NE-944-45.

"top-ranking theological institution on this continent" had been built. A grateful congregation sang "Now Thank We All Our God."

As the dedication crowd pressed into the new building for a first glance at the academic complex, they saw an architectural statement in concrete, metal, and glass which clearly revealed the seminary's self-understanding of its mission to relate the Gospel to the modern world. President Herman articulated this awareness in his description of the building:

> The architect's concept of a boldly cantilevered building clothed in steel and tinted glass has become a handsome reality. Its broad entries are designed to provide easy access to and from the world, the cantilevers serving in the twentieth century as the horizontal equivalent of the flying buttresses which distinguished the Gothic cathedrals of Europe. Religion consists in the ministry of Christian grace from man to man, as well as the worship of God.[11]

THE EDUCATIONAL IDEAL

The final decision to locate the Lutheran School of Theology in this university-urban context was made by the representatives of Augustana, Chicago Lutheran, Grand View, and Suomi seminaries on March 24, 1961.[12] The rationale for this decision would have been clearly understood by the founders of these schools. They shared a common educational ideal with their twentieth century counterparts—"a conception of the Christian ministry, and indeed, of Christian life, which would take into account and be informed by the total culture of a people."[13] In Europe, their forebearers had implemented this educational ideal in a university setting, with theological education taking its place among all the other university disciplines. In fact, from the earliest days of the Reformation, Phillip Melanchthon had made a permanent mark on Lutheran theological education with his insistence that the fruits of humanism must be used in the service of religion. Melanchthon's inaugural address at Wittenberg on August 29, 1518, had set the tone for his lifetime of concern that all the powers of the human spirit be cultivated:

> Having traced the demise of learning in western Europe, Melanchthon placed his formula for improvement of studies before the university: Learn thoroughly the ancient languages of Hebrew, Greek, and Latin; recover the original wellsprings of the classics and Christianity. He pleaded for a renaissance through a study of original sources. To drink from the sources of theology and to cultivate the liberal arts, he said, we must comprehend the Greek, Latin, and Hebrew languages, for only in this way can be avoid the frigid glosses and jangling comments interposed by men.[14]

[11]Stewart W. Herman, "From the Desk of the President," *Context*, I (Autumn, 1967), 51.

[12]*Infra*, p. 71.

[13]*Supra*, p. 2. Central Seminary representatives were not involved in these 1961 merger discussions. See Chapter X.

[14]Clyde L. Manschreck, *Melanchthon: The Quiet Reformer* (Nashville, Tennessee: Abingdon Press, 1958), p. 23, quoting *Corpus Reformatorum, Melanchthon Opera*, eds. Bretschneider and Bindseil, 1834-60, Volume 11, pp. 22-23.

By teaching from time to time both in the areas of the classics and in theology at the University of Wittenberg, Melanchthon actualized his educational ideal. His forty-two year teaching career attempted to counteract any tendencies of the Reformation toward obscurantism or hostility to culture. A firm believer in the necessity of sound education for the preservation of church and state, he insisted that theological education must be placed in the context of many academic disciplines:

> Without an understanding of language, one cannot read the Old and New Testaments; and to understand languages one needs all sorts of related knowledge in history, geography, chronology, and other liberal arts.[15]

This educational ideal permeated Lutheran theological education in Germany and Scandinavia, and was eventually brought to America by the early founders of Lutheran seminaries in this country. In attempting to incorporate this ideal in America, these patriarchs influenced successive generations of the church in theological education and thus were instrumental in shaping the 1961 merger and relocation decision.

Augustana Seminary and the Educational Ideal

The founders of Augustana Seminary came from a land and a church that had provided theological education in a university context, thus training a ministry that would be relevant to the needs of the age as well as the needs of the church. The early Swedish pioneer pastors in America were university graduates. A statute adopted by the Swedish Parliament in 1831 had provided that:

> ... every theological student, prior to presenting himself for ministerial examination before the diocese in which he will serve, must furnish to that diocese an affidavit certifying that he has been matriculated in the university by the theological faculty and has been examined in all the required courses and has been approved as possessing such competence in dogmatics, moral theology, introduction, symbolics, exegesis, church history and pastoral theology, that he can be admitted to candidacy for the ministerial examinations by the diocese.[16]

The broad cultural background of these pioneers can be seen in the person of Rev. Dr. Lars P. Esbjorn, first President of Augustana Seminary. During 1858-1860, when he served as Scandinavian Professor at Illinois State University, Springfield, a school of the Synod of Northern Illinois, he taught his regular subjects in theology and the Scandinavian lanugages, but also courses in chemistry, astronomy, and natural philosophy. His achievements as a student in Sweden in the areas of mathematics, chemistry, and astronomy, plus his lifetime

---

[15]*Ibid.*, p. 146, quoting CR, Volume 11, p. 130.

[16]Arden, *School of Prophets*, p. 32, quoting Maria Cronquist, "Teologfrekvensen i Sverige efter 1830," *Kyrkohistorisk Arsskrift* (Stockholm, 1925), p. 150, quoting "Förslag till stadga för undervisning i teol. fak," p. 15.

interests in these areas, well equipped him for these tasks. Dr. Esbjorn's colleagues shared his concerns:

> But men like Esbjorn, Hasselquist, and Erland Carlsson, with their university backgrounds, understood that religious values cannot endure in isolation, but must be dynamically related to the total life of the individual and that such relationships are predicated upon an intelligent awareness of a whole culture. Therefore, the new church in a new world must be buttressed by institutions of learning which would give, not only to the youth, but more particularly to ministers-in-training, the same broad grasp regarding their total human heritage which the educational, and especially the university, ideal of the homeland envisaged.[17]

It was no surprise, therefore, when the Augustana Synod was founded in 1860, at Jefferson Prairie, Wisconsin, that the new constitution provided that:

> The Synod shall establish and support a theological seminary for the education of ministers and school teachers of our churches.[18]

In reality, Augustana Seminary was a continuation of the Scandinavian Professorship begun two years earlier at Springfield, thus preserving the broad educational concerns of that institution. The new school, to be located in Chicago, was to have two departments, one preparatory and the other theological. In its embryonic state, Augustana Seminary was already a college and a seminary, a small scale Swedish university, though it did not adopt the name, Augustana College and Theological Seminary, until 1869. Commenting on this evolution and name change, Professor Arden observes:

> The meaning is clear. These Scandinavians were determined to provide for themselves and their children an educational program which was inspired by the university ideal of the homeland, patterned according to the lines of a typical American college, and adapted to the needs of the Church it was to serve.[19]

> This inner development reflects that liberal spirit which the founding fathers inherited from Sweden, which deemed it necessary for a Pastor to know not only the meaning of the Gospel, but to be aware, as well, of the relevant and "existential." This was the very genius of the "University Spirit" which prevailed in both Uppsala and Lund; this was also the ideal of the best American theological schools of that day. The leaders of Augustana did not make the mistake which so often was evident on the American frontier a century ago, of holding that a concentrated course in Biblical exegesis coupled with homiletical advice constituted all the training necessary for "a plain preacher to plain people." They had a great and profound vision of the Christian ministry and its needs, and their educational ideal was the University.[20]

[17]*Ibid.*, p. 23.
[18]*Ibid.*, p. 112, quoting Augustana Synod *Constitution*, Article VII.
[19]G. Everett Arden, *Augustana Heritage* (Rock Island, Ill.: Augustana Press, 1963), p. 99.
[20]Arden, *School of Prophets*, pp. 154-55.

Even when the young school moved to Paxton, Illinois, in 1863, over the bitter opposition of Esbjorn, resulting in his resignation and removal to Sweden, the educational ideal did not wane under the new president, T. N. Hasselquist. Based on his reading of Hasselquist's dedicatory address at Augustana College and Theological Seminary on June 12, 1889, Arden concludes:

> No less pronounced was Hasselquist's influence upon the educational development of the Synod. Though he differed with Esbjorn on many questions, he fully shared Esbjorn's educational ideal which involved the recognition of the vital relationship between religion and culture. Religion and theology must not be isolated from the rest of human knowledge and experience, but must inform, and be informed by, it, and education must be the handmaiden of this cross-fertilization. To this end the theological curriculum must be preceded by "preparatory courses" in science, the humanities, and the practical skills, in order that the clergy of the church may know not only the gospel, but might also become intelligently aware of the world to which the gospel is addressed.[21]

This ideal refused to die. Steeped in this tradition, Rev. Dr. Conrad Bergendoff, then President of Augustana College and Theological Seminary, pointed out the dangers of a seminary's separation from university life and the general culture of the age when he made his annual report to the Augustana Synod in Kansas City, Missouri, in 1947:

> Drawing away from the university we have made theological training a profession, a ministry within the congregation instead of a prophecy, an interpretation of God's will, to the world. Seminarians are often very narrowly trained within a certain discipline. We produce too few scientists, philosophers, historians, artists, states-men within the church because we have limited the deeds of God to a few areas of life. Our theological curriculum starts too late and ends too soon—a little piece of knowledge isolated from secondary education on the one hand and university studies on the other. We still think of the theological seminaries as supplying pastors for pioneer churches. We hardly sense the larger aim of interpreting truth to all mankind.
>
> The Seminary should be the Church's interpreter of all knowledge. But Protestant seminaries have too often cut themselves off from the current of contemporary life and become little museums of interesting periods of the past. They should rather be in the midst of the turmoil of modern thought and life and proclaim a Christ great enough to be the Redeemer of modern politics, sociology, art, literature, music, even a Redeemer of the relations between nations. I believe that all the currents of life which flow through a college should flow through a seminary. A theological faculty can not interpret a life from which it has withdrawn. If the seminary is a higher school it is so only in the sense that it has a firmer grasp on and clearer discernment of the truth in the knowledge that courses through college curricula. Some may not like

21Arden, *Augustana Heritage*, p. 98.

the designation Augustana College and Theological Seminary, but to my mind it expresses the faith of our Church that truth is one, and that all the realm of knowledge stands in relationship to the revelation of Jesus Christ. It is for the Seminary's sake that I have contended for a closer, rather than a more remote and isolated relationship to what the Church seeks to realize in and through its colleges. And it is for the Church's sake that I have sought to integrate the program of the College with the Seminary.[22]

The separation of the seminary from the college in 1948[23] was not a repudiation of this educational ideal. In the debate which brought about the separation it was asserted that the college had so thoroughly outgrown the seminary "to the extent that the seminary was completely overshadowed and pushed into the background, both as to numbers and as to demands for new resources and greater support."[24] The ideal, itself, was not lost through separation, as is evidenced by a paper drawn up by the seminary faculty at its annual retreat in 1960. This paper, "Digest of Faculty Discussion on Report of Study on Augustana Seminary," refutes an accusation by the American Association of The Theological Schools study committee that the seminary was more interested in preserving Swedish traditions than in confronting society with the Christian message. The answer, on the part of the faculty, demonstrates that this educational ideal was still a major factor in determining the purpose of the seminary and in ordering its course:

> ... we have through the years sought to adjust to the existing cultural situations and have sought to address the Gospel to life as it is ... It seems clear that the early leaders in the Seminary history were very conscious of a cultural situation to be addressed. We may have failed in carrying out this early objective; and it may well be that we are not addressing the present situation in full and real confrontation. Any such failure, however, cannot be attributed to the influence of the Swedish tradition.[25]

Augustana Seminary's representatives on the Inter-Seminary Committee voting in favor of the university-urban setting for the new Lutheran School of Theology at Chicago were acting in accord with a long standing educational ideal of the church and seminary.

Grand View Seminary and the Educational Ideal

What obtained in the Augustana tradition prevailed also in the American Evangelical Lutheran Church. A vital Christian humanism characterized the founders of the first Danish Lutheran seminary in northwestern Wisconsin in 1886, and its successor in Des Moines, Iowa, ten years later.[26] This was a

[22]Conrad Bergendoff, "Report of the President," (Augustana College and Theological Seminary), *Augustana Synod Minutes*, 1947, p. 57.
[23]Arden, *Augustana Heritage*, pp. 345-56.
[24]*Ibid.*, p. 346.
[25]Augustana Theological Seminary, *Minutes of the Board of Directors*, October 7-8, 1960, Exhibit A, p. 1.
[26]*Infra*, pp. 26-30.

Christian humanism fostered not only by their experiences in the university in Copenhagen in which their theological education took place, but was equally stimulated by the influence of N. F. S. Grundtvig and the folk school movement. That Grundtvig shared the educational ideal of the Swedish pioneers is clear from these statements by Professor Johannes Knudsen and American Evangelical Lutheran Church historian, Rev. Enok Mortensen:

> He [Grundtvig] was interested, passionately and personally, in making the gospel of Jesus Christ living and real for himself and his time. To put this in modern terms: he was concerned about making the gospel efficacious and contemporary.[27]

> In contrast to the other-worldliness of the Pietists, he [Grundtvig] believed in the value of man's life here on earth, since God had created man in his own image, and redeemed him. This concept led to a concern for a people awakened not only spiritually but culturally as well.[28]

As an expression of this concern for the totality of life the Danish pioneers established folk schools in the early days wherever Danish settlements sprang up—in Michigan, Iowa, Wisconsin, Nebraska, Minnesota, Canada, and California. In keeping with the purpose of the folk schools in Denmark "they were concerned with the wealth of the created life as received from God. Their point of departure was again the value of the human."[29] Though the folk school and the church were to remain separate, this educational ideal of concern for the totality of life prevailed among those who jointly, but separately, supported both church and folk school.

Professor Kildegaard describes the broad concerns of these folk schools and their influence upon the thinking of Danish Lutherans in America:

> If any one thing was definitive of the particular life that our church has known it has been our concept of the human. In our congregations this evidenced itself clearly in our parish facilities and programs. In addition to church and parsonage, another all-purpose building was erected. Here was to be found the center of many of the activities of the congregation. Along the walls were the stall bars used by the gym teams which met regularly under the tutorship of a member who often had a personal knowledge of gymnastics from Denmark. Blackboards were in evidence reminding one of the educational concern for the children of the church. Saturday school and vacation school centered about the old Folk School subjects of history, mythology, literature, and language. Bible stories held a central place in that curriculum, but these were not Bible schools. A stage at one end of the hall bespoke a concern for amateur dramatics and entertainments. Portable benches and chairs were often pushed aside for singing games and folk dances. Visiting lecturers were often welcomed, and their subjects were broadly defined. These were

[27]Johannes Knudsen, "Facing the Issues Today," American Evangelical Lutheran Church, *Report*, 1962, p. 246.
[28]Enok Mortensen, "Our Father's Church We Build," *Ibid.*, p. 213.
[29]Axel C. Kildegaard, "The A.E.L.C.: Its Life and Death," *Ibid.*, p. 228.

concerned with historical and cultural understandings, usually conceived within the Christian context, but rarely dealing with specifically doctrinal questions.[30]

Educationally, socially, economically, politically, we were concerned and involved. Who had time for the confessions of orthodoxy then? We suspect that the political spectrum of the AELC to this day is somewhat different from that of other Lutheran bodies, and if this could be substantiated, it could be traced to this breadth of life and concern.[31]

As heirs of this kind of willing concern for a direct confrontation of the world, society, and culture by an informed Christian faith, the representatives of Grand View Seminary saw a vote in favor of a university-urban setting for LSTC as a logical consequence of their tradition.

Maywood Seminary and the Educational Ideal

In the last half of the nineteenth century, when most Lutherans were establishing theological seminaries which used only their native languages, a group of leaders in the General Council were beginning to see the need for an English speaking Lutheran seminary in the midwest. Among those chiefly concerned was Rev. Dr. William A. Passavant. As he saw the vast numbers of English-speaking Lutherans moving to the West, and as he pondered the number of Lutherans who would be lost in succeeding generations unless the Church would be there to minister in their language, he became increasingly convinced that a theological seminary to train men for an English speaking ministry in the West was an absolute necessity.[32]

Dr. Passavant, himself, was a graduate of Lutheran Theological Seminary at Gettysburg, Pennsylvania. However, when the Synod of Pennsylvania at its spring convention in 1864, voted to establish a new Lutheran Theological Seminary in Philadephia, Passavant shifted his loyalties and concerns to this school. Professor G. H. Gerberding, later a member of the faculty of the Chicago seminary, commented on Passavant's interest in the Philadelphia school:

Dr. Passavant was deeply interested from the beginning and with his prophetic vision foresaw what an important work it was destined to do in the upbuilding of the Church. He eagerly devoted his farreaching influence and enthusiasm to its material and spiritual welfare. This interest he kept up until the day of his death. When he afterwards prayed and planned for a Western Seminary, he did not lose interest in the one in Philadelphia.[33]

Especially appealing to Passavant was Philadelphia seminary's conservative theological position in the Lutheran tradition, in contrast to Gettysburg

[30]*Ibid.*, p. 223.

[31]*Ibid.*, pp. 228-29.

[32]Marjory Weng, "Passavant's Vision, A History of the Chicago Lutheran Theological Seminary, 1891-1951," *Record*, October, 1951, p. 5.

[33]G. H. Gerberding, *Life and Letters of W. A. Passavant, D.D.* (Greenville, Pa.: The Young Lutheran Co., 1906), p. 349.

Seminary, which under S. S. Schmucker was strongly influenced by Reformed theology; its strong academic standards, which insisted from the beginning that "graduation from a college would be required of candidates for admission";[34] and its location in the heart of the city, where seminarians could be exposed to the needs for the inner mission ministry so strongly espoused by Passavant.

It was not strange, therefore, that Passavant wanted the proposed seminary in the West to be patterned after the Philadelphia seminary. When the General Council met for its Third Convention in the Swedish Immanuel Lutheran Church in Chicago, November 4-10, 1869, and adopted a series of resolutions "looking to the establishment of a Theological Seminary, in or near Chicago, 'where the future ministry of our English, German, and Scandinavian churches may be educated together, in the unity of the common Faith confessed and maintained by this Body',"[35] Passavant must surely have been pleased by Professor Charles Porterfield Krauth's appeal that the new seminary in Chicago should be a replica of the Philadelphia school. Passavant had higher regard for no man than he did for Dr. Krauth.[36] His broad range of knowledge qualified him for both a teaching position in theology at the Philadelphia seminary and as a professor of Intellectual and Moral Philosophy in the University of Pennsylvania where he also served as vice-provost. A prolific writer, his works ranged from philosophy to Biblical commentaries to journalism to theology. Truly a Christian humanist, he "developed an excellent reading knowledge of German to supplement his knowledge of Latin, Greek, and Hebrew, and, thus equipped, he read widely and deeply. He had an enormous appetite for books and amassed a private library of great value."[37] The fact that Passavant so ardently admired this man and wanted the new seminary in Chicago to be patterned after his emphases at Philadelphia seminary is a clear indication that Dr. Passavant shared this educational ideal of relating the Gospel to all knowledge and all of life. His well known concern for the work of "inner missions" was to impress upon the new seminary that it did not exist for academic pursuits alone, important as he regarded this, but to prepare men for ministering to all the various needs of men. Rev. Joel Lundeen rightly evaluated the influence of Passavant upon the new Chicago seminary when he wrote:

> ... the intense pastoral and missionary concern which characterized Passavant himself ... through him came to characterize the school. This commitment was also indicative of an honest desire to be identified with the American scene—with American church-life and with the American academic world.[38]

[34]Theodore G. Tappert, *History of the Lutheran Theological Seminary at Philadelphia 1864-1964* (Philadelphia: Lutheran Theological Seminary, 1964), p. 39.

[35]S. E. Ochsenford, *Documentary History of the General Council of the Evangelical Lutheran Church in North America* (Philadelphia: General Council Publication House, 1912), p. 229.

[36]For a moving tribute to Professor Krauth written by Dr. Passavant upon the former's death, see Gerberding, *Life and Letters*, pp. 524-25.

[37]Tappert, *Lutheran Seminary at Philadelphia*, p. 47.

[38]Joel W. Lundeen, *History of the Library of the Chicago Lutheran Theological Seminary of Maywood, Illinois* (unpublished Master's dissertation, University of Chicago,

The early founders implemented this educational ideal as best they could. From the very beginning the new seminary required a broad educational background on the part of every applicant. The catalog for the third year (1893-1894) stated:

> All students must have a good education, if possible, a full collegiate education. Exceptions will be made in cases where the student is advanced in years and has experience in teaching and in mission work, but in such cases the candidate is required to give evidence of such scholarship as will enable him to pursue all the studies of the theological course.[39]

The success of this emphasis was seen in the fact that Dr. G. H. Gerberding could report in 1904 that "of the 27 new men now in residence all but two are college graduates."[40] Gerberding also pointed out how the curriculum recognized that the minister had to be grounded in subjects of a general nature in addition to theology: "We had courses in Psychology and Sociology, in Moral Science and other lines not strictly theological but of untold value to a minister."[41] Likewise, he boasted that Chicago Lutheran Seminary offered the full range of theological courses: "Our Seminary stands, first of all, for a thorough and sound theological training. Whoever will examine the schedule of subjects and courses taught here will see that we aim to cover the whole field of Theology in all of its departments."[42]

The professor who perhaps best embodied this educational ideal in his twenty-four years of teaching, from the founding of the school in 1891, to his death in 1915, was Rev. Dr. Revere F. Weidner. Dr. Weidner graduated from Muhlenberg College in Allentown, Pennsylvania, as a member of its first class in 1869, distinguishing himself as a scholar in Greek. His academic career also flourished at Philadelphia Lutheran Seminary where he distinguished himself in Hebrew studies. His broad educational background enabled him to serve as professor of English and history at Muhlenberg College while serving simultaneously as a parish pastor. From 1882, until he became president and professor of Chicago Lutheran Seminary in 1891, he taught full-time at Augustana College and Theological Seminary in Rock Island, thus fraternizing with many who shared his educational ideal. His deep concern for a ministry exposed to all the academic disciplines, in addition to theology, is seen in the matriculation examination which he introduced in the early nineteen hundreds. "The examinations covered the entire field, Arithmetic, Algebra, Geometry, Physics, Physiology, History, English, Psychology, Geology and Astronomy, as

---

39*Ibid.*, p. 50, quotes *Catalog of the Theological Seminary of the Evangelical Lutheran Church at Chicago, Illinois: Third Year, 1893-1894* (New York: Flemming H. Revell Co., n.d.), p. 7.

40*Ibid.*, p. 52, quotes *Record*, January, 1904, p. 7.

41G. H. Gerberding, *Reminiscent Reflections of a Youthful Octogenarian* (Minneapolis: Augsburg Publishing House, 1928), p. 240.

42Gerberding, *Life and Letters*, p. 564, quoting *Record*, April, 1902.

well as languages."[43] Only college graduates with Latin, Greek, and German were admitted to the seminary without this examination. The validity of his own scholarship, both in breadth and in depth, is attested to by the fact, that Dr. William Rainey Harper, first president of the University of Chicago, invited him to lecture at the Chautauqua Institute, co-authored with him textbooks in Greek and Hebrew, and offered him several times, without success, a professorship in Hebrew at the University of Chicago at a salary three times the figure he received at Chicago Lutheran Seminary.

Rev. Dr. Henry Eyster Jacobs, in his twenty-fifth anniversary address at the school in 1916, summarized aptly the contributions of these men: "If Dr. Passavant was the architect, Dr. Weidner was the master builder."[44] Both architect and master builder were infused with the same educational ideal. Their influence was felt in the momentous decision to locate the seminary in the university-urban setting these many years later.

Suomi Seminary and the Educational Ideal

The development of theological education in America by Finnish immigrants closely paralleled the pattern of the Swedes and the Danes. In their native Finland theological education had always been conducted in the context of the university, first at Turku, founded in 1640, and then at Helsinki, when the university was transferred there in 1828.[45] Theological education was strongly influenced by the Swedish university at Uppsala during the years that the Turku diocese came under the Swedish crown.[46] The fact that theological education in Finland during the nineteenth century was based upon the same educational ideal which motivated their fellow Scandinavians who founded American seminaries in that century, is made clear in an article by Professor Erkki Kansanaho. Comparing the division of theological departments in Helsinki to a model cited by Fr. Schleiermacher in 1811, he calls philosophical theology the root of the tree which feeds the trunk—historical theology consisting of exegetics, dogmatics, and church history—and the branchy top—practical theology. The definition of philosophical theology clearly states the education ideal:

> By philosophical theology Schleiermacher meant the knowledge which theology requires for its scientific basis, and which thereby unites theology with the total body of knowledge.[47]

The nineteenth century theology professors at the University of Helsinki who trained the men coming to America were learned men of broad backgrounds in

[43]Weng, "Passavant's Vision," p. 24.
[44]Lundeen, *History of Library*, p. 18, quoting "Address by Henry E. Jacobs, D.D., Ll.D.," *Record*, October, 1916, p. 55.
[45]Esko Haapa, "Exegetics," *Finnish Theology Past and Present*, ed. by Lennart Pinomaa (Helsinki, Finland: Kirjapaino Oy Lause, 1963), p. 5.
[46]Mikko Java, *The Church of Finland* (Pieksamaki, Finland: The Bible House, 1963), pp. 3-4.
[47]Erkki Kansanaho, "Practical Theology," *Finnish Theology*, p. 109.

Christian humanism.[48] Their influence on Finnish pioneer pastors in America is seen in a statement by Rev. J. G. Nikander of Hancock, Michigan, who four years after graduating in theology from the University of Helsinki, declared to his fellow Finns in America in 1888:

> If we Finns do not get a Christian institution of learning and teachers here in America, Christianity itself will disappear from our midst, and then will disappear our nationality (kansallisuutemme) as well.[49]

The Finnish immigrant pastors obviously recognized the validity of the educational ideal they carried from Finland, for on June 2, 1891, at the second convention of the Suomi Synod, they voted to secure a site "for the establishment of an institution of learning."[50] The actual development of the school was delayed by haggling over a specific location. Finally, after rejecting proposed sites at Minneapolis-St. Paul, Minnesota; Superior, Wisconsin; Duluth, Minnesota; Little Falls, Minnesota; and several others, the fathers selected Hancock, Michigan, in 1896, for the basic reason that the principal concentration of Finns in America was in this copper country. The choice also coincided with Pastor Nikander's preference. Once the location was determined the pioneers set about ordering the structure of the school. That the school was to be patterned after the typical Scandinavian university and that they envisioned the new school to be the University of Helsinki in microcosm is seen in the fact that the director of the school was sent to Augustana College and Theological Seminary in Rock Island, Illinois, "to make comparisons and to take suggestions."[51] The first curriculum developed by the "little" University of Helsinki staff showed their concern to relate the Christian faith to all academic disciplines. It included: Religion, Finnish, English, Arithmetic, Geography, American History, Natural Science, Penmanship, Art, Bookkeeping, Voice, Piano, Physical Education, and Finnish History.[52]

A major concern of the new school which opened its doors for the first time September 8, 1896, was to provide men with the necessary broad background in all academic areas to enable them to move next to the study of theology. Therefore, when the first commencement was held May 26, 1904, seven of the ten graduates were men, and all seven were candidates for the seminary. That same Fall the seminary department was added and Suomi College and Seminary was complete. Comments Kangas about this enterprise: "It cannot be denied that, to the founders of the Suomi Synod and Suomi College, the queen of the sciences was theology . . . the Theological Seminary crowned the

---

[48]Haapa, *Finnish Theology*, pp. 5-8.
[49]Henry R. Kangas, *Blades, Ears, and Corn: Suomi Synod, 1890-1962* (unpublished history of the Suomi Synod, LSTC Library), p. 97.
1967), p. 15.
[50]*Ibid.*, p. 99.
[51]*Ibid.*, p. 107.
[52]*Ibid.*

academic posture of Suomi College, in Hancock, Michigan."[53] The educational ideal was preserved in America. Later generations would vote to implement this ideal in the setting of a modern university.

All of the pioneer leaders who founded these American seminaries would have understood the answer President Herman gave to the question, Why a new seminary? when he wrote in 1964, to the supporting synods:

Why a new seminary?

in order to pool all available resources (within our four synod area) and concentrate them on the development of the best possible training center for Lutheran pastors, missionaries, and lay leadership.

in order to take full advantage of a university, metropolitan environment and its outreach into all areas of human knowledge and contemporary life.

in order to attract the best teachers in a richer variety of fields of study, so as to attract a larger number of our ablest young men and women into the service of Jesus Christ.

in order to provide the church—and the community around it—with consecrated Christian leadership, both spiritually and intellectually.

in order that, by the Grace of God and to His Glory, more souls may be sought and healed, more communities may be transformed, more nations may be blessed and the world redeemed from self-destruction.[54]

[53]*Ibid.*, pp. 141-42.
[54]Stewart W. Herman, "Why a New Seminary," Lutheran School of Theology at Chicago Development Fund brochure, 1964, p. 4.

Chapter III

THE LONG TRAIL TO THE UNIVERSITY

I believe that it is of crucial importance to the seminary to be vitally related to a larger academic community that will sustain and challenge the intellectual life of faculty and students. This academic community is, because of the nature and level of seminary work, a graduate school. The undergraduate college cannot supply the supporting environment the seminary needs to be vitally, functionally related to this environment. This means that it must enjoy an interchange of instruction with the graduate faculty; its students must have courses offered in the graduate school open to them; its professors must have the opportunity to direct the advanced studies of graduate students, and to participate as peers with their colleagues in the graduate faculty.[1]

This judgment regarding theological education was the conviction of Dr. Ernest Cadman Colwell, President of the School of Theology, Claremont, California, and former President of the University of Chicago and long-time Dean of its Divinity School. It expressed the conclusions which were reached independently by the leaders of the four Lutheran seminaries which voted in 1961 to merge these schools. Chicago Lutheran Seminary suffered from a suburban location which was geographically isolated from any other type of academic institution. Augustana, Grand View, and Suomi seminaries, on the other hand, were located on the campuses of undergraduate colleges, but the size and varied interests of these colleges predominated over the theological schools, and failed to provide the kind of intellectual and cultural stimulation which only a graduate school could offer. The fifth seminary, to enter the merger at a later date, Central of Fremont, Nebraska, was more concerned at this time with its survival than with the choice of an optimum environment for a theological school, and thus was not a party to the original discussions and decisions of the other four seminaries.

The decision to relocate in the setting of a major urban university with a strong graduate school was finally made in 1961, by the leaders of Augustana, Chicago Lutheran, Grand View, and Suomi seminaries, but the educational ideal

---

[1]Ernest Cadman Colwell, "Seminaries in the University for the Church," *Lutheran Quarterly*, XVIII (November, 1966), p. 322.

which made this decision possible had forced each of the seminaries to face the question many times before.

In the case of Augustana Seminary, there were those in the very beginning who strove for this kind of seminary environment. Dr. Lars P. Esbjorn, one of the principal founders and first president of Augustana, was fully committed to an urban location near a great university and cultural opportunities. His convictions apparently were shared by many others, because he wrote in the early 1860's: "I have spoken to both Americans and Swedes, and all agree, that in 19 out of 20 cases, it has been found that it is far better to locate schools in principal cities."[2] His insistence that the new school be located in Chicago grew out of his belief:

> ... that according to previous experience the large cities had proven to be the most strategic places in which to locate educational institutions. Such institutions require proximity to cultural centers, such as libraries, archives, etc., and the support of a larger center of population from which both students and material aid can be solicited.[3]

It was a great personal defeat for Esbjorn and his ideal when the young school moved from Chicago, its place of origin, to Paxton, Illinois, in 1863. It subsequently moved to Rock Island, Illinois, in 1875, in search for a better financial support base and a greater supply of students.[4]

On several occasions Augustana Seminary considered a return to Chicago. The first such consideration came in connection with the proposed new English-speaking seminary in Chicago. The enabling resolution, passed by the General Council in 1869, envisioned the common education of Scandinavian ministers along with those of English and German churches.[5] Dr. T. N. Hasselquist, then president of Augustana College and Theological Seminary at Paxton, was present at this meeting. A special commission of twelve persons was appointed to work on the project and to report back at each annual meeting of the council. In 1872, after learning that Dr. W. A. Passavant had donated four acres of land on the north side of Chicago in the Lake View area, the General Council voted to accept title to the land, adopted a constitution identical to the one Professor Krauth had written for the Philadelphia seminary, elected a Board of Directors, and called its first faculty member, Rev. Professor H. E. Jacobs.[6] It appeared that all was in readiness for the development of the new seminary. As a member of the General Council the Augustana Synod was invited to merge its seminary in Paxton with the proposed school in Chicago, as stated in these resolutions adopted by the council:

---

[2]Arden, *School of Prophets*, p. 139, quoting *Tidsskrift for Svensk Evangelisk Lutersk kyrkohistoria i Nord Amerika och for teologiska och kyrkliga fragor*, ed. by E. Norelius, 1899, p. 329.
[3]Arden, *School of Prophets*, p. 137.
[4]*Ibid.*, pp. 144-73.
[5]*Supra*, p. 16.
[6]He declined the call.

1. The General Council respectfully invites the Augustana Synod to unite, if possible, the Theological Department of its school in Paxton with the new Theological Seminary in Chicago.

2. That the Board of Directors are authorized to make the necessary arrangements with the Augustana Synod for the completion of this intended project, and report its actions to the General Council.[7]

These two resolutions were countered by two resolutions passed by the Augustana Synod at its 1873 meeting. The first appeared to endorse the proposed Chicago seminary in a spirit of genuine good will, while the second pointed out that this was a most inopportune time for such a relocation to take place. The whole matter of Augustana's new charter and the imminent move to Rock Island was dependent upon the continued association of President Hasselquist, who was needed to teach in both the college and the seminary. These resolutions were reported to the General Council at its October, 1873, convention in Erie, Pennsylvania:

1. That the Synod hereby expresses its sincere gratification at the measures taken to establish the proposed Theological Seminary at Chicago, and at the election of H. E. Jacobs as its first English professor.

2. That owing to our peculiar situation, arising from the removal of our institution to Rock Island, and to the fact that Dr. Hasselquist, our only theological professor, is necessarily needed in the college department, and also from the nature and charter of our instituion, the Synod is not prepared at present to accede to the fraternal invitation of the General Council to remove its theological department at Chicago.[8]

Delay after delay ensued. The great Chicago fire, the severe financial panic, the lack of funds for endowment and buildings continued to plague the proposed venture. Finally, in 1886, when the General Council again met in Chicago, where the original resolution to inaugurate the Chicago seminary had been adopted, resolutions were passed which made the new school a live issue again. The council deeded the Lake View property to a Board of Directors to be appointed and authorized the Directors to arrange for the opening of the school, without any financial responsibility on the part of the council.[9] This latter action was to appease those bodies in the council who, already supporting seminaries, were suspicious that financial favoritism might be granted to this new school. The reaction of the Augustana Synod was instantaneous. Whether the irenic resolutions previously adopted by the synod in 1873, were based on the premise that the new school would probably never develop anyway, or whether

[7]Arden, *School of Prophets*, p. 204, quoting Augustana Synod, *Minutes*, 1873, p. 35.

[8]Ben A. Johnson, "The Augustana Synod and the Muhlenberg Tradition," *Record*, August, 1960, p. 26, quoting General Council, *Minutes*, 1873, p. 32.

[9]Ochsenford, *General Council*, p. 270.

there was a genuine change of attitude in the ensuing fourteen years, may never be known. Whatever the previous motivation, the present attitude was crystal clear: Augustana Seminary did not want a competing institution on its territory. The following year, 1887, Augustana Synod delegates to the General Council Convention in Greenville, Pennsylvania, reported the following actions taken by the synod:

Whereas, Our Synod owns a Seminary so near Chicago, and,

Whereas, This Synod has the American element well represented in its Seminary, and,

Whereas, The Synod looks upon a Seminary in Chicago, established for the purpose of taking up, at least in part, the work among us Swedish-Americans, as under the circumstances, an occasion for division and separation; therefore,

Resolved, That this synod requests its delegates to the next Convention of [*sic*] not to establish a Seminary in Chicago.[10]

The response of the General Council was a peaceful rejoinder, but it gave no hint that the council would accede to the requests:

The establishment of a Theological Seminary in Chicago was, by resolution, declared to be in no way intended to conflict with the work of the Augustana Synod among the Swedes, and the managers of the same to be permanently directed to avoid any occasion of offense in interfering with the work of the Augustana Synod among the Swedes.[11]

Not content with this reply, the Augustana Synod, through its president, Rev. S. P. A. Lindahl, sent the General Council a letter in 1889, containing a resolution adopted at its June synod convention. It contained the surprising request that the General Council turn over the Lake View property in Chicago to the Augustana Synod for the purpose of establishing a seminary there.[12] The matter was studied at the October 10-15, 1889, convention of the General Council in Pittsburgh, Pennsylvania. The request was denied, but adjacent land was offered to the Augustana Synod with the invitation extended to Augustana Seminary to relocate on this land and operate the seminary in close cooperation with the proposed council seminary. All this was contained in the following resolutions adopted at that General Council convention:

1. That the General Council is not in a position to comply with the request of the Swedish Augustana Synod, by reason of the conditions imposed by the original donation of property.

2. That the General Council learns with joy that certain members of this Council have publicly, at this twenty-second Con-

---

[10]Johnson, "Augustana and Muhlenberg Tradition," p. 27, quoting General Council, *Minutes,* 1887, p. 64.

[11]Ochsenford, *General Council,* p. 273.

[12]*Ibid.,* p. 279.

vention thereof, stated the intention to offer to donate to the Swedish Augustana Synod, in fee simple, two acres of land immediately adjoining the property, the transfer of which by this body has been requested by that Synod, for the location in the name of the Augustana Theological Seminary.

3.   That should the Swedish Augustana Synod accept the proposed gift of the said two acres of land for the location of its Theological Seminary in Chicago, and establish thereon its Seminary, the General Council would look with favor upon an arrangement which might be made in reference to the lectures and studies in the Augustana Seminary and the intended Seminary of the General Council, or under the control of the General Council on the adjoining property, which might be for the mutual benefit and advancement of both institutions.

4.   That such an arrangement of lectures and studies would be in harmony with the original design of the General Council for the establishment of a Seminary at some central point in the West "where the future ministry of our English, German and Scandinavian churches may be educated together in the unity of the common faith confessed and maintained by this body."[13]

The offer was flatly rejected by the Augustana Synod, so the General Council independently founded the Theological Seminary of the Evangelical Lutheran Church, at Chicago, Illinois, in 1891. It took exactly seventy years before the two institutions were ready to join forces in a joint theological enterprise in Chicago. The regret felt by the founders of Chicago Lutheran Seminary was expressed at a General Council meeting in 1893:

That it originally contemplated an Institution in which the ministry for the English, German, and Scandinavian peoples should be trained, and seemed to find itself exceedingly embarassed when one of the most important Synods, the Swedish Augustana Synod, not only declined to cooperate with it, but objected to its establishment.[14]

At the same meeting the council decided that it would be unwise to own and manage any theological seminary, lest there be accusations of favoritism, so the die was cast for an independent, self-perpetuating board to govern the Chicago seminary. The problems this created for the seminary, in terms of lack of financial support and lack of church control, were not solved until the school finally came under synod ownership and control in 1942. Meanwhile the Augustana Synod continued to be piqued by the presence of the Chicago seminary, and at "the 1905 convention of the Augustana Synod a resolution was passed indicating that Augustana frowned upon her men attending other sem-

[13]Johnson, "Augustana and Muhlenberg Tradition." p. 27, quoting General Council, *Minutes*, 1893, p. 53.
[14]Gerberding, *Life and Letters*, p. 562.

inaries, and wished the General Council to be informed to this effect."[15] Thus Augustana's first consideration to relocate its seminary ended in failure.

A second attempt to relocate Augustana Seminary came in 1933, when the Augustana Synod voted on a resolution to move the school. The proposal to relocate was closely connected with the question of separating the seminary from the college. During the decade preceding this vote the question of separation was a major issue, and resolutions dealing with some aspect of it were considered at Augustana Synod conventions in 1926, 1930, 1932, and 1933.[16] The resolutions considered in 1933, called for a separation of seminary from college and its removal to Chicago or environs:

1. Awaiting possible and probable developments in the field of theological education within the Lutheran Church in America we propose the following enunciation of a policy for the future:

    a) That Augustana Seminary be moved.

    b) That it be moved to Chicago or its vicinity.[17]

The resolution was defeated 125 to 110.[18] Had just eight of the delegates who voted "no" chosen to support the measure it would have passed. This close margin is all the more remarkable when it is noted that the new seminary campus was just ten years old, and the expenditures necessary for a new building program in Chicago or its vicinity would have been exceedingly difficult in that time of economic depression. For the second time efforts to relocate Augustana Seminary were frustrated, but the long trail to the university was getting shorter.

The eventual separation of seminary and college came in 1948, having been approved by Synod in 1947. Though the action did not provide for the removal of the seminary from the college campus, it did create a separate legal entity for the seminary which made it ready for the enabling action to merge and relocate which came in 1961.

There was also strong support in the early days for the location of a Danish Lutheran seminary near the campus of another academic institution. The decision to found such a school was made at the 1886 convention of the Danish Evangelical Lutheran Church of America. Meeting in Cedar Falls, Iowa, the assembly considered four different locations, but the host city itself received the most votes. In support of this location, many delegates pointed out the advantages of proximity to a college. One advantage was "that future pastors would have an opportunity in Cedar Falls to attend the normal school for

15Johnson, "Augustana and Muhlenberg Tradition," p. 28, based on General Council, *Minutes*, 1905, p. 170.
16Augustana Synod, *Minutes*, 1926, pp. 62-63; 1930, p. 96; 1932, p. 86; 1933, pp. 69-78.
17*Ibid.*, 1933, p. 76.
18*Ibid.*, 1933, p. 78.

teachers and to acquire a knowledge of the English language."[19] However, the seminary was not to locate near the budding college in Cedar Falls because a special committee "decided to rent the folk school building at West Denmark Wisconsin, temporarily, and to open the seminary there the following spring."[20] It was also decided that the president of the school should have the additional duties of teaching in the seminary and serving as pastor of the West Denmark congregation. Somewhat anxious that a subsequent relocation of the school to the Cedar Falls campus would also require the president to serve the sizeable Danish Lutheran congregation in this Iowa city, President Thorvald Helveg chose to have the seminary remain in its "temporary" location. Here the demands of a smaller congregation were not as great, and he would have more time to devote to the new seminary. Thus, the educational ideal carried to America from Denmark received a temporary setback as professors and students settled back in isolation from university, urban life, and American culture:

> ...the sylvan setting enhanced the mood of meditation and contemplation. With the outside world so far away, the seminary created its own cultural and spiritual realm. The woods were so deep and still, the lakes so pretty and placid.[21]

Although President Helveg was educated at the University of Copenhagen, and was regarded as a "brilliant speaker and an inspiring teacher,"[22] the school was handicapped in carrying out its task of relating the Gospel to all learning and all of life because the curriculum was limited practically exclusively to theological subjects.[23]

The opportunity to reconsider the seminary's location came in 1891, when the convention of the Danish Church voted to close the seminary over the strained relations between President Helveg, a Grundtvigian, and his associate, Rev. P. S. Vig, of Inner Mission leanings.[24] Two interesting proposals confronted the Church in its 1893 convention. The first was a proposal to build a seminary on the campus of the University of Iowa:

> ...a Professor Schaefer from the university at Iowa City was given permission during this discussion to suggest the possibility of establishing a Danish Lutheran seminary in conjunction with his institution.[25]

The second was an invitation from the two-year-old Chicago Lutheran Seminary. In the same spirit that Augustana Seminary had been invited to join forces with

[19]Enok Mortensen, *The Danish Lutheran Church in America: The History and Heritage of the American Evangelical Lutheran Church* (Philadelphia: Board of Publication, Lutheran Church in America, 1967), p. 93.
[20]*Ibid.*
[21]*Ibid.*, p. 94.
[22]Mortensen, "Our Father's Church," p. 218.
[23]Mortensen, *Danish Lutheran Church*, p. 93. "The curriculum included Old and New Testament exegesis, church history, history of the Church of Denmark, dogmatics, the religious sects, world history, Danish, and English."
[24]Mortensen, *Danish Lutheran Church*, pp. 102-05.
[25]*Ibid.*, p. 114.

the fledgling seminary, now the Danes were asked to send their students to Chicago and "augment their training through instruction by a Danish professor—if the synod desired to add such a man to the faculty."[26] Both considerations were rejected, but not the idea that their pastors needed a more adequate education than had been provided thus far. "There must be a school which could more effectively prepare the seminarians in the broad field of academic knowledge."[27] Such a school was founded by the Danes before the end of the century.

Grand View University, as it was known during its formative stages, opened its doors in Des Moines, Iowa, to students on September 27, 1896. One Niels Jul came the first day, and thirty-three others joined him as the school year ensued, including three theological students. According to Rev. Dr. Ernest D. Nielsen, current president of the institution, it was

> ... not conceived of as a folk high school, but as an institution of higher education which will offer not only theological education for future pastors, but general education for the youth of the church . . . . Grand View embarks from the very outset on a broader base and higher educational level.[28]

Mortensen's observation that "it was meant to be nothing less than the University of the Danish Lutheran Church in America,"[29] is verified in a fund raising pamphlet printed in 1898. Bearing the title, "About a Danish University in America," it states as one of its aims:

> To augment the theological seminary with a Danish university for the study, not only of Danish and English branches, but of all subjects of interest to the human mind.[30]

Here in an urban setting, for "Des Moines was then 'a thriving city of 75,000',"[31] the theological seminary was to flourish in the context of a new American university, much the same as the theological enterprise was pursued at the University of Copenhagen, though on a smaller scale, of course.

The goals were a bit ambitious for the young school. In fact, the first president, Rev. R. R. Vestergaard, newly arrived from Denmark, felt the term "university" was a bit presumptuous. Nevertheless he set about establishing a curriculum that was unusually wide in range for a school of its size.[32] He insisted that candidates for the ministry be well grounded in the school's preparatory department before embarking upon the study of theology. The president also voiced his concern for a thoroughly adequate theological training:

---

[26]*Ibid.*, pp. 133-34.

[27]*Ibid.*, p. 134.

[28]Ernest D. Nielsen, "The Church's Concept of Grand View College Through the Years," American Evangelical Lutheran Church, *Report*, p. 236.

[29]Mortensen, *Danish Lutheran Church*, p. 138.

[30]*Ibid.*, p. 137.

[31]*Ibid.*, p. 134, quoting *Kirkelig Samler*, 1894, p. 307.

[32]*Ibid.*, pp. 138-139.

There are those who have believed it sufficient to have felt a call as a holy fire, plus a natural oratorical ability. The holy fire is necessary, and oratorical ability is a splendid medium, but they are only servants . . . A theological school must help its students not only to find and use their talents, but also to master them.[33]

Grand View was plagued by a slow growth in numbers of students, not least in the seminary department. Constant haggling over the years between supporters of the folk school tradition and supporters of a university orientation had a debilitating effect on the struggling school. The insistence, until 1939, that the language of instruction in the theological department be Danish, imposed obvious limitations on enrollment. In fact, of the six pastors who entered the ministerium of the Danish Church in 1931, only two had received all their training at Grand View.[34] The change to English as the language of instruction in 1939 was necessitated by the seminary's acceptance of its first non-Danish seminarian that Fall.

As the college grew, especially after World War II, the seminary simply did not keep pace. Voices began to be raised in support of separating the seminary from the college and relocating on a new campus. It was when the seminary enrollment in 1952-53 slipped to four students, with the prospect of adding only three new students the next Fall, that Rev. Dr. Johannes Knudsen, former president of Grand View, who became dean of the seminary in 1951, posed this question to the seventy-sixth Annual Convention of the Church:

We must ask ourselves the question whether we are giving an adequate instruction to the young men who are preparing for the ministry. This question does not involve the competency of the present instructors, which is unquestionably adequate, but the character of the Seminary as a whole. This question rests in itself, but upon it also hinges the problem of attracting the desirable number of students.[35]

Dean Knudsen pointed out in this report, which he had earlier made to the Board of Directors of the seminary February 28, 1953, that the whole matter of accreditation by the American Association of Theological Schools was a major issue. To achieve such accreditation would have meant the addition of at least one faculty member, doubling the size of the library, and adding more students. He posed three alternatives:

1. Continuation as of the present with prospects of the same average enrollment and with a total instruction that does not meet the minimum requirements of the AATS.

2. An increase and improvement of faculty and facilities with the hope of an increased enrollment. This would mean an

[33]*Ibid.*, p. 139, quoting *Kirkelig Samler*, 1897, p. 377.
[34]*Ibid.*, p. 207.
[35]Johannes Knudsen, "Grand View College and Grand View Seminary Report," Danish Evangelical Lutheran Church, *Report*, 1953, p. 132.

increased budget, enlarged facilities, and the engagement of at least one additional full-time professor.

3. The merger or federation of Grand View Seminary with another seminary.[36]

He decisively stated his preference, by adding: "It is my conviction that the function of training ministers for the D.E.L.C.A. can best be served by associating the Seminary with another Lutheran Seminary."[37] His convictions were further reinforced by his resignation to be effective May 31, 1954. When the convention met in Des Moines, Iowa, August 11-16, 1953, to consider this report, it confronted two alternatives presented by the seminary board:

Plan 1: To improve the present seminary facilities and increase the faculty to be able to teach adequately all the required subjects and provide the training needed for those who are to be ministers of the gospel to the congregations of the Synod.

Plan 2: To move Grand View Seminary to some other Lutheran Seminary and affiliate with it, and one or two of the instructors from our Synod to be engaged to teach at this institution.[38]

After a lengthy debate, the following recommendation by the Board of Directors of the seminary, which it had adopted unanimously, was passed by the convention:

The board recommends that it be authorized to explore the possibilities and responsibilities involved in maintaining Grand View Seminary under the control and direction of the corporation, but affiliated with another Lutheran seminary in order to draw effectively upon the more extensive resources of such institution, the results of such exploration to be presented to the next annual meeting of the corporation.[39]

Meanwhile, the Board of Directors at Chicago Lutheran Seminary had viewed the uncertainty at Grand View as an opportunity to renew the invitation their forebears had extended the infant seminary in 1893. At the May 7, 1953, meeting of the Maywood board, President Armin G. Weng urged the board to call Dr. Knudsen to Maywood to assist in the expanding graduate program, in the realization that Grand View Seminary might also wish to transfer to Maywood:

Were Dr. Knudsen called to the Seminary, the Danish Church would probably close its seminary (they have only 8 students) and it would be hoped that then the Danish Church would make a grant towards Dr. Knudsen's salary, giving him status of professor of the Danish Lutheran Church. The church will meet in convention in August and

36*Ibid.*, pp. 132-33.
37*Ibid.*, p. 133.
38*Ibid.*, pp. 135-36.
39Danish Evangelical Lutheran Church of America, *Minutes*, 1953, p. 47.

will consider any proposition we present to them at that time. There is the possibility that the Danish Church would consider affiliation with Northwestern Seminary if we do not submit some definite proposal.[40]

No action was taken on this recommendation, though at the next board meeting it was announced that Grand View Seminary had approached the Maywood board:

A committee has been appointed by the American Evangelical Lutheran Church to confer with our Seminary among others with the possibility of their affiliating with our Seminary or another Seminary.[41]

The Maywood board responded affirmatively and appointed the president of the seminary, the president of the board, and a member of the faculty to meet with this committee. Subsequent minutes of the Executive Committee of the Chicago Seminary indicate that several meetings were held. The report of Grand View's committee indicates that Northwestern Seminary in Minneapolis, Minnesota, was also considered.[42] No mention is made of it in this report, but contacts were also made with Augustana Theological Seminary in Rock Island, Illinois:

President [Karl E.] Mattson reported on negotiations with Grand View Seminary, Des Moines, Iowa, regarding a possible arrangement whereby candidates for the ministry in the American Evangelical Lutheran Church (Danish) would be trained in our seminary.[43]

Prior to the 1954 AELC convention the Grand View seminary board voted on the two proposed plans: three board members voted to retain the present location and three voted to move the seminary. President of the Board, Dr. Erling Jensen, broke the tie with a vote in favor of relocation. The debate at the convention of the church was equally divided. Twenty-one of the fifty-two pastors present, plus sixteen laymen, participated in the animated discussion which lasted from mid-morning to late in the afternoon on Friday, August 14.[44] When the written ballots were tabulated, "The chairman announced the results as 133 votes in favor of adopting Plan I, 100 votes against."[45] The descendents of those who had originally voted at a convention in Cedar Falls, Iowa, in 1886, to establish a seminary, now decided in the same city to retain their seminary in Des Moines.

Although the seminary would not be moving to Maywood yet, its Dean would. A one year call as guest professor, was extended by the Maywood board

[40]Armin G. Weng, "Report of the President," p. 3, Chicago Lutheran Seminary, Board of Directors, *Minutes*, May 7, 1953.

[41]Chicago Lutheran Theological Seminary, Board of Directors, *Minutes*, September 16, 1953, p. 1.

[42]Alfred Jensen, "The Future of the Seminary," American Evangelical Lutheran Church, *Report*, 1954, pp. 137-143.

[43]Augustana Theological Seminary, Board of Directors, *Minutes*, February 17-18, 1954, p. 7.

[44]American Evangelical Lutheran Church, *Minutes*, 1954, pp. 44-45.

[45]*Ibid.*, p. 45. Plans 1 and 2 are detailed *supra*, p. 30.

to Dr. Johannes Knudsen.[46] Two weeks later Rev. Millard Stiles, secretary of the board, received this reply:

> With gratitude have I received your letter and with gratitude do I accept the invitation to become Guest Professor at the Theological Seminary of the Evangelical Lutheran Church in Chicago for one year beginning July 1, 1954.[47]

The call was renewed at the April 14, 1955, meeting of the Board of Directors, and then a permanent call was extended November 30, 1955. Thus AELC had an investment in theological education at the Chicago seminary which was to be influential in the decision to relocate, soon to come.

In the interim, supporters of Grand View Seminary sought to strengthen the school. Reports to the AELC Convention in 1955, indicated that classrooms, library, and married couples housing was being renovated, and Dr. Leroy Norquist was added to the faculty, but that the enrollment problem remained.[48] In his 1957 report, Dean Kildegaard expressed some optimism:

> Grand View Seminary's growth remains keyed to the future. We do not anticipate much growth in numbers for this fall but have high expectations for the fall of 1958.[49]

One year later, however, Dean Kildegaard reported that the enrollment had not increased at all, and added this word of explanation:

> The situation in which we decided to retain and improve our facilities by action of our convention in 1954 has changed. At that time our decision included the provision that we reconsider the future of the seminary in 1959. We have grown much closer to other schools and churches during the past few years. At the same time there are evidences that students who in former years would have come to Grand View Seminary will not enroll here. Some prefer the advantages of the larger school and specifically the degree that may be obtained there. More seriously, and there is no count of these, are the prospects for the ministry that are not challenged by our school and who do not consider another school . . . .
>
> The rapidly changing situation has demanded a restudy of our work and future in order that the most constructive plan available may be presented to the church by the summer of 1959.[50]

The Church was ready to act. It authorized the Seminary Committee of the Board of Directors and the Dean of the Seminary to investigate the matter of affiliating the seminary with a larger school and report back with proposals to the 1959 convention.[51] Once again the Seminary Committee went to work on the same problem assigned to it five years earlier. This time, however, church

---

[46]CLTS, Board, *Minutes*, May 5, 1954, p. 4.
[47]*Ibid.* Letter filed with *Minutes.*
[48]AELC, *Report*, 1955, pp. 155-56.
[49]Axel Kildegaard, "Grand View Seminary Report," AELC, *Report*, 1957, p. 158.
[50]Kildegaard, "Seminary Report," AELC, *Report*, 1958, pp. 175-76.
[51]AELC, *Minutes*, 1958, pp. 38, 40.

merger was in the air. Two of the seminaries of the Lutheran bodies involved in the Joint Committee on Lutheran Unity discussions, Augustana Seminary and Maywood Seminary, had initiated merger talks in January, 1958, and representatives of Suomi Seminary and Grand View Seminary had joined the talks that Summer. Further, Suomi Seminary had affiliated with Maywood Seminary in the Fall of 1958, in anticipation of this merger. Therefore, even though serious and extended conversations were held with both Central Lutheran Seminary in Fremont, Nebraska, and Chicago Lutheran Seminary in Maywood, Illinois, the preference of the committee was for Maywood. It reported its reasons to the 1959 AELC Convention in Detroit:

1. The recognized academic standing of the Seminary at Maywood. The school has long been accredited and offers a faculty which is most capable and renowned.

2. As Chicago is an important center of theological education in our country, there are opportunities afforded to students at this school which are to be coveted

3. The broader background of the larger student body at Chicago Lutheran and the advantages which fellowship with this student body offers the young men of our Church matches the academic gains which affiliation would bring.

4. The prospect for future contribution to the educational task of the new Church in a new Seminary embodying the traditions of the four merging churches can best be realized through present affiliation with Chicago Lutheran Seminary[52]

The recommendation presented at the Detroit convention on Friday, August 14, 1959, was that Grand View affiliate with the Maywood seminary on the basis of the "Principles of Agreement Between the Chicago Lutheran Seminary and Grand View College and Grand View Seminary."[53] These twenty-two principles guaranteed, among other things, the continuation of Grand View Seminary's identity, the integration of Professor Axel Kildegaard into the Maywood faculty, representation on the Maywood Board of Directors, and the assurance that AELC students would be called only to AELC congregations upon graduation. This time the vote carried 165 to 1. Grand View Seminary moved to the Maywood campus one year later, the Fall of 1960. The decision made 74 years earlier, to locate the seminary in a "university" setting, was a long step nearer fulfillment.

Founders of Chicago Lutheran Seminary were similarly impressed by the advantageous environment of a major metropolitan area for theological education.

The pioneers chose wisely when they selected Chicago as the home for the Seminary. Chicago is preeminent in education, the very center of higher learning in America. It has six universities, eight law

[52]AELC, *Report*, 1959, pp. 144-45.
[53]These Principles are recorded in toto in AELC, *Report*, 1959, pp. 145-47.

schools, six medical schools. Chicagoland is also America's center of theological education. Every leading denomination has a theological seminary here.

Chicago libraries, with their more than five million volumes, many of them cultural institutions conceived on a magnificent scale, add to the advantages at our Seminary students' disposal.[54]

This statement, which appeared regularly in the Chicago Lutheran Theological Seminary *Record* in the 1940's was a genuine tribute to Dr. W. A. Passavant, founder of the seminary. It was through his personal foresight and generosity that the seminary came to locate in the Lake View area of Chicago in 1891. Previous to this time, voices back East had been saying in criticism of the choice of Philadelphia for a new seminary: "Theological seminaries in cities have been failures. There is not a single instance of eminent success in this country."[55] Passavant obviously felt otherwise, both with regard to Philadelphia and Chicago, and his choice of an urban location served the young seminary for its first nineteen years. Professor Gerberding recalled in his later years how the location had provided a host of opportunities for relating the Gospel to the needs of the vast city:

> The professor of Practical Theology used to take his classes down town to visit the Jail, the House of Correction, the Juvenile Court, the Hull-House and Chicago Commons, the County Hospital, the Municipal Lodging House and sundry welfare agencies.[56]

In time, however, commercial interests encroached upon the seminary's limited property of three acres. Even when additional, adjacent property was purchased at the price that added $57,000 to the indebtedness of the school, the problem was not solved. The incessant noise of freight trains being switched in the adjoining freight yards, seven days a week, twenty-four hours a day, plus the other distractions and inconveniences of a heavy-commercial area, eventually convinced the Board of Directors that the property should be sold and the seminary relocated. When the sale was effected at a price of $175,000 to developers who were to build the present Wrigley Field, home of the Chicago Cubs, on the site, there was a sense of relief on the part of the seminary family:

> The Seminary in this location [Maywood], said the *Record*, will be out of reach of the smoke, dust, grime, soot, dirt, foul gasses, etc., railroading by night and day, whistles, ding-donging of bells late and early and in between times, and the ceaselessness of undersirable traffic incidental thereto that is growing more unbearable every week. The good wives of the Seminary force and the faithful matron of the Seminary dormitory will not be ceaselessly at war in their continued battle against the dirt caused by coalyards, gravelyards, sandyards, ice stations, milk stations, etc., with all the attendant shifting of freight trains and driving of teams with the unsanctified

[54]CLTS, *Record*, January, 1944, p. 15.
[55]Tappert, *Lutheran Seminary at Philadelphia*, p. 31.
[56]Gerberding, *Reminiscent Reflections*, pp. 240-41.

men in charge sending the unsterilized particles, odors, and speech into the homes, eyes and ears of the Seminary habitants. The comforts of the students could be equally enlarged upon.[57]

In the quest for a new campus forty-one sites were examined by the board before it decided to purchase a sixteen acre tract, bounded by Tenth and Thirteenth avenues and Van Buren and Harrison streets, in Maywood, for a price of $15,306.[58] The selection of this new location was not without opposition. Professor Gerberding indicated that practically all of the professors and most of the Chicago pastors were opposed to the seminary's leaving Chicago.[59] In time, all contrary forces acquiesced, ten new buildings were erected on the Maywood campus in the Summer of 1910, and classes opened on the new location that Fall.

Not until 1945, did the seminary consider a movement back to the city. Preoccupied during the intervening years with a split which led to the development of Northwestern Theological Seminary in Minneapolis, with a depressing indebtedness that forced the school to live off its endowment funds until the early 1940's, with shrinking enrollments and a mounting indifference on the part of surrounding synods, the seminary was barely able to maintain its life, much less consider a dramatic move back to the urban area and a university setting. However, in the early 1940's the school's fortunes began to reverse. Under the leadership of Rev. Dr. Armin G. Weng, President of the Illinois Synod-ULCA and acting President of the Seminary 1941-42, a long-projected and greatly-needed $100,000 fund appeal in the Illinois Synod was brought to a successful completion; the seminary became solvent again. With the arrival of Rev. Dr. Charles B. Foelsch as President of the school in 1942, the academic house was put in order; new, young faculty members were added: Professors E. Theodore Bachmann, Joseph Sittler, Jr., Carl Umhau Wolf, and Charles W. Kegley,[60] to join the veteran Dr. H. Grady Davis; much needed repairs were made to the buildings; morale and student enrollments began to climb.

At this point, in 1945, Northwestern University in Evanston, through its President, Dr. Franklyn Bliss Snyder, offered a tract of real estate on Sheridan Road, immediately opposite Garrett Biblical Institute, as a new site for Chicago Lutheran Seminary. The ideal of having the seminary in a university-urban location was not dead, for when the proposal was presented at the Board of Directors meeting in February, 1945, "all members present [gave] their hearty approval to the basic idea of relocation. The Executive committee was directed to explore the plan and if feasible prepare it for later consideration by the Board."[61] Before this action could be fully implemented, the seminary received another offer, this one from the University of Chicago through its

[57]Marjory Weng, "Passavant's Vision," p. 29.
[58]*Ibid.*, p. 29.
[59]Gerberding, *Reminiscent Reflections*, p. 258.
[60]Marjory Weng, "Passavant's Vision," pp. 68-70.
[61]Charles B. Foelsch, "Concerning the Seminary's Relocation," CLTS, *Record*, July-October, 1945, p. 3.

Vice-President, and later President Dr. Ernest Cadman Colwell. This gift was even more generous because it incluede not only the land but also a complex of buildings which were currently occupied by the Orthogenic Clinic. The Executive Committee authorized an exploration of this offer, too. Both universities offered ninety-nine year leases at the rate of $1.00 per year, subject to renewal. After a long series of consultations, "the findings seemed to warrant the preparation of a tentative agreement form looking to the relocation of the Seminary on the Chicago University campus."[62] At the request of the seminary board, the five supporting synods of the ULCA—Illinois, Indiana, Michigan, Wartburg, and Pittsburgh—at their 1945 conventions considered resolutions to grant approval for relocation. All sanctioned the move, "though on the part of the Illinois, Wartburg, and Pittsburgh Synods with the provision that in the final consideration of the plan members of the Executive committee of all the supporting synods should have a voice, before the Board finally took action."[63] The Illinois Synod also added this provision: "the Board of Directors shall provide in the agreement with the University for perpetual independence and control of the Seminary as an institution of the Evangelical Lutheran Church."[64] Many saw this as an opportunity to express more fully the educational ideal in the context of a university-urban setting. An article in the schools's publication outlined this ideal:

> The Seminary's relocation at the University of Chicago would:
>
> . . . .
>
> help to prevent the genius of Lutheranism from being isolated and rendered irrelevant to the living issues in modern life; inasmuch as evangelical theology, indeed, in order to maintain its integrity and its ability to satisfy the needs of men must be vigorously proclaimed and stoutly defended on a front where conflicting points of view are contending for the allegiance of men;
>
> make available for the Seminary's use one of America's great libraries, including a valuable theological section besides the comprehensive interest, cultural advantages, and physical convenience of an outstanding university.[65]

That some of the oldest graduates of the school still supported this ideal was evident from this letter written by Rev. W. H. Shepfer, who graduated from the seminary at Lake View when it was just ten years old:

> We should not be afraid to enlarge our horizons. The Lutheran Church has grown up. It must leave its provincialisms. We must not continue to paddle around in ponds and mud puddles, but launch out into the deep and let down our nets for a draught . . . . The time is past for us to be hiding our Light under a bushel, or to be living the life of an ecclesiastical recluse . . . . The largest Protestant

[62]*Ibid.*, p. 4.
[63]*Ibid.*
[64]Illinois Synod-ULCA, *Minutes*, 1945, p. 38.
[65]CLTS, *Record*, July-October, 1945, p. 5.

Church in the world has an obligation to assume leadership and should not be satisfied to do small things in a small way . . . The deed is done; the Rubicon is crossed . . . Unitedly let us go forward![66]

Rev. Dr. Paul Krauss, son of Rev. Dr. Elmer F. Krauss, former president and professor at the school, and President of the Board of Directors at the time, noted in his report to the supporting synods in 1946, that "academically, theologically, and financially the opportunity seems more attractive than ever."[67] Hopes to relocate on the University of Chicago campus by the Fall of 1946 were dampened by the news that the university needed the buildings a bit longer pending further construction. Further delays were announced the next year:

The relocation plan is marking time pending the provision of quarters on the campus of the University of Chicago. Both the University authorities and the Seminary continue to be strongly committed to the relocation. During the summer of 1948 the buildings which have been offered for the purposes of the Seminary are expected to be available—therefore the actual moving of the institution should take place not later than September, 1948.[68]

The delays tried the patience of many and afforded others of the opposition time to attempt to thwart the effort. A surprise resolution by the Executive Board of the Illinois Synod-ULCA calling for the seminary to remain on the Maywood campus, threw the 1947, convention into two hours and twenty minutes of heated debate.[69] Finally a substitute motion calling for the relocation of the seminary prevailed by the narrow margin of sixty-two to fifty-nine.[70] For good measure, the Synod once again went on record favoring the University of Chicago location, urging the Board of Directors to work out the best possible arrangements. This passed by a stronger margin of eighty-four to forty-eight.

However, all efforts over the three year period proved to be in vain. In the end the university was unable to turn over the property it had promised. A sizeable gift to build a new building for the Orthogenic Center, expected by university officials, never materialized, due to the death of the prospective donor.[71] The already overcrowded university could not surrender space it did

66*Ibid.*, April, 1947, p. 20.
67Illinois Synod-ULCA, *Minutes*, 1946, p. 57.
68*Ibid.*, 1947, p. 61.
69*Ibid.*, pp. 20-21. "In anticipation of the proposed campaign of the Board of Education of the United Lutheran Church in America, it is recommended that the Illinois Synod representatives on the Board of Directors of the Chicago Lutheran Theological Seminary be instructed to urge the Seminary Board to present to the Board of Education of the United Lutheran Church plans for the future development of the Seminary on its present location."
70*Ibid.*, p. 21.
71Information secured in an interview with Rev. Dr. Joseph Sittler, Jr., July 7, 1968.

not have. Rev. Harmon J. McGuire, President of the Board of Directors, sadly reported to the supporting synods:

> The relocation matter is definitely settled. The Seminary remains in Maywood. This action became necessary when the University of Chicago, due to its own overcrowding, was unable to turn over to the Seminary the buildings which had been designated for Seminary use by the University.[72]

A disappointed seminary president, Dr. Foelsch, wistfully expressed his hope that "with all the arguments for and against the controversial relocation proposal in the realm of fading yesterdays, who will doubt that the pastors and people of our several synods will now rally to the Seminary's support with a united enthusiasm not to be realized while the heated debate was on."[73]

The trail to the university ended as abruptly as it began. A decade would elapse before it would be taken up again—this time successfully.

Suomi Seminary faced the same pressures as did Augustana, Chicago Lutheran, and Grand View, to relocate into a setting which would better enable it to achieve its theological task. This concern was expressed in the call letter to the 68th Church Convention of the Suomi Synod held in 1957, in Hancock, Michigan, the home of Suomi College and Theological Seminary.

> WHEREAS the Suomi Theological Seminary in Hancock, Michigan, has for several years suffered from the difficulty of maintaining an adequate faculty that would guarantee a well-balanced theological education for the future members of the ministerium of Suomi Synod, and
>
> WHEREAS this difficulty has built up pressures among students and faculty members which eventually would make the implementation of the program of said seminary increasingly difficult, and
>
> WHEREAS conditions in modern church work have made the ministry a highly demanding and specialized service,
>
> BE IT THEREFORE RESOLVED, that Suomi Synod grant the right to the Consistory of the Suomi Synod and the Board of Suomi College and Theological Seminary to separate Suomi Theological Seminary from Suomi College with the further right to affiliate said seminary with some other larger Lutheran seminary in such a way that Suomi Theological Seminary will still continue to be a distinct institution of Suomi Synod capable of fulfilling its unique task in training ministers for bilingual work, and
>
> BE IT FURTHER RESOLVED that the large Lutheran Seminary to be chosen by the Consistory of Suomi Synod and Board of Suomi College and Theological Seminary as the site of affiliation will be determined by the decision Suomi Synod will make as to the direction of merger at the June, 1957, 68th Church Convention in Hancock, Michigan.[74]

[72]Illinois Synod-ULCA, *Minutes*, 1948, p. 48.
[73]Charles B. Foelsch, CLTS, *Record*, October, 1947, p. 6.
[74]Suomi Synod, "Minutes," 1957, *Yearbook*, 1958, p. 25.

These proposed resolutions were an attempt to complete the separation of the seminary from the college which had officially begun the previous year. At that time, according to Suomi Synod President, Dr. Raymond Wargelin, "The Board of Suomi College and Theological Seminary, having dragged its feet on this request for several years, finally gave its approval in 1956 and the division was made."[75] By division, however, was meant the separation of administrative budgets, but the retention of the same administrative personnel. The seminary saw itself drifting further apart from the college as the new four-year college graduate requirement for seminary entrance accentuated the academic difference between the junior college and seminary students, as the seminary faculty showed an increasing interest in providing its own program and promotion, and as the presence of a lay-president continued to be a source of constant irritation to the theological faculty.[76] It was inevitable that the division should be more firmly fixed. Furthermore, factors were at work that seemed to make the present location of the seminary less and less desirable: the increasing use of English in Suomi congregations minimized the need for a seminary that could train men for a Finnish ministry, thus questioning the justification for existence of a small seminary in Hancock; the recently added requirement of a college degree for entrance into the seminary was producing more demanding students, and the limited faculty in Hancock had difficulty meeting these demands; and greater numbers of Suomi Synod students were choosing to attend larger Lutheran seminaries instead of Suomi Seminary, with the result that Suomi's enrollment was small and static.[77] Matters were complicated when Rev. Dr. Walter Kukkonen, professor in the seminary, had to take a leave-of-absence in the summer of 1955, due to exhaustion caused by the excessive demands of teaching too many different courses. Rev. Karlo Keljo replaced him that fall, but left in December to accept a call to a parish. Rev. Arvo Niskanen, then doing graduate work in theology at the University of Helsinki in Finland, was called, but died unexpectedly just prior to the beginning of the school year in the fall of 1956. Professor Kukkonen, long an advocate for relocation of the seminary, returned to Hancock to preach the funeral sermon. He asked the congregation, "How plainly does God have to speak to us to show us that we cannot continue as we have been doing?"[78]

What internal arguments could not effect, external forces were soon able to accomplish. These forces were in the form of the Joint Commission on Lutheran Unity. Suomi Synod commissioners were present at the initial meeting of JCLU on December 12-13, 1956, and again for the second on March 8-9, 1957. They were convinced that the future of theological education in the Suomi Synod had to be linked to the pending merger. The Consistory of the

[75]Raymond W. Wargelin, "Two Decades of Change," Suomi Synod, *Yearbook*, 1962, p. 63.
[76]*Ibid.*
[77]Information secured in an interview with Professor Walter Kukkonen, May 29, 1968.
[78]*Ibid.*

synod, which previously had been "hesitant about projecting an action that would change the historical pattern of educational matters," but seeing that "one overt step after another to strengthen the program of the Seminary failed to materialize," knew that "steps must be taken to procure better training for the future pastors of the church."[79] The result was the series of resolutions included in the letter of call to the 1957 convention.[80] The 1957 *Yearbook* also contained a three-page report indicating the feasibility of an association between Suomi Seminary and Chicago Lutheran Seminary.[81] Chicago's willingness to entertain such an association was clearly stated.

The delegates to the Hancock convention faced the seminary issue on June 18, 1957. After a lively and lengthy debate the votes were taken on each portion of the three-part resolution:

1. Separation of the seminary from the college. Yes-249, No-81. Carried.

2. Affiliation of the seminary with a larger Lutheran seminary. Yes-227, No-97. Carried.

3. Selection of the larger seminary on the basis of the vote to be taken on the merger question.[82] Yes-259, No-40. Carried.[83]

The enabling actions came at the next convention of the Suomi Synod in Detroit in 1958. Delegates had received in advance copies of the "Principles of Agreement" drawn up between Chicago Lutheran Seminary and Suomi Theological Seminary, as well as a proposed Constitution for the now-independent seminary.[84] Rather perfunctory meetings had been held also with representatives of Augustana Theological Seminary and Hamma Divinity School during the previous months,[85] but the committee expressed a preference for the Maywood school because of its Chicago location and the contacts it had experienced over the years through Suomi students who had attended there. The Suomi Synod Consistory and Suomi College and Theological Seminary Board presented its resolution:

[79]Suomi Synod, *Yearbook*, 1957, p. 36.
[80]*Supra*, p. 38.
[81]Suomi Synod, *Yearbook*, 1957, pp. 150-52.
[82]This meant that if the Suomi Synod voted to join the American Lutheran Church merger an ALC seminary would be selected, or if the Lutheran Church in America merger would be chosen a LCA seminary would be selected.
[83]Voting results are recorded in Suomi Synod, "Minutes," 1957, *Yearbook*, 1958, p. 26.
[84]Suomi Synod, *Yearbook*, 1958, pp. 95-102.
[85]Correspondence between Suomi Synod President, Dr. Raymond Wargelin, and Augustana Seminary President, Dr. Karl E. Mattson, October, 1957-February, 1958, now contained in the LSTC Archives, as well as references in Augustana Seminary, *Minutes*, February 4-5, 1958, pp. 3-4, indicate that a meeting was held on the Rock Island campus, November 21, 1957, involving Rev. Eino M. Tuori, Rev. Ralph Jalkanen, and Rev. Dr. Bernhard Hillila of Suomi Synod and representatives of Augustana Seminary. A spirit of good will is evident in these records, and a definite invitation to Suomi Seminary is included in a letter from President Mattson, dated February 5, 1958. President Wargelin's reply of February 21, 1958, indicates both the plan to move to Maywood and the assurance of interest in a larger merger eventually involving Augustana, Maywood, and Suomi.

Since favorable action has been taken by both groups authorized by the Suomi Synod Church Convention to separate and reaffiliate Suomi Seminary, it is hereby moved that this decision be adopted as a plan of action.[86]

Action was delayed while debate centered about a proposal from the Michigan Conference to postpone action on the whole matter. Finally, when the vote was taken and the ballots were counted, the "Principles of Agreement" were adopted by the narrow margin of 167 to 149. That Fall, 1958, eight students and two professors relocated from Hancock to Maywood in a move called the "Event of the Year at Maywood."[87] The long trail to the university was suddenly shortened by five hundred miles.

[86]Suomi Synod, "Minutes," 1958, *Yearbook*, 1959, p. 19.
[87]Donald R. Heiges, "Event of the Year," Suomi Synod, *Yearbook*, 1959, pp. 86-87.

Chapter IV

MERGER BEGETS MERGER

On September 5, 1962, Charles F. Carpentier, Secretary of State of the State of Illinois, signed the documents that legally consolidated Augustana, Grand View, Maywood, and Suomi seminaries into the Lutheran School of Theology at Chicago.[1] The four seminaries were still located on two campuses, Rock Island and Maywood, but it was understood that in a short time, hopefully by 1966,[2] the new campus would be completed and the consolidated school could begin its work in the university-urban setting adjacent to the campus of the University of Chicago.

These events would appear to be the logical consequence of the common history, tradition, and educational ideal which all the schools shared. Yet, the aspirations cherished by those who had a keen appreciation for a theological education in a university-urban setting were never, by themselves, adequate to get the task accomplished. As was the case with Grand View and Suomi seminaries, which knew theoretically that relocation was inevitable, and yet refused to take action until driven to it by the negative force of declining enrollments and the positive force of pending church merger, so in the case of the larger consolidation involving all four schools there had to be a force stronger than the educational ideal itself. The force was found in the developing merger negotiations of the Lutheran bodies that united to form the Lutheran Church in America, and the inevitable effect this merger would have on seminaries in the mid-west.

The whole Church merger development got underway on March 28, 1955, when the United Lutheran Church in America, having declared its desire to merge with any or all Lutheran church bodies in America, issued an invitation to the Augustana Lutheran Church to join it in issuing invitations to all other Lutheran church bodies to participate in merger discussions looking toward organic union. At its annual convention in June, 1955, the Augustana Church accepted the invitation, and on the following December 16, letters of invitation were issued over the signatures of Oscar A. Benson and Franklin Clark Fry, Presidents of Augustana and ULCA. Two of the fourteen bodies invited

---

[1]See Appendix II.
[2]The first target date set. Later it was changed to 1967.

43

responded affirmatively,[3] the American Evangelical Lutheran Church and The Finnish Evangelical Lutheran Church of America—Suomi Synod. One year later, after informal preliminary meetings had been held to prepare for the undertaking, forty-six commissioners, representing these four churches, assembled in Chicago on December 12, 1956, to organize the Joint Commission on Lutheran Unity (JCLU) and begin negotiations.

At its second meeting, March 8-9, 1957, JCLU confronted the seminary question for the first time. In adopting a series of guidelines, which were retained throughout the merger negotiations, JCLU declared that:

1. Ownership and primary responsibility for administration and control of theological seminaries shall be vested in the constituent units of the united church.

2. The general body shall have a major board, or division of a board, with the following powers:

   a. Construct a master plan of location of theological seminaries.

   b. Approve the establishment and relocation of seminaries within the united church.[4]

. . . .[5]

Thus, it was established at the outset that the task of determining the number and location of seminaries would be delegated to the new Church and would not be assumed by JCLU. Individual commissioners and churches resisted this ruling at times during the merger negotiations, expressing the conviction that JCLU should take a firm hand in these matters, but the original rule prevailed. Also, the rule made clear that seminaries would be owned by regional synods, as in the case of ULCA, not by the national church body, as in the case of the other three churches. The implication for the midwestern seminaries became readily apparent. Four of the eleven American seminaries—Augustana, Grand View, Maywood, and Suomi—would be located in the state of Illinois,[6] while three others—Central, Fremont, Nebraska; Hamma, Springfield, Ohio; and Northwestern, Minneapolis, Minnesota—would be in nearby states. For the seminaries in Illinois this posed an immediate problem. The three seminaries which received financial support and recruited students on a national basis would now have a limited, regional base. The one seminary, Chicago Lutheran, that was accustomed to regional support would now be in competition with three other

---

[3]Four other bodies were currently engaged in merger negotiations of their own which led to The American Lutheran Church in 1960, and these bodies preferred to follow their own course.

[4]Joint Commission on Lutheran Unity, *Minutes*, March 8-9, 1957, p. 24.

[5]Six additional sub-points are listed in the *Minutes*.

[6]Actually at this time Grand View was still in Des Moines, Iowa, and Suomi was in Hancock, Michigan, but negotiations regarding their relocation to Maywood were underway and their eventual move could be safely assumed. *Supra*, Chapter 3, pp. 30-33 and 40-41.

seminaries on the territory. President Karl E. Mattson of Augustana Seminary articulated the problem in his report to the Augustana Church:

> The pattern of seminary life in the new church calls for synodical ownership and control of the seminaries. If we expect to continue with the status quo we will find ourselves in a position where we must share financial support and students with at least one or more seminaries who will be serving the same area. The prospect, if the status quo is to be maintained, is a smaller and weaker seminary.[7]

Later experience verified President Mattson's apprehension. In the case of Augustana Seminary, incoming Junior classes which had averaged fifty-two students per class during the decade 1953-63, suddenly after the LCA merger in 1962, until the relocation to Chicago in 1967, dropped to an average of twenty-nine students per class, a reduction in enrollment of 44 per cent. During the same period Maywood Seminary showed a slight average gain of five incoming students per year, but these figures included former AELC and Suomi students who were now attending Maywood. (See Table 1, page 46.)

In addition to the obvious problem which the pending LCA merger posed for the Illinois seminaries, it also provided a unique opportunity: only on this territory of the new Church could all four merging traditions be represented in one theological seminary.

> Although the immediate occasion for the seminary merger discussion was the imminent church merger, it early became apparent to the members of the Inter-Seminary Committee that a unique opportunity for creative action in the field of theological education had been granted the church. The area of the four seminaries is the only area within the Lutheran Church in America where all four of the merging churches have a seminary. Only in this area is it possible for the Lutheran Church in America to bring together four seminaries representing distinct heritages in American Lutheranism. This new seminary of the Lutheran Church in America thus becomes a significant visible symbol of the new unity in the Lutheran Church in America.[8]

It became increasingly clear to more and more people that the only way to solve the problem of competition, and the best way to capitalize on the opportunity to blend four theological traditions, was to merge the four seminaries into one. President Armin G. Weng of the Maywood campus spoke for these when he later made this observation about those formative years:

> Administration, professors and students alike have followed with keen interest the progress toward merger, the origin of which was in the minds of several of us as early as the beginnings of J.C.L.U.

[7] Karl E. Mattson, "Augustana Seminary President's Report," Augustana Lutheran Church, *Minutes*, 1960, p. 366.
[8] *Official Documents of the Lutheran School of Theology at Chicago*, 1961, p. 5.

TABLE 1

AVERAGE NUMBER OF INCOMING JUNIOR STUDENTS AT MERGING SEMINARIES, BEFORE AND AFTER LCA MERGER

Seminary/Location	Average 1953-1963	62-63	63-64	64-65	65-66	66-67	67-68
Augustana 1953-1967 Rock Island	52	35	41	23	17	30	–
Central 1953-1967 Fremont	13	17	13	7	10	8	–
Chicago Lutheran 1953-1967 Maywood	29	22	46	32	26	38	–
Grand View 1953-1960 Des Moines 1960-1967 Maywood	3			Included in CLTS			–
Suomi 1953-1958 Hancock 1958-1967 Maywood	4		Included in CLTS				–
LSTC 1967-1968 Chicago	–	–	–	–	–	–	82
Total	101	74	100	62	53	76	82

46

discussions. That there should be but one strong seminary on the territory was self-evident.[9]

"That there should be but one strong seminary on the territory was self-evident," but how should this seminary come about? Who would take the initiative to begin merger negotiations? JCLU would not and really could not. Its crowded agenda would not permit the addition of such matters without creating undue delays in the merger schedule. Secondly, the matter of seminary merger and relocation was a perennial subject of controversy in the United Lutheran Church in America. There were many who were adamant in their resistance to any movement on the part of the national church to exercise control over the regionally owned and operated seminaries.[10] In the light of these circumstances, caution prevailed. Rather than taking the risk of scuttling the entire church merger by a premature confrontation of this controversial issue, JCLU declined the role of initiator. President Fry assured his fellow-clergy of the ULCA:

> It is an open-secret that many in JCLU are unhappy at the present number and geographical pattern of our United Lutheran seminaries. They believe that they are too numerous, in view of the resources of theological scholarship available, and in some cases too close to each other. As a result, there was a strong sentiment in favor of a free vote on this issue prior to the merger. That desire has been abandoned in deference to the principle, which has been mentioned repeatedly, that good faith in a church union calls for the acceptance of the status quo on the day on which the new church comes into existence.[11]

At the same time he voiced the appeal that members of the ULCA would honestly examine the question of the number and location of seminaries in the light of present needs, and thus he gave an impetus to any regional groups who were willing on their own to face up to the question in their own areas:

> In the same spirit of justice and magnanimity, we in the United Lutheran Church ought not to be oblivious of the good judgment of our friends and (we hope) future partners in the church-to-be, all the more so when, in candor and honesty, a host of us have unquiet minds about it ourselves. Is not this the hour, our shining opportunity that ought not to be allowed to slip away, for us to re-examine our own seminaries while we are responsible only to ourselves, to the future and to God? With due respect to our fathers, let us remember that the high calling of theological education in 1958 is not to perpetuate the past but to serve the vibrant and expanding generation in which we ourselves live—and, further beyond, to build for a still more imposing century to come.[12]

---

[9]Armin G. Weng, "Report of the President," Chicago Lutheran Theological Seminary, Board of Directors, *Minutes* April 26, 1961, p. 2.

[10]*Infra*, p. 56.

[11]Franklin Clark Fry, "The State of the Church," *Desk Book*, September, 1958, p. NE-944.

[12]*Ibid.*

This much was clear—if Augustana, Grand View, Maywood, Suomi, and any other mid-west seminaries were to begin merger conversations, the initiative must come from outside JCLU.

MERGER TALKS BEGIN

The first invitation to consider consolidation and relocation came from the University of Chicago, eleven years after its initial invitation to move to the university had been extended to the Maywood campus.[13] At the suggestion of Lutheran faculty members in the university's Divinity School, Chancellor Lawrence A. Kimpton called a luncheon meeting on October 25, 1956.[14] Since neither Suomi Seminary nor Grand View Seminary had yet relocated to Maywood, the invitations were limited to Augustana and Maywood seminaries. Representing Augustana were its President, Dr. Mattson, and its board Chairman, Rev. Dr. O. O. Gustafson; representing Maywood were its President, Dr. Weng, and a board member, Rev. William J. Boldt; Chancellor Kimpton and Dean Brauer represented the university. The university's interest was precipitated in part by the urban renewal program which was just developing[15] and in part by a desire to accent the humanities in an environment that was becoming increasingly weighted in the direction of the physical sciences. As Dr. Kimpton later expressed it:

> We wanted to attract good groups because of our urban renewal program. We thought the Lutherans were a splendid group and we were eager to have them as members of our community. At the same time we felt the existence of numerous protestant faiths, a large library, an academic community, etc., would be of benefit to the Lutherans.[16]

Discussion at the luncheon centered about the possibility of both schools moving to the university, the availability and costs of land, and the serious desire of the University of Chicago to have the seminaries relocate on its campus.[17] The meeting, though cordial, produced no immediate results beyond establishing

---

[13]*Supra*, pp. 35-36.

[14]These professors were Dean Jerald Brauer, Joseph Sittler, Jr., and Granger Westberg. In the light of pending JCLU merger negotiations, they saw an opportunity to achieve a seminary merger and relocation to a university-urban setting and thus better implement the educational ideal cherished by the merging churches. Information is based on personal interviews with Dr. Westberg, June 4, 1968; Dr. Brauer, June 24, 1968; Dr. Sittler, July 7, 1968; and correspondence from Dr. Westberg, May 28 and June 21, 1968; Dr. Kimpton, June 7 and 12, 1968; and Rev. William J. Boldt, May 29, 1968.

[15]This urban renewal program was being launched in the entire Hyde Park area of Chicago where the University of Chicago is located. Hyde Park is the area bounded by Hyde Park Boulevard, Cottage Grove Avenue, the Midway, and Lake Michigan. Here the first large-scale Urban Renewal Project in the country was developed. The program had the result of stabilizing the population and property values by stopping the exodus of white families as black families purchased property in the area. The consequence was a relatively successful integrated residential area.

[16]Letter from Dr. Kimpton to the writer. June 12,1968

[17]Based on letter from Rev. William J. Boldt to the writer, May 29, 1968, and a personal interview with Dean Brauer, June 24, 1968.

the university's good will and interest.[18] Minutes of the boards of directors of Augustana and Maywood simply record the following:

> Augustana: Dr. Gustafson and President Mattson reported on their conference with Chancellor Kimpton with respect to the invitation to move the Seminary to Chicago. They indicated that a cordial meeting was held on October 25, 1956.[19]

> Maywood: Dr. Weng told of a meeting that he and Pastor Boldt attended by invitation of Dr. Kimpton, Chancellor of the University of Chicago. Present in addition were Dean Brauer and President Mattson of Augustana Seminary. He stated there was no interest in pursuing conversation any further.[20]

Augustana's reticence can best be understood in light of the fact that JCLU negotiations were just in the planning stage at the time, and the eventual merger which produced the Lutheran Church in America was by no means envisioned as a certainty. This was also true for Maywood Seminary, but in addition, in their case the memories of the bitter controversy less than a decade earlier, over that seminary's relocation to the University of Chicago, and the subsequent withdrawal of the agreement by the university, were still fresh in the minds of many. Then, too, there were the twin attractions on the Maywood campus of a new library, completed four years earlier, and the largest B.D. enrollment in its history, 105, as compared with a low of nineteen just ten years before. Conditions had never been better on the Maywood campus. There was a natural reluctance to move.

One year later a second meeting was called at the University of Chicago. This time it was to be in the nature of an informal discussion with representatives of Augustana and Maywood seminaries, the Illinois Synod-ULCA, the Central Conference-Augustana Lutheran Church, with Dean Jerald Brauer serving as host. The purpose of the meeting, scheduled for October 30, 1957, was stated by the convener: "It was our hope that we might have discovered some way to present certain concerns to the various boards responsible for making any decisions regarding our Lutheran Theological Seminaries."[21] President Weng was unable to attend the meeting and President Mattson declined. In doing so, President Mattson stated the position of the

---

[18]This is verified in a letter of June 13, 1968, from Dr. Robert Mortvedt, Secretary of the Augustana Seminary Board of Directors at the time, to the writer:
"I can tell you that I remember very well some of the conversations following the visit with Chancellor Lawrence Kimpton . . . . I recall very well [President] Karl Mattson's comments about the enthusiastic response which he received from Chancellor Kimpton relative to the possibility of having a Lutheran Seminary near or on the University of Chicago campus."
[19]Augustana Theological Seminary, Board of Directors, *Minutes*, February 5-7, 1957, p. 6.
[20]Chicago Lutheran Theological Seminary, Board of Directors, Executive Committee, *Minutes*, December 13, 1956, p. 1.
[21]Letter from Dean Brauer to President Mattson, November 1, 1957, in LSTC Archives.

Augustana Church's Commission on Ecumenical Relation, at the time, that Augustana favored Church ownership and control for all seminaries, and that this question should have precedence over the matter of individual and regional seminary concerns. There was still the hope among Augustana leaders, despite the "Guidelines" for theological seminaries adopted at the March 8-9, 1957, JCLU meeting,[22] that the seminary question could be dealt with on a national level. Despite the absence of the chief administrators of the two seminaries the October 30, 1957, meeting at the University of Chicago had the salutary effect of keeping the merger and relocation question alive. It also enabled the university to reaffirm its invitation to the seminaries to locate on its campus.

When JCLU met December 12-14, 1957, the seminary issue arose again, as Augustana commissioners attempted to offer a substitute motion to replace the "Guidelines" adopted in March. The substitute would have provided for Church ownership of seminaries, but it was defeated. In its place a motion was passed to study the matter further.[23]

Time was fleeting. One year of JCLU negotiations had passed, and still there were no definite signs that JCLU would be willing to take the initiative on the seminary problem. Yet, the church merger seemed more assured than ever, which meant that the problem of having several seminaries on the same geographic territory was growing more acute. The time seemed to be right for some kind of action. It came in January, 1958.

THE INVITATION

In the January 15, 1968, *Minutes,* of the Executive Committee of Chicago Lutheran Theological Seminary appears this simple entry:

> It was moved and seconded that a letter be sent to the Board of Directors of the Augustana Theological Seminary: Motion carried.[24]

The historic letter follows:[25] (See page 51.)

Although the letter was signed by the Chairman and Secretary of the Board of Directors, the pride of authorship belonged to President Weng who commented just weeks before his death in 1967:

> It will always be a matter of satisfaction to me that I was the one, on behalf of the Board of Chicago Lutheran Theological Seminary, who wrote the letter to Augustana Seminary suggesting a merger.[26]

The Board of Directors of Augustana Seminary heard the letter at its February 4-5, 1958, meeting, and voted to accept "subject to the approval of and possible

---

[22]*Supra*, p. 44.
[23]JCLU, *Minutes*, December 12-14, 1957, p. 44.
[24]CLTS, Executive Committee, *Minutes*, January 15, 1958, p. 5.
[25]The original letter is in the LSTC Archives.
[26]Armin G. Weng, "Memories of Twenty Years at Maywood," LSTC-Maywood Campus, *Record*, May, 1967, p. 23.

CHICAGO LUTHERAN THEOLOGICAL SEMINARY
1644 South Eleventh Avenue
MAYWOOD, ILLINOIS

January 28, 1958

Phone
FIllmore 4-4200

The Reverend Oscar O. Gustafson
President, Board of Directors
Augustana Theological Seminary
P. O. Box 415
Dassel, Minnesota

Greetings:

Remembering the many instances of helpful consultation mutually
enjoyed by our Seminaries in times past and mindful of the great
significance to Lutheran Theological Education which arises out of
the progress being achieved in the work of the Joint Commission on
Lutheran Unity, the Executive Committee of the Board of Directors
of Chicago Lutheran Theological Seminary believes that the time is
now at hand when our two Theological Institutions might well enter
into discussion concerning the future Institutional possibilities
for Theological Education in the framework of a merged Church.

We, therefore, earnestly extend to you cordial invitation to create
with us an Inter-Seminary Committee whose purpose shall be to discuss, explore and survey the whole area of our mutual concerns for
Theological Education in the light of merger possibilities.

Such a committee might include the Presidents and Secretaries of the
two Boards, two additional members from each Board, the President of
each Seminary and a member from each of the two faculties.

Our next regular meeting of our full Board will occur on April 30,
1958 and any report of content which a joint committee might be prepared to make at that time would doubtless receive solid support
from our Board.

May we have your reaction to this proposal, and of course, any suggestions which you may feel would be more feasible than those
presented above.

Sincerely yours,

Lyman Grimes, President

Alfred Stone, Secretary
The Executive Committee
Board of Directors
Chicago Lutheran Theological Seminary

cc to: Dr. Mattson
        Dr. Weng

51

instruction by the Church's Commission on Ecumenical Relations."[27] A letter from President Mattson, February 12, 1958, to Maywood Seminary verified the acceptance, while a second letter to Dr. Oscar Benson, Augustana Church President, requested immediate approval by the Ecumenical Commission, stating: "It is imperative we meet with Chicago or otherwise they are going out on a big drive to spend more on their own campus." [28]

INTER-SEMINARY COMMITTEE FORMED

The historic, first meeting of the Inter-Seminary Committee was April 23, 1958, in the conference room of Christ the King Lutheran Church in the Loop, 327 South LaSalle Street, Chicago. Nineteen meetings would follow before the committee would complete its tasks on March 26, 1962.

Present at the initial session were Augustana Representatives: Dr. Karl E. Mattson, President; Dr. O. O. Gustafson, Board Chairman; Dr. Arthur O. Hjelm, Board member substituting for Dr. Granger Westberg; Dr. Arthur Arnold, Faculty; Mr. Lloyd A. Schwiebert, Board member; and Dr. Robert Mortvedt, Executive-Secretary of the Board of Christian Higher Education of the Augustana Lutheran Church; Maywood Representatives: Dr. Armin G. Weng, President; Rev. Lyman H. Grimes, Board Chairman; Dr. A. Howard Weeg, Board member; Dr. Johannes Knudsen, Faculty; Dr. Gould Wickey, Executive Secretary of the Board of Christian Education of the United Lutheran Church. Over the years others would join the committee as additional personnel or replacements until finally a total of seventy different men would serve on the committee. This included AELC–6, Augustana–27, Suomi–8, and ULCA–29.[29] Officers of the committee elected at the meeting were Grimes, Chairman, and Arnold, Secretary. Mortvedt became Chairman in 1960, when Grimes moved to Florida.

ORGANIZATIONAL PRINCIPLES

It was apparent at the first meeting that the two seminaries would be functioning in the merger conversations under two different sets of principles. As the only seminary of the Augustana Church and completely under the ownership and control of the church, Augustana Seminary's representatives had to function within the framework of the authority given to it. This was clearly stated in the enabling resolution passed by the Church's Commission on Ecumenical Relations:

> Voted: that we recognize the authority of the Seminary Board to engage in exploratory conversations begun with other seminaries and that information useful to the work of the Commission may be derived therefrom and request that all such conversations bear in mind the authority to be assigned to the church at large with

[27] Augustana Seminary, Board of Directors, *Minutes*, February 4-5, 1958, p. 5.
[28] Letters in LSTC Archives.
[29] This list of seventy men and a list of meetings attended may be seen in Appendix III. The only representative to attend all twenty meetings was President Mattson.

reference to theological education and institutions, and providing also that no attempt be made during these conversations to arrive at a consensus regarding the eventual pattern with regard to particular seminaries.[30]

This meant that the Church must be kept constantly informed and that approval must be given for any major decisions. The situation with respect to Chicago Lutheran Seminary was somewhat different. Responsibility was limited to the five supporting synods who elected members to the Board of Directors. Under its charter and constitution the Board possessed full authority to proceed with merger negotiations. Progress reports were to be made to the Board of Directors for information purposes only. In the end only the definite legal actions required for merger would have to be approved by the synods.[31]

As an entity in itself the Inter-Seminary Committee was a creation of the two seminary boards. It had no powers and authority of its own. Any decisions it made were not binding until another body—the seminary boards or the supporting synods and churches—ratified them. Yet without any vested authority the committee worked through all the details of merger, formulated legal documents, recommended the location for the new school, and even selected building sites—all decisions that required ratification by the duly constituted authorities—and not once was a decision or recommendation of this committee denied. This success was due to the committee's extreme sensitivity to principles which it later enunciated:

A. The Inter-Seminary Committee should take no action which would:

    1. Commit the board of the new seminary to any obligations which it might not have to or want to assume, whether as to finances, personnel, policy, or any other matter; or

    2. Presume on the prerogatives of the board.

B. Within the limitations of the above statement, and in accord with previously adopted decisions of the Inter-Seminary Committee, especially those which have been included as a part of the basic aggreements on which the merger of the seminaries was approved, the committee should do all that it can to facilitate the actual establishment of the merged seminary by:

    1. Taking such action as is in keeping with the merger agreements, which the board would necessarily have to take and which can with advantage be done without delay; and

[30]Augustana Lutheran Church, Commission on Ecumenical Relations, *Minutes*, March 19, 1958, p. 2.
[31]Armin G. Weng, "From the President's Desk," CLTS, *Record*, May, 1960, p. 25.

2. Making such further studies as might be helpful, on the basis of which the board can act wisely and quickly.[32]

In addition to sensing their responsibilties to their seminary boards and constituencies, the representatives on the Inter-Seminary Committee recognized an obligation to JCLU and its Committee on Seminaries. President Mattson, a member of JCLU, cautioned the committee at the first meeting that its work was to be "purely exploratory to provide useful information to the Commission [JCLU], and that by order of the Commission 'the Committee shall make no attempt to arrive at a consensus regarding the eventual pattern with regard to particular seminaries'."[33] Inherent in this statement was the conviction that JCLU should, and the hope that it would, play a major role in the whole seminary question. In this spirit the committee at its second meeting notified JCLU of the preliminary merger discussions and requested "guidance and counsel."[34] One year later representatives of JCLU's Committee on Seminaries—Dr. Oscar Benson, Dr. Franklin Clark Fry, and Rev. Ronald Jespersen—met with the Inter-Seminary Committee. It was clear that the JCLU committee saw its role as advisory. Chairman Benson explained: "We have agreed to ask the JCLU to make available to various seminaries the services of this committee in unofficial discussions regarding merger and relocation or realignment of seminaries. We would urge that they avail themselves of such services before arriving at any findings."[35] Nothing was said to discourage these seminaries from continuing their talks leading to eventual merger. In fact, Dr. Fry "expressed the hope that the constituent churches involved in the merger discussions may have given consent prior to the merger of the church to the merger of seminaries."[36] The meeting clarified the point that seminary mergers, if they were to take place before church merger, would do so only at the initiative of the individual seminaries, not under the guidance of JCLU. Those who were not ready to accept this ruling, especially the Augustana commissioners, proposed a motion at the JCLU meeting the next month, that "JCLU enunciate the principle that the new Church operate and support a maximum of five or six seminaries."[37] The motion gained some support, but it was deferred until the December, 1959, meeting. At this meeting the proposal was withdrawn and in its place a motion was passed authorizing the new Board of Theological Education to make recommendations to the second convention of the new church regarding the number and location of seminaries. The decision was final and irrevocable. JCLU would not under any circumstances take the initiative in

[32]Inter-Seminary Committee, *Minutes*, August 31, 1961, Exhibit A, "Report of the Committee to Study the Limits of Jurisdiction of the Inter-Seminary Committee," p. 1.
[33]Inter-Seminary Committee, *Minutes*, April 23, 1958, p. 1.
[34]*Ibid.*, June 23, 1958, p. 2.
[35]*Ibid.*, June 25, 1959, p. 1.
[36]*Ibid.*, p. 3.
[37]JCLU, *Minutes*, July 16-18, 1959, p. 145.

merging and relocating seminaries. The Inter-Seminary Committee must proceed on its own, but with the blessing of JCLU.

OTHER SEMINARIES INVITED

At its first meeting the Inter-Seminary Committee considered very seriously the matter of inviting other mid-western seminaries to participate in the merger conversations. At this time it was generally known that the Suomi Synod Consistory was ready to propose the relocation of Suomi Seminary to the Maywood campus[38] and that AELC was considering the same.[39] A motion passed to invite Grand View and Suomi seminary representatives met with approval by the boards of Augustana and Maywood. Grand View accepted and became a permanent member of the committee at the next meeting through its representatives: Grand View Dean, Axel Kildegaard, and AELC President, Alfred Jensen, who was replaced on the committee by Dr. A. E. Farstrup when he became AELC Presiden in 1960. Suomi Synod, which held its annual convention during the week of the Inter-Seminary Committee's second meeting and voted to relocate on the Maywood Campus at that convention, also accepted permanent membership. Its representatives, Professors Karlo J. Keljo and Walter Kukkonnen, were present at the Fall meeting, and in 1960-61, were joined by Dr. Raymond Wargelin, Suomi Synod President.

Hamma Invited

Many members of the Inter-Seminary Committee hoped that the merger of seminaries might be even more inclusive of mid-western seminaries. At the second meeting, when all presidents of synods supporting Chicago Lutheran Seminary joined as permanent members, Dr. Walter Wick of Indiana raised a question regarding the possible involvement of Hamma Divinity School, Springfield, Ohio, in these talks. Action was taken at a subsequent meeting requesting the presidents of the Indiana and Michigan synods to "arrange for a representative or observer from the Hamma Divinity School at future meetings of this committee," and to assure Hamma that "such a representative or observer would be most welcome."[40] In response, the Wittenberg University Board, which governed Hamma, appointed President Clarence Stoughton and Dr. Carl Satre, Chairman of the Seminary Committee, as observers, with Dr. Donald Elder, Secretary of the Committee, serving as alternate. Hamma was represented at three meetings in 1959. That the Ohio school did not enter seriously into the merger discussions is explained partly by the fact that its representatives were appointed strictly as observers, not as participants, and in part by fear on behalf of some that the presence of a second ULCA seminary might threaten the balance of power in the delicate negotiations among the other seminaries. There is also a strong indication that many Hamma supporters believed that the continuation of the school on the Ohio territory was necessary for the sake of

---

[38]*Supra*, pp. 39-41.
[39]*Supra*, pp. 32-33.
[40]Inter-Seminary Committee, *Minutes*, November 25, 1958, p. 2.

the Church.[41] These supporters welcomed the announcement made in Chicago on January 20, 1960, by JCLU's Committee on Seminaries that "all the theological seminaries of the merging church bodies and their constituent synods shall be recognized by the Lutheran Church in America as institutions of the church," and that "financial provision will be made in the first budget of the church to assure each seminary of as much income from church sources during each year of the first biennium of the Lutheran Church in America as that seminary received from its supporting constitutency in the last year preceding the merger."[42] Thereafter, the Hamma Board of Directors chose not to be represented any longer on the Inter-Seminary Committee.

The conviction that Hamma should retain its identity and serve the Ohio area was firmly fixed in the consciousness of many in the Ohio Synod–ULCA. Dr. Conrad Bergendoff, in his studies of LCA seminaries immediately after the Church merger, made this observation in his 1963 report:

> The action of the Church in assigning only one supporting synod to Hamma may be interpreted as confidence in the Ohio Synod to bear this burden. Certainly this synod has demonstrated its willingness to give substantial aid. On the other hand evidence points to Hamma as largely an Ohio institution. While this situation is not unique at Hamma, the degree to which it is true here is greater than at the seminaries so far surveyed. I do not have a remedy to suggest, but I call it to the attention of the BTE.[43]

This "Ohio consciousness" had frustrated previous attempts at merger with Chicago. In the late twenties, when a movement was started toward seminary consolidation in the ULCA, a meeting of mid-western seminaries, including Maywood and Hamma, was held in Chicago in 1929, and it was agreed that "a thorough study should be made."[44] Subsequently the Board of Education of ULCA made a series of recommendations to the Philadelphia Convention in 1932. Among those adopted was the resolution that "Hamma and Chicago seminaries be merged, and be supported by the following synods: Ohio, Indiana, Michigan, Illinois, Wartburg."[45] The action was ruled unconstitutional in 1934 by the ULCA Court of Adjudication on the grounds that the "powers of the general church body were advisory only."[46] This ruling nullified an action taken by the Illinois Synod in 1933, to approve the principle of merger and enter into negotiations,[47] but the Board of Directors of Chicago Lutheran was able to report favorable news in its 1935 *Report*:

[41]Information based on interviews with Dr. Satre and Dr. Elder on July 22, 1968.
[42]JCLU, Volume 7, *Pensions, Publications, Social Ministry, Theological Education, World Missions*, Committee on Seminaries, "Report of Consultations," Exhibit B, p. 1.
[43]Conrad Bergendoff, *Executive Secretary's Reports, 1-11, To The Board of Theological Education*, October, 1962-May, 1963, "Report No. 4," pp. 14-15.
[44]Marjory Weng, "Passavant's Vision," p. 59.
[45]ULCA, *Minutes*, 1932, p. 453.
[46]LCA, *Bulletin of Reports*, 1968, p. 493.
[47]Illinois Synod-ULCA, *Minutes*, 1933, p. 21.

In response to a resolution of Synod at its 1934 convention, representatives of the Board of Directors of the Chicago Lutheran Seminary met at Fort Wayne, Indiana, with representatives of the Board of Directors of Hamma Divinity School and Secretary Wickey of the Board of Education. After a most frank and friendly discussion it was deemed advisable to ask the Board of Education to recommend a synchronized curriculum, especially for Chicago Seminary and Hamma Divinity School, and to recommend to the Board of Education the desirability of making provisions for the exchange of professors for lecture purposes between these two institutions.[48]

The expressions of harmony and good will continued, and finally in March, 1940, representatives of all the synods supporting the two schools chose to attend an unofficial meeting in Chicago regarding the question of merger. Out of this meeting came the creation of an Inter-Synodical Seminary Merger Committee, with President Weng as Chairman. At the request of the constituent synods at their 1940 conventions this committee drew up a report. When completed it called for a merger of Chicago Lutheran and Hamma, with the merged school occupying the Maywood campus. The report's proposal and plan of merger received the unanimous approval of the representatives of the Synods of Illinois, Wartburg, Indiana, Michigan, Ohio, Kentucky-Tennessee and West Virginia who were members of the Inter-Synodical Seminary Merger Committee. Presented to the synods at their 1941 conventions, the plan received approval from all Synods except Ohio. This synod voted to defer action for one year and provided for a discussion of the question at all of the Conference meetings that Fall.[50] At the Toledo Convention the next year the question was met with vigorous debate over a period of two days. When the vote was finally taken and tabulated it was announced that the measure lost by one vote.[51] Hamma would remain as an independent institution in Ohio.

Memories of this 1942 struggle were still fresh in the memories of many when Hamma was invited to participate in the Inter-Seminary Committee talks in 1958, and was a major factor in the response Hamma gave to this invitation.

Northwestern Invited

Three months after the Inter-Seminary Committee invited Hamma representatives to participate in the merger discussions it voted on February 23, 1959, to include Northwestern Lutheran Theological Seminary of Minneapolis, Minnesota. The invitation was to be conditional upon the endorsement of the

[48]*Ibid.*, 1935, p. 37.
[49]Inter-Synodical Seminary Merger Committee, *Report*, 1941, p. 11.
[50]Ohio Synod-ULCA, *Minutes*, 1941, pp. 77-78
[51]*Ibid.*, 1942, pp. 110-17. The one vote margin in not recorded in the Minutes, but the information was cited in a letter to the writer from Dr. E. Rudolph Walborn, Ohio Synod-LCA Secretary, and in a personal interview, July 7, 1968, with Dr. Joseph Sittler, Jr., who strongly supported the issue but had to be absent from the convention on the day of the vote, May 21, 1942, due to the birth of his son, Joseph Andrew, that day. His vote would have caused a tie in the balloting. Dr. Sittler referred to the baby as "a child of destiny."

Augustana Commission on Ecumenical Relations.[52] When the Augustana
Commission was approached for its reaction it declared: "It is our opinion that
invitations such as the one suggested should be extended by JCLU through the
committee they have duly authorized for this purpose."[53] This action was
consistent with Augustana's position desiring Church ownership and control of
seminaries, but inconsistent with the free policy which had governed the
issuance of previous invitations to Grand View, Suomi, and Hamma, and
certainly inconsistence with the position which JCLU had taken to date, and
would continue to take, that JCLU's role would be purely advisory, and that any
serious conversations for actual mergers would have to arise at the initiative of
the seminaries themselves. Augustana's Commission took this unusual and
unprecedented action early in 1959 when it still hoped that JCLU could be
persuaded to change its position and adopt Church control over the number and
location of seminaries.[54] By asking the Inter-Seminary Committee to request
JCLU to invite Northwestern Seminary to the merger discussions, Augustana was
in effect encouraging a church-wide strategy for theological education. The
Inter-Seminary Committee acquiesced and petitioned JCLU to issue an inclusive
invitation so that all mid-western seminaries could be brought together under
JCLU auspices for merger considerations.[55] JCLU responded affirmatively,[56] so
no direct invitation to Northwestern from the Inter-Seminary Committee was
extended. By the time JCLU actually issued the invitations in late 1959, it had
made its final decision that it would not take the initiative in merging and
relocating seminaries,[57] and therefore invited all thirteen seminaries, not just the
mid-western schools as had been requested, to a "consultation session" in
Chicago on January 20, 1960. There the sixty representatives of these seminaries
heard brief reports on the status and prospect of each school, participated in a
discussion of practical considerations confronting each seminary in the light of
merger, and received copies of the "Principles" governing the number, location,
and alignment of Theological Seminaries in the LCA. No effort was made at this
meeting to encourage specific seminaries to consider merger conversations with
one another, though the promise was made that the Committee on Seminaries
would "include in its report to JCLU on the fulfillment of its mandate a
mention of the specific situations possibly involving seminary relocations or
combinations to which the Board of Theological Education of the [LCA] should
give special consideration in connection with the construction of the master plan
of theological education for the new church."[58] However, the meeting did not
achieve the purpose of involving Northwestern in the Inter-Seminary Committee

[52]Inter-Seminary Committee, *Minutes*, February 23, 1959, p. 2.
[53]Augustana Lutheran Church, Commission on Ecumenical Relations, *Minutes*,
March 4, 1959, p. 4.
[54]*Supra*, pp. 54-55.
[55]Inter-Seminary Committee, *Minutes*, June 26, 1959, p. 4.
[56]*Ibid.*, p. 2.
[57]*Supra*, pp. 54-55.
[58]Committee on Seminaries, *Report*, p. 3.

discussions as the authors of the request had hoped. As a result, almost one year had passed since the Inter-Seminary Committee first chose to invite North-western and the Minneapolis seminary still had not received an invitation to participate. This was not particularly discouraging to Northwestern Seminary, since it really preferred to perpetuate its work in the Minneapolis-St. Paul area. In fact, during this very same time in 1959, Northwestern had approached Augustana Seminary unilaterally, with the proposal that Augustana merge with Northwestern in Minneapolis and preserve its traditions in a territory where the Augustana Church had considerable numerical strength. Duly authorized discussions by the two seminaries were held, but the cordial conversations produced no action.[59] Further evidence of Northwestern's desire to remain as a separate seminary in Minnesota was the resolution adopted by the Board of Directors of Northwestern Seminary on September 25, 1959:

> Be it resolved that the Board of Directors of the Northwestern Theological Seminary express its judgment that a seminary of the merged church, located in the Minneapolis-St. Paul area, is of great strategic advantage to the merged church, and

> That this expressed judgment be conveyed at once to the members of the Joint Commission on Lutheran Unity.[60]

Nevertheless, Northwestern Seminary officials were interested in the progress of the Inter-Seminary Committee conversations, especially as they might have implications for their school. The lack of a formal invitation in 1959 to attend these meetings prevented their attendance. President Zeidler later explained Northwestern's plight:

> We ourselves waited for such an invitation, and receiving none, finally requested permission to attend several of the meetings in order to discover (1) if the thinking of the [Inter-Seminary] Committee included Northwestern in its plans, and (2) if cogent reasons could be found that would reverse the unanimous advice that was being given to continue our life in the Twin City area.[61]

The approach was made by Rev. Ingolf B. Kindem, Chairman of Northwestern's board, who did finally receive the long-awaited letter of invitation from the Inter-Seminary Committee Chairman. Zeidler and Kindem attended the July 7, 1960, Inter-Seminary Committee meeting. However, their interest in partic-ipating in the Inter-Seminary conversations began to wane in the light of these recent developments:

1. JCLU's assurance in January that all LCA seminaries would be recognized as institutions of the Church.

[59]Inter-Seminary Committee, *Minutes*, June 26, 1959, p. 1, and interview with President Clemens H. Zeidler, July 22, 1968.

[60]Northwestern Lutheran Theological Seminary, *Minutes*, September 25, 1959.

[61]Clemens H. Zeidler, "Comment on Report No. 11," p. 3, Bergendoff, *Executive Secretary's Reports.*

2. Northwestern's reaffirmation, at its May, 1960, board meeting, of the principle that the merged church needed a seminary in the Minneapolis-St. Paul area.

3. The absence of arguments at the Inter-Seminary Committee meeting that Northwestern was moving in the wrong direction.

4. The action of the Augustana Lutheran Church at its June, 1960, Convention which directed Augustana Seminary to explore merger possibilities with Northwestern, as well as other seminaries.

Fortified by these factors, Northwestern looked confidently to the further development of its own campus in the Twin City area, and withdrew from the Inter-Seminary Committee after its representatives attended their first meeting.

Northwestern Seminary, which traced its origin to a schism in Chicago Lutheran Seminary in 1920,[62] had made its decision to fulfill its destiny on its own territory. The depth of feeling behind this decision was perceived by Dr. Bergendoff when he wrote some time later in his evaluation of Northwestern: "There is no doubt that Northwestern has a determined following, and recommendations that it be merged with Chicago, in the interest of the Church-at-large, will be vigorously resisted."[63]

All efforts to make the merger of mid-western seminaries more inclusive had resulted in failure. The Lutheran School of Theology would embrace only Augustana, Chicago Lutheran, Grand View, and Suomi at the time of consolidation, though before the new campus could be occupied Central Seminary of Fremont, Nebraska, would become a part of the venture.[64]

---

[62]Gerberding, *Reminiscent Reflections*, pp. 264-71, and Marjory Weng, "Passavant's Vision," p. 52.

[63]Conrad Bergendoff, *Reports to BTE*, Report No. 10, Northwestern Seminary, 1963, p. 15.

[64]*Infra*, Chapter X.

Chapter V

TO MERGE OR NOT TO MERGE

"Remembering the many instances of helpful consultation mutually enjoyed by our Seminaries in times past . . ." Thus began the cordial and earnest letter of invitation from Chicago Lutheran Seminary to Augustana Seminary to engage in "discussion concerning the future Institutional possibilities for Theological Education in the framework of a merged church."[1] The friendly reference to mutual associations in the past could easily be misconstrued by the chance reader to mean that the two seminaries were in a close working relationship which could then be easily solidified into organic merger in the light of current church merger talks. It was not this simple. The relationships between the two schools, though located 150 miles apart in the same state, were really limited to participation in the same professional and student organizations of the type that would as easily relate the two schools to other seminaries as with each other. The correspondence which flowed between the two seminaries and boards immediately after this initial invitation of January 28, 1958, had the formal format and rather stilted language of correspondents who, though relatively unacquainted, wanted to establish relationships but not cause offense in the process. The two schools had lived in relative isolation from each other for so long that a major task at the beginning of Inter-Seminary Committee sessions was establishing the personal relationships of friendship and trust out of which major decisions could be reached. It is a tribute to the churchmanship of these seventy different men, who attended one or more of these meetings over a four year period, that the climate was sufficiently positive and conducive to effect a merger.[2]

The stern realities of the future were faced at the initial meeting of the committee on April 23, 1958. The discussion was predicated upon the presupposition that the proposed church merger of AELC, Augustana, Suomi, and ULCA would be consummated. It was announced that in all likelihood the only synod in America that would have at least two, if not four, seminaries on its territory would be Illinois. Further, it was emphasized that time was of the

[1]*Supra*, p. 51.
[2]Interview with Dr. Arthur Arnold, Inter-Seminary Committee Secretary, July 22, 1968.

essence, since any plan involving merger should be completed by 1960, so that churches and synods could properly act upon it.

Then followed a serious exploration and evaluation of the options, problems, and opportunities such a church merger would present to the two seminaries:[3]

1. Both seminaries could continue their independent existences. This was ruled out as being unrealistic. Two schools on the same territory simply could not successfully compete for students and financial support.

2. Augustana could continue as the B.D. level school and Chicago Lutheran could concentrate on the graduate level. The consensus of the committee was that B.D. level and graduate school work were interdependent, and a graduate school could not function properly apart from a B.D. School.

3. Discontinue one of the schools. No one was prepared to support this alternative.

4. Merger of Augustana and/or Chicago with another seminary in some other synod. This was met by resistance on the part of those who were convinced that a seminary was needed in the Illinois area and by those who felt that such a seminary, strengthened by such a merger, would create a competitive situation with non-LCA Lutheran seminaries in the area. A preferred alternative to this option was the transfer of portions of the two faculties to several existing seminaries, but this was greeted with little enthusiasm, also.

5. Possible merger of Augustana and Chicago. It was clear at the outset that this was the most attractive of the alternatives, for the discussion centered immediately upon the location for such a new school, and a resolution called for presentations at the next meeting of various sites for a new, merged school.

In a final action the committee voted to invite Grand View and Suomi to future meetings.[4]

Motivated perhaps more by expediency than by the educational ideal which had informed their mutual theological traditions, the representatives of Augustana and Maywood seminaries had faced the crucial question of their future in the life of a merged church, and had seen merger as the best of several alternatives. Though no formal action had been taken at this first meeting in which they registered their preference or desire for merger, the assumption seemed to be implicit in all future meetings. Though it would be threatened at times by strong and genuine differences over the location of the new school, and though the differing church polities of the synods and churches would cause numerous delays and involvements in mechanics, especially as related to Augustana, the sense of a common destiny experienced from the beginning would enable the merger to become a reality.

[3]Inter-Seminary Committee *Minutes* April 23, 1958, p. 4.
[4]*Supra*, p. 55.

Each of the four seminaries involved in the inter-seminary discussions had a particular stance regarding seminary merger which informed its role in the deliberations. The Suomi Synod participated in the talks with a definite commitment to a consolidation of seminary resources. It had decided at its 1957 convention that the future of theological education in the synod must be tied to any decision it would make with regard to its involvement in church merger.[5] When the Suomi Synod made the decision to continue in JCLU and to affiliate Suomi Seminary with Chicago Lutheran,[6] the 1958 Convention was acting in the full awareness that merger conversations between Augustana and Maywood seminaries had begun and that Suomi had been invited to join the discussions. In a real sense those who voted for association between Suomi and Maywood seminaries were also voting for participation in discussions which could well lead to a merged seminary in the new church. Suomi representatives joined the Inter-Seminary Committee September 30, 1958, with the assumption that their relationship with Chicago Lutheran was leading them into a larger merger. Professor Karlo J. Keljo revealed the Suomi Synod's awareness of these facts at the second meeting he attended: "Should there be a merged seminary in the context of the proposed merged church, it follows logically that there would be no Suomi Theological Seminary as it now exists."[7]

Professor Keljo's concerns did not involve the seminary merger or the surrender of his seminary's identity—these were assumed. Rather, Suomi was concerned that the Finnish language work which remained in the Suomi Synod would not be forgotten in the training of future pastors, and secondly that the maximum amount of academic and religious freedom allowed by the confessional position of the Lutheran Church would be preserved in the new seminary.

> We enjoy this freedom now at Maywood and deem it of great importance that such an atmosphere of freedom be characteristic of the proposed merged seminary also. Our small church body includes a great variety of emphases among laity and clergy alike. This variety of outlooks can exist in the Suomi Synod without splintering the church because there is a spirit of permissiveness and freedom.[8]

To merge or not to merge was not the question. Suomi was ready in 1958.

When Grand View representatives joined the merger discussions of the Inter-Seminary Committee at its June 23, 1958, meeting the situation with respect to their seminary was not unlike that of Suomi's. The actions of AELC regarding the future of Grand View Seminary were following the same course as those of the Suomi Synod, but on a somewhat delayed time schedule. Grand View's future as being aligned with Maywood's was clear in the minds of the seminary's leadership and was becoming increasingly clear in the minds of the AELC constituency. When the decisive vote to locate Grand View on the

[5]*Supra*, p. 40.

[6]*Supra*, p. 41.

[7]Karlo J. Keljo, "Problems of Merging the Seminaries Viewed from the Standpoint of the Suomi Synod and Suomi Theological Seminary," Inter-Seminary Committee, *Minutes*, November 25, 1958, p. 1.

[8]*Ibid.*

Maywood campus was taken at the AELC convention in 1959,[9] the Inter-Seminary Committee had been functioning for one and one-half years. The direction in which the committee was moving had become increasingly clear, so AELC also, in a sense, cast a joint ballot for relocation of its seminary and for participation in serious seminary merger talks.

As in the case with Suomi, Grand View representatives had only positive interest in the seminary merger question. They could see only advantages in the areas of curriculum and academic concerns. Professor Kildegaard voiced some minor concern about the size of the seminary, in contrast to the extremely low faculty-student ratio at Grand View, and the hope that the new seminary would remain close to the life of the church.

Grand View seminary moved to Maywood in 1960, in the full realization and hope that this was just the first step in a larger relationship.

Chicago Lutheran Seminary over the years had developed an impressive record of concern for merger. In addition to the early attempts to involve Augustana Seminary and the Danish Lutheran Seminary in the life of its infant school,[10] the contituency of this seminary supported the action of the ULCA in 1932, which, until ruled unconstitutional, would have involved Maywood in its first merger.[11] Likewise, the seminary's governing synods supported the unsuccessful merger attempt with Hamma Divinity School in 1941.[12] In 1954, when the Board of Education of the ULCA held a meeting with all seminary presidents and representative board members, in connection with the Toronto convention, to explore the attitudes of the schools toward a church wide study of theological education and institutions, the only seminary to express an interest in such a study was Chicago Lutheran.[13] Most recently Maywood's inclusive attitude had been demonstrated in its desire to receive Grand View and Suomi seminaries as associated schools. In addition to its commendable ecumenical concern, Maywood was also motivated by some very practical considerations. In light of the pending LCA merger it faced keen competition for students and financial support on the same territory with Augustana Seminary in nearby Rock Island. President Weng of Maywood later voiced his seminary's conviction at this point, "That there should be but one strong seminary on the territory was self-evident."[14] The question of the very survival of Maywood and Augustana seminaries was tied to the possibility of a successful union between them. It was not strange, therefore, that Chicago Lutheran Seminary initiated merger discussions with its letter of invitation to Augustana Seminary.

[9]*Supra*, p. 33.

[10]*Supra*, pp. 23 and 27-28.

[11]*Supra*, p. 56.

[12]Supra, p. 57.

[13]Letter to the writer from Rev. Lyman H. Grimes, former Chairman of CLTS Board of Directors and a representative at this meeting in Toronto, June 25, 1958.

[14]Armin G. Weng, "Report of the President," Chicago Lutheran Theological Seminary, Board of Directors, *Minutes*, April 26, 1961, p. 2.

As Chairman of ths school's Board of Directors, Rev. Lyman H. Grimes was able to state unequivocally at the outset of these discussions that "merger of seminaries, as a single question, would have immediate consent of our Supporting Synods and endorsement by our wider constituency."[15] In answer to the specific question of merger with Augustana, Grand View, and Suomi seminaries, he stated emphatically, "Yes! From our point of view no impediment obstructs a quick assertion of 'readiness' as we survey the prospect of merger with these sister Seminaries."[16] In fact, the same paper voiced concern that the merger not be limited to the four seminaries, but ought to reach out to include Hamma, Northwestern, and Central.[17]

Chicago Lutheran had made its position clear. It recognized that a host of problems relating to location, facilities, financial support, integration of faculties, students, and libraries would still have to be solved, but on the basic question of merger with the other three seminaries it had made its decision. It, too, was ready to merge.

Augustana Seminary approached the merger discussions from a somewhat different perspective than the other three schools. As the largest of the thirteen seminaries of the four merging church bodies, it approached the Inter-Seminary Committee from the position of unique strength. Augustana representatives knew that this was one of the few areas in the pending church merger—otherwise largely dominated by the sheer numerical strength of ULCA, even though at ULCA's insistence the representation of JCLU was practically equally divided among the four church bodies—that Augustana had an opportunity to make a significant contribution. It had to be certain that it was making the right one. Also, as the only theological seminary of the Augustana Lutheran Church it was subject to pressures of several regional groups who wanted to continue the Augustana theological tradition on their own territories.[18] Then, too, other seminaries of ULCA were bidding for Augustana Seminary's participation in

[15]Lyman H. Grimes, "The Problems of Merging the Seminaries Viewed from the Standpoint of the Cooperating Synods of the ULCA and Chicago Lutheran Seminary," Inter-Seminary Committee, *Minutes*, November 25, 1958, p. 1.

[16]*Ibid.*

[17]*Ibid.*, p. 2.

[18]Augustana Lutheran Church, *Minutes*, 1960, pp. 378, 379. See also correspondence in the LSTC Archives from Dr. Carl Segerhammar, President of the California Conference of the Augustana Lutheran Church, to Dr. Karl E. Mattson, October 7, 1959, November 12, 1959, regarding a merger with Pacific Lutheran Seminary in Berkeley, and from Dr. George Hall, Executive Director of the Lutheran Student Foundation of Minnesota, to Dr. Mattson, November 21, 1960, regarding the transfer of Augustana Seminary's resources to create a Graduate School in Theology at the University of Minnesota, and Augustana Seminary *Minutes*, May 28-29, 1959, p. 10, regarding a relocation to Minneapolis and a merger with Northwestern Seminary.

their programs.[19] These factors made it a bit more difficult for Augustana to commit itself too early to the four-way merger of seminaries, even though remaining in the State of Illinois and becoming a part of the only school to preserve all four church traditions was a most natural attraction.

It also must be noted that Augustana representatives had certain restrictions placed upon them by the polity of the Augustana Church.[20] All major discussion and decisions had to be reported to the Commission on Ecumenical Relations, the Executive Council, and the Augustana Lutheran Church in convention. Likewise, direction and guidance had to be secured from these entities. The process was sometimes painstakingly slow, but it had to be observed.

A further hindrance to rapid progress was the rigid position Augustana commissioners took in JCLU during 1958-59 regarding church ownership and control of seminaries. The issue, though resolved several times, was opened again and again, until the final and absolute decision was made in December, 1959, and announced at the consultation for the thirteen seminaries of the merging bodies January 20, 1960.[21] Until this issue was fully and finally resolved, Augustana representatives were not ready to commit themselves to the Chicago merger.

Despite all these factors, Augustana continued to play a dominant role in Inter-Seminary Committee discussions and decisions, and interest in the prospective merger continued to grow. As President Karl E. Mattson wrote to Dr. P. O. Bersell, when the latter assumed the chairmanship of the Committee on Seminaries of JCLU in late 1959:

> If Augustana [Seminary] is left in its present situation, the net result over the years will be that Augustana and Chicago will both be weak institutions. After the merger we would get progressively weaker as a seminary. The other alternative is to merge Augustana, Chicago, Grand View and Suomi Seminaries. If there is a choice between establishing a new seminary that could be the strongest theological institution in the new church or leaving two weak institutions, I would vote every time for a merger. After careful study we have come to the conclusion that Chicago would be the best location for the merged seminary. It has university facilities. It is near a center of Lutheranism and there would be no competition as far as other seminaries are concerned in this area.[22]

[19]Northwestern Lutheran Seminary of Minneapolis, Minnesota, and Pacific Lutheran Seminary of Berkeley, California, requested consultations with Augustana Seminary in 1959. See Augustana Seminary, Board of Directors, *Minutes*, May 28-29, 1959, p. 10, October 6-7, 1959, p. 4, and letter in LSTC Archives from Dr. Charles B. Foelsch, President of Pacific Lutheran Seminary, to Dr. Oscar Benson, President of the Augustana Lutheran Church, July 17, 1959, and Dr. Benson's reply, July 26, 1959, regarding a proposal of merger between Augustana and Pacific at the Berkeley location.

[20]*Supra*, pp. 52-53.

[21]*Supra*, pp. 44, 47, 50, 54, 55, 57, 58.

[22]Letter from Dr. Karl E. Mattson to Dr. P. O. Bersell, October 28, 1959, LSTC Archives.

By February, 1960, Augustana's representatives were ready to take formal action recommending the four-way merger in Chicago. Any hope that JCLU would take decisive action regarding location and number of seminaries had vanished with the Committee on Seminaries' statement of the previous month. The *Minutes* of the Board of Directors of Augustana Seminary records the decisive action:

> Report on merger negotiations by President Mattson. Motion made, seconded and carried that in the event, that the Augustana Church at this 1960 synod approves the proposed merger, we recommend to the Church that the Seminary Board be authorized to proceed with negotiations of specific terms for the merger of four or more seminaries to be located in the Chicago area, and report to the 1961 Synod for approval.[23]

President Mattson, in his report to the Augustana Lutheran Church at its centennial convention in Rock Island that Summer, informed the delegation:

> No decisions have been made but our studies seem to make this conclusion rather self evident. A merger of four or more seminaries in the Chicago area seems to be the best answer to the questions of our future existence.
>
> In the event that the Augustana Church at this 1960 synod approves the proposed [church] merger, we recommend to the Church that the Seminary Board be authorized to proceed with negotiations of specific terms for the merger of four or more seminaries to be located in the Chicago area, and report to the 1961 synod for approval.[24]

The Church was not ready to act quite so readily. Under the pressure of Memorials from the California and Columbia Conferences urging the Church "to give consideration to the merging of the Augustana Theological Seminary with the Pacific Lutheran Theological Seminary at Berkeley, California,"[25] coupled with pressures from other regions of the Church which wanted the seminary on their own territories, the assembly directed the Board of Directors of the seminary to explore a variety of alternatives and report back to the 1961 synod. The specific instructions were:

> 2a. The Church authorize and direct the Board of Directors of Augustana Theological Seminary to explore and to study the various options for the future existence of Augustana Theological Seminary in the proposed new church as follows and to report its findings to the Executive Council and the Church:
>
> (1) A possible merger of four or more seminaries in the Chicago area.
>
> (2) A possible merger with Central Seminary, Fremont, Nebraska, at a new location.

---

[23]Augustana Seminary, Board of Directors, *Minutes*, February 2-3, 1960, p. 2.
[24]Augustana Lutheran Church, *Minutes*, 1960, p. 366.
[25]*Ibid.*, p. 379.

(3) A possible merger with Pacific Lutheran Seminary to be located in Berkeley, California.

(4) The possibility of the continued existence of Augustana Theological Seminary in its present location and the possibility of merger with other seminaries to be located in the Rock Island area.

(5) A possible merger with Northwestern Seminary, Minneapolis, Minnesota.

b. The Board of Directors of Augustana Theological Seminary be further authorized and directed to arrive at a conclusion with regard to the future of Augustana Seminary at the earliest possible opportunity and report this conclusion and the reasons therefor to the Executive Council and to the Church.

c. The Board of Directors of Augustana Theological Seminary be further authorized and instructed to prepare specific terms of a possible merger of seminaries, if this option is chosen, and to report to the Executive Council and the Church.

d. All decisions and conclusions of the Seminary Board shall be subject to review and approval, disapproval, or amendment by the Executive Council and the Church at its 1961 synod.[26]

Following this directive of the Church, the Board of Directors created a special Augustana Seminary Inter-Seminary Committee with representatives from the board, faculty, administration, and church-at-large.[27] Sub-committees of this special committee, together with President Mattson, held consultations with each of the three seminary presidents, presidents of supporting synods or surrounding conferences, and other representatives of the designated seminaries:

1. Northwestern Seminary, July 26, 1960

2. Pacific Lutheran Seminary, September 20, 1960

3. Central Seminary, September 27, 1960

Previous consultations had been held in 1959, with Northwestern and Pacific Lutheran Seminaries at the request of these schools,[28] so only Central was being approached for the first time in this series of meetings. A summary of these consultations was made by President Mattson at a plenary session of the Augustana Inter-Seminary Committee on October 7, 1960. [29]He indicated that

[26]*Ibid.*, p. 378.

[27]Augustana Seminary, Inter-Seminary Committee, *Minutes*, July 6, 1960, p. 1. Committee members were: Board members—Dr. Oscar Benson, Rev. Clarence Hall, Rev. Ralph Lindquist, Dr. Granger Westberg, Dr. Richard Pearson. Faculty—Dr. Eric H. Wahlstrom, Dr. Arthur O. Arnold. President—Dr. Karl E. Mattson. Church-at-large—Dr. Malvin Lundeen, Dr. O. V. Anderson, Dr. Robert Mortvedt. Legal consultant—Mr. Tage Joranson.

[28]Augustana Seminary, Board of Directors, *Minutes*, May 28-29, 1959, p. 10, October 6-7, 1959, p. 4.

[29]*Ibid.*, October 7-8, 1960, Exhibit C, "Reports."

all of the seminaries visited "indicated joy at the prospect of merger with Augustana and that the meetings were pleasant and profitable."[30] The seventeen page report was referred to the board and faculty for joint study at the October 7-8, 1960, board meeting. Following the discussion, in which each faculty member gave his personal reactions to the report, the faculty was polled. The vote was unanimous that Augustana should merge with Maywood, Grand View, and Suomi in a Chicago area location.[31] A subsequent straw vote among the board members indicated that ten favored the Chicago merger, one the California merger, and one preferred to remain in Rock Island. When the formal motion was placed before the board the vote was unanimous in favor of the merger in Chicago:

> That the Board of Directors of Augustana Theological Seminary, following long and careful consideration and study including consultations with other seminaries involved in the current unity negotiations, concludes that participation in a merger of four or more seminaries in the Chicago area offers the most promising possibilities for Augustana Theological Seminary to make its maximum contribution to the new Church; and that the chairman report this resolution to the Executive Council of Augustana Lutheran Church.[32]

This definite action, that Augustana would be a part of the four-way merger, pending final approval by the Church in 1961, received the concurrence of the Augustana Lutheran Church Executive Council at its October 27-28, 1960, meeting, and was reported to the Inter-Seminary Committee at the November 7, 1960, meeting.[33]

The crucial question, to merge or not to merge, had now been settled by representatives of all four seminaries. What remained was the development of the necessary legal documents and the official action on the part of supporting synods and churches.

MAKING IT LEGAL

Serious merger negotiations began to take place the moment Augustana representatives made their eventful announcement on November 7, 1960. Ground rules were established to insure total agreement and satisfaction on the part of all four seminaries:

a. A delegation may request the privilege of withdrawing for consultation in order to determine more exactly the opinion of their constituency and of one governing Board of the Seminary.

b. A delegation representing a single seminary may notify the chairman that they do not concur in an action taken by the

[30]*Ibid.*

[31]*Ibid., Minutes*, p. 1.

[32]*Ibid.*, pp. 2-3. The corrected form of the motion as reproduced above is recorded in *Minutes*, February 10-11, 1961, p. 1.

[33]Inter-Seminary Committee, *Minutes*, November 7, 1960, pp. 1-2.

Joint Committee. When such notification is given the action shall not be binding for the seminary whose delegation has given such notice. The question shall be re-opened for discussion, negotiation and decision in order that an agreement acceptable to all may be reached.[34]

At the same time a merger time-table was adopted calling for the preparation of articles of consolidation and a new constitution before May 1, 1961, so that the proper judicatories could take action that Spring and Summer. The following committee was appointed to develop the appropriate legal documents: Dr. Karl E. Mattson—Chairman, Dr. Armin G. Weng, Dr. Walter J. Kukkonen, Dr. Walter Wick, Professor Axel Kildegaard, and Mr. Tage Joranson—attorney.

In drafting a constitution for the new school, the committee leaned heavily, for format and content, on Augustana's constitution which had been drawn up in 1947 by a committee which included two members of the present committee, President Mattson and Attorney Joranson.[35] Initial drafts were presented and revised at Inter-Seminary Committee meetings on December 21, 1960, and February 21, 1961. The constitution in its final form was carefully edited by Dr. Robert Mortvedt and Dr. Donald Heiges, and was approved by the Inter-Seminary Committee at the March 23-24, 1961, meeting.[36]

A review of the evolution of the document indicates that there was some uncertainty regarding a name for the new school. Augustana's representatives to the Inter-Seminary Committee had admitted during the early days of merger discussion, "we would, of course, appreciate it if this new seminary were given the name of Augustana, but the name is relatively unimportant."[37] In a gesture of good will, the Maywood faculty went on record December 19, 1960, preferring the name Augustana Lutheran Theological Seminary.[38] These preferences were ignored by the first two drafts of the constitution which bore the name, "The United Seminary of the Lutheran Church in America," but the third draft suggested a compromise, "Augustana-Chicago Theological Seminary." None of these names proved to be acceptable so a special committee consisting of Dr. Donald Heiges, Dr. Granger Westberg, and Dr. A. E. Farstrup was appointed. They proposed two names: "Lutheran School of Theology at Chicago" and "Lutheran Theological Seminary at Chicago." Acceding to the recommendation of the committee, the Inter-Seminary Committee adopted the first of the names suggested and ordered that it be inserted in the proper place in the documents.[39]

---

[34]*Ibid.*, p. 3.

[35]A comparison of the two constitutions reveals the same general outline and similar, often the same, language.

[36]Inter-Seminary Committee, *Minutes*, March 23-24, 1961, p. 2.

[37]Eric H. Wahlstrom, "Problems of Merging the Seminaries Viewed from the Standpoint of Augustana Lutheran Church and Augustana Seminary," Inter-Seminary Committee, *Minutes*, November 25, 1958, p. 2.

[38]CLTS Faculty, *Minutes*, December 19, 1960, p. 1.

[39]Inter-Seminary Committee, *Minutes*, March 23-24, 1961, p. 2.

Notable changes in the stated objects of the new school, as compared with the predecessor seminaries, were the statements dealing with the four divisions in the seminary—B.D. program, graduate school, school of missions, and continuing education ("instruction in theology for laymen")—plus the recognition that both men and women could receive training at LSTC. The doctrinal basis departed from the traditional language of Lutheran constitutions and employed the more dynamic language of the new LCA constitution. In keeping with the regional ownership of the seminary, board members were to be elected by the supporting synods, but in recognition of the principle of supervision and regulation of standards by the Board of Theological Education of the LCA a few board members were to be nominated by BTE. In deference to the wishes of the four merging church bodies to perpetuate their traditional loyalties, a special provision required the synods to give consideration for four years after merger to proper representation of the groups uniting to form the school. In accordance with the practice on the Maywood campus the constitution called for both a President and a Dean of Faculty. In thoughtful provision for the period of time prior to the functioning of the first Board of Directors, the framers of the constitution stipulated that a special Administration and Liaison Committee should be appointed.

In addition to the Constitution, the committee drew up a Summary of Agreements which summarized the history of the merging seminaries and the work of the Inter-Seminary Committee, provided detailed instructions for the election of the initial Board of Directors, listed the professors of the four schools who would be retained as members of the faculty, and enumerated a series of legal principles relating to merger.

The other assignment completed by the committee was the drafting of the Plan of Consolidation. This outlined the legal steps necessary in order to effect the consolidation of the schools. Technically the plan called for consolidation, not a merger, under Illinois law. The Inter-Seminary Committee gave its approval to all these documents when it adopted the following resolution at its March 23-24, 1961 meeting:

> That the Summary of Agreements, the Constitution and the Plan of Consolidation be approved and recommended, and that they be submitted to the boards of directors of the four seminaries and by them to their supporting churches and synods for adoption or rejection as presented.[40]

The committee had completed its herculean task well in advance of the May 1, 1961, deadline. The documents would move now to the seminary boards for approval and then to the various synodical and church conventions where Dr. Robert Mortvedt, Dr. Donald Heiges, and Dr. Walter Kukkonen would make the verbal presentations at the committee's request. The procedure varied slightly

[40]*Ibid.*

for Grand View Seminary since it did not have a corporate existence apart from the Grand View College and Seminary corporation.

The boards of directors of the seminaries discharged their duties by approving the Summary of Agreements, taking action recommending that the Board of Directors of the new school adopt the Constitution, and then adopting a special adaptation of a resolution approving the Plan of Consolidation.[41]

When the documents reached the churches and synods, each group took the necessary actions prescribed for them.[42] In almost every instance the votes were unanimous. In an unusual display of harmony and good will the constituencies of the four schools supported the formation of the new Lutheran School of Theology.[43] The last group to take action was the American Evangelical Lutheran Church at its convention in Tyler, Minnesota. Appropriately the vote taken on Friday, August 18, 1961, was without a single dissenting ballot.[44] The enabling actions were then completed and the consolidation was guaranteed. In just one more year the Lutheran School of Theology at Chicago would become a corporate reality. Three years and seven months after the Board of Directors of Chicago Lutheran Theological Seminary voted to send a letter of invitation to Augustana Seminary to "enter into discussion" the challenging task was completed. The question, to merge or not to merge, was settled.

[41]See Appendix IV, *Official Documents of the Lutheran School of Theology at Chicago*, 1961, "Action By Boards of Directors: Augustana, Maywood, and Suomi," pp. 22-23.

[42]*Ibid.*, p. 24.

[43]Augustana Church, *Minutes*, 1961, p. 388. Illinois Synod-ULCA, *Minutes*, 1961, p. 33. Wartburg Synod-ULCA, *Minutes*, 1961, p. 64. Michigan Synod-ULCA, *Minutes*, 1961, p. 159. Indiana Synod-ULCA, *Minutes*, 1961, p. 69. Pittsburgh Synod-ULCA, *Minutes*, 1961, p. 141. Suomi Synod, *Minutes*, 1961, in *Year Book*, 1962, p. 194.

[44]AELC, *Minutes*, 1961, p. 45. "Dean Axel Kildegaard commented: This is a merger of four schools, but not four corporations. In effect, if this motion is passed, it will amount to dismissing Grand View Seminary from the Grand View College and Grand View Seminary Corporation," p. 45.

Chapter VI

CHOOSING THE UNIVERSITY

Second in importance only to the basic decision of merger itself was the decision to locate the new school adjacent to the campus of the University of Chicago. Steeped in the educational ideal which American Lutherans had inherited from their European forebears, members of the Inter-Seminary Committee became increasingly convinced that a university setting was imperative for the training of pastors in modern society. Dr. Karl E. Mattson became a spokesman for the committee when he later enunciated this principle and the reasons for it.

> As the Lutheran Church more and more enters the maelstrom of modern life it will need pastors who can face modern America with power. America must be addressed in the name of Jesus Christ if we are to keep and to adapt our Christian heritage.
>
> Where can a young man be trained so that he becomes such a man? The answer came easily. The best place for such training is a university environment since it is here that the various movements and tendencies which shape the future meet and engage in dialog. The pastoral candidate must also engage in such dialog if he is to speak forcefully to modern America. Insights such as these elicited the decision to locate in a university setting.[1]

That the Lutheran Church in America, through its Board of Theological Education, was pleased with this decision is seen in the resolution of commendation extended to the Lutheran School of Theology at Chicago at the Second Biennial Convention,[2] and the resolutions encouraging other LCA seminaries to consider university locations, too.[3] Dr. Conrad Bergendoff, the Board's Executive Secretary, revealed his confidence that the decision to locate at a university was informed by a deep consciousness in the Church of the ideal that theological education must inform, and be informed by, all of life, learning, and culture in society today, when he wrote:

[1]Karl E. Mattson, "The New Location," LSTC Development Fund Brochure, 1964.
[2]LCA, *Minutes*, 1964, Resolution 6, p. 589.
[3]*Ibid.*, Resolutions 2 and 3a., pp. 588-89.

73

And on every hand there is an insistence that theological seminaries must pay attention to laymen, their needs, their understanding, their participation. The shift towards pastoral counseling, clinical training, chaplaincies in church and state institutions, reveals a demand created by our times. At the same time there is a demand that in this scientific age and cultural atmosphere the ministry know how to preach also to men and women who come from our univeristies.

I am persuaded that these are the kinds of factors which are leading our synods to create a new kind of theological school close to one of the world's great universities. It is a venture of faith—faith that the Word of God belongs on all levels of culture and learning, faith that the church can meet the problems of radical change in our great cities, faith that the youth who prepare for the ministry in the church can go on in clarity and power when confronted by the "powers" of the age in which they must serve.[4]

Though the decision to locate in a university setting was a very logical one in the light of this educational ideal, the choice of the specific university was not easy. Chicago offered two great universities, Northwestern University in Evanston and the University of Chicago in Hyde Park. Further complicating the choice were minority voices supporting the Maywood or other suburban location.

The opportunity to confront this difficult choice came at the second session of the Inter-Seminary Committee on June 23, 1958. The following papers were presented and discussed:[5]

"The Case for a Chicago Location"—Dr. Frank Madsen

"The Case for a Rock Island Location"—Mr. Lloyd Schwiebert

"The Case for a Location on the South Side of Chicago"—Dr. Granger Westberg

"The Case for a Location on the North Side of Chicago"—Dr. Johannes Knudsen

"The Case for the Present Maywood Campus"—Dr. A Howard Weeg

Certain factors became clear as a result of this and the two subsequent meetings:

1. The Augustana Seminary campus in Rock Island was not considered suitable as a location for the new school. Its own representatives admitted this,[6] and no serious consideration was given further to the matter.

2. The Maywood campus was strongly proposed as the site by its president and some of its representatives. This conviction was retained until the final decision on location was made in 1960.[7]

[4]Conrad Bergendoff, " . . . What will happen at Chicago," LSTC Development Fund Brochure, 1964.
[5]Inter-Seminary Committee, *Minutes*, June 23, 1958, Exhibits.
[6]Wahlstrom, "Problems of Merging," p. 2.
[7]Interview between Dr. Armin G. Weng and the writer June, 1960.

3. Augustana representatives were equally convinced that the new school should not be located on the Maywood campus.[8]

4. All representatives agreed that the school should be located in Chicago or in the Chicago area. There was partisan support for Northwestern University, University of Chicago, Maywood Seminary, and a western suburban acreage.

In order to give committee members an opportunity to view all these sites, meetings were held on the campus of Maywood, September 30, 1958, which included a bus tour of the western suburbs; on the Rock Island campus, November 25, 1958; on the University of Chicago campus January 22, 1959; and on the Northwestern University campus on February 23, 1959. At this point a committee was appointed to obtain specific data on all available locations.[9]

NORTHWESTERN UNIVERSITY

Fourteen years earlier Northwestern University had taken the initiative and invited Chicago Lutheran Seminary to relocate the school on its campus, directly across from the Garrett Biblical Institute. The offer was rejected in favor of a similar offer from the University of Chicago.[10] This time the Inter-Seminary Committee was making the approach to the university, but the circumstances had totally changed. The representatives learned this as they met February 23, 1959, with Dr. Moody Prior, Vice-President of Northwestern; Dr. Charles Harris, President and Dean of Seabury-Western Theological Seminary; and Dr. Dwight Loder, President of Garrett Biblical Institute. The usual advantages gained through promixity to a university were pointed out—university libraries, lectures and concerts, health services, dialogue between students and faculties of the various schools—but the university was not prepared to offer any special relationships nor provide any assistance with respect to the purchase of land. Rather the group was informed that land was both exceedingly limited and expensive, and generally was available only at some distance from the campus. Though both seminaries expressed great interest in the coming of a Lutheran seminary to the campus, the university itself was cordial but not encouraging.[11]

Undaunted, the special Site Committee met the following Summer and went on record, after reviewing all the available sites in and around Chicago, that "It is our opinion that a location near Northwestern University would be preferable from the viewpoint of the total seminary program."[12] It cited the following reasons for this choice:

[8]Wahlstrom, "Problems of Merging," p. 2, and Augustana Seminary, Board of Directors, *Minutes*, October 7-8, 1960, p. 3.

[9]Inter-Seminary Committee, *Minutes*, February 23, 1959, p. 2. Committee: Lloyd Schwiebert—Chairman, Arthur O. Arnold, O. V. Anderson—Consultant, Frank Madsen, A. Howard Weeg, Johannes Knudsen, Walter Kukkonen, Axel C. Kildegaard.

[10]*Supra*, p. 35.

[11]Inter-Seminary Committee, *Minutes*, February 23, 1959, pp. 1-2.

[12]Site Committee, *Minutes*, June 8-9, 1959, Exhibit, "Recommendations," p. 1, attached as Exhibit to Inter-Seminary Committee, *Minutes*, June 26, 1959.

1. The structure of relationships extant between existing seminaries and Northwestern University would allow the measure of freedom and theological self-determination necessary for a significant Lutheran Seminary.

2. The Evanston Institute for Ecumenical Studies is located in this area.

3. Proximity to the emerging Lutheran College at Kenosha, Wisconsin.

4. Housing and the family welfare of the faculty would be favored by this location.[13]

This decision was predicated on the presuppositions that the new seminary should not be a federated part of a university, that the Maywood campus was not acceptable to the Augustana representatives, that the possibility of locating the seminary in a western suburb was not totally ruled out, and that the advantages of being near a university were significant.[14]

Favorable sociological factors in Evanston entered very strongly into the decision for the Northwestern location. Committee members warned that locating the seminary near an inner city situation would produce a commuting faculty and a bad sociological situation for students, and that the academic advantages of a university location would be vitiated by difficult living conditions.[15] The accuracy of their judgment was validated by a poll later taken of the faculties on both campuses:[16]

If the decision is finally made to locate the new seminary in close proximity to the University of Chicago, would you have any objections to establishing your residence in the Hyde Park area?

Summary: No objections   6
         Strong objection   5
         Reluctant   12
         Doubtful   1

If the decision is finally made to locate the new seminary in close proximity to Northwestern University, would you have any objections to establishing your residence in Evanston?

Summary: No objections   26

By the October 16, 1959, meeting of the Inter-Seminary Committee, the representatives were ready to agree that the new site should be identified with the metropolitan area, that it should not be on the campus of any of the existing seminaries, that there were advantages in being near a university, and that "a location near Northwestern University is preferable in the light of the total

[13]*Ibid.*, p. 1.
[14]Site Committee, *Minutes*, June 8-9, 1959, pp. 1-2.
[15]*Ibid.*, p. 3.
[16]Inter-Seminary Committee, *Minutes*, February 21, 1961, Exhibit, "Report on Faculty Opinion Regarding the Site of the Merged Seminary," p. 9.

seminary program."[17] Their serious intentions to locate at Northwestern was demonstrated further by their assignment to a new committee to investigate property in the Evanston area.[18]

Hopes to locate near Northwestern began to vanish quickly as the committee set about its task to investigate property. Only small, isolated parcels of land were discovered—none adequate in size for a seminary campus—and land prices were considered exhorbitant for the portions available.[19] Dr. Mortvedt, chairman, finally reported to the Inter-Seminary Committee that he saw only two alternatives: "The lines are becoming increasingly clear, indicating that the merged seminary will either have to settle for a small plot of ground, allowing for practically no campus but in close proximity to a recognized university [Northwestern], or to locate on some more spacious tract of land on the outer fringe of the Chicago area such as the Bethany Biblical Seminary location."[20] There was no disposition to purchase small parcels of land in Evanston, thus splintering the campus and losing the possibility of establishing a consolidated seminary community. Fleeting glances were cast in the direction of Northwestern thereafter for some months, but no further serious investigations were made. Had the land been available in 1959, there is little question that this location would have been selected. Now the committee had to turn elsewhere.

WESTERN SUBURBS

At the third meeting of the Inter-Seminary Committee, Dr. Gould Wickey, consultant to the committee, presented a paper dealing with the financial needs of a merged seminary. The paper presumed that the new seminary would be located on a tract of approximately fifty acres on the edge of the city.[21] That many shared his thinking at the time is revealed in an excerpt of a letter to Dr. Oscar Benson, Chairman of the Committee on Seminaries of JCLU, reporting the progress on the seminary merger question:

> Next is the matter of location. Our best thinking on this point seems to indicate Chicago as the logical place. The next question is where in Chicago? We have proceeded under the assumption that we should not affiliate directly with any university. Seminary education would also require relationship with all the cultural and educational advantages of Chicago, and at the same time a certain amount of isolation. The best suggestion in our studies so far is to buy a tract of about fifty acres on the North or West sides of Chicago.[22]

[17]Inter-Seminary Committee, *Minutes*, October 16, 1959, p. 3.

[18]*Ibid.*, Augustana: Robert Mortvedt, Karl E. Mattson; Chicago: A. Howard Weeg, Armin G. Weng; Grand View: Alfred Jensen, Ronald Jespersen; Suomi: Karlo Keljo, Walter Kukkonen.

[19]Committee to Survey Evanston Property, "Report," Inter-Seminary Committee, *Minutes*, December 16, 1959.

[20]Inter-Seminary Committee, *Minutes*, December 16, 1959, p. 3.

[21]Gould Wickey, "The Financial Needs of a Merged Seminary," Inter-Seminary Committee, *Minutes*, September 30, 1958, p. 1.

[22]Letter from Dr. Karl E. Mattson to Dr. Oscar A. Benson, December 12, 1958, LSTC Archives.

The opportunity to explore this possibility came in a letter from Dr. Paul M. Robinson, President of Bethany Biblical Seminary, Chicago, October 21, 1959. Dr. Robinson indicated that his seminary had also considered locating near Northwestern University, but rejected this when it, too, failed to discover available land. Bethany also considered the University of Chicago, but rejected it on the grounds of adverse sociological conditions and the fear of being in proximity to an undenominational divinity school. At that point the school purchased fifty-five acres of land about seventeen miles west of Chicago in a residential, suburban area. Dr. Robinson asserted that the location afforded opportunities to be in touch with universities, but provided also the isolation they desired for a denominational seminary.[23] When he appeared before the Inter-Seminary Committee December 16, 1959, the President extended a personal invitation to the merged seminary to purchase adjacent land and begin the development of a seminary complex.[24] The Site Committee which considered the invitation ruled it out two months later on the bases that the location was too far from the metropolitan area, that proximity to Bethany Biblical Seminary might create undesirable tensions, that such a completely self-contained theological community might be undesirable, and the lack of assurance of a metropolitan water supply.[25] The committee did not rule out the possibility of selecting a site of some thirty to fifty acres nearer to the metropolitan center, but a subsequent meeting with a group of real estate specialists revealed the futility of such a search. A decision to locate in the western suburbs was becoming less likely and less desirable.

UNIVERSITY OF CHICAGO

The perennial attraction of the University of Chicago location, in addition to the obvious resources of the great academic institution, was the desire on the part of university officials to have the seminary there. The desire had not died with the abortive attempt in 1955, to attract Maywood seminary.[26] Twice, before merger talks had even began, the university had invited representatives of Maywood and Rock Island to consider moving to this campus.[27] The same cordial reception was accorded the Inter-Seminary Committee when it met for the first time on the University of Chicago campus on a blustery Winter day, January 22, 1959. University officials and faculty members,[28] on hand to meet the committee, almost outnumbered the guests whose numbers were severely

[23]Letter from Dr. Paul M. Robinson to Dr. Gould Wickey, October 21, 1959, LSTC Archives.

[24]Inter-Seminary Committee, *Minutes*, December 16, 1959, Exhibit B, p. 4.

[25]Site Committee, "Report," February 17, 1960, Inter-Seminary Committee, *Minutes*, March 15, 1960.

[26]*Supra*, pp. 35-38.

[27]*Supra*, pp. 48-50.

[28]Inter-Seminary Committee, *Minutes*, January 22, 1959, p. 1. Administration: John Kirkpatrick, Vice-Chancellor; Thomas Filbey, Vice-President; R. Wendell Harrison, Vice-President and Dean of Faculties; Charles Gibson, Real Estate Officer. Faculty: Granger Westberg, Markus Barth, P. S. Beaver, Jerald Brauer, Dean of the Divinity School. Executive Director of the South East Chicago Commission: Julian Levi.

reduced by the inclement weather. Dr. Filbey expressed the genuine welcome of the university to the new Lutheran seminary, and Dr. Kirkpatrick assured the committee that the university would be pleased to work out an affiliation with the new seminary on one of many different kinds of bases available. Turning to the academic scene, Dean Brauer cited the advantages offered by the University of Chicago, Dr. Beaver explained the resources available to the School of Missions, and Dr. Barth spoke of the nature of theological education at the theological seminaries on campus and its meaning for a Lutheran seminary. Finally, Mr. Levi assured the committee that sites were available and that fresh insitutional investments were being solicited. The welcome by the University of Chicago was definite and pronounced. The assurance of its full cooperation and assistance was guaranteed.

The Inter-Seminary Committee did not question the genuineness of the invitation nor the highly respected academic atmosphere, but was frankly very disturbed by what it regarded as adverse living conditions in the area. For this reason the invitation was never really taken seriously. Ten months later when the committee went on record favoring the Northwestern location only two voices were raised in favor of retaining an interest in the University of Chicago.[29] As late as February 17, 1960, the Site Committee reported that the disadvantages of a location there outweighed the advantages, and concluded the report with these words: "The sociological situation in the vicinity of the University is a recognized problem of enormous proportions. It is not an inviting prospect."[30]

Until the Fall of 1960, there was no serious indication that the merged seminary would ever be located adjacent to the University of Chicago in Hyde Park.

A TIME FOR DECISION

Two and one-half years had passed since the Inter-Seminary Committee began to consider a location for the new seminary, and still no solution appeared to be in sight. Northwestern University was a highly desirable location, but land was not available. The western suburbs were available, but not desirable for this seminary with its unique educational ideal. The Maywood campus was available, but all existing seminary sites were ruled out, largely at Augustana's insistence, but with the ready support of most of the committee members. The University of Chicago had stated very candidly its welcome, but the sociological conditions were regarded as a severe liability. What was the solution?

The pressure for decision came at the November 7, 1960, meeting of the Inter-Seminary Committee when Dr. Karl E. Mattson announced that Augustana was definitely ready to enter the merger.[31] Immediately a new Site Committee

[29]*Ibid.*, October 16, 1959, p. 1.

[30]Site Committee, "Report," February 17, 1960, Inter-Seminary Committee, *Minutes*, March 15, 1960, p. 1.

[31]*Supra*, p. 69.

was appointed[32] and charged with the responsibility of studying both the Northwestern University and University of Chicago locations, and was directed to bring a specific recommendation to the committee by March 15, 1961, so that it could be noted in the articles of consolidation.[33] In December, when the new Site Committee recommended that the Inter-Seminary Committee go on record definitely limiting the choices to the two university locations, there was a very animated discussion and finally a decision to defer action until later. Those holding out for a Maywood location, or even a western suburb, were not ready to yield. However, the committee did accept the recommendation to seek the help of professional consultants with the location problem:

> It was moved, seconded and carried that we accept the offer of the AATS [American Association of Theological Schools] to furnish consultants to make recommendations concerning the specific university (either the University of Chicago or Northwestern University) near which the proposed seminary should be located; that we request these consultants to evaluate the validity of the reasoning leading to the conclusion to locate the proposed seminary near either the University of Chicago or Northwestern University, and that we request a report of their recommendations by February 16, 1961, if possible.[34]

It was not difficult for the members of the new Site Committee to engage a study that would consider the University of Chicago as seriously as Northwestern. These were men, in the main, who felt so strongly that the Hyde Park location offered so many more advantages that nothing, even somewhat undesirable living conditions which could easily change in the future, should deter its being thoroughly studied. Dr. Heiges, a new member of both the Inter-Seminary Committee and the Site Committee, having replaced Dr. Johannes Knudsen who had left on a Sabbatical, was convinced that the University of Chicago was the proper location.[35] Dr. Madsen and Dr. Westberg had been the two outspoken advocates of this university when the rest of the committee endorsed Northwestern in October, 1959, and they remained firm in their convictions.[36] Professor Scherer saw the advantages for the School of Missions in Chicago's Asian Studies program and other similarly helpful resources.[37] Dr. Anderson, Dr. Weeg, and Professor Keljo knew by experience the difficulty of securing land in Evanston, having served on one of the previous site committees, and were very impressed by the willingness of the University of

[32]Inter-Seminary Committee, *Minutes*, November 7, 1960, Exhibit C. Site Committee: A. Howard Weeg—Chairman, O. V. Anderson, Frank P. Madsen, Granger E. Westberg, Donald R. Heiges, Karlo J. Keljo, and James Scherer.

[33]*Ibid.*, pp. 3-4.

[34]Inter-Seminary Committee, *Minutes*, December 21, 1960, p. 2.

[35]Interviews between Dr. Donald Heiges and the writer, April 24, 1958, and June 24, 1958.

[36]Inter-Seminary Committee, *Minutes*, October 16, 1959, p. 1.

[37]Letter from Professor Donald Flatt, Acting Director, LSTC School of Missions, May 16, 1968.

Chicago to help secure land in that area.[38] The Site Committee was as ready now to face the possibility of a University of Chicago location as the entire Inter-Seminary Committee had previously been ready to avoid it.

The committee engaged three men to serve as consultants and make an objective, in-depth study of Northwestern and Chicago universities: Dr. Charles L. Taylor, Executive Director of the American Association of Theological Schools; Dr. Herman N. Morse, consultant to the Council on Theological Education of the United Presbyterian Church in the U.S.A.; and Dr. Oren H. Baker, President Emeritus of Colgate-Rochester Theological Seminary.

Their written report[39] was presented at the February 21, 1961, meeting of the Inter-Seminary Committee. The consultants revealed a keen grasp of the educational ideal which had governed the thinking of so many in Lutheran theological education.

> We are in hearty agreement with the thinking that has led you hitherto to investigate the possibility of a site for the new seminary within easy walking distance of a university. On theological grounds we believe that the student preparing for the ministry should not only be thoroughly at home in the Christian Gospel and the history of the Church, but should also be prepared to follow the Lord whom we preach into the world to which He came and to the people whose predicament He addressed. Therefore, it behooves us to know the world in which we live, to speak a language intelligible to it, and to profit by the studies which may reveal to us the depths and complexities of man's plight. Bluntly, the sociological and psychological sciences are important for the ministry. Moveover, the universities which teach these sciences are representative of the total secular order, into which we believe the theological students should be plunged long before the time after graduation when they will encounter, often traumatically, the realities of modern life to which they should earlier have been exposed.[40]

> Proximity to a university also means close involvement in the life of the city. Again, we heartily concur in your judgment that, if theological students are to minister effectively upon ordination to the urban and suburban areas in which so many Lutheran churches are located, they should learn the problems of these churches while yet students. Further, we live in a culture which, whether we like it or not, is increasingly urban-dominated.[41]

After carefully weighing the advantages and disadvantages of both university locations, the consultants admitted that in many areas either location would be equally suitable, but academically they felt the University of Chicago had a distinct edge, for these reasons:

[38]Letter from Dr. O. V. Anderson to writer, May 17, 1968, and interview June 14, 1968.

[39]Appendix V.

[40]Inter-Seminary Committee, *Minutes*, February 21, 1961, "Report of Advisory Committee to the Committee on Site of the Inter-Seminary Committee," p. 1.

[41]*Ibid.*, p. 2.

a. For the B.D. student, who is the man we have chiefly in mind, we believe the professionally oriented setting of the University of Chicago offers a more suitable mental climate than does Northwestern which is primarily an undergraduate institution, increasingly interested in engineering. There is now considerable dialogue on the South Side among the faculties of theology, law, medicine and business to the enrichment of each and the profit of their pupils.

b. If you are right—as we think you are—in your emphases and your presuppositions of theological education, the strength of Chicago in the social sciences meets your need, but is balanced by corresponding excellence in philosophy, history and classical studies.

c. It is when we contemplate advanced theological studies that the manifold advantages of the University of Chicago are clearest. As we earlier noted, it already has about 110 divinity students working for the Ph.D. degree, of whom 45 are Lutherans. There is an atmosphere of mental excitement and mutual stimulation at this advanced level, a flexibility and applicability of doctoral programs born of long competence together with great resources representing every field of scholarship which has importance for theological education. Moreover, for a strong Lutheran seminary to be in a position to maintain direct contact with this considerable number of Lutheran doctoral candidates should have great value both for them and for the Lutheran Church. This is a situation ready-made for your advantage.

d. For the students of the School of Missions, it seems plain that the resources of the University of Chicago in languages, education, comparative religions, anthropology, history and related fields will more than adequately meet their interests and needs.

e. There seems to us to be a sharper focus here than at Northwestern on various specialized aspects and needs of the ministry and a greater opportunity for technical training when desired (as in the chaplaincy, social work, research, etc.). This is facilitated by the significant emphasis in the University on research and on a close working relationship among all faculties. Further, from this location there is easy access to many institutions for clinical and field work experience.[42]

Without overlooking the current adverse sociological circumstances, the consultants expressed confidence that improvements would be forthcoming shortly.

When the paper had been analyzed and discussed by the Inter-Seminary Committee, the first recommendation of the Site Committee was adopted:

That the Inter-Seminary Committee reaffirm its previous action asserting its preference for the merged seminary's orientation to a university in the Chicago area.[43]

[42]*Ibid.*, pp. 6-7.
[43]Inter-Seminary Committee, *Minutes*, February 21, 1961, p. 3.

The second recommendation, "That it [the Inter-Seminary Committee] record its preference at this time for a location in proximity to the University of Chicago," met with some resistance. When the vote was taken, fifteen supported it and three cast negative votes.[44] The decision was finally made. At last a Lutheran seminary in America would be located in a university-urban setting. What the force of the educational ideal alone could not accomplish, the added pressures of church and seminary mergers had achieved. The Lutheran School of Theology at Chicago was destined for the campus of the University of Chicago.

PUBLICIZING THE DECISION

The matter of announcing and interpreting this decision to the constituencies was a delicate and difficult task. In the first place the Inter-Seminary Committee had voted a "preference" for the University of Chicago location. Though the action revealed the final thinking of the committee it could not be regarded as official until a duly constituted authority had voted upon it. There was some considerable reluctance to write this decision into the provisions of the articles of consolidation lest the synod and church conventions be side-tracked from a consideration of the main merger issue to a debate on a specific geographic location. The greater issue could be lost over a preoccupation with the lesser issue, especially since the articles of consolidation would have to pass through four seminary boards, five synod conventions, and three national church conventions. Consequently the "Official Documents," which were distributed at all synod and church conventions in 1961, did not include a recommendation that the school be located precisely at the University of Chicago, but it did summarize the thinking of the Inter-Seminary Committee and the conclusions it had reached:

1. That the new seminary would not be located at Maywood or Rock Island. "The new corporation shall not permanently establish or maintain its theological seminary, or any part thereof, on or near any site now owned or used by any of the parties hereto as and for a seminary, except that on a temporary basis only the new Corporation may conduct its operation on the present sites of Augustana Seminary and Maywood Seminary until it has established a seminary elsewhere."[45]

2. That a university location was being seriously considered. "In connection with the discussion of a new site for the united

44*Ibid.* Dr. Armin Weng, long hopeful that the merged school would eventually locate on the Maywood campus, was keenly disappointed by the action, and requested that his negative vote be recorded on the grounds that the matter should have been discussed longer. His convictions, however, did not interfere with his support of the relocation to the University of Chicago. In a letter from Dr. Weng to the writer, February 1, 1963, he made reference to a pastor who sought his assistance in resisting the move: "He mentioned that he understood that I had originally been opposed to the location, and I tried to make it plain that a decision made is a decision, and we certainly must get behind this thing and do all we can . . . ." Such displays of churchmanship and good will enabled the Inter-Seminary Committee to accomplish its tasks despite occasional differences on crucial issues.

45*Official Documents of the Lutheran School of Theology at Chicago*, 1961, p. 19.

seminary ... the matter of proximity to a university was seriously considered. At this point it appeared that a unique opportunity for creative action had been granted the church."[46]

3. That the university would be in the vicinity of Chicago. " ... looking toward the consolidation of these and other interested seminaries of the new church into a new seminary in the general Chicagoland area."[47]

At the synod and church conventions, by order of the Inter-Seminary Committee, the representatives of the committee reported orally that the present preference was for the University of Chicago.[48] Therefore, the vote to adopt the articles of consolidation and thus merge the seminaries, was done in the full awareness that the University of Chicago location was being proposed by the Inter-Seminary Committee to the new LSTC Board of Directors.

The one large body, which circumstances prohibited from entering into this important decision, was that portion of Northwest Synod-ULCA congregations and pastors which was located in the State of Wisconsin. Since the Northwest Synod-ULCA was not one of the supporting synods of Chicago Lutheran Theological Seminary it did not vote on the articles of consolidation. Yet, by action of the Lutheran Church in America's constituting convention in Detroit, the Wisconsin congregations of the former Northwest Synod became part of the new Wisconsin-Upper Michigan Synod, one of the synods aligned with LSTC, and thus inherited ownership and support for a seminary they had not been able to help create.[49]

The opportunity for the supporting synods to ratify the decision of the Inter-Seminary Committee regarding location at the University of Chicago, which was concurred in by the initial Board of Directors of LSTC, came at the synod conventions in the Spring of 1963. Resolutions were presented requesting the synods to "memorialize the Board of Directors of the Lutheran School of Theology at Chicago to exercise the Option Agreement with the University of Chicago and purchase the property offered under the terms of said option, so that the new seminary may be built as soon as feasible at this new location."[50] Indiana-Kentucky Synod and Michigan Synod supported the resolutions overwhelmingly and with very little debate.[51] The Wisconsin-Upper Michigan Synod chose not to act on the issue since so many of the synod's congregations and pastors had not been a part of the action that brought the seminary to this point, and also because synodical action was not required in the light of the Board's power to purchase land without synodical approval. At the Illinois

[46]*Ibid.*, p. 5.
[47]*Ibid.*, p. 3.
[48]Inter-Seminary Committee, *Minutes*, March 23-24, 1961, p. 5.
[49]LCA, *Minutes*, 1962, p. 225.
[50]LSTC Board of Directors, Executive Committee, *Minutes*, March 11, 1963, Exhibit A.
[51]Indiana-Kentucky Synod-LCA, *Minutes*, 1963, p. 82. Michigan Synod-LCA, *Minutes*, 1963, p. E-24.

Synod Convention a heated discussion ensued over the relative merits of the proposed location and the abandoning of the Maywood campus, but when the vote was taken it was decisively in favor of the Board's recommendation.[52] This settled the issue once and for all. With the knowledge that the synods would back up its decision to locate on the University of Chicago campus, the Board moved forward in the securing of land and the development of plans for the new campus.

[52]Illinois Synod-LCA, *Minutes*, 1963, p. 54.

Chapter VII

SITE PURCHASES IN HYDE PARK

By the end of 1961, the Inter-Seminary Committee had completed its work. It had made the basic decision to merge the four seminaries, chosen the university setting, drafted the legal documents and successfully guided them through the judicatories. Representatives had even made initial approaches to the University of Chicago for aid in procuring land. The committee was now ready to turn over the task of site purchase and the general assignments of governing the new school to the newly elected Board of Directors.

NEW BOARD OF DIRECTORS

The articles of incorporation provided that an interim board of eighteen members should be elected by the Boards of Directors of the four merging seminaries. The following were elected in the Fall of 1961:[1]

American Evangelical Lutheran Church Representatives

Rev. Harry Andersen, Chicago, Illinois
Mr. Harry Gjelsteen, Menominee, Michigan

Augustana Lutheran Church Representatives

Dr. Kermit Almos, Western Springs, Illinois
Rev. Dr. O. V. Anderson, Chicago, Illinois
Mr. Paul Kotila, Marquette, Michigan[2]
Rev. Dr. Malvin H. Lundeen, Minneapolis, Minnesota
Rev. Philip Nelson, Bay City, Michigan
Rev. Dr. Richard B. Pearson, Waltham, Massachusetts
Rev. Harold C. Skillrud, Bloomington, Illinois

Suomi Synod Representatives

Rev. Thomas Asuma, Marquette, Michigan
Mr. V. Richard Hietikko, DeKalb, Illinois

United Lutheran Church in America Representatives

Mr. Carl Bergendoff, Glen Ellyn, Illinois
Mr. Fred Drinhaus, Highland Park, Illinois

---

[1]LSTC Board of Directors, *Minutes*, February 23, 1962, Exhibit A.
[2]Mr. Kotila resigned, and was succeeded by Dr. Gustof A. Peterson, Madison, Wisconsin.

Mr. Harold Jordan, Elgin, Illinois
Rev. Dr. Frank Madsen, Detroit, Michigan
Rev. Dr. Luther Mueller, Harvard, Illinois
Rev. Dr. A. Howard Weeg, Chicago, Illinois[3]
Rev. Dr. Walter M. Wick, Indianapolis, Indiana

These men served until the Spring conventions of the supporting synods in 1963, when the permanent board was elected. At this time some were re-elected, others were replaced by their successors, and six additional men were elected upon the nomination of the Board of Theological Education of LCA. They were joined by the presidents of the four supporting synods as ex-officio members, and by the Executive Secretaries of the Boards of Theological Education and World Missions as consultative members.[4]

The interim board of eighteen men held three joint meetings with the Inter-Seminary Committee in late 1961, and early 1962, to prepare for the takeover. At the official organizing meeting, February 23, 1962, officers were named—Chairman, Rev. Skillrud; Vice-Chairman, Mr. Jordan; Secretary, Mr. Gjelsteen[5]—and an invitation was extended to the Wisconsin-Upper Michigan Synod to appoint observers to serve until the 1963 elections, so that all synods would have representation during the initial year of operation.[6] Rev. Robert Anderson, Milwaukee, and Rev. D. C. Kalweit, Racine, were appointed.[7]

At its twentieth meeting, March 26, 1962, the Inter-Seminary Committee heard its final report from the chairman, Dr. Robert Mortvedt, who declared that the work of the committee had been completed. After four years of significant service and historic decisions, representatives passed the following resolution:

> Whereas, the basic tasks assigned to the Inter-Seminary Committee have been substantially completed; and
>
> Whereas, the Board-elect of the Lutheran School of Theology at Chicago is now holding regular meetings;
>
> Be it, therefore, resolved: That this be the final meeting of the Inter-Seminary Committee unless a necessity for a further meeting or meetings should arise and that the Boards of Directors of Augustana, Chicago, Suomi, and Grand View Seminaries be so informed by the secretary of this Committee.[8]

One era had ended, another was just beginning.

IN QUEST OF LAND

The first major task assigned to the new Board of Directors was the securing of property near the University of Chicago. The Inter-Seminary

---

[3]Dr. Weeg resigned, and was succeeded by Rev. Eldred Trede.

[4]Appendix VI contains a list of all Board members 1963-1968.

[5]LSTC Board of Directors, *Minutes*, February 23, 1962, p. 2. At a subsequent meeting Mr. Julian Kating, Chicago, was elected Treasurer, *Minutes*, May 24, 1962, p. 1.

[6]*Ibid.*, February 23, 1962, p. 4.

[7]*Ibid.*, March 26, 1962, p. 1.

[8]Inter-Seminary Committee, *Minutes*, March 26, 1962, p. 2.

Committee passed on its recommendation that "a site of two blocks is highly preferable,"[9] having learned previously that the cost of property in the area might range anywhere from $195,000 to $825,000 per block depending upon

FIGURE 1

FIRST SITE PROPOSAL FOR LSTC CAMPUS

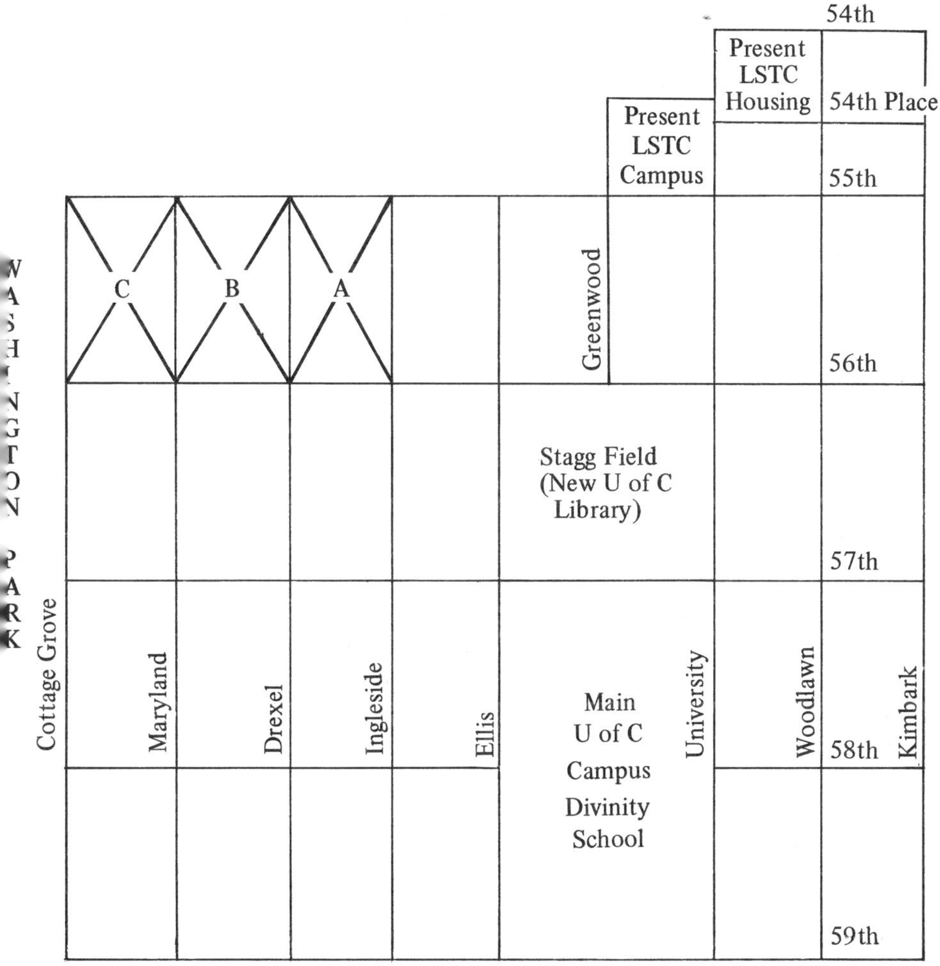

First Preference: Blocks A and B
Second Preference: Block A
Third Preference: Block B
Fourth Preference: Block C

[9]*Ibid.*, August 31, 1961, p. 5.

the location and whether it were obtained through urban renewal or from private owners.[10] These prices, though exorbitant when compared with the $5,000 per block price in Hyde Park in 1875,[11] the time when some Chicago voices were wooing Augustana Seminary to Chicago, were to rise even higher by the time the real estate transactions would be completed.

The initial formal approach to the Board of Trustees of the University of Chicago, after a series of informal negotiations had been held, was made in a letter to Dr. George W. Beadle, President of the university, November 21, 1961. A brief which accompanied the letter indicated that the seminary felt it must be located in close proximity to the university and on a main artery of university traffic. A specific request was made for land within the four block area bounded by 55th Street, Ellis Avenue, 56th Street, and Cottage Grove Avenue, in the northwestern part of the campus, strategically near the University Medical School and the University hospitals.[12] These specific blocks had been requested because university officials had thought they might be available. However, at the time LSTC made its formal request circumstances had changed. The university had received a major government project in connection with the National Aeronautics and Space Administration which would require the expansion of the university campus westward, including the three blocks proposed by LSTC. The land could not be made available to the seminary. However, the university expressed continued interest in the seminary's need for land, and promised its full cooperation, including the assigning of Mr. Albert Svoboda, Assistant Treasurer, to work as a consultant with LSTC representatives:

> All of us here at the University are quite anxious to have you locate the new Lutheran School of Theology adjacent to the campus of the University. We believe that the school would make a definite contribution to the academic life of the University and to the cultural life of the University community. For this reason, we are anxious to work out a solution that will be most satisfactory to you.[13]

By the time of the next joint meeting of the Inter-Seminary Committee and the interim Board of Directors January 29, 1962, the university had several sites to offer. All were north of 55th Street and the then existing 54th Place and were adjacent to University and Woodlawn Avenues.

LSTC representatives were favorably impressed with these proposals, but in the course of the meeting became increasingly convinced of the merits of fronting the school on 55th Street, a main thoroughfare. They voted to approve the acquisition of the sites immediately available, take options on the others,

---

[10]Report of Mr. Julian Levy. *Ibid.*, April 13, 1961, p. 1.

[11]Arden, *School of Prophets*, p. 175.

[12]Inter-Seminary Committee, *Minutes*, November 7, 1961, pp. 3-4, and Exhibit B. Letter and "Site Proposal" to Dr. George W. Beadle from Dr. Robert Mortvedt, November 21, 1961.

[13]Letter from Dr. Ray E. Brown, Vice-President for Administration, University of Chicago, to Dr. Robert Mortvedt, December 27, 1961, LSTC Archives.

FIGURE 2

SECOND SITE PROPOSAL FOR LSTC CAMPUS

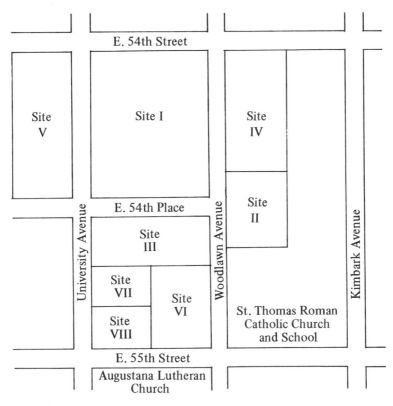

Site   I—Contains several apartment buildings, some owned by the university and others to be acquired by the university. Site available for purchase by LSTC.

Site   II—Contains two apartment buildings owned by the university. Site available for purchase by LSTC.

Site   III—Contains several apartment buildings not currently owned by the university, but LSTC could receive an option to purchase after the university acquired the property.

Site   IV—Same arrangement as Site III above.

Site   V—Same arrangement as Sites III and IV above.

Site   VI—Not offered by the university.

Site   VII—Not available. Reserved for Child Care Center.

Site VIII—Not available. Reserved for Chicago Fire Station.

and encourage the university to do everything within its power to secure the land and buildings fronting on 55th Street, Site VI, even though the university had not included this area in its proposal.[14]

The Site Committee, under the chairmanship of Dr. A. Howard Weeg, went to work, and at the May 10, 1962, meeting of the Board of Directors was able to report that most of Site I and all of Site II were now available, Site III was being procured with no difficulty, and the strategic corner of 55th Street and Woodlawn was being acquired by the university and would be available soon. In haste and secrecy, lest common knowledge of the transaction force the real estate prices upward, the Board voted to negotiate an option with the University of Chicago at $50,000 or less, with prices for the property to be the same as the cost to the university plus a fair increase for improvements.[15] It was understood that the exercising of the option would be contingent upon the action of the supporting synods at the 1963 conventions.[16] In exactly two weeks the completed option agreement was enacted by the Executive Committee of the Board,[17] and the Board of Directors of Chicago Lutheran Seminary advanced the $50,000.[18] Six days later Attorney Joseph Cox sent a letter to the LSTC Board Chairman assuring him that the task was completed:

> This is to advise you that Mr. Harold Jordan [Chairman of CLTS Board of Directors] and myself in conference with Mr. Svoboda, Treasurer of the University of Chicago, this morning executed on behalf of The Theological Seminary of The Evangelical Lutheran Church, the Option Agreement with the University, a copy of which you have.
>
> Mr. Jordan also paid to the University the sum of $50,000.00 on behalf of the Seminary.[19]

Meanwhile the building on 55th Street suddenly became available. Its purchase was a necessity if the seminary were ever to front on 55th Street. A quick mail vote among members of the Augustana Seminary Board this time, produced unanimous approval for the $146,000 purchase. Thus the seminary's first piece of property was a building housing "Jimmy's Tavern," a popular haunt of university students, a super market, an apparel shop, an art gallery, and a small grocery.[20] By the end of the year two lots at the north end of the block were also purchased.

Beginning in January, 1963, the Board made a serious effort through the university to purchase the properties north of 54th Place, Site I. All but the southwest corner were secured.

[14]Inter-Seminary Committee, *Minutes*, January 29, 1962, pp. 4-5. LSTC Board of Directors, *Minutes*, March 26, 1962, p. 7.
[15]LSTC Board of Directors, *Minutes*, May 10, 1962, p. 3.
[16]*Supra*, pp. 84-85.
[17]LSTC Board of Directors, Executive Committee, *Minutes*, May 24, 1962, p. 2.
[18]CLTS Board of Directors, *Minutes*, July 25, 1962, pp. 1-2.
[19]Letter from Mr. Joseph W. Cox to Rev. Harold C. Skillrud, July 30, 1962.
[20]The building was later sold back to the university at the same price when the seminary decided to locate one block west. *Infra*, p. 95.

As more and more property was being purchased by the seminary a certain uneasiness was developing in the Hyde Park community. The Board had continued the policy of no publicity with respect to real estate purchases in hopes of keeping prices at a minimum. In keeping with this policy not even the supporting synods were officially notified until the Spring of 1963 concerning the definite decision to locate at the University of Chicago and the specific tracts being purchased. However, information inevitably slipped out, and those residents in the Hyde Park community who resisted any further expansion of institutional building in the area began to protest. The opposition grew in intensity following the first public announcement to the press on May 6, 1963, of the seminary's land acquisition. Within days several families living in the block being acquired for the seminary academic buildings, Sites III and VI, organized the 5400 Woodlawn-University Block Club, and under its volatile and vocal chairman launched its attack against LSTC. Claiming that the seminary was threatening residential security and destroying "the few remaining well-kept, moderately priced integrated housing units in the Hyde Park community," the block club took its appeal to the public through the press and to LCA pastors through the mails.[21] Other community organizations joined the protest. A steady flow of letters and phone calls poured into the offices of Rev. Dr. Robert Marshall, Site Committee Chairman, and Rev. Harold Skillrud, Board Chairman. In a letter sent July 8, 1963, to the Hyde Park-Kenwood Community Conference and other organizations and individuals concerned about the seminary's plans, Dr. Marshall attempted to explain the Board's actions:

1. All purchases have been made on the private market. Prices paid have been arrived at by direct negotiation with owners willing to sell. No right of public acquisition, eminent domain or condemnation, or any element of public subsidy has been or will be involved.

2. While we have hoped that owners of property we desire to purchase would be prepared to sell at reasonable, fair prices, no element of coercion or compulsion is or will be involved.

3. The structures which we have acquired to date involve 199 units. 112, or 56.5% of the total, consist of student housing operated by the University of Chicago. The University of Chicago has advised us that it has already made plans for the rehousing of the persons here concerned when required. The balance of 87 units are located in other structures where it is our intention, working in collaboration with the University of Chicago and the appropriate city agencies, to develop and carry out an appropriate program of relocation services when required.

4. In the selection of site and the formulation of our plans, we have sought to minimize any impact upon non-white families. You will be interested to know that of the 199 units, only 31 involve

[21]Delores McCahill, "Hyde Parkers Appeal Lutheran Building Plan," *Chicago Daily News*, July 13, 1963.

non-white families. Relocation services, again, will be available here. You will also note that since our school includes Negroes among its students, the block will continue to be integrated.

5. Prediction as to timing is difficult because we do not know yet when sufficient funds will allow us to proceed. It appears at this time, however, that possession at the earliest will not be required for more than a year. It is our intention, moreover, to provide the most adequate notice of our need for possession of any premises, hopefully a year in advance.

6. Required architectural work and studies are now only in the formative stages. In due course we will, of course, be in a position to describe our plans with much greater precision.[22]

The absence of a President[23] or any other official representative of the seminary in the Hyde Park community provided a decided handicap in attempting to deal with opposition forces in the community. Letters of explanation were not adequate. The controversy raged on.

By the Summer of 1964, the only properties actually acquired in the block north of 55th Street, Sites III and VI, were three of six lots in the north portion of the block facing University Avenue, the commercial building at 55th and Woodlawn, and one house facing Woodlawn. Under considerable pressure, because at that time the school was scheduled to move to the new campus by the Fall of 1966, the Board authorized the architects to sketch plans employing only those portions of the block owned by LSTC, with plans to build on these parcels and wait until the other properties became available. In one last attempt, Mr. Frank Zimmerman,[24] who had joined the LSTC staff as business manager that year, and Mr. Henry Kennedy of McKey and Poague real estate agents, met July 11, 1964, with the owners of the three family cooperative apartment on the lot adjacent to the 55th Street corner building. This building had to be secured if even the latest modified building plan were to be effected. When an inflated offer by the seminary of $60,000 for the building, which had cost the occupants only $20,000, was refused, it was obvious that the organized community pressure against the seminary was effective, and it appeared that all hopes for immediate construction had vanished.

That evening, at midnight, as Mr. Zimmerman and Mr. Kennedy stood at the corner of 55th Street and University Avenue commiserating together over the unsuccessful evening, they began to gaze longingly at the block across the street to the west. Here was a block, also fronting on 55th Street, consisting entirely of apartment buildings. Scheduled for the future, beginning at this block

[22]Letter from Dr. Robert J. Marshall to Hyde Park-Kenwood Community Conference and Others, July 8, 1963.

[23]The school's president, Dr. Stewart Herman, did not take office until January 1, 1964.

[24]Much of the detailed information from this point on in this chapter was provided by Mr. Zimmerman in an interview with the writer, April 24, 1968, and a letter from Mr. Zimmerman to the writer, July 31, 1968.

and continuing westward, was a broad parkway with lawn and trees. If this new block could be obtained, as President Herman had originally suggested some months earlier, the academic building could have an entire, square block, and not be forced to share its frontage with a fire station, as on the original block. Both men agreed it was worth a try.

FIGURE 3

THIRD SITE PROPOSAL FOR LSTC CAMPUS

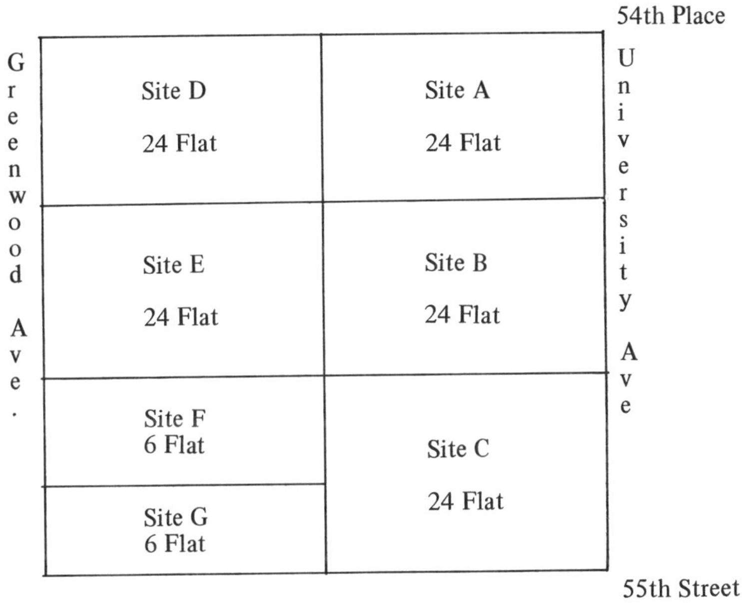

54th Place

Greenwood Avenue	Site D 24 Flat	Site A 24 Flat	University Avenue
	Site E 24 Flat	Site B 24 Flat	
	Site F 6 Flat Site G 6 Flat	Site C 24 Flat	

55th Street

The next day Mr. Zimmerman and Mr. Kennedy contacted the University of Chicago, owners of Sites C, D, and F. University officials agreed to sell these properties to the seminary on the condition that they be permitted to purchase back the 55th Street business property on the original block and the two apartment buildings on Woodlawn. This presented no hardship for the seminary, since if it were to build on the new site it would no longer need the properties requested by the university. However, the outlook for securing the other properties was not favorable. The university warned that Site B, a cooperative apartment, was owned by families that would not sell to the university or anyone else. Undaunted, the two seminary representatives proceeded to contact the private owners of the other Sites—A, E, and G—and were able to negotiate sales in a short period of time. As the university predicted, residents of the cooperative, Site B, were definitely not interested in selling. Impressed by the new proposal, the Board of Directors at its Fall meeting took unanimous action favoring the new site and authorized the administration of the seminary to proceed with the acquisition.[25] By the end of 1964, the seminary had purchased all the property on the new block, except Site B, and additional properties in the block north of 54th Place fronting on University Avenue. Property acquisitions were nearing completion for both the academic building and the residential, so the President could state in his report for 1964:

> The new 6 acre site fronts splendidly on 55th Street where it has been widened and landscaped as a two-lane boulevard. The northern edge of the main campus of the University of Chicago is directly across the street. Stagg Field, projected site of the new University Library, is only one block south. The LSTC location consists of almost two entire city blocks plus several other pieces of property in the immediate vicinity. The principal block (on 55th Street between University and Greenwood Avenues) will contain the "academic" structure. Measuring 346 by 360 feet, it now holds seven apartment houses, of which LSTC already has six in hand. Efforts are being made to acquire the seventh but possession of it is not immediately essential.

> The second block (fronting on University Avenue between 54th Place and 54th Street) consists of large apartment houses which will be renovated for use as residential halls. LSTC now owns all but two of the 12 apartment houses in this block.[26]

Soon after the public announcement of the new LSTC site in mid-September, 1964, there were immediate repercussions from both the University of Chicago students living in some of the apartments purchased by the seminary and from individuals and groups in the community who were ready to carry on the battle of the previous year against any institutional expansion in the neighborhood. Articles in the university newspaper, such as "Dear Lutherans, Please Try Elsewhere," and photographs, news stories, and letters-to-the-editor in the Hyde Park community newspaper continued to fan the flames of controversy. A new block club of residents on the proposed site attached itself to the block club which had successfully resisted the efforts of the seminary to purchase the property one block east the previous year. At one point the President received a delegation of three persons who presented petitions signed by 4,267 students and other residents, protesting the seminary's designs on this property.

Patiently and methodically seminary and university officials attempted to deal with the question. In January, 1965, University of Chicago students, administration, and seminary administration met to discuss the issue. Dean Brauer of the Divinity School pointed out that the educational ideal of the Lutheran Church required the presence of a seminary on a university campus, such as the University of Chicago:

[25]LSTC Board of Directors, *Minutes*, September 30-October 1, 1964, p. 63.
[26]Illinois Synod-LCA, *Minutes*, 1965, pp. 168-69.

Merger has opened the opportunity for Lutheran theological education to return to the place of its origin—the university.

By locating a seminary at a university, the church need not sacrifice any of its independence or conviction, but it can attract a faculty and students who desire broader cultural relationships that the church's school can provide.[27]

It was stated further that the advantage of a university location would be destroyed unless the seminary campus were in close proximity to the university campus, hence the need for the school's present choice of location. Students were assured that no other adequate sites were available. Arguments that the seminary would destroy the integration achieved by the housing on this site were answered with the information that the seminary, too, was an integrated community. Fears that university students and other families would be evicted without provision for housing were allayed with the announcement that the seminary had a program in operation of relocating students into other apartments owned by the school and other residents would be assisted in securing housing through the Department of Urban Renewal. Mr. C. H. Anderson, Business Manager of the Rock Island Campus, established a housing office at the new site in January, 1965, and began the process of visiting personally each of the one hundred eight families living in the seminary property scheduled for later demolition. Confronting rumor with facts and hostility with charity, he gradually won the confidence of most tenants and successfully arranged for the relocation of all university students into larger and improved seminary apartments in the residential block. When the Department of Urban Renewal, under pressure of vocal elements in the community, removed its offer to assist in the relocation of non-student families, Mr. Anderson and the seminary staff accomplished this feat as well. One hundred thirty-three families were successfully relocated by the end of the year through the concerned efforts of Mr. Zimmerman, Mr. Anderson, and Mr. Alfred Pfenner, Business Manager of the Maywood campus.

To assist in the development of better community relations the Board created a Lutheran Neighborhood Committee to which the President appointed a number of highly respected citizens in the community who were members of LCA congregations.[28]

Against this background of controversy and opposition the seminary attempted to negotiate the purchase of the one remaining apartment building on the new site. All efforts were fruitless, so the Board considered building its new academic building around the co-op apartment, fronting on University Avenue. The plan became public information when it was publicized in the community newspaper February 10, 1965.[29]

[27]*Chicago Maroon*, January 22, 1965, pp. 1,3.

[28]Mr. Hubert L. Will, Federal Judge; Mrs. Oliver Crawford, wife of a medical doctor; Mrs. Philip Williams, wife of a medical doctor; Dr. Richard Moy, Head of Student Health Service at the University of Chicago; and Mr. Leonard I. Carlson, Social Worker.

[29]*Hyde Park Herald*, February 10, 1965, p. 1. See Figure 4, p. 98.

FIGURE 4

INITIAL SITE DEVELOPMENT PLAN FOR LSTC CAMPUS

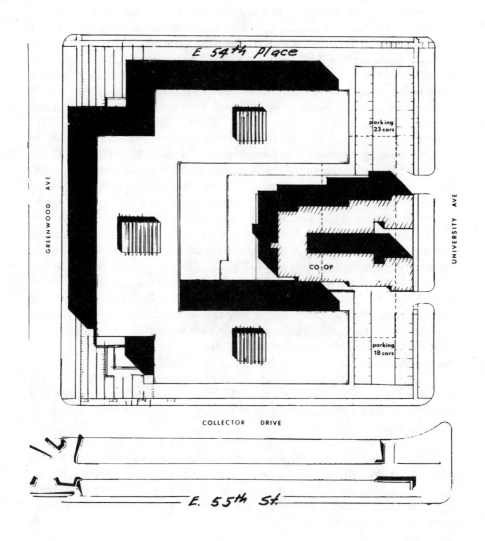

The publication of the plan which indicated the serious intention of LSTC to proceed with its building program fanned the flames of controversy again. In an effort to inform the community of its specific plans, the seminary scheduled a public meeting at which the President, the Business Manager, and a representative of the architectural firm would present information and answer questions about the proposed construction. Despite one of the worst snow storms of the Winter, more than 150 persons, mainly University of Chicago students, crowded Swift Hall commons on the university campus February 25, 1965, for the meeting. Efforts to confine the meeting to the stated purpose were fruitless as it became obvious that most of those attending wanted to voice opposition to the seminary's interests in building on its chosen site. However, the seminary's announcement of a firm policy in following through with its plans, plus the assurance that seminary personnel were dealing personally with each family involved in the need for relocation, convinced some in the community that the project was inevitable and ought to be accepted. On March 10, 1965, the local newspaper ran a surprising, but welcome, editorial, "Let's End the Controversy." Admitting that the seminary's public relations had been poor, it nevertheless commended the school for its good faith in relocating tenants, and it scored some block clubs for "a lack of responsibility and a tendency to inflame the issue unnecessarily by some unsupported statements and actions."[30] It concluded with a final appeal to the community:

> The fact now remains that the Lutherans own two blocks of housing in Hyde Park which they intend to keep and develop. Asking the Lutherans to move to another site in Hyde Park at this point is unrealistic.
>
> In our opinion, the block clubs and other concerned residents ought to recognize the economic realities of the situation. An institution which has invested over one million dollars in property is not about to abandon its investment and move elsewhere.
>
> This community has many serious problems now and will have for years to come. The energy and effort spent on what is an accomplished fact could be more profitably used on other aspects of community life.[31]

The editorial brought forth a volley of opposition from individuals, but it was clear that the major controversy had ended. A few remaining opponents quietly distributed a mimeographed protest at the Groundbreaking ceremonies some months later on October 6, 1965, and a dozen good-natured pickets marched in orderly fashion at the Cornerstone rites April 24, 1966, but with this the opposition died away. The following Summer a large Chicago daily commented in summary:

[30]*Ibid.*, March 10, 1965, p. 4.
[31]*Ibid.*

Plans for the school prompted a three-year controversy in Hyde Park over land acquisition. The school got more urban involvement than it bargained for.

But now, with classes due to begin in the 3.5 million dollar center Oct. 1, debate has died in the community, said Ald. Leon Despres (5th).

Residents of the affected area, he said, are quietly resigned.[32]

About the time that the community opposition began to wane, the Board of Directors recognized that its original goal of moving on to the new campus in the Fall of 1966, was unattainable. As a consequence of shifting the site one block westward and the impossibility of relocating all tenants before October 31, 1965, so that the buildings could be demolished, the target date was postponed from September, 1966, to June 1, 1967.[33]

Even before the newspaper publicity concerning the possible plan of building the seminary around the cooperative apartment appeared on February 10, 1965, producing this latest round of community controversy, the Board of Directors of LSTC was exploring ways of purchasing the co-op, so that the seminary could utilize the entire block and front the new building on 55th Street. Negotiations which had appeared fruitless for the first six months, suddenly produced a letter from the co-op owners January 4, 1965, indicating a friendly relationship, the assurance that they would not be influenced by the block clubs' pressure tactics, and would be open to negotiation for a trade or possible sale. This welcome news prompted the Board to direct the Business Manager to do everything within his power to secure the apartment, even to the point of offering a somewhat inflated price.[34]

The unpleasant prospect of having a large theological seminary building in their back yard, and the pleasant prospect of being able to trade off their present building for apartments with larger rooms, combined to make the co-op owners receptive to a new offer from the seminary. In an extremely complex real estate transaction Mr. Zimmerman was able to effect a trade with the co-op owners.[35] First, after securing the approval of the co-op members, LSTC purchased a thirty-six apartment building in the neighborhood. At this point one-third of the co-op members saw an opportunity to secure a premium price, and filed suit against the seminary on the charges of misrepresentation of facts. The charges could not be substantiated, so at the counsel of the judge they did not press their case, and instead merely sold their apartments in the new building to the seminary. This meant that LSTC owned twenty of the thirty-six apartments in a building more than six blocks away. Selling, however, presented a problem because under a co-op arrangement potential purchasers could not borrow

[32]*Chicago Sunday Tribune*, July 23, 1967.
[33]LSTC Board of Directors, *Minutes*, April 20-21, 1965, p. 90.
[34]*Ibid.*, January 27-28, 1965, p. 75.
[35]Frank Zimmerman, Memo to Messrs. Soderberg and Wohlers, Dr. Herman, Pastor Skillrud, August 5, 1966, p. 1.

FIGURE 5

FINAL SITE DEVELOPMENT PLAN FOR LSTC CAMPUS

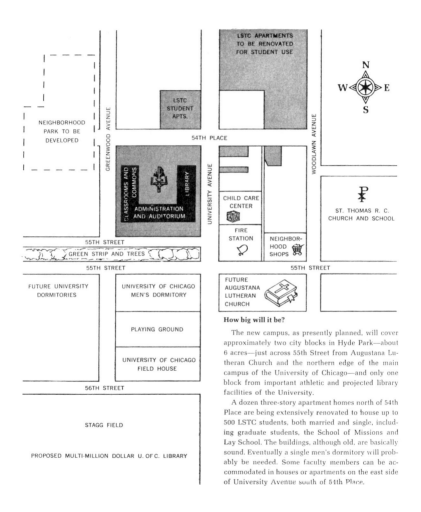

How big will it be?

The new campus, as presently planned, will cover approximately two city blocks in Hyde Park—about 6 acres—just across 55th Street from Augustana Lutheran Church and the northern edge of the main campus of the University of Chicago—and only one block from important athletic and projected library facilities of the University.

A dozen three-story apartment homes north of 54th Place are being extensively renovated to house up to 500 LSTC students, both married and single, including graduate students, the School of Missions and Lay School. The buildings, although old, are basically sound. Eventually a single men's dormitory will probably be needed. Some faculty members can be accommodated in houses or apartments on the east side of University Avenue south of 54th Place.

Acquistion Costs:

Land for academic building and parking lot	$1,272,051
Land and buildings for student housing	1,685,774
	2,957,825

101

money by mortgaging their apartments. This could be achieved, however, by converting the property into a condominium. This was done with the assurance that a local financial firm would make the necessary loans to prospective purchasers, so that the seminary could withdraw from ownership of the twenty apartments. However, the financial institution did not have sufficient funds to make the loans, and to make this possible LSTC invested some $215,000 of its endowment fund at 5½ per cent interest with the firm for a two year period. When the entire transaction was finally completed, the cooperative members had either roomier apartments or cash settlements, the twenty apartments in the condominium were sold through loans provided by the seminary to a lending institution, and above all, LSTC had purchased the last remaining piece of property on the new site. The Executive Committee of the Board of Directors took its official action authorizing the real estate transfer June 17, 1965. Mr. Zimmerman had achieved the improbable within the alloted time, November 1, 1965, and well within the maximum payment allowed. With this strategic purchase completed, demolition could be scheduled and construction could be authorized. The new building would front on 55th Street where passers-by could have a proper view of the impressive structure. A relieved and thankful board and administration announced the new and permanent site.[36]

[36]The property was later enlarged even further when 54th Place was closed July 7, 1967, by action of the City of Chicago at the seminary's request, making possible a spacious parking lot on the north side of the academic complex.

Chapter VIII

COUNTING THE COST

Merger and relocation to a university-urban setting was a costly enterprise. It demanded the surrendering of deep attachments to specific campus locations, long cherished by their respective constituencies. It demanded the willingness to adjust to a new type of seminary community created by the blending of several theological traditions, faculties, and student bodies. It demanded a sensitive relationship to a new sociological and academic environment. It also demanded the expenditure of huge sums of money.

The experiences associated with the acquisition of land proved that the financial costs were even greater than the highest estimates. This came to be true in most other areas, too, as the following table indicates.

TABLE 2

ESTIMATED AND ACTUAL COSTS

Project	1964 Estimate	1968 Actual
Land and Buildings	$2,500,000[a]	$2,957,825
New construction, demolition, parking lot, architectural fees	3,901,800	4,810,002
Renovation and furnishing of student housing	1,026,100	381,590
School Equipment	350,000	323,797
Moving expenses	–	86,525
Landscaping	–	14,729
Total	$7,777,900	$8,574,468

[a]Estimate based on purchase of block east of final site, a smaller piece of property.

Substantial savings were realized in the renovation and furnishing of student housing by skillful seminary management. However these savings were more than offset by the increased costs in the area of land acquisition, due to the move westward one block, and in the area of construction, due to the inflationary spiral and larger than anticipated construction costs. The total actual financial requirements proved to be about $800,000 more than estimated in 1964.

However, even on the basis of the lower estimated figure in 1964, seminary officials and board realized that a monumental task confronted them, especially when they learned that no financial assistance could be expected from the Lutheran Church in America. In 1961, when JCLU representatives were present at a meeting of the Inter-Seminary Committee, the question was asked:

> Would any funds from the national church be available for the seminary apart from the above operating budget, Graduate School, and School of Missions either for construction or operational purposes?[1]

The following answer was given:

> The proposed by-laws of the LCA (Section X, G, Item 4, b, and Section XVIII, Item 5) open the way for the provision of funds for special purposes for theological education, either from the church budget or from special appeals. The JCLU confidently expects that the future church will give serious attention in one way or another to the general welfare of theological education.[2]

This favorable response was based upon action taken by JCLU at a meeting earlier in the month.[3] However, any hopes that Church support would go beyond operating budget assistance and include funds for construction were dashed to the ground the next year. A meeting November 17, 1962, between Rev. Dr. Franklin Clark Fry, Rev. Dr. Conrad Bergendoff of the Board of Theological Education, and Rev. Harold Skillrud of the seminary board dealt with this specific question. Dr. Fry explained that developments at other LCA seminaries calling for capital funds were beginning to appear, and that the only way to be fair to all seminaries was to encourage them to conduct their own regional appeals for construction purposes; LCA could help only in the area of operating budget assistance.[4]

LSTC DEVELOPMENT FUND

Realizing now that all the funds to defray the costs of the new campus development must be raised within the four synods which then supported the school, LSTC's Board of Directors immediately appointed a committee to investigate the matter, and by March, 1963, was ready to act favorably on the recommendations:

---

[1]Inter-Seminary Committee, *Minutes*, March 23-24, 1961, p. 4.
[2]*Ibid.*
[3]JCLU, *Minutes*, March 3-4, 1961, p. 218.
[4]LSTC Board of Directors, *Minutes*, November 21, 1962, p. 5.

1. That a financial campaign begin not later than January, 1964, and that the four supporting synods take action in the Spring of 1963, to authorize it.

2. That the goal of the campaign be established at $3,200,000.

3. That a professional fund raising firm be employed to direct the campaign.

This proposal to the synods, coming as soon after the LCA merger as it did, and calling for a substantial financial contribution to the new seminary, was a test both of the success of church merger and the concern of the synods for this unique venture in theological education.

The Indiana-Kentucky Synod was the first to confront the resolution. Presidents Mattson and Weng of the Rock Island and Maywood campuses presented the cause to the assembly. Since this synod recommended a concurrent campaign for LSTC and its synod camping program, most of the debate centered about the division of funds to each cause. The measure was strongly supported when the vote was taken.[5] The Synod's goal was set at $423,000 for LSTC, and Rev. Robert Cassell and Mr. Donald E. Kern were designated co-chairmen for the appeal. The appeal resulted in a substantial over-subscription. LSTC did not participate in amounts exceeding its goal of $423,000.

The next synod to act on the resolution, May 14, 1963, was Michigan. Here President Mattson and Board Chairman Skillrud addressed the assembly. Michigan Synod also decided to relate the appeal to other causes, camping and social services, and adopted the recommendation launching the appeal.[6] Under its co-chairmen, Rev. R. Edward Carlstrom and Mr. James A. Heller, the Synod accepted a goal of $360,000 for the seminary, but received pledges for $430,141, an over-subscription of 19 per cent.

The climate at the Wisconsin-Upper Michigan Synod convention was definitely affected by the peculiar set of circumstances which gave many of the synod's congregations and pastors an official voice in the affairs of the seminary for the first time on May 16, 1963. Having not voted on the merger documents in 1961, nor participated directly and officially in the decisions of the seminary up to this point, these congregations were being asked to support a venture financially which they had not helped to create.[7] The debate was lively as Rev. Dr. Robert Marshall, Site Committee Chairman; Rev. Dr. Jerald Brauer, Dean of the University of Chicago Divinity School; and Rev. Harold Skillrud, Board Chairman, answered questions and provided information. Finally, on the conviction that a premature campaign could fail in this synod, delegates unanimously passed a substitute motion authorizing a fund appeal to begin one year later.[8] The good will of the synod in support of the new venture became

---

[5]Indiana-Kentucky Synod-LCA, *Minutes*, 1963, pp. 77, 82.
[6]Michigan Synod-LCA, *Minutes*, 1963, pp. E-24-E-25.
[7]*Supra*, p. 84.
[8]Wisconsin-Upper Michigan Synod-LCA, *Minutes*, 1963, p. 120.

manifest as it accepted its goal of $938,000, and then under the leadership of its co-chairmen, Rev. William B. Downey and Mr. Russell M. Rutter, raised pledges of $1,755,700 over the goal by 87 per cent.

Dr. Marshall had prepared the Illinois Synod for its vote on May 21, 1963, with this strong appeal: "To provide a campus for the new Lutheran School of Theology is the single greatest demand our synod must meet in the immediate future."[9] After some animated debate, which questioned the necessity of employing professional fund raising counsel, the recommendation was voted upon and passed decisively.[10] Adopting a goal of $1,479,000 the Illinois Synod went on to pledge $2,731,438, or 85 per cent above the goal, under the leadership of co-chairmen Rev. Glenn Gilbert and Mr. Leonard Olson.

A summary of the Development Fund appears in Table 3.[11] (See page 107.)

CAMPUS SALES

Another major source of revenue for the development of the new campus was the sale of the seminary campuses about to be vacated. Grand View Seminary's share of the assets of Grand View College was estimated at $15,000 and this amount, plus a special AELC thank offering gift of $4,000 was transferred to the LSTC building fund. Likewise, Suomi's assets were limited to its partial holdings, and this fund of $12,415 was also turned over for new campus development. A special fund appeal of the former Illinois Synod of the ULCA, "United For Christ's Tomorrow," had produced over $400,000 for Maywood seminary, and after some funds were removed for Maywood Campus operations, about $300,000 was remitted to LSTC for the new campus. It was recognized that the sale of the campuses in Rock Island and Maywood would produce the greatest revenue.

The Rock Island campus was sold first. Since it was located at the very center of Augustana College campus, all parties recognized that the college was obviously the only buyer. To explore the sale and possible purchase price with college officials, a special committee was appointed by the Augustana Seminary Board of Directors as early as October, 1961.[12]

A survey of the campus revealed that two-thirds of the buildings had been erected in 1923, and the balance in 1953-54. Original construction costs were $895,406 and estimated replacement costs were $1,246,700. The college representatives estimated its value to the school, on the basis of age and utility, at $520,000.

In an effort to assist the college in the purchase of the buildings the Executive Board of the Augustana Lutheran Church-Central Conference, at the recommendation of its President, Rev. Dr. O. V. Anderson, voted to contribute

[9]Illinois Synod-LCA, *Minutes*, 1963, p. 74.

[10]*Ibid.*, p. 54.

[11]Figures provided by LSTC Business Office September 5, 1968. Estimates call for an additional $450,000 in receipts by the end of 1968.

[12]Augustana Seminary Board of Directors, *Minutes*, October 6-7, 1961, p. 4.

TABLE 3

DEVELOPMENT FUND REPORT AS OF SEPTEMBER 5, 1968

Synod	Members	Goal	Per Member	Intents	Per Member	Paid	Per Member	Due	Per Member
Illinois	144,996	$1,479,000	$10.20	$2,731,438	$18.50	$2,212,329	$15.25	$ 519,109	$3.25
Ind.-Kentucky	43,290	423,000	9.80	423,000	9.80	377,862	8.75	45,138	1.05
Michigan	41,592	360,000	8.65	430,141	10.35	314,915	7.60	115,226	2.75
Wisc.-U. Mich.	101,628	938,000	9.25	1,755,700	17.25	927,324	9.10	828,376	8.15
Totals	331,506	$3,200,000	$ 9.70	$5,340,279	$16.10	$3,832,430	$11.55	$1,507,849	$4.55
Alumni						1,011			
Special Gifts						46,986			
Total Receipts						$3,880,427			

107

its surplus funds of approximately $400,000 for this purpose.[13] To this, Augustana College added $100,000 as the maximum its representatives concluded the college could afford.[14] The sale was consummated and LSTC ultimately received a total of approximately $525,000. The seminary buildings became a part of the Augustana College campus in the Summer of 1967.

The Maywood campus held greater potential for an excellent sale price. Its large acreage was located adjacent to the Eisenhower Expressway and was within easy distance to the Chicago loop. The American Appraisal Company appraised the land and buildings at $1,001,000, the land itself being valued at one-half that amount.

The first group with serious intentions to purchase was the Lutheran Church-Missouri Synod, but after holding an exclusive right to negotiate for its purchase for several months, terminated its interest. Subsequent efforts to sell the property for commercial or residential purposes failed to produce a buyer.

During the last school year on the Maywood campus, 1966-67, the seminary conducted serious negotiations with the Board of Education of Cook County School District Number 89, and the sale was finally consummated in September, 1967. The school board purchased the the entire campus, with the exception of the library, for a total price of $850,000. The appraised value of the library which remained was $150,000.

The old chapel pipe organ, first given to the seminary by St. Mark's Lutheran Church, ULCA, in Chicago in 1955, and installed on the Maywood campus by seminary students, was sold for $25 in the Summer of 1967, to Rev. Arthur Kreinheder, the only Lutheran monk in the United States, who has since installed it in St. Augustine's House near Oxford, Michigan.[15]

BOARD OF WORLD MISSIONS

A final source of funds for the building project was the Lutheran Church in America's Board of World Missions. It was heavily involved in the Maywood Seminary program since it placed its School of Missions there in 1957. A major part of its financial investment in Maywood was the School of Missions Dormitory, valued in 1967, at $118,500 when it was sold as a part of the total campus to the Maywood Board of Education. A sum of $261,000 was earlier paid to LSTC by the Board of World Missions as a contribution toward its fair share of the total new campus development; the contribution of the Mission Dormitory brought the Board's total investment at the new seminary to $379,500.[16] LSTC, in accepting this assistance from the Board, became contingently liable to repay this amount, minus two per cent per year

---

[13]Executive Board, Central Conference, Augustana Lutheran Church, *Minutes*, December 5, 1962.

[14]Rock Island Campus Sale Committee, *Minutes*, January 22, 1963, p. 2.

[15]Oxford, Michigan, *Leader*, April 25, 1968, p. 24.

[16]Letter from Mr. Frank Zimmerman, LSTC Business Manager, to Mr. John V. Lindholm, Board of World Missions Treasurer, November 9, 1967.

amortization in the event that the School of Missions were to withdraw from LSTC within ten years after November, 1967.

INDEBTEDNESS

Funds from all these sources were not adequate to meet the total costs of land and building acquisition, new construction, furnishings, campus development, and moving. A one million dollar indebtedness had been anticipated in 1964, but the actual indebtedness proved to be double that amount. A combination of increased construction and land costs and a reduction in receipts anticipated from the Development Fund produced the increased debt.

Land costs rose when the decision was made to purchase the complete block west of the original partial block. Original architectural estimates of construction costs proved to be too low, and even though the Building Committee and the Board of Directors scaled down the architect's recommendations on several occasions, the costs for building and site development increased twenty-five per cent over the original estimates of 1964. The Board could be criticized for letting the contract when the increased costs became known. It could have rejected the architectural drawings and insisted on a complete revision of plans. This alternative was rejected for two reasons: 1) This would have delayed the move to the new campus far beyond the 1967 deadline, resulting in more apprehension on the part of prospective students and added inconveniences for the new owners of the Rock Island and Maywood campuses. 2) A delay in architectural drawings would have resulted in higher construction bids since the Chicago construction market was increasing at approximately seven to eight per cent per year. Then, too, the Board was encouraged by Development Fund pledges which were $1,140,000 over the original goal. These increased pledges actually exceeded the net increased costs of land purchase and construction by some $300,000. It appeared that the increased costs could be borne by the increased gifts. If the Board is to be blamed for the fact that the final indebtedness was approximately $2,000,000 instead of the estimated $1,000,000 it is due to the fact that it took too seriously the Development Fund pledges. By late 1968, $1,500,000 in unpaid pledges remained, and the estimate indicated that only about $400,000 of this would ultimately be collected.[17]

Several explanations were offered for the reduction in Development Fund receipts.[18] A large number of congregations interpreted their Declarations of Intent to mean goals rather than firm commitments, and thus did not sense an obligation to remit the entire amount of the pledge. This confusion appeared to be the result of a misunderstanding by some congregations of the procedures outlined by the Development Fund campaign organization. Secondly, a number of urban congregations during the three to four year collection period suffered a significant reduction of members caused by a flight to the suburbs, and thus many pledges went unmet. Thirdly, other local programs requiring financial

[17]LSTC Executive Committee, *Minutes*, September 5, 1968, p. 3.
[18]Oral report to the LSTC Board of Directors, October 16-17, 1968, by Dr. Stewart Herman, President, and Mr. Frank Zimmerman, Assistant to the President.

support developed in many congregations, and the Development Fund was bypassed in favor of these programs. Fourthly, during this collection period a greater emphasis was placed on the church's role in the urban crisis, coupled with a growing disdain for institutional building, and the financial support of urban programs took precedence over the Development Fund in some congregations. Part of this deficit might have been taken up by the solicitation of large gifts, as is frequently done with financial appeals of this type. However, in this case the Development Fund program was conducted, at the insistence of the fund raising counsellors, on the congregational level only. It was feared that the solicitation of large gifts from members of congregations would hamper each congregation from achieving its corporate goal.

The result was an indebtedness of some $2,000,000. Consequently, the Board of Directors in late 1968, was forced to authorize long-term financing for the eradication of the indebtedness,[19] and to create an Office of Development for the procuring of funds to meet the amortization schedule.[20]

[19]LSTC Board of Directors, *Minutes*, April 24-25, 1968, p. 177, and Executive Committee, *Minutes*, September 5, 1968, pp. 2, 3.

[20]LSTC Executive Committee, *Minutes*, September 5, 1968, pp. 3, 5, and Board of Directors, *Minutes*, October 16-17, 1968, p. 5.

Chapter IX

A TIME TO BUILD

After the decision to merge the four seminaries had been made by the Inter-Seminary Committee in early 1961, and subsequently approved by the judicatories of the churches, a full year elapsed before public announcement was made that the new site would be adjacent to the University of Chicago. Even then there was no assurance regarding the exact date when the school would open at the new location, so students enrolling at the Maywood and Rock Island campuses had difficulty making precise plans for the future. Such uncertainties had an adverse effect on enrollments at both schools. In his final report as Dean of Chicago Lutheran Seminary, Dr. Donald Heiges spoke for both campuses when he predicted a decrease in enrollment for the 1962-63 school year and thereafter until plans for the future could be finalized:

> The decrease in admissions has probably been due to a number of factors .... The third, and I think **the most serious factor,** has been the uncertainty surrounding the merger of CLTS with three other seminaries and the consequent relocation of the campus. Almost all prospective students show anxiety at this point, and my assurances have not seemed to allay their concern. We cannot assume that, because we have confidence in the future of the Lutheran School of Theology, prospective students feel the same way. As a result, I predict that there will be a drop in enrollment in 1962-1963, and perhaps for several years thereafter.[1]

Enrollments did drop. In the Fall of 1962, 35 new students enrolled at Rock Island and 22 at Maywood, compared with average incoming classes during the previous decade of 52 and 29 respectively.[2]

SELECTION OF ARCHITECT

Factors such as these put added pressure on the new Board of Directors of the school to proceed immediately with building plans and construction. After authorizing a preliminary site study and master plan for completion in early 1963, so that cost estimates could be included in the publicity materials for the

---

[1]CLTS Executive Committee, *Minutes*, May 15, 1962, "Report of the Dean," p. 1.
[2]*Supra*, p. 46, Table 1.

development fund campaign, the board appointed a Committee on Selection of Architect, chaired by Dr. O. V. Anderson. The committee met five times in 1963, utilizing the consultative services of Dean Leonard J. Currie of the College of Architecture and Art of the University of Illinois, Chicago Campus, and interviewed six architectural firms of international reputation. Projects completed by these firms included the Air Force Academy Chapel at Colorado Springs, Colorado, buildings at Harvard College, Massachusetts Institute of Technology, and the University of Chicago. Upon recommendation of this committee the Board of Directors authorized the employment of a Chicago firm, The Perkins and Will Partnership, specialists in school building.[3]

At the very outset there were several conferences with the architects at which the educational ideal of the school was set forth. Seminary representatives insisted that the building must express the school's basic concern for relating theology to all of life, the importance of the inter-relationship between the seminary, the world, society, and other academic disciplines. President-elect Stewart W. Herman voiced these same concerns:

> My vision of the new seminary leads me to suggest the general idea that everything about its new buildings should express the fullest possible communication between our theological training, the world around us and God "above" us. Architecturally, it seems to me that this may be indicated by avoiding the usual cloistral or sequestered effect.[4]

Inital architectural studies and plans were made on the basis of the original location, one block east of the final site. The difficulties experienced in securing all of this property required the architects to make a series of tentative sketches, each dependent on the amount of land secured. With the abandonment of the original site in favor of the present location, the architects had to begin afresh, thus causing necessary but serious delays. The ultimate solution was a "U" shaped building which could front either on Greenwood Avenue or on 55th Street, depending on the outcome of attempts to purchase the last remaining building on the new site.[5] The Building and Site Committee[6] was ready to

---

[3]LSTC Board of Directors, *Minutes*, January 30-31, 1964, p. 34.
[4]Letter from President Herman to Dr. O. V. Anderson, October 18, 1963.
[5]*Supra*, pp. 95, 100, 102.
[6]Building and Site Committee: Robert Marshall (Chairman), Kermit O. Almos, C. H. Anderson, O. V. Anderson, Robert B. Anderson, Fred Drinhaus, Harry Gjelsteen, Stewart Herman, Paul H. Krause, Frank P. Madsen, Theodore E. Matson, Harold C. Skillrud, Walter M. Wick, Frank K. Zimmerman.

Executive Committee: Robert Marshall (Chairman), Stewart Herman, Frank K. Zimmerman.

Advisory Committee: Berthold E. Roeselar, Augustana Congregation, Hyde Park; Dr. Howard Schomer, Chicago Theological Seminary; Dr. Jerald C. Brauer, Divinity School, University of Chicago; Irving M. Gerick, Hyde Park Community Conference; Dr. Donald L. Houser, LCA Board of American Missions; Dr. E. Theodore Bachmann, LCA Board of Theological Education; Dr. Earl S. Erb, LCA Board of World Missions; Dr. Robert P. Roth, LCA Commission on Church Architecture; Dr. Armin G. Weng, Maywood Faculty; Dr. Karl E. Mattson, Rock Island Faculty; Dean James Scherer, School of Missions; Rev. Joel Lundeen, LSTC Librarian; Dr. Joseph Sittler, Divinity School Faculty; Dr. Martin Marty, Divinity School Faculty; Dr. A. R. Kretzmann, Pastor, St. Luke's Lutheran Church.

recommend the general design at the April, 1965, board meeting. The design concept envisioned a three-story, three-building complex with a curtain wall facade of glass and metal containing an interior open court. The building according to the architects, would "look both outward to the variety and vitality of the city life all around it, and inward to the quiet solitude of its own central court." It provided for a balanced theological pursuit of confrontation with the world and quiet reflection.

Each of the three units forming the building was designed to rest on four giant concrete pedestals capable of supporting three million pounds each. This cantilever construction would permit a cut-away entrance at each corner of the building, providing an open view of the interior court. The center wing of the structure provided for a chapel-auditorium seating 500, administration and faculty offices; the east wing included the dining hall, student lounge, classrooms, and faculty offices; and the west wing was reserved for the library and the great lounge. Total floor space was 136,000 square feet.[7]

PLATE II
COMPLETED BUILDING

SELECTION OF CONTRACTOR

By the Summer of 1965, the architectural drawings were sufficiently advanced to permit the consideration of contractors. The Building and Site Committee had carefully studied a recommendation of the architectural firm

---

[7]Appendix VII contains detailed floor plans of the entire building.

that the seminary award a "negotiated" contract, rather than release the plans for open bidding. This plan had two major advantages: 1) Only firms capable of handling the massive concrete and structural demands of the complex design would be considered. 2) The contract could be negotiated at once on the basis of schematic drawings completed at that point, while open bidding would require that all detailed, working drawings be completed. When the recommendation came to the Board of Directors at a special August, 1965, meeting, prices had been secured on a negotiated contract basis from two major Chicago contractors. The board awarded the contract to the lower bidder, the James McHugh Construction Company.[8] At the same time it authorized the creation of an Executive Construction Committee. The chairman appointed Mr. Frank Zimmerman, LSTC Business Manager, Chairman; Dr. Stewart Herman, LSTC President; Dr. Harold Lohr and Mr. Albert Wohlers, board members; and Rev. Philip Anderson, Pastor of Augustana Lutheran Church on 55th Street. These men met regularly with the architects and consultants during the entire construction period.

GROUNDBREAKING

Against the background of partially demolished buildings, the result of a demolition project begun September 17, 1965, to ready the property for new construction, members of the Board of Directors and guests assembled on the 55th Street site for a Groundbreaking Ceremony at 1:30 p.m. on October 6, 1965.

Speaker at the event was Dr. Walter Wick, President of the Indiana-Kentucky Synod, member of the Board of Directors and previously of the Inter-Seminary Committee. Pointing out that the seminary site was just a few hundred feet from Stagg Field, where the first controlled nuclear chain reaction had taken place in 1942, he noted how significant this location would be in implementing the seminary's educational ideal:

> We stand in the shadows of a mighty university where in colloquy with world renowned minds our faculties and students will sharpen theirs. Here we listen to the subdued rumble and undertones of a great city where flow the cross currents of many races, creeds, and cultures. This is exactly why the place is ideally qualified to fashion leaders for the increased urbanization of our culture and church.

> Here a new venture of our Church will spring forth. In this place shall arise the true symbol of the amalgamators of the four groups that formed our Lutheran Church in America. Here will be the heart and future of the church.

[8]LSTC Board of Directors, *Minutes*, August 13, 1965, p. 95. The contract, when awarded the following October, was for $4,107,675 including demolition of old buildings and protective fencing. During construction, due to additions and alternates, plus the demolition of an additional building to make room for the construction of a parking lot not included in the original bid, expenditures rose another $329,294. However, the early date of the negotiated contract resulted in a savings of several hundreds of thousands of dollars due to radical construction cost increases the next year.

Here is the seed-bed of the church, for here will be shaped and molded the shepherds of our congregations, the missionaries for far places, the leaders of a great church. Here will be the storehouse of our treasures and traditions, the tools of our workshops, in our libraries. Here are the anvils of theological dialogue where our faculties will hammer out the principles of the future.

I feel that I stand on sacred ground, and like Moses, I seem to see a fire that consumes not, but perpetually enlightens and brightens the contemporary scene and designates the very presence of God.[9]

Dr. Stewart Herman, President, turned the first shovel of earth, and was joined by the Presidents of the four supporting synods and the chairman of the board. Dignataries assisting in the ceremony included Dr. E. Theodore Bachmann, Executive Secretary of the Board of Theological Education-LCA; Dr. Jerald C. Brauer, President of the BTE board and Dean of the nearby Divinity School of the University of Chicago; and Mr. Leon Despres, City Alderman from the area.

The brief ceremony concluded with the prayer:

O God, in whom every good thing has its beginning, and by whom it increases and advances to greater worth: Grant us, thy servants, that what we have this day undertaken to the glory of thy Name, may, by the aid of thy fatherly wisdom, be successfully completed; through Jesus Christ, our Lord. Amen.[10]

The Lutheran School of Theology had arrived at a university site at long last.

CORNERSTONE LAYING

Heavy rain clouds vanished and bright sunlight broke forth just minutes before 4:00 p.m. on Sunday, April 24, 1966, allowing over 500 friends of the seminary to attend the out-door Foundation Festival of Praise at the southwest corner of the developing new building.

Highpoint of the inspiring service was the address by Dr. Conrad Bergendoff, former President of Augustana College and Theological Seminary, entitled, "The Throne and the Faculties." Pointing to the huge structure arising behind him, he said that the remarkable feature of this project was not its size, but its location next to a major university. He saw in this decision the fruition of an educational ideal long implanted in the life of the Lutheran Church:

The remarkable fact about our proposal is the placing of it alongside one of the world's great universities. This is itself a declaration of faith which not all of our Church recognizes. Not that the earlier founders of our seminaries would have hesitated to do so. But let me emphasize that in 1860 there was no University of Chicago, nor a University of Illinois . . . . But it has required sacrifice and a clear sense of purpose to move from original sites to this one, from

[9]*LSTC News Release*, October 7, 1965, p. 1.
[10]See Appendix VIII for copy of Groundbreaking brochure.

familiar and cherished campuses into the heart of this strange and changing metropolis. And to do so with the avowed intention of placing future theological students next door to the world-renowned laboratories, libraries, and lecture halls of the University of Chicago means that the Church believes its message is not secondary to the pronouncements of the leaders of thought and action of our generation. Church and university belong together in the creation and redemption of the thought, the feeling, the aspirations, and the faith of our nation.[11]

The purpose of the Lutheran School of Theology at Chicago on the campus of a university, he asserted, "is to witness to Christ as the sovereign of the spirit of man. And that witness is not in any declaration of superior power over other faculties, but in a demonstration of service to mankind, in His name who came not to be ministered to but to minister."[12]

In a special Litany of Thanksgiving, written for the occasion by Professor Morris Niedenthal, gratitude was expressed for

the God-given abilities to build:

For the glory with which Thou dost invest the things of the earth.
For the mystery of the creative process, and the wonders of design,
For the eye that beholds, and the mind that conceives and delights,
For the hands that draw blueprints, and the hands that weld steel,
For the materials of concrete, steel and glass, and the labor of men
    who build with them,
    We praise Thee, O God.

the traditions of the four merging seminaries:

For the streams of religious tradition merged in the building of this
    school,
For the Suomi tradition of intimate, personal comradeship with the
    living Christ,
For the Danish tradition of awareness that we are living stones of
    God's house,
For the Augustana tradition of faith in the Heavenly Father whose
    children we are,
For the United Lutheran tradition of ecumenical concern and
    Lutheran unity,
    We praise Thee, O God.

the privileges of dialogue, confrontation and service:

For the University of Chicago, and all the neighboring schools of this
    community,
For education, and all the privileges we enjoy through literature,
    science and art,
For all true knowledge of Thee and Thy love which we are permitted
    to learn and to teach,

[11]Conrad Bergendoff, "The Throne and the Faculties," *The Seminary Review*, 18:4 (1966).
    [12]*Ibid.*

For every opportunity this new school will have of serving our
generation in its concern for social justice, human dignity and
international peace,

For every occasion this school will have of manifesting the love of
Christ to men in our city and in all the world.

We praise Thee, O God.[13]

As the service neared the conclusion, President Herman placed a copper
box containing a copy of the Holy Scriptures into the cornerstone and Dr.
Marshall sealed the cornerstone with a bronze plaque and said, "In the faith of
Jesus Christ I do now seal the Cornerstone of this house of prayer and study, to
be known as the Lutheran School of Theology at Chicago." Even the plaque
bore its silent witness to the educational ideal of the new school through the
engraving of the official school seal upon it. At the center was the open Bible
against the background of the urban skyline. Superimposed upon both was the
Chi Rho, symbol of the Lordship of Christ over all of life. A four-pointed star
identified the four merging seminaries, and the date 1860 referred to the
founding of the first of the four schools.[14]

PLATE III
OFFICIAL SCHOOL SEAL ON CORNERSTONE

With the completion of the Cornerstone Ceremony one more significant
milestone in the continuing development of the new campus had been reached.

CONSTRUCTION COMPLETED

By the Fall of 1966, construction progress had fallen behind almost one
month. Despite the constant, urgent pleas of the Building and Grounds
Committee and the continued vigilance of Mr. Frank Zimmerman, labor and
material shortages caused endless delays. The first official meeting at the new
site, the seminary Building and Grounds Committee, on April 26, 1967, was
conducted in an unfinished room, piled high with materials yet to be installed. It
was obvious that the June 1, 1967, deadline would not be met.

Nevertheless school had to begin that Fall. During the Summer months the
100,000 volume library arrived and was arranged in the new library wing just
nearing completion. Administrative offices were set up temporarily during the

[13]Foundation Festival of Praise program folder. See Appendix IX.
[14]The official school seal was executed by Mr. Will Schaeffer of Lakewood,
Colorado, in 1963.

Summer months and early Fall in the west lounge awaiting the completion of the permanent offices. A sufficient number of classrooms were finished to house the pre-session Greek and Hebrew classes on September 5. Temporary food services were set up in the basement of one of the apartment buildings until the permanent refectory could be used.

Despite the incomplete state of the building the school opened on schedule October 1, though the classroom chairs arrived just the previous day. The historic, first opening convocation was held in the yet-unfinished Chapel-Auditorium. Speaking from a make-shift pulpit to a congregation of faculty, students, and friends sitting on paper covered concrete risers, President Herman compared the design concept of the new school in which they were gathered to the task it was built to serve: "Theology to be healthy must be thoroughly engaged in life." He pointed out that this concept was incorporated in the design of the new building with its glass walls and cantilevered entrances which were intended not to shut the world out, but to let it in, and to give the seminary easy access to the world. Noting also the seminary's location in the city, he called attention to the seminary's need to indentify with the urban crisis. In a reference to the proximity of the University of Chicago with its accent on science, he pleaded that the seminary enterprise relate its theology to the knowledge explosion of the age.

Finishing touches were added to the building as the first school year unfolded, but even in its unfinished state the school was causing a stir and excitement in the church. A century-long ideal had been achieved. The Lutheran School of Theology at Chicago was at long last adjacent to the campus of a great university in a major urban center.

Chapter X

CENTRAL JOINS LSTC

On June 30, 1967, three months before the Lutheran School of Theology at Chicago, officially opened its doors for the first school year on the new campus, Central Lutheran Theological Seminary of Fremont, Nebraska, became the fifth LCA seminary to enter the merger.

Central joined LSTC as the result of an action taken by the Lutheran Church in America at the 1966 convention. In response to a resolution adopted at the 1964 LCA Convention, the Board of Theological Education recommended that the 1966 Convention effect a merger between Central and LSTC. The adoption of this recommendation, "with the understanding that the merger be completed not later than the end of the year 1967,"[1] brought Central to the Chicago campus in time for the initial year at the new site.

CENTRAL'S BACKGROUND

The similarities in the origin of Central Lutheran and Chicago Lutheran seminaries are striking. Both were founded in the same decade—Chicago Lutheran in 1891, and Western Seminary, as it was initially named, in 1893—by men who were deeply concerned that settlers in the West should be provided churches and pastors. Also both schools saw the importance of an urban location. What could be said about Passavant—"He wanted the Church, a century ago, to be at home in the inner city and there, he thought pastors should be educated"—could also be said about the founders of Western who chose Omaha, Nebraska, as the site.[2] Only the inability to complete arrangements in time to begin work in Omaha, by October, 1893, forced the founders to "make temporary provision for theological instruction at Midland College"[3] in Atchison, Kansas. This association with the college continued until it was made a department of the college in 1910, a relationship which not broken until Western became a separate institution in 1949, and changed its name to Central Lutheran Theological Seminary. Thus Central Seminary also shared the

---

[1]LCA, *Minutes*, 1966, p. 666.
[2]Thomas D. Rinde, *After Seventy-Four Years* (Fremont, Nebraska: n. publ., 1967), pp. 7-8.
[3]*Ibid.*, p. 8.

stimulation of a collegiate relationship, as did Augustana, Grand View, and Suomi seminaries, though for most of the years it occupied a separate campus. In a real sense the educational ideal which characterized the four seminaries that formed LSTC was also present in Central Seminary.

There was sufficient common ground between Central Lutheran and Chicago Lutheran seminaries that merger between the two institutions was seriously considered as early as 1928. Western Seminary was then thirty-five years old, having been established by the Board of Education of the General Synod in 1893, which transferred its ownership and control to the Board of Trustees of Midland College in 1910. With Midland the seminary moved to Fremont, Nebraska, in 1919, and two years later was established on the spacious campus of what had formerly been the beautiful Ray Nye property. The more favorable location had not attracted more students. In fact, enrollments had been declining since the peak year of 1906, when the largest graduating class in the history of the school included twelve students. Whereas the average graduating class in the Atchison location numbered four, the average had fallen to less than three since the move to Fremont.[4] Faced with one graduate in 1928, the Board adopted the following resolution:

> That the Board of Trustees of Midland College, relative to the Western Theological Seminary, favor the advisability of conferring with institutions of like character, relative to the consolidating the forces and resources of the seminary with theological seminaries in contiguous territory, in order to further the interests of our Lutheran Church in the West;
>
> Therefore, be it resolved that a committee of five be appointed consisting of three clergymen and two laymen, for the purpose of accomplishing such object by and with the advice and action of the proper authorities of the United Lutheran Church in America, and to report back as soon as progress is made in this direction, and be it further resolved that this Board commands the committee appointed to proceed without delay.[5]

At this point the special committee elected to contact Chicago Lutheran Seminary, whose average graduating class since the 1920 schism[6] had declined to twelve.[7] It appeared that both schools would stand to gain by a merger if there were a suitable basis for the consolidation. Representatives of both schools met in Chicago on August 28, 1928, and after a full discussion agreed upon a set of proposals for merger.[8]

In keeping with the board's resolution to act in concert with the United Lutheran Church in America, the proposals were submitted to the ULCA Board of Education. Through a series of enactments involving the Board of Education,

[4]*Ibid.*, pp. 62-64.
[5]*Ibid.*, p. 27.
[6]*Supra*, p. 60.
[7]Lundeen, *History of CLTS Library*, p. 31.
[8]Rinde, *After Seventy-Four Years*, p. 28.

the ULCA in convention, the ULCA Executive Board, and the ULCA Theological Commission a meeting was held in Chicago, April 19, 1929, involving five mid-western seminaries.[9] The discussion centered about a larger merger, involving possibly all five seminaries. The group finally concluded, however, "that the facts in hand do not justify the consolidation of these institutions,"[10] and instead urged the Theological Commission to investigate the matter further. The conclusions reached by the Theological Commission in its three year study came in the form of recommendations to the United Lutheran Church in American 1932 Convention. Under the resolutions adopted Chicago and Hamma were to merge, while Western was to consolidate its school with Martin Luther and Northwestern seminaries.[11] Even though these resolutions were two years later declared unconstitutional,[12] the momentum of the Chicago-Central merger proposals was lost, not to be regained for another thirty-five years. When efforts to terminate Western Seminary and then to merge it with Martin Luther Seminary were both defeated by narrow margins in 1934, the Nebraska Synod took forthright action declaring to the seminary's constituency and to the ULCA that it had no intentions of discontinuing Western Seminary and would dedicate its resources toward the strengthening and preserving of the institution "for the welfare of the future extension and upbuilding of the church in this vast territory of the West."[13]

During the ensuing years the seminary was indeed "strengthened and preserved." Faculty members were gradually relieved of additional teaching duties in Midland College, and through the addition of other professors, were able to limit the number of seminary departments in which they taught. Enrollments gained as is evidenced by the fact that the average graduating class from 1935 to 1967 increased to eight. In fact, three classes in the last decade reached a total of fifteen. Likewise the physical campus was substantially improved. Largely through the ULCA Christian Higher Education Year appeal during 1950-51, supplemented with sizeable private gifts, Central Seminary erected a multi-purpose building housing a chapel, library, administrative and professors offices, and four classrooms. Dr. Franklin Clark Fry, ULCA President, gave the dedicatory address on September 2, 1952. A twelve unit apartment building for married students was added in 1956, to augment the campus building program. Central was making every effort to build a strong institution.

NEW MERGER OPPORTUNITIES

In the midst of this expansion program came an opportunity for Central to participate in merger discussions leading to the creation of LSTC. On February 23, 1959, the Inter-Seminary Committee approved a motion inviting Central and

---

[9]*Supra*, p. 56.
[10]Rinde, *After Seventy-Four Years*, p. 29.
[11]ULCA, *Minutes*, 1932, p. 453.
[12]*Supra*, p. 56.
[13]Rinde, *After Seventy-Four Years*, p. 31.

121

Northwestern seminaries to the June, 1959, and subsequent meetings, subject to the approval of the Ecumenical Commission of the Augustana Lutheran Church.[14] Augustana's response was that such invitations should come through JCLU's Committee on Seminaries. [15] Consequently, no formal invitation was extended to Central Seminary by the Inter-Seminary Committee, and the seminary's correspondence files and minutes are devoid of any reference to such an action and invitation.[16] Such an invitation would not have been welcome anyway in the light of the school's recent campus development with its new buildings, expanded faculty, and increased student enrollment. To the Central constituency and leadership these were marks of strength to support a continuing mission in the present geographic area. Merger was no longer a practical necessity. Central could go it alone.

Central was invited, however, along with all other seminaries of the merging church bodies, to the January 20, 1960, consultation session sponsored by the JCLU Committee on Seminaries. Dr. E. Bryan Keisler, Central's President, attended the meeting, and reported to the Faculty the decision that "all present seminaries are to remain for the present and would be supported by the Church for the first biennium after the merger is effected in an amount equivalent to that received by each seminary during the last year previous to the merger."[17]

Knowing that its future was secure, at least for the present, seminary officials took no initiative to request participation in the merger talks in Chicago. This grew out of Central's conviction that its continuing existence in that area was necessary for the well-being of the Church. A summary of the discussion held between Central representatives and Augustana Seminary representatives in late 1960,[18] reveals this conviction:

1. That a seminary located on the territory now served by Central is a necessity for the whole Church, particularly for this area of the Church.

2. That a merger with Augustana Seminary, in a location within the area now served by Central would be highly advantageous for the whole Church.

3. That such a seminary should be fully accredited and as strong, in every way, as any seminary of the Church. That, although it should serve this area particularly, it should not become a seminary specializing in a ministry to the rural church, but should prepare men to serve in the rural as well as the urban areas of the whole church.[19]

[14]Inter-Seminary Committee, *Minutes*, February 23, 1959, p. 2.
[15]*Supra*, p. 58.
[16]Verified by Dr. Arthur O. Arnold, Inter-Seminary Committee Secretary, in an interview July 16, 1968, and in a letter April 29, 1968, from Dr. Gerhard Gieschen, former Acting President of Central.
[17]Central Lutheran Theological Seminary Faculty, *Minutes*, February 3, 1960.
[18]*Supra*, pp. 68-69.
[19]Central Seminary Board of Directors, *Minutes*, October 4, 1960, p. 3. (Underlinings by the writer.)

At the same meeting of the Central Seminary Board of Directors, President Keisler stated with guarded optimism, "What the future holds in store for Central Seminary perhaps no one knows with any degree of certainty. It is generally agreed by all that a good, Lutheran seminary somewhere in this vast area is essential to the development of our Church."[20] However, he had also pointed out in his report one year earlier that there was "at least one in high places who wanted the number of seminaries in the new Church not to exceed five," and that it might be necessary to "fight" for Central's continuance.[21]

BTE RECOMMENDATION

History revealed that there was not unanimity of opinion that a seminary must continue in Central's region, and that there were several in "high places" who questioned the wisdom of continuing the seminary. Dr. Conrad Bergendoff, Executive Secretary of the Board of Theological Education-LCA, concluded his study of Central Seminary with these words:

> In any case, it must be recognized that Central as now existing is a weak institution. It is not accredited by the AATS and will need many changes before it can be. If it is to remain in Fremont, the Church must be prepared to spend large amounts to make it an institution comparable with the other seminaries. Would the wise course at present be a merger of Central with the Lutheran School of Theology at Chicago?[22]

Whereas Central's leaders saw the school's strength in relation to its relative gains over former years, the BTE report saw the school's weakness in relation to the relative strengths of other LCA seminaries. On the basic criteria employed by BTE to justify a seminary's existence, Central simply did not measure up:

> We are brought to a conclusion that the minimum standard of an LCA seminary should have an enrollment of not less than 75, preferably 100 students. Such a student body would call for a faculty and staff of at least 10, or 12, and an operating budget of 150 to 200 thousand dollars. This figure is based on a faculty of at least two professors in each of the four usual departments, and an administrative staff of president, librarian, business manager and secretarial staff. If operation and maintenance of an adequate campus is added, it is difficult to see how any seminary can operate on less than $200,000 a year.[23]

Central's average total enrollment over the previous decade, 41.2, was less than half of the preferred standard, and "there are no indications that Central will increase."[24] The faculty of six was 25 per cent lower in number than the

[20]E. Byran Keisler, "President's Report," Central Seminary Board of Directors, *Minutes*, October 4, 1960, p. 8.

[21]*Ibid.*, October 6, 1959, pp. 8-9.

[22]Conrad Bergendoff, "Report Number Eight," Central Lutheran Theological Seminary, 1963, p. 13.

[23]Bergendoff, *LCA and Theological Education*, p. 31.

[24]*Ibid.*, pp. 30-31.

accepted standard, meaning that there were not at least two professors in each of the four departments. The teaching load per professor was second highest among all LCA seminaries.[25] Its educational expenditures of $106,994 were only one-half of the recommended minimum for a strong seminary, resulting in the lowest paid professors of all LCA seminaries in America.[26] On the other hand, because of the small enrollment, the per-student cost was among the highest.

Stimulated by these findings, Central Seminary and its five supporting synods, launched a major research project in October, 1963.[27] The "Lutheran Regional Survey" was published in March, 1964. Although "it was not the purpose of the study to justify the location of Central Seminary in Fremont, Nebraska, or to formulate specific courses of action,"[28] it did conclude that "a strategically located seminary within the region can be a vital factor in the LCA's realization of its responsibility in the region," and that "a regional seminary has advantages in recruiting, educating and returning a greater proportion of pastors to congregations in its region."[29] This survey was presented to the Board of Theological Education at its March 12, 1964, meeting[30] at which BTE formulated the following resolution which was later adopted at the 1964 LCA Convention:

> The Board of Theological Education bring recommendations con-
> cerning the Central Lutheran Theological Seminary to the 1966
> convention of the Church.[31]

The LSTC Board of Directors saw in this resolution an opportunity to consider serious merger conversations with Central Seminary as one of the alternatives BTE could consider, and at its October, 1964, meeting voted to inform BTE of this interest.[32] Dr. E. Theodore Bachmann, newly installed successor to Dr. Conrad Bergendoff as Executive Secretary of BTE, conveyed the request of LSTC to his board. Dr. Bachmann reported the following January to the LSTC board that it was quite free to communicate directly with Central Seminary and

[25]*Ibid.*, p. 20.

[26]*Ibid.*, pp. 21, 29.

[27]T. Earl Sullenger, Vernon L. Strempke, and G. Gordon Parker, *Lutheran Regional Survey: A Summary*, 1964, p. 1.

[28]*Ibid.*, p. 3.

[29]*Ibid.*, p. 17.

[30]*Ibid.*, p. 2.

[31]LCA, *Minutes*, 1964, p. 593. At the same time a resolution was passed requesting Hamma Divinity School "to explore the possibility of merger with the Lutheran School of Theology at Chicago, or with the Ev. Lutheran Theological Seminary, Columbus, Ohio." (p. 593) At the invitation of LSTC, with the approval and encouragement of BTE, these two LCA seminaries finally met in Chicago, October 4, 1965. However, the Hamma Board of Directors at a July 15, 1964, meeting declared its preference for broadening the cooperation with the ALC seminary in Columbus, "believing that the Lutheran Church needs, and will continue to need, a school of theology centrally located within the vast concentration of population in Ohio and neighboring states." Discussions at the meeting were cordial but unproductive of serious merger consideration in the light of Hamma's desire to remain in Ohio. Though a continuing committee was established, no future meetings were held.

[32]LSTC Board of Directors, *Minutes*, September 30-October 1, 1964, pp. 64-65.

that BTE would follow the conversations with interest and support. The board took immediate action requesting the President and Chairman of the Board of LSTC to communicate with the Board and Administration of Central Seminary "inviting them to enter into discussions looking forward to closer cooperation."[33] The next week letters were on their way to Dr. Gerhard Gieschen, Acting President, and Rev. Russell J. Olson, Chairman of the Board. When the Executive Committee of the Central board met with Dr. Bachmann on February 22, 1965, it voted unanimously to recommend to the Board of Directors that the invitation be accepted. Chairman Olson warned, however, that the subject was a most controversial one:

> We would call to your attention the fact that we had a very lively and spirited discussion of this invitation, of what we personally believe to be the need of theological education in this mid-America area of our nation, and of the part that we believe that Central should play in it. At the same time we are mutually agreed as an Executive Committee that we will enter into these discussions completely without prejudice. In other words we will be objective and will attempt to enter into these meetings with a primary concern for the total program of theological education in the Lutheran Church in America. At the same time we do trust that the representatives of the Chicago Lutheran School of Theology will also meet with us "without prejudice." Unfortunately we are aware of pressures brought by certain members of the Board of the institution in Chicago where they feel very strongly (just as strongly as some of our men do in the continuation of Central) that the only possible solution is a merger on the campus in Chicago. Quite obviously unless all parties concerned are honest, objective, and without prejudice these discussions cannot bear fruit.[34]

The Central Board of Directors did vote to accept the invitation, but qualified the motion with the addition of the phrase, "as one step in the investigation of possible alternatives in meeting our responsibilities in Theological Education."[35] The total list of possible alternatives included: "a) Build up Central, b) Relocate, c)Merge with ALC on relocated campus, d) Merge with Lutheran School of Theology—Chicago."[36] All but the last alternative supported the findings of the "Lutheran Regional Survey," that a seminary on the territory of Central's five supporting synods was desirable.

The historic, first meeting of the representatives of both schools[37] was held June 17, 1965, in the conference room of Christ the King Lutheran Church

---

[33]*Ibid.*, January 27-28, 1965, p. 79.

[34]Letter from Rev. Russell J. Olson to the writer, March 1, 1965.

[35]Central Seminary Board of Directors, *Minutes*, April 21-22, 1965, p. 2.

[36]*Ibid.*

[37]Central Representatives: Dr. Everett Hedeen, Dr. Raynold Lingwall, Dr. Leeland Soker, Dr. Reuben Swanson, Dr. Philip Wahlberg, Dr. Gerhard Gieschen, Rev. Russell Olson, Rev. Walter Rowoldt, Dr. Gilbert Monson, Rev. Sherman Frederick, and Mr. Marius Christensen. LSTC Representatives: Dr. Frank Madsen, Dr. Robert Marshall, Dr. Theodore Matson, Dr. Walter Wick, Dr. Stewart Herman, Rev. Harold Skillrud, Dr. Harold Lohr, Rev. Robert Anderson, and Mr. Frank Zimmerman.

in Chicago. Each seminary explained its program as well as its understanding of the two schools' mutual concerns. Problems and opportunities associated with a merger of the two institutions were discussed. Major attention was focused on the concern for church-wide strategy in seminary education. The cordial and harmonious meeting concluded with the assurance that Dr. Bachmann of BTE and representatives of Central would meet in September to discuss further the matter of possible merger with LSTC and the other alternatives facing Central in the future.[38]

By the time of the October, 1965, meeting of the Board of Theological Education several consultations with individuals and groups had been held and extensive study had been made. The members were ready to make their recommendation to the 1966 LCA Convention:

> That the Board of Theological Education, in the implementation of the Master Plan for number and location of the LCA theological seminaries, recommend to the 1966 convention of the Lutheran Church in America that the Central Lutheran Theological Seminary at Fremont, Nebraska, merge with the Lutheran School of Theology at Chicago.

> That the synods of the LCA (namely, Iowa, Nebraska, Central States, Texas-Louisiana and Rocky Mountain) now constituent to Central Lutheran Theological Seminary be aligned with the merged Lutheran School of Theology at Chicago.[39]

Dr. Bachmann communicated this significant decision personally to both seminary presidents, chairmen of the boards, the synod presidents, and the Central Board at its November 5, 1965, meeting. He explained that BTE reached this decision on the basis of its developing Master Plan which called for fewer and stronger seminaries:

> In doing so, it takes into account such factors as: the drastic changes currently transforming higher education as a whole; the resulting demands on professional-graduate education; the rising costs of quality theological education; the avoidance of duplication of effort at the B.D. level so as to make available new ways of continuing theological education as well as developing new forms of field (intern) education; and, above all, to see and serve the needs of the LCA as a whole in the education of its [clergy].[40]

The Position Paper also outlined three possible options for the Central Board to pursue in the light of the BTE recommendations.

1. Note these recommendations as information—and do nothing more.
2. Reject them—and take whatever steps would be necessary to alter or defeat them.

---

[38]LSTC and Central Representatives Meeting, *Minutes*, June 17, 1965.
[39]E. Theodore Bachmann, "Central Seminary and BTE Recommendations," a Position Paper, November 5, 1965, p. 1.
[40]*Ibid.*, p. 7.

3. Receive them as recommendations likely to be accepted by the church convention—and in anticipation initiate steps to actualize them.[41]

The BTE decision and options met with an animated response by board members, including a strong and impassioned plea to retain Central in Fremont, a review of constitutional rights and procedures as they pertain to seminaries and synods, and a complete review of the advantages and disadvantages available under each of the three options. The motion which eventually prevailed partially embraced option number three:

> That a committee be appointed to explore the possibilities of merger of Central Lutheran Theological Seminary, Fremont, Nebraska with the Lutheran School of Theology, Chicago, Illinois, and that the appointed committee report its findings to the Board of Central Lutheran at its next meeting.[42]

Chairman Olson reminded the committee that the key word in the resolution was "explore."

President Stewart Herman, on behalf of LSTC, reacted to the news with gratitude and guarded optimism: "The response from Central Seminary is the answer to many prayers that more careful thought be given to the preparation of Lutheran ministers in the tasks that lie ahead. It must be kept in mind, however, that a proposal to negotiate is not yet a merger, which even under most favorable conditions may be as much as two years away."[43]

A subsequent meeting on December 10, 1965, in Chicago, between representatives of both seminaries sparked a lively discussion throughout the day-long session. Major areas of concern included the question of serving the Great Plains-Southwest constituency from a Chicago based seminary, curriculum, preservation of the heritages of the respective seminaries, transfer of faculty to Chicago, library needs, student needs—including housing, transfer of academic credits, increased cost-of-living in the Chicago area—disposition of the Fremont property, and constitutional changes. By the end of the meeting it became apparent that a smaller committee would have to negotiate further with respect to these matters, and a motion prevailed authorizing a Committee of Five, consisting of the two seminary presidents, the two board chairmen, and the executive secretary of BTE.[44]

The Committee of Five held meetings on December 21, 1965, and January 13, 1966, the second in consultation with the nine presidents of the supporting synods. The committee's work was summarized in its "Committee of Five Report to the LSTC-CLTS Boards, January, 1966." The report presumed the ultimate passage of the BTE recommendation at the 1966 LCA Convention. Dr.

[41]*Ibid.*, p. 2.
[42]Central Seminary Board of Directors, *Minutes*, November 5, 1965, p. 2.
[43]LSTC, *News Release*, November 19, 1965, p. 3.
[44]Special Committee to Explore Merger of LSTC and Central, *Minutes*, December 10, 1965.

Bachmann's statement on behalf of BTE's recommendation summarized the rationale of the decision to recommend the merger of LSTC and Central:

1. In a time when fewer but stronger seminaries are needed for basic B.D. education it is appropriate that the strong elements in Central's program should be combined with another strong school.

2. Since LSTC embodies institutionally the predecessor bodies of the LCA merger and provides a major base in Mid-America, Central's place in this company makes sense.

3. Such a merger would not reduce service to the five-synod area, since even at the present time fifteen of the twenty-three men interning in the area are from LSTC. Nor do students resist attending a seminary outside the area, since at present seventeen of the thirty senior seminarians from the five-synod area are attending seminaries outside the area, including ten at LSTC, compared with thirteen at Central. Furthermore there should be no reduction in the supply of pastors for the area, since even at present only 30% of the Nebraska pastors are Central graduates 25% of the Central States pastors, 18% of the Rocky Mountain pastors, 12% of the Texas-Louisiana pastors, and 10% of the Iowa pastors.

4. Regarding the future service of Central's faculty, BTE and LSTC by responsible action will see that all faculty members are treated fairly.[45]

The following specific proposals, to implement the action of the LCA Convention if it approved the BTE recommendation, were adopted unanimously by the Committee of Five at its January 13, 1966, meeting.

A. General

1. that, dependent upon LCA approval of the BTE recommendation, Central Seminary become the Fremont campus of LSTC on September 1, 1966, and that consolidation be completed at the new LSTC site no later than September 1, 1967.

2. that the Fremont campus continue to operate during the academic year 1966-67 under its present Board and Administration under overall LSTC administration, especially the President, the Business Manager and in academic matters, the Dean of Faculty.

3. that all faculty on the Fremont campus be retained, if they so desire, at least until June 30, 1968, their participation being seen as making a valuable contribution to a genuine merger of institutions. Meanwhile the LSTC will complete its study of future needs under the new curriculum and give thoughtful consideration to the possibility of further service on the part of the Fremont faculty members as well as of the present LSTC teaching staff. In this

---

[45]These four points are the writer's summary of Dr. Bachmann's statement in "Committee of Five Report," pp. 2-3, and LCA, *Minutes*, 1966, p. 657.

connection the faculty is assured that all the resources of the BTE and of LSTC will be brought to bear in securing useful and appropriate service for such men who may wish to take advantage of available opportunities in other areas of Christian service.

4. that students on the Fremont campus who have not yet terminated their work be invited to transfer to the Chicago campus with the assurance that courses and credits already completed will be fully honored and that graduation requirements will not be altered. Furthermore, that in such cases allowances or grants be made by LSTC to compensate for differences in tuition, board and lodging.

5. that the present Middler class be given the option of either going out on internship in 1966-67 or returning to CLTS to complete their Senior year prior to going out on internship.

6. that the Fremont campus in accepting new students for the academic year 1966-67 do so in consultation with and approval of the LSTC dean of students.

7. that all Central alumni be regarded as alumni of LSTC, receive all publications and be invited to participate in alumni activities of the school.

B. Fiscal

1. that LSTC receive from Central Seminary Board title to plant at Fremont, Nebraska and all equipment belonging to the seminary and be at liberty to use or dispose of it.

2. that all obligations and commitments, e.g., pensions, annuities, specified by Central Seminary be assumed by LSTC.

3. that endowment funds likewise be transferred and incorporated with the LSTC general endowment fund. All identified funds will be maintained as such in LSTC records.

4. that $39,000 of the proceeds from sale of plant be placed in the endowment fund as annuity for Mr. and Mrs. Stelk.

5. that Central Seminary as a Nebraska Corporation be dissolved upon completion of all necessary transfers.

C. Synodical

1. that the synods which have heretofore supported Central Seminary initiate steps to adopt the LSTC constitution, and petition the LCA through the BTE for realignment in support of LSTC.

2. that the financial support of the Fremont campus continue in the usual way until consolidation is effected or no later than September 1, 1967, and that, upon consolidation of the campuses, each synod undertake to assume responsibility for its proportionate share of the total LSTC budget.

3. that the question of participation in the capital building fund by means of a special campaign be reserved for later discussion, certainly not before the present college fund drive has been terminated, and that the proceeds of the sales of Central Seminary plant and equipment, except as herein designated for the general

endowment fund, be regarded as a donation to the LSTC building fund.

4. that the LSTC assure the five synods of a sincere desire to serve all supporting synods to the best of its ability and to cooperate closely with all appropriate synodical authorities in the preparation and continuing education of Lutheran pastors for the parish ministry; further that special efforts will be made to develop contact with the greatly increased LSTC constituency through forms of field representation, pastors' institutes and a strategically devised internship program; further that LSTC is ready to cooperate in the planning and execution of a senior placement program.

5. that LSTC make every effort to preserve continuity with the history, ethos and tradition of CLTS through representation on the Board, the faculty and the preservation of archives and significant memorial articles.

6. that the proposed by-law of the LSTC constitution regarding synodical representation on the LSTC Board of Directors be approved, as follows:

By-Law I a.

1. For 25,000 or fewer confirmed members on the active roll each supporting synod shall be represented by its president ex officio and two elected members.

2. For each additional 25,000 confirmed members on the active roll, or major fraction thereof, each supporting synod shall elect one additional member.

3. The LCA-BTE shall have a representation equivalent to not less than 20% of the elected membership of the LSTC Board. These members shall be elected by synods upon nomination by the BTE in consultation with the presidents of the synods concerned.

4. Representation among the elected members shall be arranged so as to maintain clergy and laymen in approximately equal numbers.

5. For three years following the consolidation of Central Seminary on the LSTC campus the BTE representatives shall be nominated to the supporting synods as follows: Illinois 2, Wisconsin-Upper Michigan 1, Iowa 1, Nebraska 1, Indiana-Kentucky 1, and Michigan 1.[46]

The LSTC Board of Directors was the first board to receive the Report of the Committee of Five at its January 26-27, 1966, meeting. After carefully scrutinizing the document and making a few, minor changes, the Board unanimously approved the report and timetable.[47] At this same meeting Dr. Bachmann predicted that the Central Board would have a serious struggle with

---

[46]"Committee of Five Report," pp. 3-5. This report is reproduced in LCA, *Minutes*, 1966, pp. 657-60.
[47]LSTC Board of Directors, *Minutes*, January 26-27, 1966, p. 114.

this document, for many of the members considered the proposals "not so much a merger as a closing."

His prediction was accurate. Despite the recommendations of the seminary president and the chairman of the board who, as members of the Committee of Five, had helped draft the document and approved it, the Board of Directors balked at adopting it. Motivated by a hope that the LCA Convention might vote down the BTE recommendation, and disturbed because the document did not guarantee perpetual teaching positions at LSTC for all Central faculty with rank and tenure preserved, many Board members did not wish to give tacit approval to the merger of the schools by adopting the provisions of the report. Instead it voted to "inform the students and faculty that it anticipates observance of the timetable stated in the proposals of the Committee of Five, if the LCA in convention adopts the recommendation of the Board of Theological Education," and that action on the proposals should be deferred until after the LCA convention.[48] Meanwhile Central Seminary faced a major morale problem with students and faculty due to the uncertainty of the future. Positive statements by Acting-President Gerhard Gieschen, including convincing arguments citing the advantages of theological education in the university-urban setting, did much to allay fears and create a spirit of anticipation. He admonished the seminary community, "Let us face the future unafraid and hopefully. It may be God Himself Who is directing us to Chicago."[49]

Meanwhile, two of Central's five supporting synods, went on record opposing a merger with LSTC. Central States Synod on April 27, 1966, adopted a Memorial requesting of LCA:[50]

1. That the present operation of Central Lutheran Theological Seminary in Fremont, Nebraska, be continued;

2. That a more advantageous location and improved facility, other than the Lutheran School of Theology in Chicago, be sought in the Great Plains and the Southwest region;

3. That Central Lutheran Theological Seminary be supported.

On June 2, 1966, the Nebraska Synod adopted the following resolution:[51]

The Nebraska Synod memorialize the LCA at its 1966 convention to recognize the need of a seminary in the Great Plains area and to continue and strengthen the support of Central Seminary in Fremont, Nebraska.

THE LCA CONVENTION

On Monday morning, June 27, 1966, the BTE resolution to merge Central with LSTC came before the LCA Convention in Kansas City. Interest in the

[48]Central Seminary Board of Directors, *Minutes*, February 17, 1966.
[49]Gerhard Gieschen, "A Word of Clarification and Encouragement to the Students of Central," February, 1966, p. 3.
[50]LCA, *Minutes*, 1966, p. 57.
[51]*Ibid.*, p. 63.

assembly ran beyond the recommendation itself, for being tested here for the first time was the authority and power of the Church over regionally owned and controlled institutions. Delegates of AELC, Augustana, and Suomi background were accustomed to making decisions regarding their seminaries at national conventions, but those of ULCA heritage were confronting this for the first time since the 1932 action regarding seminary merger was declared unconstitutional.[52] If this recommendation were to pass and be implemented successfully the Church might well recommend similar action with regard to other seminaries in the future. Thus, those from Central's territory who opposed the merger were joined by some delegates from other regions who resisted the principle. Extensive discussion followed the presentation of the recommendation, but when the vote was finally taken, the measure passed 473 to 120.[53]

One of the most telling arguments employed by the proponents of the resolution was the emphasis upon Central's lack of accreditation by the American Association of Theological Schools, with the inference that Central was academically inferior. Though the charge was not answered on the convention floor, Acting-President Gerhard Gieschen set the record straight in the September, 1966, issue of the *Bulletin*:

> Central Seminary has been an Associate Member of the American Association of Theological Schools for many years and, thus, has met at least "minimal standards" in theological education. The granting of full accreditation was held in abeyance through no fault of the Seminary. When it was sought several years ago, the Seminary was advised by the AATS to postpone its request for the required inspection and evaluation schedules on the grounds that Central's future was in doubt. Consequently, no inspection was ever made, nor was accreditation ever denied. The implication that Central Seminary could not and did not measure up to accepted standards is altogether gratuitous.[54]

However, Central Seminary's reputation and service to the Church were vindicated on Wednesday, June 29, 1966, when the following resolution was adopted by a rising vote and a spontaneous ovation on the part of convention delegates:

> Whereas, the action of the church in its development of a Master plan for Theological Education will merge Central Lutheran Theological Seminary with the Lutheran School of Theology at Chicago; and

> Whereas, Central Lutheran Theological Seminary has made notable contributions to the life of our Church through graduates who man posts throughout our Church at home and abroad; and

---

[52]*Supra*, p. 56.
[53]LCA, *Minutes*, 1966, p. 666.
[54]*Central Seminary Bulletin*, September, 1966, p. 2.

Whereas, Central Lutheran Theological Seminary has been served by dedicated men of high scholastic competence who have labored faithfully through difficult times in her history; therefore, be it

Resolved, that this convention of the Lutheran Church in America record its deep appreciation for the notable contributions Central Lutheran Theological Seminary has made to the life and growth of the church, offer its commendation to the members of the faculty and staff for their dedication and zeal, and pray that God will richly bless the enlarged Lutheran School of Theology at Chicago as it now embraces the thrust and strength of Central Lutheran Theological Seminary.[55]

IMPLEMENTING THE ACTION

On Monday evening, June 27, 1966, following the action of the convention to merge Central and LSTC, the Central Board of Directors held a special meeting in Kansas City, in which it unanimously adopted the "Report of the Committee of Five" as a guideline in preparing merger documents, and re-affirmed "its responsibility with regard to the tenure of the Central Seminary Faculty, and [that] in consultation with the Lutheran School of Theology, Chicago, Illinois, administration, [it would] attempt to resolve this matter satisfactorily."[56]

A Joint Executive Authority, consisting of representatives from each school,[57] set to work on the formulation of merger documents.[58] Though the matter of the placement of Central's faculty was of major concern to this committee, the Central Board of Directors at its October, 1966, meeting had eased the load by passing a motion calling for personal conferences between the LSTC administration and each Central faculty member to discuss his place of service at LSTC, and "that each faculty member be free to exercise his option under tenure or to take steps to relate his ministry at a place other than LSTC."[59] These conferences were held with Dean L. Dale Lund and President Stewart Herman, and by the Spring of 1967, all faculty members had made their decisions regarding their future service:[60]

---

[55]LCA, *Minutes*, 1966, p. 816.

[56]Central Seminary, Board of Directors, *Minutes*, June 27, 1966.

[57]Central Representatives: Mr. Marius Christensen, Dr. Gerhard Gieschen, Dr. N. Everett Hedeen, Mr. Tom Irwin, Dr. Theodore Johnson, Dr. Raynold J. Lingwall, Rev. Russell Olson, Rev. Walter Rowoldt, Dr. Leeland Soker, Dr. Reuben Swanson, Rev. Norman Ullestad, and Dr. Philip L. Wahlberg. LSTC Representatives: Mr. A. Roy Anderson, Rev. Robert B. Anderson, Dr. Robert Borkenstein, Dr. Stewart W. Herman, Dr. Harold R. Lohr, Dr. Frank P. Madsen, Dr. Robert J. Marshall, Dr. Theodore E. Matson, Rev. Harold C. Skillrud, Dr. Walter M. Wick, and Mr. Albert H. Wohlers. Officers: Chairman, Rev. Harold Skillrud; Vice-Chairman, Rev. Russell Olson; Secretary, Rev. Dr. Harold Lohr.

[58]Three meetings were held: November 21-22, 1966, in Chicago; January 20, 1967, in Maywood; and May 31, 1967, in Chicago. In addition, presidents and board officers of each seminary attended board meetings of both schools during 1966-67.

[59]Central Seminary, Board of Directors, *Minutes*, October 13, 1966, p. 5.

[60]*Ibid.*, February 17, 1967, p. 2, and *Central Seminary Bulletin*, June, 1967, and LSTC Board of Directors, *Minutes*, April 26-27, 1967, p. 160.

Dr. Gerhard Gieschen, Retirement, Professor Emeritus

Dr. Wilhelm C. Linss, LSTC

Dr. Richard R. Syré, LSTC

Dr. Martin E . Lehmann, Luther and Northwestern Seminaries, St. Paul Minnesota

Dr. Vernon L. Strempke, Pacific Lutheran Seminary, Berkeley, California

Dr. Charles A. Chamberlin, Lutheran Theological Seminary, Saskatoon, Saskatchewan, Canada

Another Central Faculty Member, Dr. Wesley Fuerst, had previously been called to LSTC in 1966, and taught on the Maywood campus for one year before joining the rest of his colleagues when the school opened on the new campus the following year.[61]

In an effort to give broad representation to the five synods which had supported Central, the Joint Executive Authority incorporated in the merger documents a provision that each synod would have at least one lay representative, one pastoral representative, and the synod president on the Board of Directors. Larger synods would have more representation in proportion to their size. The original four supporting synods of LSTC remained at the same strength, except the Illinois Synod which was reduced by one representative. This action increased the total size of the LSTC Board of Directors to forty-six members plus consultants and advisory members.

In planning for financial support, JEA noted that the five Central synods had 173,000 persons on the active roll of confirmed members, compared with 331,506 for the LSTC synods, or a grand total of 504,516 members. Whereas the four LSTC synods' 1966 grant of $314,582 was an average per capita of $0.95, Central's grant of $128,904 was an average of $0.75 per capita from members of the five synods. These figures excluded contributions to the LSTC Development Fund. JEA asked all synods to become equally supporting partners as soon as possible. Meanwhile, Central Seminary made a major financial contribution to the new seminary's building program in Chicago through the sale of the Fremont campus and library. Though interest in the campus was expressed by private and public educational institutions, the major portion of the seminary property was retained for church use. Timothy Chapel ,and the seminary offices and classrooms were purchased in the Summer of 1967, by the Board of American Missions-LCA for the development of a new congregation in west Fremont. Also included in the purchase price of $128,500 was one-third of the land on the campus. A second sale, of the old Nye residence and about half of the land, for a housing development, resulted in an additional $55,375. The sale was completed with the purchase of the married couples apartment building in the Spring of 1968, by a real estate investor at a price of $67,500. The Central Seminary library continued in the service of the church as it was purchased by

---

[61]Professors Fuerst, Linss, and Syre were later granted tenure at LSTC. See LSTC Board of Directors, *Minutes*, October 16-17, 1968, p. 7.

Wittenberg University of Springfield, Ohio, for approximately $1.00 per volume, or a total of $16,250.

Necessary changes in the LSTC Constitution were voted upon and approved by all nine synods,[62] and the five new supporting synods of LSTC at their 1967 conventions elected their fourteen board members who would join the five synod presidents on the Board of Directors. Thus with 34 per cent of the total membership of one-half million members residing within these five synods, the former Central constituency had 41 per cent of the membership on the board elected from its territory.

The Articles of Merger,[63] voted upon unanimously by the Boards of Directors of both schools, called for the actual merger to take place on June 30, 1967. This made each event in those closing days highly significant. At the final Commencement Service, fifteen men, including those who chose to graduate one year early by taking their intern year after graduation, received their degrees. Some bitterness, remorse, and melancholy was expressed over the discontinuance of the work in Fremont,[64] but in the main a spirit of confidence and optimism prevailed, such as was expressed by Rev. Russell Olson, Chairman of the Board of Directors, in his final report:

> These have been difficult days and yet they have also been moments of glory. It is exciting but demanding to experience the real meaning of the Gospel where we lose our life in the larger life of the work of the Church. June, 1967, is not the end of Central Lutheran Theological Seminary. It is rather the end of a glorious chapter of excellent service and it is the beginning of a service with greater dimensions, a more significant ministry and a more glorious life in the service of our Lord.[65]

> Next year the report will be the first chapter of a larger life for Central in the Lutheran School of Theology at Chicago where the fine traditions, excellence in service to the Church, and the spirit of our seminary will continue in larger dimensions.[66]

On October 1, 1967, the new seminary in Chicago officially opened its doors for the first time. Members of Central's faculty and student body were there as an integral part of the Lutheran School of Theology at Chicago. After twenty-six years in Atchison, and forty-eight years in Fremont, the Central tradition was beginning a new and expanding life in Chicago's university-urban setting.

---

[62]Illinois, Indiana-Kentucky, Michigan, and Wisconsin-Upper Michigan in 1966. Central States, Iowa, Nebraska, Rocky Mountain, and Texas-Louisiana in 1967.

[63]Appendix X.

[64]Rinde, *After Seventy-Four Years*, pp. 60-61.

[65]Russell J. Olson, "Annual Report of Central Lutheran Theological Seminary," 1967, p.3.

[66]*Ibid.*, p. 1.

Chapter XI

CAMPUS PERSONNEL

THE FIRST PRESIDENT

Rockefeller Chapel was the setting for the first service of worship of the Lutheran School of Theology on the University of Chicago campus on Sunday afternoon, May 3, 1964. The occasion was the Inauguration of the first President of the school, Rev. Stewart Winfield Herman, Litt.D.

Over 1000 members of the congregation participated in the inspirational service which began with a processional of 170 vested pastors and representatives of educational institutions and ecclesiastical organizations. The induction ceremonies were cast in the setting of Vespers conducted by Dr. Harold Lohr, Secretary of the Board of Directors, and were immediately preceded with an address by the President of LCA, Dr. Franklin Clark Fry. President Fry commended the school for its wisdom in choosing to locate in the cultural environment of the University of Chicago and praised the leadership of the new seminary president. Rev. Harold C. Skillrud, Chairman of the Board of Directors, conducted the Order of Induction in the chancel of the Chapel:

STEWART WINFIELD HERMAN, by the action of the Board of Directors of the Lutheran School of Theology at Chicago you were elected on April 23, 1963, as the first President of this institution. Your official acceptance has been received by the Board of Directors.

Hear therefore, the aims and goals of the seminary as stated in the Constitution:

To Prepare men for the Gospel ministry, especially in the Lutheran Church;

To equip men and women for missionary service;

To prepare men and women for leadership in Christian education, parish service, and such other areas as may be required by the Church;

To provide instruction in theology for laymen;

To encourage and assist in the in-service training of pastors; and

To establish and maintain a program of graduate study in theology.

You have read the Constitution, including the Doctrinal Basis, of the Lutheran School of Theology at Chicago as set forth in the Official Document;

I therefore ask you:

DO YOU, STEWART WINFIELD HERMAN, accept the office and ministry to which you have been called, and do you promise to uphold and defend the Constitution of the Lutheran School of Theology at Chicago and to discharge faithfully the duties of the office of President?

Answer: YES, BY THE HELP OF GOD.

BY THE AUTHORITY vested in me, and as the representative of the Board of Directors, I declare you installed as the first President of the Lutheran School of Theology at Chicago.

President Herman demonstrated his grasp of the school's educational ideal in his Inaugural Address when he affirmed the seminary's intention to relocate to this area: "In direct contrast to the general trend in the resettlement of seminaries, we are moving into the city, not away from it."[1] He emphasized the program of the seminary to be the relating of the Christian message to the world and all human knowledge, and the eager anticipation with which the school was preparing for this confrontation and dialogue:

> The substance of the dream, the Lutheran School of Theology at Chicago, is accurately summed up and adequately described by its name .... Chicago is one of the most vigorous and envigorating metropolitan areas of the world, and the University which bears its name is renowned as a dazzling international exchange of the most precious of all commodities, human knowledge .... We trust that our school in its turn will give to this civic and academic environment as much as it gains from them—or more. This we must do if we understand our task to be the proclamation of the Gospel.[2]

Decrying any efforts to limit the new seminary to the work of a "trade school or replacement depot," the new president declared that the seminary itself must be involved in the struggle for change in a revolutionary age:

> The LSTC comes into a complicated world of rapid social change. Interaction between the church and the world must constantly be encouraged for the welfare of both. The LSTC has no intention of avoiding such interaction.[3]

As the recessional hymn was sung, "Lead on, O King eternal, the day of march has come," it was apparent that the Lutheran School of Theology at Chicago was entering a new day of testing and challenge. The seminary was moving from an era of relative isolation to a direct confrontation with academic and urban forces. In confidence and anticipation the congregation sang:

Lead on, O King eternal:
We follow, not with fears,

[1]Stewart W. Herman, "Inaugural Address," May 3, 1964, p. 3.
[2]*Ibid.*, p. 2.
[3]*Ibid.*, pp. 4-5.

For gladness breaks like morning
Where'er thy face appears:
Thy Cross is lifted o'er us;
We journey in its light;
The crown awaits the conquest;
Lead on, O God of might.[4]

Selection of the President

The inauguration of President Herman marked the end of a lengthy and thorough search for the man to fill the key position in the new school. Some two years earlier a special committee for the selection of a president was appointed by the interim Board of Directors.[5] The committee was aware that faculty members at both Maywood and Rock Island campuses were encouraging the consideration of their administrators for the post. President Armin G. Weng of Maywood was nearing retirement age, but Dr. Donald Heiges, Dean of Chicago Lutheran Seminary, was strongly recommended by his colleagues.[6] The Rock Island faculty, while voicing no objection to Maywood's choice, indicated their confidence in the leadership of their President, Dr. Karl E. Mattson.[7] At its first meeting of the Committee on Nomination of President, March 15, 1962, the suggestion was made that the president ought not be selected from either of the present campuses, on the basis of the same logic which ruled out both campuses from consideration as the permanent site of the new school. The argument that a new seminary on a new campus demands new leadership prevailed in the committee's subsequent actions, though not without some considerable protest and debate.

On the basis of the following qualifications for the new president, the committee began its quest:

1. A Pastor of the LCA (although this requirement need not limit the search)
2. Proven executive competence
3. Recognized stature as a theologian
4. Able educator
5. Earned doctorate or its equivalent
6. Broad contacts in academic circles and in the church-at-large
7. Cooperative, ability to delegate authority and to work well with others
8. Living faith

[4]For a copy of the Inauguaration Service program see Appendix XI.

[5]The initial committee consisted of Rev. Harry Andersen, Mr. Harry Gjelsteen, Mr. V. Richard Hietikko, Mr. Harold Jordan, Dr. Malvin H. Lundeen, Rev. Harold C. Skillrud, and Dr. A. Howard Weeg. Subsequently Dr. Walter Wick succeeded Dr. Weeg on the committee and as its chairman. Dr. E. Theodore Bachmann served as consultant to the committee.

[6]CLTS Faculty, *Minutes*, December 20, 1961, p. 5.

[7]Letter from Augustana Seminary faculty to Dr. Malvin H. Lundeen, March 20, 1962, subsequent to vocal expressions of support for Dr. Mattson.

The committee first turned its attention to Dr. Edgar M. Carlson, President of Gustavus Adolphus College in St. Peter, Minnesota. His name had been submitted to committee members from all areas of the Church. It was obvious that President Carlson held the confidence and enthusiastic support of church leaders from all the merging bodies. After serious discussion between the committee and representatives of the faculties at Maywood and Rock Island, members voted unanimously to nominate Dr. Carlson, and requested Dr. A Howard Weeg, Dr. E. Theodore Bachmann, and Rev. Harold C. Skillrud to interview the candidate. The interview was held and the committee impressed upon the candidate the unanimity of the Church, Board, and Faculty in support of his election. After long and thoughtful consideration, Dr. Carlson replied that he could not accept the nomination in deference to his commitment to his present position.[8]

Out of the conviction that the presidency of the new seminary was potentially the most strategic theological post in the Church, the committee renewed its task with deliberateness and prayerful concern. A sizeable number of candidates were considered during the ensuing months,[9] but the interest eventually settled upon Dr. Stewart Herman, then Executive Secretary of the Division of Lutheran World Federation Affairs of the National Lutheran Council. An experienced churchman of international repute, Dr. Herman had served in Europe directing post-war relief and reconstruction work for the World Council of Churches in Geneva, and then the Service to Regugees sponsored by the Lutheran World Federation. Through his efforts in resettling refugees in South America, the Lutheran World Federation created a special Latin America Committee and named Dr. Herman as its first director. Conversant by experience and inclination with the challenge of relating the Gospel to the various needs and conditions of men and society, he was viewed as the leader who could best implement the seminary's educational ideal in its new university-urban setting. Upon the unanimous recommendation of the Committee on Nomination of President,[10] the Board of Directors elected Dr. Herman at its April, 1963, meeting as the first president of LSTC.[11] A thankful Board received the good news of his acceptance:

> Convinced—despite all my misgivings—that such an opportunity to be of further service to our Lord and His Church cannot lightly be declined, my decision is to accept the call which the Board has so graciously extended to me. Now, more than ever, I shall be needing the support and the prayers of which so many persons have assured me![12]

[8]Letter from Dr. Edgar M. Carlson to the LSTC Board Chairman, May 10, 1962.
[9]Correspondence with candidates is on file in the LSTC Archives.
[10]Committee on Nomination of President, *Minutes*, March 27, 1963, pp. 1-2.
[11]LSTC Board of Directors, *Minutes*, April 23-24, 1963, p. 4.
[12]Letter from Dr. Stewart Herman to the LSTC Board Chairman, June 13, 1963.

President Herman assumed his duties January 1, 1964.

ADMINISTRATIVE STAFF

Prior to the election of the seminary president, Dr. Karl E. Mattson of the Rock Island campus and Dr. Armin G. Weng of the Maywood campus were designated Administrative Vice-Presidents of their respective institutions.[13] While President Herman concentrated on the developments of the new school, the two campus administrators provided leadership for the continuation of the seminary's program on their respective campuses.

With the arrival of the new president on January 1, 1964, the Board of Directors initiated action to complete the administrative team. Rev. L. Dale Lund, Ph.D., President of Bethany College in Lindsborg, Kansas, the only candidate seriously considered for the post, was recommended for the position of Dean of Faculty by President Herman and the Policy and Personnel Committee. The Board of Directors unanimously elected the new Dean at its April, 1964, meeting.[14] Dr. Lund's acceptance was contingent upon concluding one more year of leadership at Bethany College, and he took over his new position at LSTC in July, 1965, and was installed the following October 5, in Christ the King Lutheran Church in the Loop. Rev. Dr. Paul Krauss, fifty year veteran pastor preached the sermon, and board chairman, Rev. Skillrud, performed the rite of installation. Dr. Lund revealed his understanding of the educational ideal of the school when he declared that one of his first objectives as Dean was to "move theological education out of isolation (ghetto) and into the light and criticism of university life."[15] Dean Lund's major responsibilities during his three years of service included development of the new curriculum,[16] preparation for the total academic program of the new campus, oversight of the dean's office on the Maywood campus 1965-67, and recruitment of faculty. Dr. Lund resigned in the Spring, 1968, to accept the presidency of Midland College in Fremont, Nebraska. He terminated his services at LSTC July 31, 1968. In accepting his resignation the Board of Directors adopted this resolution of appreciation:

> To a richly endowed and ever gracious servant of our Lord, who daily planned, labored, spent himself for his seminary, for our seminary, we give thanks. We acknowledge him who is universally admired, because of his spirit, his leadership and companionship, in the critical and trying days of the forging of this seminary, with all its antecedent traditions, into a distinguished seminary. This leader is the Reverend Doctor Dale Lund, academic dean of the Lutheran School of Theology at Chicago. The Board of that school now bestows its unqualified gratitude upon Dr. Lund as he leaves his post

---

[13]For a summary of the contributions of Dr. Karl E. Mattson and Dr. Armin G. Weng see Appendix XII.
[14]*Ibid.*, April 28-29, 1964, p. 43.
[15]*The Illinois Lutheran*, November, 1964, p. 1.
[16]*Infra*, pp.

and assumes leadership in the church and education elsewhere. To you, Dr. Lund, our affectionate and grateful farewell.[17]

Dr. Wesley Fuerst, member of the LSTC faculty, was elected Interim Dean.[18]

After joining the administrative staff in 1964, as Business Manager, Mr. Franklin K. Zimmerman was elected two years later to a newly created position, Assistant to the President, with responsibilities of planning and programming in the areas of business and finance, development, property management, public relations and publicity.[19] As he announced the new position, President Herman commended his new assistant:

> No man has made a greater practical contribution to the realization of the Lutheran School of Theology at Chicago than Mr. Zimmerman . . . . His job, in short, is to strengthen the physical and financial framework within which young men and women may receive the best possible training for Christian service.[20]

Having completed his major objectives—supervision of the new campus construction, arrangements for long-term financing on the indebtedness, organization of the business office—Mr. Zimmerman resigned in late 1968, to accept a new position with an LCA synod.[21]

Three additional administrative appointments were made by the Board of Directors at its January, 1966, meeting. Dr. Arthur O. Arnold, who had served as administrator of the Rock Island campus since the death of Dr. Karl E. Mattson, and who had represented that faculty on the Inter-Seminary Committee on which he served as secretary, was elected Dean of Students effective June 1, 1966.[22] For Graduate School Dean, the board elected Dr. Johannes Knudsen who had held that post on the Maywood campus. Dr. Knudsen chose to retire from that position in the Spring of 1968, just prior to his 1968-69 sabbatical year, so that he could devote his few remaining years before retirement to full-time teaching. In recognition of his service the Board of Directors adopted this tribute:

> The graduate program of the Lutheran School of Theology has been personified in one man . . . . Dr. Johannes Knudsen became the builder and zealous advocate of the graduate school . . . . To him the Board of Trustees of the Lutheran School of Theology owe an imminent measure of appreciation and with this inadequate tribute offers its lasting gratitude.[23]

On the recommendation of President Herman, the board appointed Dr. G. Everett Arden, Professor of Church History, as Interim Director of Graduate

[17]LSTC Board of Directors, *Minutes*, April 24-25, 1968, p. 186.
[18]*Ibid.*, p. 184.
[19]*Ibid.*, January 30-31, 1964, p. 35; April 24-26, 1966, p. 134; and Executive Committee, *Minutes*, July 1, 1966, p. 2.
[20]*LSTC Epistle*, Fall, 1966, p. 5.
[21]LSTC Board of Directors, *Minutes*, October 16-17, 1968, p. 3.
[22]*Ibid.*, January 26-27, 1966, p. 115.
[23]*Ibid.*, April 24-25, 1968, p. 185.

Study, effective August 1, 1968.[24] The third administrative position went to Dr. Theodore Conrad as Director of Admissions and Registrar.[25] After completing the task of coordinating all student and academic records and establishing a new system of admissions for the merged school, Dr. Conrad resigned. Upon the executive committee's acceptance of the resignation,[26] Dr. Herman expressed the appreciation of LSTC for his outstanding service:

> President Herman paid . . . tribute to Dr. Conrad especially for his . . . achievement in establishing efficient admissions and registry procedures. His well known competence in and love for Greek requires no comment after long years in the classroom.[27]

Dr. Wilhelm C. Linss, member of the faculty, was appointed Acting Registrar.

Professor James A. Scherer, Dean of the School of Missions since its inception in 1957, continued in this position after the formation of LSTC, until he resigned in the Spring of 1968, in order to return to full-time teaching. Appreciation for Dean Scherer's service as director of the missions school was expressed in a resolution by the Board of Directors:

> To the Reverend James Scherer, . . . the members of the Board of the Lutheran School of Theology, Chicago, submit herewith their highest expression of appreciation. We recognize, Mr. Scherer, teacher and director of missionaries, for his devoted service as dean of the School of Missions, a position he has now relinquished.[28]

Professor Donald Flatt, also of the School of Missions, was elected Acting Director of the School.[29]

Completing the administrative team were Rev. Joel Lundeen, M.A., Director of Library and Associate Archivist of the LCA Archives located in the LSTC Library, and Dr. Robert I. Tobias, Director of Continuing Education.

FACULTY

The articles of consolidation adopted by the judicatories of the merging seminaries in 1961,[30] provided that "Members of the faculties of Augustana Theological Seminary, Grand View Theological Seminary, Suomi Theological Seminary and the Theological Seminary of the Evangelical Lutheran Church at Chicago shall be retained as members of the faculty of the Lutheran School of Theology at Chicago."[31] Of the twenty administrators and professors listed in the document in 1961, only ten actually were a part of the merged seminary

[24]*Ibid.*, p. 184.
[25]*Ibid.*, January 26-27, 1966, p. 116, and Executive Committee, *Minutes*, July 1, 1966, p. 2.
[26]LSTC Executive Committee, *Minutes*, May 29, 1968, p. 2.
[27]*LSTC Epistle*, Summer, 1968, p. 6.
[28]LSTC Board of Directors, *Minutes*, April 24-25, 1968, p. 185.
[29]LSTC Executive Committee, *Minutes*, March 27, 1968, p. 2.
[30]*Supra*, pp. 71, 72.,
[31]*Official Documents*, p. 7.

when it moved on the new campus in 1967. The other half had taken positions elsewhere, retired, or died.

The 1967-68 faculty roster listed thirty professors, three part-time instructors, and seven former teachers with professor emeritus standing.[32] The thirty professors included nine who came from the Rock Island campus, twelve from the Maywood campus, one from the Maywood campus with a Suomi background, two from the Maywood campus with a Grand View background, one from the Maywood campus with a Central background, one who taught at both Maywood and Rock Island, two from the Central campus, and two new professors.

The successful merger of faculties on the new campus in 1967, was due in no small measure to the harmonious relations which had been established during the years prior to the relocation. The Maywood faculty, including the Suomi faculty then on the Maywood campus, had taken the initiative in inviting the Rock Island faculty to a colloquy on the Maywood campus May 1-2, 1959. The Maywood faculty clarified for itself the purpose of the meeting in a statement of presuppositions:

> The contemplated merger of our church bodies will inevitably bring about vast changes in our patterns of theological education. The merger of seminaries in the Illinois-Iowa area, while not a foregone conclusion, is a strong possibility.

> The task of drawing up plans and policies for the church's future theological education does not lie within the jurisdiction of the seminary faculties. Nevertheless, the faculties should be in a position to express their minds clearly on educational matters affecting the church's plans and policies. In this realm, if we are not in a position to say what we would like, we shall have to take what we get.

> To clarify our own minds we should also think together. Our task demands more than sharing information and ideas. We must genuinely know one another before we can achieve a genuine and creative meeting of minds.

> This colloquy's purpose is strictly exploratory. It is no caucus. It seeks no commitments. It will formulate no consensus. We hope, however, that it will inaugurate a useful conversation among our faculties on basic academic matters in the church's task of theological education.[33]

The colloquy provided an opportunity for faculty members to become better acquainted and to discuss issues of mutual concern: seminary curriculum, seminary admission policies, and purposes of theological education.

The Augustana Board of Directors reciprocated with an invitation to the Maywood, Suomi, and Grand View faculties.[34] At this December 5, 1959,

---

[32]See Appendix XIII for a complete listing of faculty as listed in LSTC, *Catalog*, 1968-69, pp. 84-89.

[33]CLTS Faculty, *Minutes*, April 23, 1959, p. 1.

[34]Augustana Seminary Board of Directors, *Minutes*, May 28-29, 1959, p. 10.

session on the Rock Island campus, a serious discussion was held on the topic, "The Pattern of the Merged Seminary," with special emphasis on the merged seminary's different schools and various departments, the general organization of the faculty, and curriculum. The session was concluded with a business meeting in which a special faculty committee with representatives from all four seminaries was commissioned to begin a joint study of curriculum.[35] These joint sessions were continued thereafter, and were augmented with joint committee meetings and joint consultations on the selection of new faculty and other academic concerns.

STUDENTS

In the Fall of 1967, when the number of students entering LCA seminaries in the United States declined from the previous year in six out of the eight schools, only Pacific Lutheran Theological Seminary and the Lutheran School of Theology at Chicago showed increases.[36] An analysis of the Junior Class members by home states provided the answer for LSTC's favorable enrollment. Whereas 76 per cent of the Senior Class, 67 per cent of the Intern Class, 66 per cent of the Middler Class came from the nine synod area which supports LSTC, the percentage dropped to 55 per cent for the incoming Juniors.[37] Almost one-half of the new class chose LSTC instead of the seminaries in their own regions. This was highly significant, since this was the first class that deliberately chose to attend LSTC because of its new university-urban location.

The incoming Juniors also differed from the upper classmen in that less of them were graduates of Lutheran colleges. The percentages of Lutheran college graduates dropped from 70.6 per cent in the Senior Class, to 62.8 per cent and 62.5 per cent in the Intern and Middler classes, down to 54.9 per cent for the Juniors.[38] Taking into account the total 1967-68 student body at LSTC, 61.7 per cent were Lutheran College graduates, compared with 81.6 per cent at Rock Island, 67.7 per cent at Fremont, and 55.2 per cent at Maywood the previous year.[39] It is obvious that LSTC was attracting a greater number of seminarians who had done their undergraduate work in state and private non-church-related colleges. It appeared that the challenge of a theological education in a university-urban setting was beginning to attract more students with a secular university background.

The total enrollment of B.D. students at LSTC during the 1967-68 year was 242, a significant drop from the total of 321 B.D. students who were attending the seminaries in Fremont, Maywood, and Rock Island in 1962-63, the year of the seminary merger. A part of the explanation was the universal drop in

---

[35]Joint Faculties Meeting, *Minutes*, December 5, 1959, p. 1.

[36]E. Theodore Bachmann, "Report of the Executive Secretary," Appendix I, p. 6, BTE, *Minutes*, October 10-11, 1967.

[37]*LSTC Catalog*, 1968-69, pp. 95-105.

[38]*Ibid.*

[39]*Ibid.*, 1967-68, pp. 74-85.

seminary enrollments during this five year period, but the major factor was the change of status for Rock Island from a national to a regional seminary.[40]

The proportion of married students at the new campus was fairly similar to the pattern at the predecessor schools. Fifty-three and three-tenths per cent of the students in 1967-68 were married,[41] whereas 54.3 per cent of the students in 1962-63 were married.[42] A part of the reduction is explained by the fact that the Juniors in 1967-68 represented a much higher proportion of the total student enrollment than did the Juniors in 1962-63, and the percentage of married Juniors is always lower than that of upper classmen.

Regarding the college academic achievement of the 1967-68 incoming Juniors the averages were as follows:[43]

7 students (9%) had an A average, based on 3.25-4.00
18 students (23%) had a B average, based on 2.75-3.24
53 students (68%) had a C average, based on 2.00-2.74

After only one year's experience it was premature to judge whether or not the new university-urban location was attracting students of better academic quality.[44]

Forty-two different major fields in college were represented among the 242 B.D. students at LSTC during 1967-68. History, Philosophy, Sociology, English, and Psychology were the most popular, in that order, and accounted for well over half of the students. The broad range of major fields represented in the student body provided fertile soil for the seminary's attempt to relate the Gospel to all academic disciplines, the world, and society.

[40]Augustana Seminary alone had 184 students in 1962-63, which had come from all regions of the United States.

[41]Figures supplied by Dr. Theodore E. Conrad, LSTC Director of Admissions and Registrar, in a letter to the writer May 13, 1968.

[42]Bergendoff, *LCA and Theological Education*, p. 17.

[43]Figures supplied by Dr. Conrad.

[44]Dr. Arlan Helgeson, Dean of the Graduate School, Illinois State University, Normal, Illinois, indicated to the writer in an interview May 15, 1968, that the distribution of A and B students is slightly higher than the average college graduating class.

Chapter XII

ACADEMIC PROGRAM

RELATIONSHIP TO THE UNIVERSITY OF CHICAGO

All negotiations between LSTC and the University of Chicago were predicated on the premise that the seminary did not wish to become a part of the University's structure, but wished to create relationships that would be mutually beneficial. Dr. Jerald Brauer, Dean of the university's Divinity School, but also Chairman of the Board of Theological Education of LCA, clearly understood this distinction and summarized it in his first meeting with LSTC representatives:

> I am beginning with the assumption that if a Lutheran Theological School were to move adjacent to The University of Chicago, its primary concern would be to retain full academic autonomy, as represented in complete control over its own faculty and its own students. With a full autonomy over its academic program as well as over its entire corporate and institutional life, it would like to have available those facilities and resources of the University which make the University community an attractive place, in which Lutheran theological education for the ministry should take place. Therefore, all of our discussion ought to proceed on this basic premise. I am certain that it will, then, be possible to develop mutually advantageous relationships which in no way threaten the integrity or the autonomy either of the Lutheran Theological School or of the University's theological program.[1]

As a theological seminary of the Church whose first object was "To prepare men for the Gospel ministry, especially in the Lutheran Church,"[2] the protection of the school's autonomy was critical. According to Dr. Ernest Cadman Colwell, who had spent twenty years in university administration and more than twelve years in seminary administration, such a "seminary should not be a university school, but should have some corporate responsibility to the church. The ideal relationship is that of the seminary located on the edge of the university campus as an autonomous institution engaged in a vigorous and lively partnership in higher education in religion with the graduate school of the

[1]Inter-Seminary Committee, *Minutes*, April 13, 1961, Exhibit C.
[2]LSTC Constitution, Article I, Section 3a.

147

university."[3] It is quite obvious that LSTC was strategically located according to these standards. Dr. Colwell's arguments reinforced the decision of the seminary's leadership to be "in" but not "of" the university.[4]

The cooperative agreement between the University of Chicago and LSTC, which was approved by the LSTC Board of Directors in April, 1965,[5] guaranteed the autonomy of both institutions:

> The University and the LSTC are separate entities and each is separately responsible for its faculties, degree requirements and all other aspects of its administration. Either party may mention in its publications the fact that there is a cooperative arrangement between the institutions, which provides that under certain conditions, courses and facilities of the other party will be available to its students, but neither party shall represent that there is an administrative or academic affiliation between the parties.[6]

The major advantages for students of both institutions was the privilege to use libraries of both schools and enroll in courses on each campus, providing fees and requirements of each school had been met. LSTC students were permitted use of university athletic and health privileges according to a prescribed quarterly fee. Likewise faculty members of the two schools have access to all libraries in accordance with the applicable regulations, and employment of the other's faculty members by each school is permissible when cleared through the proper administrative channels.[7]

The document makes adequate provision for dialogue and communication between both schools, and the way was opened for full implementation of the seminary's historic, educational ideal.

---

[3]Colwell, "Seminaries in the University for the Church," p. 323.
[4]*Ibid.*, pp. 323-24.
"The University has only one lord, and its name is research, and the university bows the knee to this lord seven times a day. Contributions to the knowledge of the experts are both the road to advancement and the badges of distinction in the life of the university, and the school that has no countervailing force to hold it to its professional objective will inevitably succumb to the constant pressure of the university's ideals upon its faculty and staff and student body. There is plenty of empirical evidence in the history of schools of religion in these United States today to demonstrate the accuracy of this statement. The nondenominational university-related schools have served an exceedingly valuable function in the development of scholarship in the field of religion. They are providing teachers and also men for specialized ministries who are splendidly equipped for their tasks, but they are not today educating men for the parish ministry in numbers large enough to be worth serious consideration.

"If the primary task of the theological school is the education of men for the ministry of the church, the so-called parish ministry, then the theological school as it moves into relationship with the university needs to throw out a sea anchor in the shape of responsibility to the church to keep it true to this primary function."
[5]LSTC Board of Directors, *Minutes*, April 20-21, 1965, p. 86
[6]*Cooperative Agreement*, pp. 3-4.
[7]*Ibid.* pp. 1-3.

LSTC CURRICULUM

Inter-faculty discussions on a new curriculum for the new seminary began in 1959, while merger negotiations were still being held,[8] and continued at joint faculty meetings and retreats. However, with the arrival of Dean L. Dale Lund in 1965, an ad hoc committee on Curriculum and Internship was revitalized and serious work began.[9] Progress was hampered by the problem of the geographic distance between Maywood and Rock Island, which limited the number of joint sessions. Likewise, the composition of the committee—some conservative members who wanted few innovations and others who favored radical change—produced a number of delays in reaching conclusions. The end result was a curriculum that was a "blend of conservatism and experimentation."[10]

In formulating the new curriculum, the committee first set down the aims and objectives of theological education, based on the assumption that LSTC was a graduate-professional school and its program should partake of both elements. These became the stated aims and objectives:

1. To assume the theological task of the times by asserting and explaining the Christocentric meaning of existence.

2. To serve the church by being sensitive to its needs and seeking to offer a program which will bring forth a steady supply of candidates for the ordained ministry as well as for other specialized services which require or profit by seminary education.

3. To keep sharp and fresh the concept of the ministry as a theological concern, a service to the church and a practical imperative for its recruits.

4. To keep alive and fresh a concept of church life—parish, congregation, etc.—which stresses the idea of a ministering and serving church and gives appropriate place to the ministry of the layman.

5. To so teach, guide, counsel and influence the student that he will become a theologian in his own right and be able to make a sound appraisal of his own place in the ministry of the church and offer himself freely to its accomplishment.[11]

---

[8]*Supra*, p. 145.

[9]Members of the committee during 1965-66 which formulated the curriculum included: Carl Braaten, Maywood faculty; Arnold Carlson, Rock Island faculty; Theodore Conrad, Rock Island faculty; Richard Deines, student, Rock Island; Robert Fischer, Maywood faculty; Gerhard Gieschen, consultant, Central Seminary; David Granskou, Maywood faculty; Stewart W. Herman, ex officio; Harold R. Lohr, board representative; L. Dale Lund, chairman; Robert J. Marshall, board representative; Morris Niedenthal, Maywood faculty; N. Leroy Norquist, secretary, Rock Island faculty; Leonard Peterson, student, Maywood; and Paul Swanson, Rock Island faculty.

[10]*The Lutheran*, October 11, 1967, p. 8, and interview by the writer with Dr. Lund, May 29, 1968.

[11]L. Dale Lund, Curriculum, 1966, p. 2.

Having established the aims and objectives of the curriculum, the committee moved next to a consideration of the processes, procedures, and methods for achieving these ends. These became the following:

1. The curriculum must relate to the students, build on his education and previous experience in order to meet him where he is as well as build on what he is.

2. The curriculum and the efforts put forth to accomplish its purposes must respect the teaching-learning process and devise the most appropriate and effective approach to each course or area of academic endeavor.

3. The curriculum will stress and illustrate the historical-sociological-emotional context of the theological enterprise and of the life of faith which is the arena of experiencing, learning and living the meaning of the gospel.

    (Here we acknowledge and set forth the existential nature of theology as against the scholastic.)

4. The educative process of the LSTC can be strengthened and enriched by capitalizing on the location adjacent to the University of Chicago and in proximity to such other schools as Chicago Theological Seminary.

    In addition to library and public lecture resources and the privilege of fellowship and dialog with fine people with similar problems and interests, there will be the policy of permitting LSTC students to take a limited number of courses at neighboring institutions. Cooperation will be possible in several areas .... These matters deserve frequent study and will require constant attention if they are to be worked out properly for all concerned.

5. Courses should be so planned and taught that they will help the young student-theologian to grow in his understanding of the gospel, world and church as they interrelate.

    Insights and help should be offered for the understanding of man in society and the relevance of the gospel thereto as well as the ministry of word and sacrament which will helpfully provide the ingredients for reconciliation, acceptance and fellowship in profound ways.

    Practical subjects and problems will be dealt with in any field or area, but they will come in for most attention during the internship and in courses framed to improve a man's capacity for ministry.[12]

Here was stated most explicitly the committee's understanding of the historic educational ideal that had prevailed through the years. There was the recognition that the university location afforded the opportunity to carry on a dialog with

---

[12]*Ibid.*, pp. 2-3.

other disciplines and to relate the Gospel to all areas of man's exploding field of knowledge. Likewise the stress on relevance recognized the need to understand and to serve men in today's world and society. This was seen against the background of the unusual opportunities presented by the changing society which is Chicago. "Here are social, cultural, ecclesiastical, artistic, industrial and public resources for study and field education which are almost incomparable."[13] Flexibility was built into the curriculum to meet the needs of students with varying backgrounds and interests. This was exceedingly important for students coming from colleges which did not offer certain pre-seminary courses, for students who decided upon the ministry rather late in life, for students who wished to accelerate their studies by carrying a heavier load or taking advanced courses in lieu of core requirements, and for the increasing number of students who were interested in studying theology but were uncertain about their place in the ordained ministry of the institutional church. The curriculum also reflected a change in pedagogical policy by placing a maximum emphasis upon seminar and tutorial methods of instruction on campus, and on clinical training in hospitals and a direct involvement in community affairs off campus. The broad range of electives kept in mind the increasing number of specialized ministries within the church.

Graduation requirements in the B.D. program included 108 quarter credit hours plus one year of field education. Thirty-six courses were required, with seven of these in each of the biblical, historical-systematic, and functional fields, plus three interdivisional courses and twelve elective courses. In the selection of electives each student was limited to taking no more than one half of these in any one of the three divisions—biblical, historical-systematic, or practical. A comparison of graduation requirements between the new LSTC curriculum and that of the Maywood and Rock Island campuses at the time of merger in 1962, is listed in the following table. (See Table 4, page 152.)

The new elements in the curriculum which best served to implement the seminary's educational ideal were the Interdisciplinary courses and the Church and Society courses. The three interdisciplinary courses were designed to "illustrate the lively relationship which exists among theological disciplines and between theology and certain other academic disciplines which also concern themselves with matters of intense importance to humanity."[14] However, this concern to relate theology to other academic disciplines was not limited to these interdisciplinary courses, as can be seen by the general course offerings in other divisions such as, "Theology and Natural Science," "Doctrine of Man in the Light of the Life Sciences and the Social Sciences," "The Development of Secularism in the Modern Era," "Theology and Philosophy in the 20th Century," "Radio and TV Communications," "Christianity and Tragedy," "Personality

---

[13]*LSTC Catalog*, 1968-69, p. 5.
[14]*Ibid.*, p. 39.

TABLE 4

COMPARISON OF GRADUATION REQUIREMENTS

	Maywood 1962-63	Rock Island 1962-63	LSTC 1968-69
Total Quarter Credit Hours Required for Graduation	139	135	108
Hours of Biblical Courses	39	26	21
Proportion of Total Courses	28%	19%	19.5%
Hours of Historical-Systematic Courses	39	41	21
Proportion of Total Courses	28%	30%	19.5%
Hours of Division of Ministry Courses (Functional)	43	28	21
Proportion of Total Courses	31%	21%	19.5%
Hours of Inter-disciplinary Courses	0	0	9
Proportion of Total Courses	0%	0%	8.3%
Hours of Elective Courses	18	40	36
Proportion of Total Courses	13%	30%	33.2%
Year of Field Work	Optional	Required	Required

Theory and Psychotherapy," "Religious Education of the Exceptional Child."[15] The other new element, a broad range of courses in the area of Church and Society, was an attempt to analyze, interpret, and discover ways of serving contemporary society and to understand the ways in which the church is conditioned by its social, cultural, economic, and political environment. The vast resources of the city of Chicago were seen as a giant laboratory in which this study could take place through both observation and involvement.

Quite apart from the formal curriculum, LSTC in its university-urban setting provided unlimited opportunities for spontaneous involvement of students and faculty. In the first year on the new campus there were men involved in released time teaching in local parishes, in "Head Start" programs in the ghetto, in integrated confirmation classes meeting on campus, and a host of other community-involvement programs.

The intern program—which called for the seminarian to spend one year of supervised work in a parish, campus center, institutional chaplaincy, industrial mission, or even in an overseas assignment—was pioneered in 1934, by Augustana Seminary of Rock Island,[16] became a compulsory part of the program at Maywood in 1963, having been available as an optional program and

15*Ibid.*, pp. 38-72.
16Arden, *School of Prophets*, p. 233.

strongly recommended for years, and was made an integral part of the new curriculum at LSTC. Innovations included the expansion of the "cluster plan" which called interns, pastoral supervisors, and seminary representatives together by regions for regular discussion, evaluation, and planning. It normally also provided for three months of clinical training.[17]

The proposed curriculum and plan for internship was adopted by the entire faculty on May 26-27, 1966, and the Board of Directors gave its approval at the September, 1966, meeting. One year later the new Lutheran School of Theology at Chicago began its first year in the university-urban setting with a new curriculum ready to meet the challenge of the new context for life and thought.

THE GRADUATE SCHOOL

Proponents of post-graduate education in the Lutheran theological seminary saw in the LSTC merger-relocation proposal an unprecedented opportunity for growth and development in the university setting. Dr. Johannes Knudsen, Dean of Graduate Studies on the Maywood campus, expressed his hopes for the future in his 1962 report:

> ... the graduate studies of CLTS, continued in the new, merged seminary, show promise of fulfilling the dream of a top-level Lutheran graduate school . . . .

> Access to the resources of the university in a general way, and through negotiations in special ways, will not only create a situation of general scholarly and cultural significance, but it will enable us to live within the total activity of learning and discussion so essential to academic development, which no isolated school, however competent, can achieve on its own.[18]

A strong post-graduate program had been the ideal of LSTC and its predecessor schools for many years prior to the 1967 move to Chicago. Augustana Seminary's program had been largely a correspondence school approach until 1935, when the Doctor of Sacred Theology degree was dropped entirely and the requirements for the Master of Sacred Theology degree were substantially increased.[19] However, though the catalogs continued to carry information on the graduate school program, course offerings at Rock Island were primarily limited to regular, Senior B.D. courses, and the number of students pursuing serious graduate work was extremely limited.[20] Two Master of Sacred Theology degrees were given in 1966 and 1967. Central Seminary in Fremont began a program of advanced theological education for pastors in 1963. Regular class sessions on a semester basis were conducted on the Fremont

[17]Axel Kildegaard, "Intern Program Design LSTC," 1968, pp. 1-4.

[18]Inter-Seminary Committee, *Minutes*, January 29, 1962, Exhibit C, "Graduate Studies Report," p. 2.

[19]Arden, *School of Prophets*, pp. 234-35.

[20]*Augustana Seminary Review*, Volume 12, Number 1, First Quarter, 1960, Catalog Number, p. 38.

campus, as well as other centers such as Omaha and Lincoln. The graduate level courses were taught by Central Seminary faculty, as well as professors from other seminaries, universities, and clinical training centers. Central awarded no degrees, but grades and credits were given "for possible use toward advanced theological degrees."[21] A sizeable number of clergymen, many non-Lutheran, participated in the program over the four and one-half years of its existence. Grand View and Suomi Seminaries had no post-graduate departments.

By far, the most ambitious program was offered on the Maywood campus. Its origin lay in the formative years of the Theological Seminary of the Evangelical Lutheran Church when it was still located in Chicago. As early as the first decade of the school's existence, Rev. Dr. Revere Franklin Weidner, President, made provision for advanced studies for pastors.

> A close friend of the University of Chicago's first president, William Rainey Harper, Weidner picked up the interest in ongoing education by correspondence courses which Harper was promoting as an extramural department of the University. The perfecting of the mails in those years opened up an entirely new field for the pursuit of education beyond the scope of formal instruction on an academic campus. The Chicago Lutheran Seminary was quick to take advantage of the new situation.[22]

The seminary's Extra-Mural Department was for over three decades under the supervision of Rev. Dr. Elmer F. Krauss, Professor of New Testament. The home study courses offered through this department supplemented the occasional on-campus offerings in advanced theological study. The popularity of the program grew rapidly and within five years of the origin of the school there were fourteen pastors in residence and 102 pastors in the correspondence school program.[23] During the Gruber administration, 1926-41, the graduate department greatly expanded and a large number of Master of Sacred Theology degrees and some Doctor of Sacred Theology degrees were awarded. However, like Augustana, the Maywood Seminary began to question its doctoral program, and in 1939 announced that no new candidates for the S.T.D. would be accepted.[24]

In the summer of 1942, Rev. Dr. Charles B. Foelsch became president and introduced a number of new educational policies. These included the phasing out of the Extra-Mural Department and the introduction of a summer graduate program. Rev. Dr. E. Theodore Bachmann, who came to the seminary in 1942 as professor of Church History, drew up this new program with the assistance of Dr. Krauss. According to Dr. Bachmann, "The format was borrowed, at least in part, from the wartime program of accelerated education at the University of Chicago."[25] The initial summer program called for three weeks of campus study combined with a self-directed home study program.

---

[21]*Central Seminary Bulletin*, Volume 18, Number 8, April, 1965, Catalog Issue, p. 28.

[22]Notes from E. Theodore Bachmann to the writer, November 3, 1968.

[23]Marjory Weng, "Passavant's Vision," p. 11.

[24]Lundeen, *History of CLTS Library*, p. 60.

[25]Notes from Bachmann.

The graduate program developed into a graduate school following the arrival in 1945, of Rev. Dr. Charles W. Kegley, professor in the field of philosophy of religion, and the full accreditation of the school in 1946. The S.T.D. program was resumed, and stringent academic requirements were stipulated and enforced.[26] The practice of securing visiting professors from other seminaries and universities for the summer graduate program also served to strengthen the academic standards.[27]

Under the presidency of Dr. Armin G. Weng, which began in 1948, the summer school program was expanded into two three-week sessions and the Tuesday program was enlarged. Finally, the program required more time and leadership than a professor could give as an extra-curricular activity. With the cooperation of the ULCA Board of Higher Education, funds were made available to add a Dean of Graduate Studies, and the post went to Dr. Johannes Knudsen in 1956.

During the period 1954-67, the Maywood campus granted the following number of advanced degrees:[28]

Doctor of Sacred Theology	11
Master of Sacred Theology	53
Master of Arts	16
Master of Arts in Clinical Education	9
Total	89

Average enrollment in Tuesday and summer session graduate courses during these same years was 160 students per year.[29]

LSTC adopted Maywood's successful program of graduate studies when it moved on the new campus in 1967. A major change was the rule requiring doctoral students to take a minimum of one year of full time graduate work in residence at LSTC,[30] a significant step in the school's ever rising academic standards.

Just prior to the beginning of the first school year on the new campus, the Board of Theological Education, LCA adopted a statement for discussion and reaction by LCA seminaries, in which it asserted that "normally, Lutheran seminaries ought not to offer research degrees alone or in conjunction with other seminaries, especially when the Lutheran school is in the context of a university that offers such a research degree."[31] Rather, BTE encouraged its seminaries to concentrate on the improvement of education for ministry and continuing professional education of ministers in the field. Reactions to the statement

26Lundeen, *History of CLTS Library*, p. 61.
27Notes from Bachmann.
28LSTC Board of Directors, *Minutes*, April 26-27, 1967, Exhibit 6, pp. 1-3.
29Lundeen, *History of CLTS Library*, p. 40. Some students are included more than once in these records, if they attended more than one session in a year.
30*LSTC Catalog*, 1967-68, p. 21.
31BTE, *Minutes*, February 14-15, 1967, p. 31.

assumed that the major criticism of BTE was toward the granting of doctoral degrees by Lutheran seminaries, not the S.T.M., but Dean Knudsen of LSTC was not ready to curtail any part of the seminary's graduate program.

> There are special factors that cause us to feel that the time is not yet ripe for determining long-range policy on graduate study. We are only now (autumn, 1967) able to work as a fully united faculty; we have only begun to acquaint ourselves with our new environment at The University of Chicago; and we are presently engaged in putting into effect a new B.D. curriculum. We therefore propose to devote further time to reflection and investigation before reaching final conclusions on these matters, and we invite the BTE to join us in these discussions.[32]

The distinction between research and professional graduate degrees was difficult to articulate for both the BTE and the seminaries, indicating that the discussion and controversy would continue for some time. Meanwhile, the Lutheran School of Theology at Chicago, with its long standing tradition of graduate studies and its present ideal proximity to library and other scholarly resources of the University of Chicago, was not readily prepared to surrender its assets. The place of graduate education at LSTC and other LCA seminaries would remain an issue for serious study and dialog for some time to come.

SCHOOL OF MISSIONS

An integral part of the Lutheran School of Theology at Chicago when it relocated adjacent to the University of Chicago campus was the School of Missions, operated under the aegis of the Board of World Missions. It was partially the advantage of proximity to the resources of the University of Chicago that had brought the school to Maywood in the first place in 1957,[33] so it was not unexpected that the newly organized LCA board at its first meeting July 9-10, 1962, adopted this resolution:

> that the Board of World Missions of the LCA request the Board of Directors of the Lutheran School of Theology at Chicago to include in the planning a School of Missions in the Lutheran School of Theology at Chicago.[34]

The Board of Directors of LSTC took action at its September, 1962, meeting by accepting the invitation and adopting the principles of agreement.[35] Although its presence in the merged seminary was assumed by the new LSTC Constitution and Articles of Consolidation, this action made it official. The School of

---

[32]LSTC Board of Directors, *Minutes*, October 11-12, 1967, Exhibit, "Response of the Lutheran School of Theology at Chicago to the BTE Statement on Graduate Theological Education," p. 2.

[33]CLTS Executive Committee, *Minutes*, June 17, 1955, and *LSTC Record*, May, 1967, pp. 24-25.

[34]LCA Board of World Missions, *Minutes*, July 9-10, 1962, and letter from Dr. Earl S. Erb to the LSTC Board Chairman, August 2, 1962.

[35]LSTC Board of Directors, *Minutes*, September 12, 1962, p. 11, and Exhibit D.

Missions was now a division of LSTC and would relocate subsequently with the seminary to its new location.

Action which originally created the School of Missions had been taken, after years of preliminary discussion by many groups including the Lutheran Foreign Missions Conference, by the United Lutheran Church in America at its 1954 Convention:

> To satisfy a recognized need, the Board of Foreign Missions, with cooperative study and possible subsidy by the Board of Education, shall seek to have established upon the campus of an existing Lutheran educational institution a Lutheran missions school.
>
> Such a school for present and prospective missionaries should provide specialized courses of study which would benefit both the individuals enrolled and the missions work of the Church. The number of estimated students could be readily accommodated at any one of the several existing Lutheran educational institutions.
>
> The share of the subsidization to be borne by the Board of Foreign Missions should be primarily through tuition payments for students placed in this school. The Board of Education should subsidize such an enterprise if necessary, through part of its grants-in-aid to the educational institution to which the school is related.[36]

After reviewing a prospectus drawn up by Dr. Rober Fischer of the Maywood campus, in which were cited the advantages that such a school would experience in the Chicago area near so many other schools having missions departments, the ULCA Board of Foreign Missions decided at its October 18-20, 1955, meeting to request Chicago Seminary to establish the School of Missions on its campus. The CLTS Board of Directors readily accepted the offer at its November, 1955, meeting,[37] and President Weng in his report to the board called this decision "probably the most far reaching development at the Seminary in recent years."[38]

The initial task of working out a curriculum for the new School of Missions was undertaken by Dr. Robert Fischer in consultation with a number of experts: Dr. Earl S. Erb, Executive Secretary of the ULCA Board of Foreign Missions; Dr. Kenneth Scott Latourette, Yale Divinity School; Drs. Joseph Kitagawa and Pierce Beaver, University of Chicago; Dr. Wilbur C. Harr, Evangelical Theological Seminary, Naperville, Illinois; Dr. Theodore Romig, Presbyterian Mission Board; and Dr. Worth Frank, McCormick Seminary. At the outset, Dr. Latourette set forth two objectives which shaped the goals and policies of the new school: 1) preparation of missionaries, 2) missions research.

> I would hope that the School would be both a place for the preparation of missionaries for their respective fields with such facilities as are needed for language and for an introduction to the

---

[36]ULCA, *Minutes*, 1954, pp. 570-71.
[37]CLTS Board of Directors, *Minutes*, November 30, 1955, p. 4.
[38]*Ibid.*, May 6, 1955, "President's Report," p. 1.

cultures, religions and history of their respective countries, and for research into the problems of missions . . . . I would hope that the School of Missions would make possible research for one or more students each year in problems particularly affecting the missions of the U.L.C.A. and that they should be furthering the entire Christian World Mission.[39]

The curriculum called for studies in Bible and Biblical theology in relation to world missions; the history of missions; the confrontation of Christ with cultures viewed from the theological, anthropological, and practical aspects; world religions; missionary methods; and linguistics.

Called as the first Dean of the new school was Rev. James A. Scherer, former teacher in China and missionary in Japan, and at the time of election a graduate student at Union Theological Seminary.[40] The *Seminary Record* commented enthusiastically on his appointment:

This rich background in missionary experience, plus his outstanding academic record, combined with a charm of personality, and humility of spirit, made him the unanimous choice of all who were giving consideration to filling this important post.[41]

When the initial day of classes began, September 10, 1957, at the first Lutheran school of missions on the American continents, twenty students were present for the historic occasion. Twelve were under assignment by the ULCA Board of Foreign Missions, and the other eight were missionary candidates of the Augustana Lutheran Church which had recently approved the school as its missionary training center.[42] The new faculty consisted of Professor Scherer, History and Theory of Mission; Dr. Richard Syré, Biblical Theology; and Dr. Paul P. Anspach, Missionary Practice and Evangelism. As vacancies occurred from time to time, the following men served on the School of Missions staff: Rev. Donald C. Flatt, Rev. Eino Vehanen, Dr. George Hall, Rev. Orville Nyblade, and Rev. David L. Lindberg. Professors Flatt, Hall, Lindberg, and Scherer constituted the School of Missions faculty in 1967, when LSTC moved to its new location.

During the first decade of the school's existence, 258 missionaries received training in the School of Missions. The roster included sixty-four pastors, thirty-nine lay missionaries, fifty-six single women, and ninety-nine wives of missionaries.[43] (See Table 5, pages 159-160.)

[39]Letter from Dr. Kenneth Scott Latourette to Dr. Robert Fischer, 1955, cited in "The Policy and Long-Range Planning for the School of Missions and Its Future Relationship to the Lutheran School of Theology," p. 3.
[40]CLTS Board of Directors, *Minutes*, May 2, 1956, p. 3.
[41]*Record*, October, 1956, p. 13.
[42]*Ibid.*, October, 1957, p. 9.
[43]*Ibid.*, May, 1967, p. 34.

TABLE 5

SCHOOL OF MISSIONS STUDENTS, AREAS OF SERVICE GEOGRAPHIC AND OCCUPATIONAL[a]

Country			
Africa:	Couples	Single Missionaries	Total
Tanzania	20	21	61
Liberia	18	14	50
Addis Ababa	1	1	3
Total Africa			114
South America:			
Guyana[b]	8	3	19
Peru		1	1
Argentina	3	1	7
Chile	1		2
Uruguay	4		8
Total South America			37
Asia:			
India	16	5	37
Japan	7	1	15
Taiwan	2		4
Malaysia	16	3	35
Hong Kong	1		2
Total Asia			93

Occupations	
Pastors	64
Medical	33
Doctors	3
Nurses	23
Medical technicians	4
Dietician	1
Physical therapist	1
Pharmacist	1
Teachers	30
Business administrators, accountants, secretaries, etc.	13
Argiculturists, veterinarian	5
Deaconess, social workers, youth workers, etc.	14

Among the wives of the missionaries many occupations were represented, which included 9 nurses, 1 medical doctor, 27 teachers, and various other occupations.

---

[a]*Record*, May, 1967, pp. 34-35.

[b]Pastor Henne formerly in Guyana, now in the new field of Trinidad.

Enrollment in the School of Missions during the first year on the new campus fell to fourteen, largely due to a change in the number and the character of missionaries requested by overseas churches, reflected in the recruitment policies of the LCA Board of World Missions. With more short-term, technical-assistant type of missionary being requested, allowing for only brief periods of orientation rather than serious academic study, fewer candidates were sent to the School of Missions. As originally constituted the school was not equipped to meet the changing needs. A further modification in Board of World Missions policy, that of sending "pre-field missionaries" for just the Summer and Fall sessions, did not bode well for student enrollments. Therefore, the School of Missions completed its first year in the new location facing a crisis regarding its present role and future place in the service of the Church. Acting Dean Flatt expressed the regrets of the school to LSTC and World Missions leaders:

> The crisis comes at a time when the new location of the Lutheran School of Theology at Chicago, near the University of Chicago, gives us new resources and opportunities, and when a greater degree of integration and co-working in the new seminary is opening fresh doors of influence in a broader sphere for the world mission cause.[44]

The School of Missions Consultative Committee in a January, 1966, meeting had indicated its eagerness to utilize the vast resources of the University of Chicago in two major areas:

1. That the new curriculum make the fullest possible use of the regular introductory courses to various civilizations offered by the University of Chicago, and of relevant offerings related to other areas.

2. That advantage be taken of relevant linguistic and language offerings for those who are scheduled to have a full year of study at the School of Missions prior to departure for their overseas assignments.[45]

Just at the point when the School of Missions, through its decade of experience and new location adjacent to the university, was best equipped to fulfill its original mandate, circumstances and policies were changing which seemed to preclude that possibility.

[44]Donald Flatt, "School of Missions—Notes On Its Future Role In Preparation of Short and Long-Term Missionaries, and Other Possible Roles," April 24, 1968, p. 1.

[45]Donald Flatt, "Towards A Curriculum For Pre-Field Training," May 17, 1968, p.

In facing alternatives for the future, school and world missions leaders recognized the growing cooperation between Lutheran church bodies in the Division of Mission Services of the Lutheran Council in the U.S.A. One early evidence of this mutual concern was the cooperation of the American Lutheran Church, Lutheran Church in America, and Lutheran Church-Missouri Synod at an annual summer orientation program for short or one-term missionaries, the first session of which was held on the LSTC campus in the Summer of 1968. Such cooperation posed the question of possible future collaboration in the sponsorship of a world mission institute or center for world mission and international studies. Possible functions and responsibilities for such an institute, tentatively envisaged by school leaders in the Summer of 1968, were:

1. **Ecumenical:**

   This should be an emphasis throughout the entire program and overarching the whole. Specific activities would be:

   a. Dialog.
   b. Cooperation in specific action projects.
   c. Campus evangelization aimed at students from overseas.
   d. "Joint Action for Mission" concerns.

2. **Training of Professionals in World Mission:**

   a. Graduate study in Missiology, World Religions and Ecumenics.
   b. Pre-field training.
   c. Continuing education of missionaries.
   d. In-service study for teachers of missiology, etc.
   e. Counseling and rehabilitation opportunities for missionaries.

3. **Evangelization and Church Planting:**

   a. Study and application of insights and tools of social sciences.
   b. Training missionary teams to move in and follow-up specific evangelistic opportunities.
   c. Organization and training of non-professional missionaries. Creation and coordination of a world-wide missionary fellowship, and provision of short orientation courses.

4. **Interpretation:**

   a. Generally among synods and congregations.
   b. Training study group leaders.
   c. Colloquies for seminary and college professors.
   d. Among the various commissions and boards of the church, to develop a six-continent mission concern.

5. **Research, Advisory Duties, and Publication:**

   a. Research is the necessary basis of the whole Institute.
   b. There must be rich resources of scholarship available to the BWM and other bodies when needed.

     c.   Advice and practical steps to develop on-field training programs should be offered on request.

     d.   Publication represents both fruit and the seed of further endeavors.[46]

Such a proposal would drastically change the character of the School of Missions, but the school was seen as the "existing base from which to advance . . . in which it may be possible to help the cause of world mission and international relations."[47]

The question of the new shape of the School of Missions or its successor was discussed at a meeting of the School of Missions Consultative Committee September 19, 1968. In an attempt to deal with the concern for exploring new ways of meeting the present and future needs in the field of World Missions, the committee adopted these resolutions:

> For purposes of future planning we recognize that there is a need for a program of Teaching, Research and Publication in the field of the Church in Missions which continues to be the responsibility of the LCA Board of World Missions and the LSTC.

> That to provide the basis for a decision on how these responsibilities shall be executed there be retained a Task Force of three in number to prepare an analysis and proposal for action, and to report to this committee at its next meeting on February 27, 1969.[48]

The Task Force, consisting of Dr. Martin L. Kretzmann, Dr. Wayne A. Ewing, and Rev. Donald C. Flatt, began its work in October, 1968, with a scheduled completion date of January 31, 1969.[49] No decision regarding the future of the School of Missions will be made until the completion of this study.

CONTINUING EDUCATION

In addition to a strong B.D. curriculum, a division of graduate studies, and a school of missionary education and research, the founders of LSTC envisaged as its fourth division a "program of theology for laymen preparing for or engaged in part or full time work in the church."[50] The objects of the seminary included a mandate "To provide instruction in theology for laymen."[51] Traces of such a program could be found in the Chicago Lutheran Seminary's summer program for lay campus workers, its Master of Arts curriculum for laymen, and a short-lived experiment, 1958-60, in evening school for laymen with collegiate degrees who might ultimately become interested in the ministry.[52]

1.

[46]Donald Flatt, "School of Missions" or "World Church/World Mission Institute?" May 15, 1968, pp. 3-4.

[47]Flatt, "Notes on Future Role," p. 4.

[48]School of Missions Consultative Committee, *Minutes*, September 19, 1968, p. 2.

[49]Steering Committee of the School of Missions Consultative Committee and Task Force, *Minutes*, October 4, 1968, pp. 1-2.

[50]*Official Documents*, p. 5.

[51]*LSTC Constitution*, Article I, Section 3d.

[52]CLTS Board of Directors, *Minutes*, April 30, 1958, p. 5, and Executive Committee, *Minutes*, January 15, 1958, pp. 2-4.

As a joint board, administration, and faculty committee studied the proposal, it became apparent that this division of the school could also be the vehicle for implementing another object of LSTC: "To encourage and assist in the in-service training of pastors."[53] This coincided with a growing, widespread interest in continuing education for clergy, as reflected at that time in this excerpt from a prominent religious journal:

> One of the most stirring developments in theological education today, one which holds great promise for the renewal of the church, is the growth in theological schools of programs for the continuing education of its ministry. Such programs speak directly to the needs of the average parish minister, who is so caught up in daily responsibilities that his hope of pursuing serious study has been reduced to a desperate clutching at straws. They also reflect an increasing awareness on the part of seminaries and churches that the work of the theological school is inseparable from the life and thought of the church and that the tasks of the pastor require renewal of theological understanding . . . .[54]

The end result was the creation in September, 1966, by the Board of Directors of a new Division of Continuing Education which would offer non-credit courses and a variety of colloquys, seminars, and study programs to both clergy and laity. Dr. Robert Tobias, visiting professor at LSTC-Rock Island Campus since 1964, was named to direct the school and was elected Associate Professor in Ecumenical Theology.[55] Possessing a doctorate from the University of Geneva Faculty of Theology, Dr. Tobias had served in post-World War II France in relief and reconstruction, was Assistant Director of the Department of Inter-Church Aid for the World Council of Churches, and completed eleven years of teaching as Professor of Ecumenics at Christian Theological Seminary, Indianapolis, before joining the Rock Island faculty.

After a full year of consultation with the Board of Theological Education and synodical committees responsible for continuing education, LSTC launched its new program in January, 1968, at the mid-point of the first year on the new campus. The first course was designed for laymen and was an exposure to the theological tasks of the Church, ranging from Bibilical scholarship to missions to ethics. Successive institutes attempted to implement the school's ideal of education by relating theology to other disciplines and today's society, such as the February, 1968, colloquy which focused "on the life sciences, the achievements and prospects of medical work, and the problems involved between the population explosion and the life-death paradox."[56] The themes of the Summer Pastors' Theological Institutes, sponsored jointly by the division and BTE, also grew out of the educational ideal, focusing on the relation of

---

[53]*LSTC Constitution*, Article I, Section 3e.
[54]*Christian Century*, April 25, 1962, p. 518.
[55]LSTC Board of Directors, *Minutes*, September 21-22, 1966.
[56]*Ibid.*, October 11-12, 1967, Exhibit G, Sub-Exhibit A, p. 2.

theology to science, politics, and the new morality. Other experimental programs, such as a cooperative course with Wartburg Seminary for pastors in the regions of Dubuque and Rock Island, pointed to the ever-expanding potential of the Division of Continuing Education.

THEOLOGICAL JOURNAL

In an effort to reach out beyond the campus, and yet reflect the life within the school, LSTC faculty members began the first year at the new location with the publication of a journal, *Context*. The editor, Dr. Franklin Sherman, stated the magazine's purpose in the initial issue:

> We are concerned to speak to the practicing clergyman, whether in the parish ministry or in some form of specialized service, who is himself concerned with the explosion of knowledge in theology and who may find in this journal an instrument for keeping abreast of current trends and, we hope, a stimulus to renewal.[57]

> We hope that some of the excitement of theological education in the new context in which our School is set—the secular city and the modern university—will be conveyed within these pages.[58]

Through the vehicle of this scholarly journal LSTC was prepared to confront the issues of the day, the other academic disciplines, and the structures of society, from the perspective of Christian theology. Articles during the first year of publication—"Speaking of God in a Secular Age," "Black Power: Crisis or Challenge for the Churches?" and "Theological Perspectives on Social Ministry"—were illustrative of the fact that the journal was one more consistent portion of the academic program that would implement the school's historic educational ideal.

A shortage of funds at the seminary forced a temporary suspension of publication of the journal after its first year, but an action of the Board of Directors in October, 1968, assured the continuance of the publication when adequate financing would become available.[59]

AFFILIATIONS WITH OVERSEAS SEMINARIES

At the initiative of President Herman, whose world-wide travels had provided numerous contacts with overseas churches and educational institutions, the Board of Directors adopted resolutions in January, 1965, creating a special relationship between LSTC and two overseas seminaries: Lutheran Theological College at Makumira, Tanzania, and Facultad Luterana de Teologia at Jose C. Paz, Argentina. The purposes of the new relationships were stated in the board's resolutions:

> *Be it Resolved*, That the Board express its desire to establish a special relationship with the *Facultad Luterana de Teologia* at Jose C. Paz, Argentina in order to foster a closer fellowship with this

---

[57]*Context*, I (Autumn, 1967), 1.
[58]*Ibid.*
[59]LSTC Board of Directors, *Minutes*, October 16-17, 1968, p. 10.

sister institution for the purpose of promoting regular contact, exchange of publications, and as occasion permits, visits between members of the faculties and student bodies.

To, this end, *Be it Resolved,* That LSTC award scholarships from time to time, including an annual scholarship of $1,000 plus tuition, board and lodging to a graduate of the FLT who desires to pursue post-graduate work at the LSTC and whose application for such purposes is regularly approved by the faculties of both institutions.[60]

Be it Resolved, That the Board expresses its desire to establish a special relationship with the Lutheran Theological College at Makumira, Tanzania, in order to foster a closer fellowship with this sister institution, particularly in support of its efforts to develop a B.D. program.

To this end, LSTC is ready to assist Makumira in working out a coordinated curriculum to be offered to students who have successfully completed at least Standard XIV upon entrance. At the conclusion of the Middler year a comprehensive examination will be given to determine whether and under what circumstances a student could be accepted for a final year or two at LSTC, with reasonable assurance that he might qualify for a B.D. degree. Moreover, LSTC is prepared, in principle, to offer limited financial aid from its scholarship fund. To one highly qualified and deserving Makumira student each year is offered a travel grant of $1,000 plus board, room and tuition for a maximum of two years of study leading to the B.D. degree, to be reviewed at the conclusion of the first year.[61]

Letters from the overseas seminaries gratefully acknowledged the special relationship. Rector Bela Lesko of the Argentina school stated that "it is a special satisfaction for us that now we will have for the first time a scholarship in a foreign country at our disposal," and that "the possibility of an exchange of publications and faculty members will open new horizons—beyond our reach until now—to our institution."[62] Likewise Principal E. E. Mshana of the Makumira seminary responded with enthusiasm: "We were all thrilled to know that our request has met your sympathetic consideration and action, and for that we are thankful."[63]

During the three school years which followed the adoption of these agreements there were eight students from Makumira and one from Jose C. Paz studying at LSTC. Though several of the Makumira students were in America under provisions other than the special agreement, the program was underway, and LSTC was assuming some measure of responsibility of strengthening theological education in younger overseas seminaries.

[60]LSTC Board of Directors, *Minutes,* January 27-28, 1965, p. 71.

[61]*Ibid.*

[62]LSTC Executive Committee, *Agenda,* June 17, 1965, p. 3., letter from Rector Bela Lesko to President Stewart Herman.

[63]*Ibid.*, March 8, 1965, p. 1, letter from Principal E. E. Mshana to President Stewart Herman.

FIRST YEAR AND FUTURE

A centuries old ideal of Lutheran theological education, conceived in Europe and transported to America by immigrant pastors—that theology must inform and be informed by all academic disciplines, and that theology must be living in constant relationship with the world and society of its day—had found expression in the Lutheran School of Theology at Chicago in its university-urban setting. One decade after the initial proposals for merger and relocation had been made, the seminary completed its first year on the new campus. The decade of negotiation, planning, construction, and organization was completed, and the seminary had demonstrated in this initial year that it was willing to accept the challenge of its new environment.

In addition to the formal academic program the school sponsored a number of events that were in harmony with the historic educational ideal. Convocation speakers, including Lord Caradon, United Kingdom representative to the United Nations; Mr. Ray Scherer, NBC White House Correspondent; Dr. Nathan Wright, Jr., Executive Director of the Department of Urban Work of the Episcopal Diocese of Newark, New Jersey; related theology to life in the contemporary world. A conference on January 10, 1968, co-sponsored by the National Conference of Catholic Bishops and the 450th Anniversary of the Reformation Committee, attracted over 300 priests and pastors to the seminary for addresses by Professor Carl Peter of Catholic University in Washington and Professor Arthur Piepkorn of Concordia Seminary in St. Louis, accenting the seminary's concern in the field of ecumenics.

In addition to convocations and addresses related to the church's role in social issues, there were several action oriented programs during the first school year. In mid-March, 1968, a military exhibit at the Museum of Science and Industry featured a helicopter equipped with a machine gun whose light ray could be aimed by children at a Vietnam village. Protesting, through public demonstration and petition, that the exhibit taught children "to condone violence and destruction as a solution to world problems," LSTC faculty members and students awakened public concern to close the exhibit. Following the assassination of Dr. Martin Luther King on April 4, 1968, students and faculty sponsored a memorial service and a series of seminar sessions on the racial problem. In the wake of ensuing riots in Chicago, LSTC students, together with students from sixteen other Chicagoland seminaries, organized a program of emergency community service.

In other community-oriented programs LSTC opened its doors to a course in Afro-American history, and also provided meeting space for Saturday morning breakfast rallies of "Operation Breadbasket," an economic program on behalf of developing black industry and commerce, sponsored by the Southern Christian Leadership Conference. The seminary also provided its facilities as a base for college students who came to explore Chicago's social agencies and urban problems. A student-sponsored conference on the military draft in April, 1968, enabled seminarians and visiting pastors to focus on the options of service faced by draft-age men in the light of Christian conscience and responsibility to country.

In the light of these and other social questions posed by contemporary American society, President Stewart W. Herman asked at the end of the first year on campus:

> What is the role of a theological seminary—specifically LSTC—in this situation? Blithe indifference? Does it confine itself to Old Testament, New Testament, and homiletics? Or does it test Christian faith and theology in the brawling marketplace of secular ideal?[64]

LSTC had given its answer. Theology in this school would be related to life.

With the first school year completed, the Lutheran School of Theology turned to the future with a sense of concern and responsibility, as voiced by its President, Dr. Stewart W. Herman in his 1968 Annual Report.

> One task has been completed; another is just beginning.
>
> The new seminary has been "blest and dedicated" to service of Almighty God. Henceforward, its sole purpose is the better preparation of men and women for many forms of Christian service, chiefly the parish ministry. Future generations may regard it as extraordinarily providential—in view of the present trend of national and international events—that this school was readied for such purpose at this particular time. God grant to all of us, who bear some measure of responsibility for this holy institution, the will and the vision not to fail or to falter in the never finished task.[65]

[64]*Context*, I (Spring/Summer, 1968), 47.
[65]Stewart W. Herman, "Report of LSTC Board of Directors," Illinois **Synod**, *Bulletin of Reports*, 1968, p. 96.

BIBLIOGRAPHY

BIBLIOGRAPHY

Books

Arden, G. Everett. *Augustana Heritage. History of the Augustana Lutheran Church.* Rock Island, Illinois: Augustana Book Concern, 1963.
_____. *The School of the Prophets. The Background and History of Augustana Theological Seminary 1860-1960.* Rock Island, Illinois: Augustana Book Concern, 1960.
Gerberding, George H. *Life and Letters of W. A. Passavant, D. D.* Greenville, Pennsylvvania: The Young Lutheran Company, 1906.
_____. *Reminiscent Reflections of a Youthful Octogenarian.* Minneapolis: Augsburg Publishing House, 1928.
Juva, Mikko. *The Church of Finland.* Pieksamaki, Finland: The Bible House, 1963.
Manschreck, Clyde. *Melanchthon: The Quiet Reformer.* Nashville: Abingdon Press, 1958.
Mortensen, Enok. *The Danish Lutheran Church in America. The History and Heritage of the American Evangelical Lutheran Church.* Philadelphia: Board of Publication, Lutheran Church in America, 1967.
Ochsenford, S. E. *Documentary History of the General Council.* Philadelphia: General Council Publication House, 1912.
Pinomaa, Lennart, ed. *Finnish Theology Past and Present.* Helsinki, Finland: Kirjapaino Oy Lause, 1963.
Rinde, Thomas D. *After Seventy-Four Years. A History of Western Seminary and Central Seminary 1893-1967.* Fremont, Nebraska: no publisher, 1967.
Schwiebert, E. G. *Luther and His Times: the Reformation from a New Perspective.* St. Louis: Concordia Publishing House, 1950.
Stupperich, Robert. *Melanchthon.* Translated by Robert H. Fischer. Philadelphia: The Westminister Press, 1965.
Tappert, Theodore G. *History of the Lutheran Theological Seminary at Philadelphia 1864-1964.* Philadelphia: Lutheran Theological Seminary, 1964.

Minutes, Catalogues, and Reports

Church and Synod Minutes

American Evangelical Lutheran Church Minutes, 1952-1963.
American Evangelical Lutheran Church Report, 1953-1962.
Augustana Evangelical Lutheran Church Minutes, 1947-1961.
Augustana Lutheran Church Commission on Ecumenical Relations Minutes, October 5, 1953-March 4, 1959.
Finnish Evangelical Lutheran Church in America-Suomi Synod Yearbook, 1957-1962.
Illinois Synod-LCA Minutes, 1962-1967.
Illinois Synod-ULCA Minutes, 1930-1962.
Indiana Synod-ULCA Minutes, 1961.
Indiana-Kentucky Synod-LCA Minutes, 1963-1964.
Lutheran Church in America Bulletin of Reports, 1968.
Lutheran Church in America Minutes, 1962-1966.
Lutheran Church in America Yearbook, 1968.
Michigan Synod-LCA Minutes, 1963.
Michigan Synod-ULCA Minutes, 1961.
Ohio Synod-ULCA Minutes, 1935-1942.
Pittsburg Synod-ULCA Minutes, 1961.
Report of the Sub-Committee of the Inter-Synodical Seminary Merger Committee In re Merger Hamma Divinity School and Chicago Lutheran Semimary.
United Lutheran Church in America Minutes, 1932.
Wartburg Synod-ULCA Minutes, 1961.
Wisconsin-Upper Michigan Synod-LCA Minutes, 1963-1965.

170

Seminary Minutes

Augustana Theological Seminary Board of Directors Minutes, November, 1947-October, 1959.

Augustana Theological Seminary Board of Directors Minutes, February, 1960-May, 1962.

Augustana Theological Seminary Executive Committee of the Board of Directors Minutes, July, 1948-August, 1954.

Augustana Theological Seminary Inter-Seminary Committee Minutes, 1960.

Central Lutheran Theological Seminary Board of Directors Minutes, 1959-1960, 1965-1967.

Central Lutheran Theological Seminary Faculty Minutes, 1959-1960.

Central Lutheran Theological Seminary and Lutheran School of Theology at Chicago "Committee of Five" Report, January, 1966.

Central Lutheran Theological Seminary and Lutheran School of Theology at Chicago Joint Executive Authority Minutes, 1966-1967.

Central Lutheran Theological Seminary and Lutheran School of Theology at Chicago Joint Meeting of Representatives Minutes, June 17, 1965, and December 10, 1965.

Chicago Lutheran Theological Seminary Board of Directors Abstract of Minutes, 1891-1916.

Chicago Lutheran Theological Seminary Faculty Meeting Minutes, June, 1954-December, 1962.

Chicago Lutheran Theological Seminary Executive Committee Minutes, February 6, 1952-May 15, 1962.

Chicago Lutheran Theological Seminary Board of Directors Minutes, 1952-1962.

Hamma School of Theology and Lutheran School of Theology at Chicago Joint Meeting of Representatives Minutes, October 4, 1965.

Inter-Seminary Committee Minutes, 1958-1962.

JCLU Minutes

Joint Commission on Lutheran Unity Minutes, 1956-1962.

JCLU, Volume 7. Pensions, Publications, Social Ministry, Theological Education, World Missions.

JCLU Register.

Catalogues

Lutheran School of Theology at Chicago Catalog, 1964-1968.

Lutheran Theological Seminary (Gettysburg, Pennsylvania) Bulletin, May, 1966.

Reports

Bergendoff, Conrad. Executive Secretary's Reports, 1-11, to the Board of Theological Education, October, 1962-May, 1963.

———. The Lutheran Church in America and Theological Education. A Report to the Board of Theological Education. New York, 1963.

Foelsch, Charles B. Chicago Lutheran Theological Seminary Report of Seminary President, 1943.

Gieschen, Gerhard. Report of the Acting President, 1965-1967.

Grimes, Lyman H. Annual Report of Board of Directors of the Chicago Lutheran Theological Seminary, 1949.

Gruber, L. Franklin. Annual Report of Board of Directors of the Chicago Lutheran Theological Seminary, 1941.

Herman, Stewart W., and Skillrud, Harold C. Annual Report of Board of Directors of the Lutheran School of Theology at Chicago, 1965-1968.

Howe, C. W. Annual Report of Board of Directors of the Chicago Lutheran Theological Seminary, 1943.

Jensen, Frank E. Annual Report of Board of Directors of the Chicago Lutheran Theological Seminary, 1930.

Keck, Albert J., Jr. Annual Report of Board of Directors of the Chicago Lutheran

Theological Seminary, 1945.
Krauss, Paul H. Annual Report of Board of Directors of the Chicago Lutheran Theological Seminary, 1944, 1946, 1947.
Leas, J. Allen. Annual Report of Board of Directors of the Chicago Lutheran Theological Seminary, 1931-1940.
McGuire, Harmon J. Annual Report of Board of Directors of the Chicago Lutheran Theological Seminary, 1948.
Olson, Russell. Annual Report of Board of Directors of Central Lutheran Theological Seminary, 1967.
Skillrud, Harold C. Annual Report of Board of Directors of the Lutheran School of Theology at Chicago, 1963-1964.
Weng, Armin George. Annual Report of Board of Directors of the Chicago Lutheran Theological Seminary, 1942.

Pamphlets and Articles

Bachmann, E. Theodore. Central Lutheran Theological Seminary and Recommendations of the Board of Theological Education (A Position Paper), November 5, 1965.
_____. "Central Seminary and the Board's Recommendation." LCA Minutes, 1966, pp. 655-660.
Foelsch, Charles Behrend. The Chicago Lutheran Seminary Record.
    "Campus Notes," January, 1947, pp. 9, 10.
    "Campus Notes," April, 1947, p. 20.
    "Campus Notes," July, 1947, p. 13.
    "Paragraphs from the President's Report," October, 1947, p. 6.
Gieschen, Gerhard. A Word of Clarification and Encouragement to the Students of Central, February, 1966.
Johnson, Ben A. "The Augustana Synod and the Muhlenberg Tradition." The Chicago Lutheran Theological Seminary Record, August, 1960, pp. 25-39.
Fry, Franklin Clark. "The State of the Church." Desk Book, September, 1958.
Lutheran School of Theology at Chicago. Development Fund.
    Skillrud, Harold C. "Introduction."
    Bergendoff, Conrad. "What Will Happen at Chicago?"
    Mattson, Karl E. "The New Location."
    Weng, Armin G. "Inadequate Facilities Plague Present Campuses."
    Knudsen, Johannes. "The Dynamics of Merger."
    Kukkonen, Walter J. "What Does the Merger Mean?"
    Herman, Stewart W. "Why A New Seminary?"
Skillrud, Harold C. "The Fruits of Merger." Theological Education, Spring, 1967, pp. 424-426.
Teresi, Richard. "This Month in Chicago: Seminarians Move to a University." The Lutheran, October 11, 1967, pp. 5-9.
Weng, Marjory R. "Passavant's Vision. A History of Sixty Years of Service to the Church." Chicago Lutheran Theological Seminary Record, October, 1951, entire issue.
_____. Progress of a Century. A History of the Illinois Synod of the United Lutheran Church in America—1851-1951.
Zeidler, Clemens H. "Comment on Report No. 11 (Northwestern Lutheran Theological Seminary, Minneapolis, Minnesota) of the Executive Secretary of the Board of Theological Education," Minneapolis, 1963.

Newspapers and Periodicals

The Central Seminary Bulletin, 1965-1967.
Chicago Daily News, 1964-1967.
Chicago Sun-Times, 1964-1967.
Chicago Tribune, 1964-1967.
Chicago's American, 1965.
Context, Chicago, 1967-1968.
Epistle, Lutheran School of Theology at Chicago, 1965-1968.

172

Hyde Park Herald, 1964-1967.
The Illinois Lutheran, 1963-1968.
Lutheran School of Theology News Releases, 1965-1968.
Lutheran Quarterly, November, 1966.
The Record, Chicago Lutheran Theological Seminary, 1935-1962; Lutheran School of
  Theology at Chicago, 1962-1967.
The Seminary Review, Augustana Theological Seminary, 1960-1962; Lutheran School of
  Theology at Chicago, 1962-1967.
The Voice, May, 1967.
University of Chicago Maroon, 1965.

Papers and Collections

(Note: The following materials are partially classified and catalogued in the Archives of the
Lutheran Church in America, Library, Lutheran School of Theology at Chicago, Chicago,
Illinois.)

Bergendoff, Conrad. Papers.
Benson, Oscar. Papers.
Bersell, P. O. Papers.
Fry, Franklin Clark. Papers.
Grimes, Lyman. Papers.
Herman, Stewart W. Papers.
Jensen, Alfred. Papers.
Lundeen, Malvin H. Papers.
Mattson, Karl E. Papers.
Mortvedt, Robert. Papers.
Skillrud, Harold C. Papers.
Wargelin, Raymond. Papers.
Weng, Armin G. Papers.

Unpublished Material

Kangas, Henry R. Blades, Ears, and Corn: Suomi Synod, 1890-1962. LSTC Library.
Ketchum, Incorporated. Manual of Reports.
Lundeen, Joel W. "History of the Library of Chicago Lutheran Theological Seminary of
  Maywood, Illinois." Unpublished Master's dissertation, University of Chicago, 1967.
Lutheran School of Theology at Chicago Revised Constitution and Bylaws, 1967.
Official Documents of the Lutheran School of Theology at Chicago—Summary of Agree-
  ments, The Constitution, The Plan of Consolidation, Necessary Actions by boards,
  churches, and synods, 1961.
Sullinger, T. Earl; Strempke, Vernon L.; and Parker, G. Gordon. Lutheran Regional Survey,
  1964.

APPENDIXES

Appendix I

SERVICE OF DEDICATION

OCTOBER 22, 1967

SERVICE OF DEDICATION

for the

Lutheran School of Theology

at Chicago

Eleven Hundred East Fifty-Fifth Street

in

ROCKEFELLER CHAPEL

University of Chicago

Three-Thirty P.M.

SUNDAY, OCTOBER TWENTY-SECOND

NINETEEN HUNDRED SIXTY-SEVEN

ORGAN PRELUDE: Fantasy in G Minor . . . . *Johann Sebastian Bach*

THE PROCESSIONAL: Echo Fantasy . . . . *Samuel Scheidt*

¶ *The Procession shall enter the Chapel and the people shall rise.*

THE PROCESSIONAL HYMN *(Aurelia)* . . . . *Samuel S. Wesley*

1 The Church's one foundation
   Is Jesus Christ her Lord;
She is his new creation
   By water and the word:
From heaven he came and sought her
   To be his holy bride,
With his own Blood he bought her,
   And for her life he died.

2 Elect from every nation,
   Yet one o'er all the earth,
Her charter of salvation
   One Lord, one faith, one birth;
One holy Name she blesses,
   Partakes one holy food,
And to one hope she presses,
   With every grace endued.

3 'Mid toil and tribulation,
   And tumult of her war,
She waits the consummation
   Of peace for evermore;
Till with the vision glorious
   Her longing eyes are blest,
And the great Church victorious
   Shall be the Church at rest.

4 Yet she on earth hath union
   With God, the Three in One,
And mystic sweet communion
   With those whose rest is won.
O happy ones and holy!
   Lord, give us grace that we
Like them, the meek and lowly,
   On high may dwell with thee. Amen.

THE VERSICLES:

¶ *The Minister shall sing:*

In the Name of the Father, and of the Son, and of the Holy Ghost,
   R. Amen.
O Lord, Open thou my lips.
   R. And my mouth shall show forth thy praise.
Make haste, O God, to deliver me.
   R. Make haste to help me, O Lord.
Establish thou the work of our hands.
   R. Yea, the work of our hands, establish thou it.
Glory be to the Father, and to the Son, and to the Holy Ghost:
   R. As it was in the beginning, is now, and ever shall be, world without end.
   Amen. Alleluia.

¶ *Then shall be said responsively:*

THE PSALM: Psalm 100 *(Jubilate Deo)*

Make a joyful noise unto the Lord all ye lands. Serve the Lord with gladness:
   Come before his presence with singing.
Know ye that the Lord he is God. It is he that has made us, and not we ourselves:
   We are his people, and the sheep of his pasture.
Enter into his gates with thanksgiving, and into his courts with praise:
   Be thankful unto him, and bless his Name.
For the Lord he is good, his mercy is everlasting:
   And his truth endureth to all generations.
Glory be to the Father, and to the Son, and to the Holy Ghost;
   As it was in the beginning, is now, and ever shall be, world without end.
   Amen.

THE LESSONS:

MINISTER: Hear now the word of the Lord, as recorded in the 11th chapter of Deuteronomy, calling God's people to **remembrance.**

SPEECH
CHOIR
You shall lay my words in your heart and soul, and you shall bind them for a sign upon your hand, and they shall be as frontlets before your eyes. You shall teach them to your children, talking of them when you sit in your house, and when you walk in the street, and when you lie down, and when you rise up. And you shall write them on the door-posts of your house, and upon your gate, that your days may be multiplied in the land which the Lord has given you.

MINISTER: Hear the word of the Lord, as written in the prophecy of Isaiah, calling God's people to **obedience.**

SPEECH
CHOIR
The spirit of the Lord is upon me, because he annointed me to preach good tidings to the poor. He hath sent me to proclaim release to the captives, and recovering of sight to the blind, to set at liberty them that are bruised, and to proclaim the acceptable year of the Lord.

MINISTER: Hear the word of the Lord, as recorded in the gospel of John, a prayer for **unity.**

SPEECH
CHOIR
Sanctify them through thy truth, thy word is truth. As thou hast sent me into the world, even so have I also sent them into the world. And for their sakes I sanctify myself, that they also might be sanctified through the truth . . . that they all may be one, as thou, Father, art in me, and I in thee, that they also may be in us; that the world may believe that thou hast sent me.

MINISTER: Hear the word of the Lord, as it is written in the gospel of Matthew, calling God's people to **works of serving love.**

SPEECH
CHOIR
Go ye, therefore, and teach all nations, baptising them in the name of the Father, and of the Son, and of the Holy Ghost: Teaching them to observe all things whatsoever I have commanded you: and, lo, I am with you alway, even unto the end of the world. Amen.

¶ *The Congregation is seated.*

THE ANTHEM: *Psalm 150*..................................*Jean Berger*

THE VOICES OF OUR HERITAGE:

VOICE I
Repre-
senting
Augustana
Tradition.
Remembrance of God's mercy, grace, and purpose, unto the obedience of unity and serving love; this is God's call to his people in every age. It was this call which our founding fathers heeded when they established those institutions of learning and training which were to be the seed beds of the Lutheran Church in the New World. In 1849 there came to the American frontier of the Mississippi Valley a company of Swedish immigrants, led by their pastor, the Rev. Lars Paul Esbjorn. Here they built their homes, erected their churches, and in 1860 established the Augustana Theological Seminary, the first, and therefore the oldest of the parent schools of the Luthern School of Theology.

¶ *At the conclusion of this narrative, the choir sings one verse of Hymn 174, Ter Sanctus. During the singing of the hymn the Augustana Seminary standard bearer places his banner.*

VOICE II Representing Maywood Tradition.	The earliest Lutheran tradition in America took form in the ministry of Henry Melchior Muhlenberg, who came to Pennsylvania from Germany in 1742. From this tradition of the Lutheran Church come two of the parent seminaries of the Lutheran School of Theology. The oldest of these was founded in 1891 by the Rev. William A. Passavant of Pittsburgh, who persuaded the General Council of the Lutheran Church to establish a theological seminary in Chicago which would give special attention to the training of an English speaking ministry in the midwest. The Chicago Theological Seminary opened its doors in the Lake View area of Chicago in the fall of 1891, and in 1910 moved to the suburban community of Maywood. As the second oldest of the parent schools it has in recent years included both a graduate program and a school of missions, in addition to its regular theological curriculum.
VOICE III Representing the Central Tradition.	The second seminary from the Muhlenberg tradition was established at Atchison, Kansas, in 1893, by the General Synod of the Lutheran Church, and was given the name Western Theological Seminary. In 1910 ownership and control was vested in the Board of Directors of Midland College of Atchison. As a department of Midland College, Western Seminary was transferred to Fremont, Nebraska, when the college moved to the Nebraska campus in 1919. As the Seminary developed its own campus, its own corporate life, and in keeping with its purpose to serve the needs of the Central States area, its name was changed to Central Theological Seminary.

¶ *At the conclusion of this narrative, the choir sings one verse of Hymn 7,* Wachet Auf, *during which the two standard bearers representing Maywood and Central Seminaries place their banners.*

VOICE IV Representing Grand View Tradition.	Among the multitudes of European immigrants who came to America during the 19th century seeking greater opportunity, were many sons and daughters of the Lutheran Church of Denmark. Those Danish Lutheran immigrants who sympathized with the religious and cultural emphasis of the great Danish churchman N. F. S. Grundtvig, founded the Danish Lutheran Church in America, and in 1896 established in the Grand View area of the city of Des Moines, Iowa, the Grand View Theological Seminary.

¶ *At the conclusion of this narrative, the choir sings one verse of Hymn 151,* Kirken, *during which the Grand View Seminary standard bearer places his banner.*

VOICE V Representing Suomi Tradition.	The youngest of the parent seminaries brings to the Lutheran School of Theology the rich tradition of the Lutheran Church of Finland. Sensing the imperative need to raise up an American ministry which could effectively serve the growing Finnish-American population in this country, the Finnish Evangelical Church, popularly known as the Suomi Synod, organized its own Suomi Theological Seminary at Hancock, Michigan, in 1904 upon the campus of Suomi College. For fifty-four years Suomi Seminary was closely associated with the College, before severing these historic relations and moving to the Maywood community in 1958.

¶ *At the conclusion of this narrative, the choir sings one verse of Hymn 180,* Suomi, *during which the Suomi Seminary standard bearer places his banner. When the five representative banners have been placed in position, the ensign of the Lutheran School of Theology is brought forward and placed in the midst.*

¶ *Then the Minister standing at the altar shall say:*

Let us pray.

¶ *The congregation shall rise.*

O God, who through thy Holy Spirit dost ever call thy people to new and greater commitment, help us now to recall with humble gratitude the sacrificial obedience of our founding fathers. By their example inspire us to heed thy call, to obey thy summons in our own day, giving ourselves wholly to thy obedience.

Bless and prosper to thy purposes, we pray thee, the Lutheran School of Theology at Chicago, which is formed of the several traditions of our Lutheran heritage. By thy Spirit's guidance make it an effective instrument of thy compassionate concern for the temporal and spiritual welfare of people, in this community, this city, this nation, and throughout the world. Let the spirit of serving love be its greatest resource, and so keep it relevant and sensitive to the needs of men, rather than preoccupied with its own prosperity. By thy grace make this school a place where men shall grow in knowledge, understanding, compassion, and in dedication to thee.

Let they benediction rest upon all who in any way labor for this new school. Especially do we invoke thy blessing upon those who teach and those who learn, that they may apply themselves with diligence to the knowledge which is able to make men wise unto salvation, and submit themselves with such ready obedience to the law of thy Son, our Savior, that they may fulfill their ministry with joy, through Jesus Christ our Lord.   R. Amen.

THE HYMN: *(Ein' Feste Burg)*.............................*Martin Luther*

1 *Congregation and Choir*
A mighty fortress is our God,
A bulwark never failing;
Our helper he amid the flood
Of mortal ills prevailing:
For still our ancient foe
Doth seek to work us woe;
His craft and power are great,
And, armed with cruel hate,
On earth is not his equal.

2 *Choir Only*
Did we in our own strength confide
Our striving would be losing;
Were not the right Man on our side,
The Man of God's own choosing.
Dost ask who that may be?
Christ Jesus, it is he;
Lord Sabaoth his Name,
From age to age the same,
And he must win the battle.

3 *Choir Only*
And though this world, with devils filled,
Should threaten to undo us;
We will not fear, for God hath willed
His truth to triumph through us:
The prince of darkness grim,
We tremble not for him;
His rage we can endure,
For lo! his doom is sure,
One little word shall fell him.

4 *Congregation and Choir*
That word above all earthly powers,
No thanks to them, abideth;
The Spirit and the gifts are ours
Through him who with us sideth:
Let goods and kindred go,
This mortal life also;
The body they may kill:
God's truth abideth still,
His kingdom is forever.

THE SERMON: THE REVEREND DOCTOR FRANKLIN CLARK FRY

PRESIDENT OF THE LUTHERAN CHURCH IN AMERICA

182

GREETING: ....The Reverend Doctor Stewart Winfield Herman

¶ *Then shall the Offering be received.*

THE ANTHEM: Sing Ye to the Lord.................*Johann Sebastian Bach*

¶ *When the offering is brought to the altar, the Congregation shall rise.*

Let my prayer be set forth before thee as incense.

R. And the lifting up of my hands as the evening sacrifice.

THE CANTICLE *(Said responsively)*

NUNC DIMITTIS

Lord now lettest thou thy servant de | part in | peace,
° ac | cording to | thy | word;
For mine eyes have | seen thy sal | vation,
° which thou hast prepared before the | face of | all | people;
A light to | lighten the | Gentiles,
° and the | glory of thy | people | Israel.
Glory | be to the | Father,
° and to the | Son : and to the | Holy | Ghost;
As it | was in : the be | ginning,
° is now and ever shall be, | world without | end. A | men.

THE PRAYER

¶ *Then shall be said the Prayers.*

Lord, have mercy upon us.

R. Lord, have mercy upon us.
Christ, have mercy upon us.
Lord, have mercy upon us.

¶ *Then shall all say the Lord's Prayer.*

Our Father, who art in heaven, Hallowed be thy Name, Thy kingdom come, Thy will be done, on earth as it is in heaven. Give us this day our daily bread; And forgive us our trespasses, as we forgive those who trespass against us; And lead us not into temptation, But deliver us from evil. For thine is the kingdom, and the power, and the glory, forever and ever. Amen.

¶ *Then shall be said:*

The Lord be with you.

R. And with thy spirit.

Let us pray.

O God, our refuge and strength, who art the author of all godliness: Be ready, we beseech thee, to hear the devout prayers of thy Church; and grant that those things which we ask faithfully, we may obtain effectually; through thy Son, Jesus Christ our Lord, who liveth and reigneth with thee and the Holy Ghost, one God, world without end.

R. Amen.

The Lord will give strength unto his people.

R. The Lord will bless his people with peace.

COLLECT FOR PEACE

O God, from whom all holy desires, all good counsels, and all just works do proceed: Give unto thy servants that peace which the world cannot give; that our hearts may be set to obey thy commandments, and also that by thee, we, being defended from the fear of our enemies, may pass our time in rest and quietness; through the merits of Jesus Christ our Saviour, who liveth and reigneth with thee and the Holy Ghost, one God, world without end.

R. Amen.

Bless we the Lord

R. Thanks be to God.

The Grace of our Lord Jesus Christ, and the Love of God, and the Communion of the Holy Ghost, be with you all.

R. Amen.

THE RECESSIONAL HYMN *(Lancashire)* . . . . *Henry Smart*

1 Lead on, O King eternal,
   The day of march has come;
   Henceforth in fields of conquest
   Thy tents shall be our home:
   Through days of preparation
   Thy grace has made us strong,
   And now, O King eternal,
   We lift our battle song.

2 Lead on, O King eternal,
   Till sin's fierce war shall cease,
   And holiness shall whisper
   The sweet Amen of peace;
   For not with swords loud clashing,
   Nor roll of stirring drums,
   But deeds of love and mercy,
   The heavenly kingdom comes.

3 Lead on, O King eternal:
   We follow, not with fears,
   For gladness breaks like morning
   Where'er thy face appears:
   Thy Cross is lifted o'er us;
   We journey in its light;
   The crown awaits the conquest;
   Lead on, O God of might. Amen.

ORGAN POSTLUDE: Outburst of Joy . . . . *Olivier Messiaen*

¶ *The Congregation shall participate in the procession to the
Lutheran School of Theology at Chicago*

CARILLON RECITAL

The Four Heritage Hymns and *Ein' Feste Burg* . . . . *arr. J. Ulrich*
Prelude No. 1 in G Major . . . . *Van Den Gheyn*
Fugue . . . . *Van Den Gheyn*
Pastorale and Toccata Gaia . . . . *Johan Franco*
Toccata No. 10 . . . . *Johan Franco*

The Rite of Dedication

At Eleven Hundred East Fifty-Fifth Street
(The Southwest Entrance)

¶ *The Congregation and participants having assembled, the minister shall say:*
In the Name of the Father, and of the Son, and of the Holy Ghost,
R. AMEN.

¶ *Then shall be said responsively:*

THE PSALM: Psalm 119   *I. Beati immaculati*

Blessed are the undefiled in the way:
    Who walk in the law of the Lord.

Blessed are they that keep his testimonies;
    And that seek him with the whole heart.

They also do no iniquity:
    They walk in his ways.

Thou hast commanded us:
    To keep thy precepts diligently.

O that my ways were directed:
    To keep thy statutes!

Then shall I not be ashamed:
    When I have respect unto all thy commandments.

I will praise thee with uprightness of heart:
    When I shall have learned thy righteous judgments,

I will keep thy statutes:
    O forsake me not utterly.

II. In quo corrigit

Wherewithal shall a young man cleanse his way:
    By taking heed thereto according to thy word.

With my whole heart have I sought thee:
    O let me not wander from thy commandments.

Thy word have I had in mine heart:
    That I might not sin against thee.

Blessed art thou, O Lord:
    Teach me thy statutes.

With my lips have I declared:
    All the judgments of thy mouth.

I have rejoiced in the way of thy testimonies:
    As much as in all riches.

I will meditate in thy precepts:
    And have respect unto thy ways.

I will delight myself in thy statutes:
    I will not forget thy word.

Glory be to the Father, and to the Son, and to the Holy Ghost:
    As it was in the beginning, is now, and ever shall be, world without end.
Amen.

¶ *Then shall all say:*

I believe in one God, the Father Almighty, Maker of Heaven and earth, and of all things visible and invisible. And in one Lord, Jesus Christ, the only begotten Son of God, begotten of his Father before all worlds, God of God, Light of Light, Very God of Very God, Begotten not made, Being of the same substance with the Father, By whom all things were made: Who for us men, and for our salvation, came down from Heaven, And was incarnate by the Holy Ghost of the Virgin Mary, And was made man; and was crucified also for us under Pontius Pilate. He suffered and was buried; And the third day he rose again according to the Scriptures, And ascended into Heaven, And sitteth on the right hand of the Father. And he shall come again with glory to judge both the quick and the dead: Whose kingdom shall have no end. And I believe in the Holy Ghost, The Lord and Giver of Life, Who proceedeth from the Father and the Son, Who with the Father and the Son together is worshipped and glorified; Who spake by the Prophets. And I believe one Holy Christian and Apostolic Church. I acknowledge one Baptism for the remission of sins. And I look for the Resurrection of the dead, And the Life of the world to come. Amen.

THE DEDICATION:

¶ The Key shall be given by the Builder to the Architect, who gives it to the Chairman of the Building Committee, who hands it to the President, saying:

It is now my privilege, Mr. President, to present to you the keys to this building, The Lutheran School of Theology at Chicago.

¶ The President shall accept the keys, saying:

The Blessing of God be upon this house.

R. And upon all who enter therein.

¶ The minister shall then say:

Our help is in the Name of the Lord.

R. Who made heaven and earth.

The Lord be with you.

R. And with thy spirit.

Let us pray:

Almighty God, look with favor, we beseech thee, upon this building which has been erected to thy glory and for the use of thy people, and be thou pleased to grace it with thy presence, and accept it of our hands. Amen.

¶ The President of the Church shall then say:

And now blest and dedicate be this Lutheran School of Theology, to the glory of Almighty God, and to the service of his Holy Church: In the Name of the Father, and of the Son, and of the Holy Ghost.

R. Amen.

Let us pray:

O God, our heavenly Father, thou hast ordained that the coming of thy kingdom shall be encouraged through the labors of those whom thou dost choose to be servants and ministers of thy word. We pray thee to raise up among the people of every generation pastors and teachers who shall be humble of heart, keen of mind, disciplined of spirit, and wholly committed to thee. We humbly thank thee for the Lutheran School of Theology, and for the gifts and labors which have made this building with its many resources possible. Help us to recognize in this structure an enduring and fitting symbol of the deep concern which the people and pastors of the Lutheran Church in America have for a well-trained and spiritually devoted ministry. Grant that by thy grace, those who work, teach, and study here may truly serve thee with vision, courage, and consecration. Let thy favor rest upon this institution so that as it takes its place as a member of this university community, it shall ever exalt the quest for truth; as it finds its home in this great city, help it to be an effective expression of thy love for all men; as it is incorporated into the expanding life of thy Church, make it a faithful steward of thy gospel. Into thy hands we commit our school, our Church, and ourselves through Jesus Christ our Lord.

R. AMEN.

⁋ *The following collect shall be said by all:*

O God our Father, who art the source of Truth and Life and Love; we thank thee for the heritage of learning which has come to us from the past, whereby our knowledge has been increased, our life enriched, and our joy made more abundant. Grant unto us true humility that we may not be disdainful of whatsoever is true in that which is old, nor refuse to receive whatsoever is true in that which is new. But loving thee with our whole mind, may we rejoice in the accumulation of all true knowledge, and employ it in the service of our fellow men, to the glory of thy name, through Jesus Christ our Lord. Amen.

THE HYMN *(Nun danket alle Gott)*........................*Johann Crüger*

1 Now thank we all our God
   With heart and hands and voices,
Who wondrous things hath done,
   In whom his world rejoices;
Who, from our mother's arms,
   Hath blessed us on our way
With countless gifts of love,
   And still is ours today.

2 O may this bounteous God
   Through all our life be near us,
With ever joyful hearts
   And blessed peace to cheer us;
And keep us in his grace,
   And guide us when perplexed,
And free us from all ills
   In this world and the next.

3 All praise and thanks to God
   The Father now be given,
The Son, and him who reigns
   With them in highest heaven;
The one eternal God,
   Whom earth and heaven adore;
For thus it was, is now,
   And shall be evermore. Amen.

THE BENEDICTION:

The blessing of Almighty God, the Father, the Son, and the Holy Ghost, be with you all.

R. AMEN.

Participants in the Dedication Service

THE PRESIDENT OF THE LUTHERAN CHURCH IN AMERICA
The Reverend Doctor Franklin Clark Fry, S.T.D., D.D., LL.D., Litt.D., L.H.D., Th.D., S.J.D., D.C.L., I.R.D., Hum.D.

assisted by the Ministers:

The Reverend Harold C. Skillrud, B.A., B.D.   The Reverend Stewart W. Herman, Litt.D.

The Reverend L. Dale Lund, Ph.D.   The Reverend John W. Arthur, S.T.M.

The Reverend Robert J. Marshall, D.D., L.H.D.

and the Lectors:

The Reverend G. Everett Arden, Ph.D.   The Reverend Johannes H. V. Knudsen, Ph.D.

The Reverend Richard R. Syré, Ph.D., Litt.D.   The Reverend H. Grady Davis, D.D.

The Reverend Walter J. Kukkonen, S.T.D.

and the Speech Choir:

L.S.T.C. Students.................... Directed by The Reverend Wilhelm C. Linss, Ph.D.

The Music:

THE LUTHERAN CHOIR OF CHICAGO
Theodore M. Klinka, *Director*

ORGANIST   CARILLONNEUR

Edward Mondello, *University Organist*   Daniel Robins, *University Carillonneur*

GUEST CARILLONNEUR

Jakob Ulrich *(following the Service)*

Also:

The Marshall (the Reverend L. Dale Lund, Dean of the Faculty) assisted by members of the faculty. Members of the student body serve as Crucifer, Torch Bearers, Bearers of the Flags, Standards, and Banners, and as Ushers.

The Administration

STEWART WINFIELD HERMAN, *President*

FRANKLIN K. ZIMMERMAN
Assistant to the President

JOHANNES KNUDSEN
Dean of Graduate Studies

JAMES A. SCHERER
Dean of School of Missions

THEODORE E. CONRAD
Director of Admissions; Registrar

STANLEY J. VOGEL
Controller

L. DALE LUND
Dean of the Faculty

ARTHUR O. ARNOLD
Dean of Students

ROBERT I. TOBIAS
Director of Continuing Education

JOEL W. LUNDEEN
Director of Library

WARREN D. NELSON
Director of Communications

The Board of Directors

THE REVEREND HAROLD C. SKILLRUD, *Chairman*
THE REVEREND RUSSELL J. OLSON, *Vice-Chairman*
MR. HOWARD L. PETERSON, *Secretary*
MR. FRED W. SODERBERG, JR., *Treasurer*

CENTRAL STATES SYNOD

THE REVEREND N. EVERETT HEDEEN, *President*
DR. DEAN WERNER
THE REVEREND VERNON F. JACOBS

ILLINOIS SYNOD

THE REVEREND ROBERT J. MARSHALL, *President*
THE REVEREND SAMUEL W. JENSEN
DR. KERMIT O. ALMOS
THE REVEREND GEORGE L. LUNDQUIST
MR. FRED DRINHAUS
THE REVEREND HAROLD R. LOHR
DR. KENNETH H. ECKHERT
DR. JAMES N. BeMILLER
MR. V. RICHARD HIETIKKO

IOWA SYNOD

THE REVEREND RAYNOLD J. LINGWALL, *President*
MR. LEONARD C. LARSEN
THE REVEREND DAVID R. BELGUM
MR. RICHARD T. GRAU

NEBRASKA SYNOD

THE REVEREND REUBEN T. SWANSON, *President*
THE REVEREND LAWRENCE H. BECK
THE REVEREND WALTER E. ROWOLDT
DR. EMORY K. LINDQUIST

TEXAS-LOUISIANA SYNOD

THE REVEREND PHILIP L. WAHLBERG, JR.,
President
THE REVEREND VANCE M. DANIEL
DR. GORDON M. ANDERSON

INDIANA-KENTUCKY SYNOD

THE REVEREND WALTER M. WICK, *President*
THE REVEREND PAUL H. KRAUSS
DR. ROBERT F. BORKENSTEIN
MR. ELDON A. SWANSON
THE REVEREND ALBERT R. SWASKO

MICHIGAN SYNOD

THE REVEREND FRANK P. MADSEN, *President*
MR. PHILIP J. WARGELIN
DR. GEORGE E. MENDENHALL
THE REVEREND GODFREY E. ALBERTI
THE REVEREND SIDNEY W. JONES

ROCKY MOUNTAIN SYNOD

THE REVEREND LEELAND C. SOKER, *President*
DR. PAUL L. HULTQUIST
THE REVEREND JOHN F. FUTCHS

WISCONSIN-UPPER MICHIGAN SYNOD

THE REVEREND THEODORE E. MATSON, *President*
MR. A. ROY ANDERSON
MR. EDWARD J. SEIY
THE REVEREND O. V. ANDERSON
MR. ALAN R. ANDERSON
THE REVEREND ROBERT B. ANDERSON
THE REVEREND WILLIAM R. SARVELA

The Faculty

G. EVERETT ARDEN	Professor of Church History and Liturgics
ARTHUR O. ARNOLD	Professor of Practical Theology and Dean of Students
JOHN W. ARTHUR	Assistant Professor of Liturgics and Chaplain
ROBERT BENNE	Assistant Professor of Church and Society
CARL E. BRAATEN	Associate Professor of Systematic Theology
THEODORE E. CONRAD	Professor of New Testament Language and Literature and Director of Admissions; Registrar
ROBERT H. FISCHER	Professor of Church History
DONALD C. FLATT	Professor of Anthropology and Africa Studies in the School of Missions
WESLEY J. FUERST	Associate Professor of Old Testament
DAVID M. GRANSKOU	Associate Professor of New Testament
GEORGE F. HALL	Associate Professor of Biblical Theology in the School of Missions
PHILIP J. HEFNER	Associate Professor of Systematic Theology
RALPH W. HOLMIN	Assistant Professor of Religious Education
HORACE HUMMEL	Associate Professor of Old Testament
AXEL C. KILDEGAARD	Professor of Functional Theology
JOHANNES KNUDSEN	Professor of Church History and New Testament and Dean of Graduate Studies
WALTER J. KUKKONEN	Professor of Systematic Theology
DAVID L. LINDBERG	Associate Professor of Missions and World Religions
WILHELM C. LINSS	Professor of New Testament
L. DALE LUND	Professor of Systematic Theology and Dean of the Faculty
JOEL W. LUNDEEN	Director of Library
MORRIS J. NIEDENTHAL	Associate Professor of Functional Theology
N. LEROY NORQUIST	Associate Professor of New Testament
JAMES A. SCHERER	Professor of Missions and Dean of School of Missions
FRANKLIN E. SHERMAN	Associate Professor of Christian Ethics
PAUL R. SWANSON	Associate Professor of Pastoral Care
THEODORE N. SWANSON	Associate Professor of Old Testament
RICHARD R. SYRE	Professor of Old Testament
ROBERT I. TOBIAS	Director of Continuing Education
ARTHUR VÖÖBUS	Professor of New Testament and Church History

EMERITI

HENRY GRADY DAVIS	Professor of Functional Theology (Maywood, 1937-1966)
GERHARD GIESCHEN	Professor of Systematic Theology (Fremont, 1951-1967) Acting President of Central Lutheran Theological Seminary
HJALMAR WILHELM JOHNSON	Professor of History and Philosophy of Religion (Rock Island, 1944-1964)
E. BRYAN KEISLER	Professor of Practical Theology (Fremont, 1949-1964) President of Central Lutheran Theological Seminary
ALVIN DANIEL MATTSON	Professor of Christian Ethics and Sociology (Rock Island, 1931-1964)
THOMAS D. RINDE	Professor of Historical Theology (Fremont, 1934-1964) Dean of Central Lutheran Theological Seminary
ERIC HERBERT WAHLSTROM	Professor of New Testament Language and Literature (Rock Island, 1931-1961)

1636 HARVARD UNIVERSITY
The Reverend James Gordon Gilkey, Jr., D.D.

1794 PITTSBURG THEOLOGICAL SEMINARY
The Reverend Marcus J. Priester, Th.D.

1812 PRINCETON THEOLOGICAL SEMINARY
The Reverend William J. Larkin, D.D.

1825 LANCASTER THEOLOGICAL SEMINARY
The Reverend Howard F. Boyer, A.B., B.D.

1826 LUTHERAN THEOLOGICAL SEMINARY AT GETTYSBURG
The Reverend O. Garfield Beckstrand, II, D.D.

1829 McCORMICK THEOLOGICAL SEMINARY
The Reverend Arthur R. McKay, Ph.D., D.D., LL.D., Litt.D.

1830 THE EVANGELICAL LUTHERAN THEOLOGICAL SEMINARY
The Reverend Edward C. Fendt, D.D., LL.D.

1830 LUTHERAN THEOLOGICAL SOUTHERN SEMINARY
The Reverend F. Eppling Reinartz, S.T.M., D.D., LL.D., L.M.D.

1832 GETTYSBURG COLLEGE
The Reverend Carl T. Uehling, A.B., B.D.

1834 HARTFORD THEOLOGICAL SEMINARY
The Reverend Charles R. Stinnette, Jr., Ph.D.

1836 UNION THEOLOGICAL SEMINARY
The Reverend Helen A. Archibald, M.A.

1839 CONCORDIA SEMINARY
The Reverend Alfred O. Fuerbringer, S.T.M., L.H.D., D.D.

1839 CONCORDIA SENIOR COLLEGE
The Reverend Martin J. Neeb, LL.D., L.H.D.

1842 ROANOKE COLLEGE
The Reverend H. Grady Davis, D.D.

1845 HAMMA SCHOOL OF THEOLOGY
The Reverend Martin Luther Stirewalt, Jr., Ph.D.

1845 MEADVILLE THEOLOGICAL SCHOOL OF LOMBARD COLLEGE
The Reverend Malcolm R. Sutherland, Jr., LL.D.

1845 WITTENBERG UNIVERSITY
The Reverend Michael C. D. McDaniel, A.B., B.D.

1846 CONCORDIA THEOLOGICAL SEMINARY
The Reverend Lorman M. Petersen, Ph.D.

1847 CARTHAGE COLLEGE
The Reverend Harold H. Lentz, Ph.D., LL.D.

1847 ROCKFORD COLLEGE
Mr. LeRoy Krizka, B.S.

1847 SAINT XAVIER COLLEGE
Sister Mary Olivia, Ph.D.

1848 MUHLENBERG COLLEGE
The Reverend Donald Pritz, B.A., B.D.

1850 NORTH AMERICAN BAPTIST SEMINARY
The Reverend G. K. Zimmerman, B.A., B.D.

1851 NORTHWESTERN UNIVERSITY
Mr. John H. Perkins, B.S.

1853 GARRETT THEOLOGICAL SEMINARY
The Reverend Orville H. McKay, Ph.D., D.D., D.S.T., LL.D.

1853 LOUISVILLE PRESBYTERIAN THEOLOGICAL SEMINARY
The Reverend Harold Walker, A.B., B.D.

1854 WARTBURG THEOLOGICAL SEMINARY
The Reverend William H. Weiblen, S.T.M., Th.D.

1855 CHICAGO THEOLOGICAL SEMINARY
The Reverend Edward F. Manthei, M.A., D.D.

1858 SEABURY-WESTERN THEOLOGICAL SEMINARY
The Reverend Charles U. Harris, D.D.

1858 SUSQUEHANNA UNIVERSITY
Mr. Amos Alonzo Stagg, Jr., Ph.B., M.A.

1860 AUGUSTANA COLLEGE
Mr. C. W. Sorensen, Ph.D., L.H.D.

1860 WHEATON COLLEGE
The Reverend Merrill C. Tenney, Ph.D.

1861 NORTH CENTRAL COLLEGE
The Reverend Jacob Sackmann, Ph.D.

1862 GUSTAVUS ADOLPHUS COLLEGE
The Reverend Robert Esbjornson, M.A.

1864 CONCORDIA TEACHERS COLLEGE
The Reverend Ralph D. Gerke, Ph.D.

1864 LUTHERAN THEOLOGICAL SEMINARY AT PHILADELPHIA, PA.
The Reverend John M. Kalny, B.A., B.D.

1865 VIRGINIA UNION UNIVERSITY
The Reverend Kenneth B. Smith, A.B., B.D.

1866 THE DIVINITY SCHOOL, THE UNIVERSITY OF CHICAGO
The Reverend Jerald C. Brauer, Ph.D., D.D., LL.D., S.T.D., L.H.D.

1866 WESTERN THEOLOGICAL SEMINARY
The Reverend Herman J. Ridder, Th.M., D.D.

1867 CROZER THEOLOGICAL SEMINARY
The Reverend Ronald V. Wells, Ph.D .

1869 CHICAGO STATE COLLEGE
Mr. Warren Strandberg, Ph.D.

1869 LUTHER THEOLOGICAL SEMINARY
The Reverend Kent S. Knutson, Ph.D.

1870 LOYOLA UNIVERSITY
The Reverend Joseph J. DeVault, S.J., Ph.D., S.S.L.

1871 BERKELEY BAPTIST DIVINITY SCHOOL
The Reverend John Nastari, B.D.

1871 SAN FRANCISCO THEOLOGICAL SEMINARY
The Reverend Arthur C. Johnson, M.A.

1871 UNITED THEOLOGICAL SEMINARY
The Reverend George E. Jacobs, A.B., B.D.

1873 EVANGELICAL THEOLOGICAL SEMINARY
The Reverend Wayne K. Clymer, Ph.D.

1874 ANDREWS UNIVERSITY
The Reverend William G. C. Murdoch, Ph.D.

1874 ST. OLAF COLLEGE
The Reverend Ansgar Sovik, S.T.D.

1883 MIDLAND LUTHERAN COLLEGE
The Reverend Paul M. deFreese, D.D.

1884 DANA COLLEGE
The Reverend Arne K. Jessen, M.Th.

1885 SCHOOL OF THEOLOGY AT CLAREMONT
The Reverend Richard S .Ford, Ph.D.

1890 GEORGE WILLIAMS COLLEGE
The Reverend John W. Dubocq, M.A.

1890 PACIFIC LUTHERAN UNIVERSITY
The Reverend Fredric M. Norstad, M.Th., D.D.

1891 LENOIR RHYNE COLLEGE
Mr. Robert V. Mauney, M.B.A.

1891 NORTH PARK THEOLOGICAL SEMINARY
The Reverend Sigurd F. Westberg, M.A.

1891 UNIVERSITY OF CHICAGO
Mr. George W. Beadle, Ph.D., D.Sci., LL.D.

1892 ILLINOIS INSTITUTE OF TECHNOLOGY
Mr. Marion H. Groves, Ph.D.

1893 CHURCH DIVINITY SCHOOL OF THE PACIFIC
The Reverend John W. Pyle, D.D.

1893 CONCORDIA COLLEGE
The Reverend Paul A. Lassanske, Ph.D.

1893 UPSALA COLLEGE
The Reverend O. V. Anderson, S.T.M., D.D.

1896 SUOMI COLLEGE
The Reverend Robert E. Schlichter, B.A., B.D.

1898 DePAUL UNIVERSITY
The Reverend Hugo Amico, O.S.B., D.Th., D.C.L.

1900 NEW YORK THEOLOGICAL SEMINARY
The Reverend Homer K. Shafer, B.A., B.D.

1901 CENTRAL BAPTIST THEOLOGICAL SEMINARY
The Reverend Robert G. Middleton, D.D.

1901 DIVINE WORD SEMINARY
The Reverend John J. Bukovsky, S.V.D., S.T.L., S.S.L.

1911 WATERLOO LUTHERAN UNIVERSITY
The Reverend J. Ray Houser, D.D.

1913 NORTHERN BAPTIST THEOLOGICAL SEMINARY
The Reverend D. George Vanderlip, Ph.D.

1920 NORTHWESTERN LUTHERAN THEOLOGICAL SEMINARY
The Reverend Dorris A. Flesner, Ph.D.

1924 CHRISTIAN THEOLOGICAL SEMINARY
The Reverend Beauford A. Norris, Ph.D., LL.D.

1930 MUNDELEIN COLLEGE
Sister Ann Ida Gannon, B.V.M., Ph.D.

1939 AQUINAS INSTITUTE OF PHILOSOPHY AND THEOLOGY
The Reverend Benedict M. Ashley, O.P., Ph.D.

1945 MENNONITE BIBLICAL SEMINARY
The Reverend Erland Waltner, Th.D.

1945 ROOSEVELT UNIVERSITY
Mr. George H. Watson, Ph.D.

1946 CALIFORNIA BAPTIST THEOLOGICAL SEMINARY
The Reverend Leland D. Hine, Ph.D.

1950 PACIFIC LUTHERAN THEOLOGICAL SEMINARY
The Reverend Harry J. Mumm, Ph.D.

1967 GOLDEN VALLEY LUTHERAN COLLEGE
The Reverend Bernt C. Opsal, B.A., B.Th., M.A.

Representatives from The Church

THE BOARD OF THEOLOGICAL EDUCATION,
LUTHERAN CHURCH IN AMERICA
The Reverend E. Theodore Bachmann, Ph.D., D.D., D.Sc.Ed.

THE BOARD OF WORLD MISSIONS, LUTHERAN CHURCH IN AMERICA
The Reverend Earl S. Erb, D.D.
The Reverend Arne Sovik, Ph.D.

THE BOARD OF COLLEGE EDUCATION AND CHURCH VOCATIONS,
LUTHERAN CHURCH IN AMERICA
The Reverend Louis T. Almen, Ph.D.
The Reverend Paul L. Roth, D.D.

THE SOUTH CHICAGOLAND DISTRICT, THE ILLINOIS SYNOD (L.C.A.)
The Reverend Robbin W. Skyles, III, Ph.B., B.D.

THE LUTHERAN COUNCIL OF GREATER CHICAGO
Mr. Clifford E. Dahlin, B.A.

THE CHURCH FEDERATION OF GREATER CHICAGO
The Reverend William Barnett Blakemore, Ph.D.
Dean, Disciples Divinity House, The University of Chicago

THE AMERICAN LUTHERAN CHURCH,
SOUTH CHICAGO CONFERENCE
The Reverend Donald M. Weber, A.B., B.D.

THE CHICAGO BAPTIST ASSOCIATION
The Reverend Richard R. Haworth, B.A., B.D.

THE GREEK ORTHODOX ARCHDIOCESE
OF NORTH AND SOUTH AMERICA
The Reverend Theodore Thalassinos, B.A., B.D.

THE EPISCOPAL DIOCESE OF CHICAGO
The Reverend John W. Pyle, D.D.

THE EVANGELICAL COVENANT CHURCH OF AMERICA
The Reverend Sigurd F. Westberg, M.A.

THE LUTHERAN CHURCH—MISSOURI SYNOD,
NORTHERN ILLINOIS DISTRICT
The Reverend Theodore Bornemann, A.B., B.D.

THE UNION OF AMERICAN HEBREW CONGREGATIONS
Rabbi Robert J. Marx, Ph.D.

THE UNITED CHURCH OF CHRIST, NORTHEAST ASSOCIATION
The Reverend Harold F. Dobstaff, A.B., B.D.

Representatives from Other Organizations

THE AMERICAN ASSOCIATION OF THEOLOGICAL SCHOOLS
The Reverend Jesse H. Ziegler, Ph.D.

THE NORTH AMERICAN ACADEMY OF ECUMENISTS
The Reverend William G. Topmoeller, S.J., S.T.D.

THE SOCIETY OF BIBLICAL LITERATURE
The Reverend Paul Schubert, Dr.phil., Ph.D.

THE AMERICAN SOCIETY OF CHURCH HISTORY
The Reverend Robert M. Grant, Th.D.

THE LUTHERAN HISTORICAL CONFERENCE
The Reverend Dorris A. Flesner, Ph.D.

ALL PERSONS ATTENDING THE DEDICATION ARE INVITED
TO PARTICIPATE IN THE RECEPTION IMMEDIATELY FOLLOWING.

ARCHITECT

THE PERKINS AND WILL PARTNERSHIP – ARCHITECTS

Wilmont Vickrey, Partner in charge of project
James L. Caron, Architect in charge of project
Raymond C. Ovresat, Architect in charge of design
Jim K. Maeda, Architect in charge of contract documents

BUILDER

THE JAMES McHUGH CONSTRUCTION COMPANY, Chicago, Illinois

The Lutheran School of Theology at Chicago expresses its deep appreciation to the many individuals and groups whose gifts have made this Dedication Day possible; and, to the Reverend Professor G. Everett Arden who prepared the Service and Rite of Dedication.

Appendix II

ARTICLES OF CONSOLIDATION

Certificate Number   67

STATE OF ILLINOIS

OFFICE OF
THE SECRETARY OF STATE

To all to whom these Presents Shall Come, Greeting:

Whereas, Articles of _Consolidation_ duly signed and verified of

AUGUSTANA THEOLOGICAL SEMINARY AND THE THEOLOGICAL SEMINARY OF THE
EVANGELICAL LUTHERAN CHURCH AT CHICAGO, ILLINOIS, Illinois corporations, and SUOMI LUTHERAN THEOLOGICAL SEMINARY, a Michigan corporation, consolidated into LUTHERAN SCHOOL OF THEOLOGY AT CHICAGO, an
Illinois corporation

have been filed in the Office of the Secretary of State on the ___4th___
day of ___September___ A. D. 19_62_, as provided by the GENERAL NOT
FOR PROFIT CORPORATION ACT of Illinois, approved July 17, 1943 in force
January 1, A. D. 1944.

Now Therefore, I, ~~EDWARD J. HUGHES~~ CHARLES F. CARPENTIER Secretary of State of the State of Illinois,
by virtue of the powers vested in me by law, do hereby issue this Certificate
of ___Consolidation___ and attach thereto a copy of the Articles of
___Consolidation___ of the aforesaid corporations.

In Testimony Whereof, I hereto set my hand and cause to
be affixed the Great Seal of the State of Illinois.
Done at the City of Springfield this ___4th___
day of ___September___ AD 19_62_ and
of the Independence of the United States
the one hundred and ___87th.___

(SEAL)

Charles F. Carpentier
SECRETARY OF STATE

200

ARTICLES OF CONSOLIDATION

OF DOMESTIC AND FOREIGN

CORPORATIONS

Date Paid *9-4-62*
Filing Fee $ *10 -*
Clerk

2609 16

To CHARLES F. CARPENTIER, Secretary of State,

The undersigned corporations, pursuant to Section 42a
of the General Not For Profit Corporation Act of the State of
Illinois, hereby execute the following articles of consolidation:

ARTICLE ONE

The names of the corporations proposing to consolidate
and the names of the States under the laws of which such corporations are organized, are as follows:

Name of Corporation	State of Incorporation
Augustana Theological Seminary	Illinois
The Theological Seminary of the Evangelical Lutheran Church at Chicago, Illinois	Illinois
Suomi Lutheran Theological Seminary	Michigan

ARTICLE TWO

The laws of Michigan, the State under which such foreign
corporation is organized, permit such consolidation.

ARTICLE THREE

The name of the new corporation shall be LUTHERAN SCHOOL
OF THEOLOGY AT CHICAGO, and it shall be governed by the laws of
the State of Illinois.

ARTICLE FOUR

The plan of consolidation is as follows:

PAID
SEP - 4 1962

201

PLAN OF CONSOLIDATION

The Parties of this Plan of Consolidation are:

Augustana Theological Seminary, an Illinois Corporation and herein sometimes referred to as "Augustana Seminary";

The Theological Seminary of the Evangelical Lutheran Church at Chicago, Illinois, an Illinois Corporation and herein sometimes referred to as "Maywood Seminary"; and

Suomi Lutheran Theological Seminary, a Michigan Corporation and herein sometimes referred to as "Suomi Seminary,"

WITNESSETH:

1--WHEREAS, each of the parties hereto is a non-profit corporation incorporated for the purpose of educating persons for the Christian ministry and other specific Christian service, and owns and is possessed of a theological seminary and of assets, real and personal; and

2--WHEREAS, each of the parties hereto is supported by one or more synods as follows:

a--Augustana Seminary by Augustana Evangelical Lutheran Church, a Minnesota Corporation, formerly known as Augustana Synod, and herein sometimes referred to as "Augustana Synod;"

b--Maywood Seminary by the Illinois Synod of the United Lutheran Church in America, an Illinois Corporation and herein sometimes referred to as "Illinois Synod," the Wartburg Synod of the United Lutheran Church in America, an Illinois Corporation and herein sometimes referred to as "Wartburg Synod," the Michigan Synod of the United Lutheran Church in America, a Michigan Corporation and herein sometimes referred to as "Michigan Synod," the Indiana Synod of the United Lutheran Church in America, an Indiana Corporation and herein sometimes referred to as "Indiana Synod," and the Pittsburgh Synod of the Evangelical Lutheran Church, a Pennsylvania Corporation and herein sometimes referred to as the "Pittsburgh Synod;"

c--Suomi Seminary by the Finnish Evangelical Lutheran Church of America--Suomi Synod, a Michigan Corporation and herein sometimes referred to as the "Suomi Synod;"

The delegates from time to time to the respective synod or synods aforementioned supporting each party hereto, constitute the members having voting rights of each such party, as that term is used in the Illinois statute hereinafter mentioned.

3--WHEREAS, the American Evangelical Lutheran Church, an Iowa Corporation and herein sometimes referred to as "A.E.L.C.," The United Lutheran Church in America, a New York Corporation and herein sometimes referred to as "U.L.C.A." and the aforementioned Augustana

202

Synod and Suomi Synod, are now engaged in consolidation proceedings under the laws of the State of Minnesota for the purpose of
consolidating said four corporations into a new corporation as a
Minnesota Corporation under the name of Lutheran Church in America;
and the aforementioned Illinois Synod, Wartburg Synod, Michigan
Synod, Indiana Synod and Pittsburgh Synod are synods within the
said U.L.C.A., which is a national church body; and

4--WHEREAS, it is the desire of the parties hereto that they
be consolidated into a new non-profit corporation under and in
accordance with the General Not for Profit Corporation Act of the
State of Illinois and as may be permitted by the statutes of the
State of Michigan in such case made and provided.

5--THE PARTIES HERETO HEREBY AGREE to consolidate into a new
corporation under and in accordance with the General Not for Profit
Corporation Act of the State of Illinois, upon the following terms,
conditions and provisions, namely:

6--The name of the new Corporation is LUTHERAN SCHOOL OF
THEOLOGY AT CHICAGO.

7--The period of duration of the New Corporation is perpetual.

8--The address of the Initial Registered Office of the New
Corporation in the State of Illinois is: 105 West Adams Street,
in the City of Chicago, County of Cook, and the name of its initial
Registered Agent at said address is: A. HOWARD WEEG.

9--The purpose or purposes for which the new Corporation is
organized are to establish and maintain a theological seminary in
the State of Illinois.

10--The new Corporation shall not permanently establish or maintain
its theological seminary, or any part thereof, on or near any site
now owned or used by any of the parties hereto as and for a seminary,
except that on a temporary basis only the new Corporation may conduct its operation on the present sites of Augustana Seminary and
Maywood Seminary until it has established a seminary elsewhere.

11--The voting rights of the members of the new Corporation
shall be established, determined and regularized by the constitution
of the new Corporation.

12--The number, election, terms of office and qualifications
of the directors of the new Corporation shall be fixed by the constitution of the new Corporation, except that the number of directors of the initial board of directors shall be eighteen and they
shall be elected prior to the execution of the Articles of Consolidation, in the following manner:

A) Seven by the board of directors of Augustana Seminary,
Seven by the board of directors of Maywood Seminary,
Two by the board of directors of Suomi Seminary, and
Two by the board of directors of Grand View College and
Grand View Seminary, an Iowa Corporation.

B) The directors so elected shall be named in said Articles
of Consolidation as constituting the initial board of directors
of the new Corporation.

13--This Plan of Consolidation shall be adopted in the following manner: The board of directors of each of the parties hereto
shall adopt a resolution approving this Plan of Consolidation and
directing that it be submitted to a vote at the 1961 annual convention of the synod or each of the synods whose members have the
voting rights of such respective party. Such synod or synods are
named in Paragraph 2 hereof. Each such convention shall be called
and notice thereof shall be given to each delegate entitled to
vote at each such meeting within the time and in the manner provided in the statutes of Illinois or Michigan in such case made
and provided. This Plan of Consolidation shall be and constitute
the plan adopted for the corporate consolidation of Augustana
Seminary, Maywood Seminary and Suomi Seminary, upon receiving at
the 1961 annual conventions aforementioned, the affirmative vote
of at least two-thirds (a) of the total number of delegates to
such convention of the Suomi Synod and (b) of the votes entitled
to be cast by members present or represented by proxy at each such
convention of the other six synods named in paragraph 2 hereof.

14--When the Consolidation has been effected, the new Corporation by virtue of the statutes of Illinois and Michigan in such
case made and provided, succeeds to all the property and liabilities
of the Consolidating Corporations by operation of law or otherwise.
Grand View College and Grand View Seminary, an Iowa Corporation,
shall be deemed to have approved and accepted the provisions of this
Plan of Consolidation when with the authorization therefore by A.E.L.C.
it has transferred and conveyed to the new Corporation, all property,
real and personal, which it holds for the use and benefit of the
Grand View Seminary. The property acquired by the new Corporation
by virtue of the consolidation and as herein provided, shall be
devoted by the new Corporation for the establishment and maintenance
of a new seminary in accordance with this Plan of Consolidation and
provisions of the Articles of Consolidation.

15--The procedure for consolidation hereunder shall be so timed
that the consolidation shall become effective on September 1, 1962
or as soon thereafter as shall be reasonably possible.

16--The new Corporation shall consolidate institutionally into
one new united seminary the four institutions commonly known as:

a) Augustana Seminary of Rock Island, Illinois

b) Maywood Seminary of Maywood, Illinois

c) Suomi Seminary now affiliated with the said
Maywood Seminary

d) Grand View Seminary now affiliated with the said
Maywood Seminary.

ARTICLE FIVE

As to each corporation, the Board of Directors, by majority vote, passed a resolution adopting the foregoing Plan of Consolidation on the date set forth after the name of each corporation, respectively, directing that the Plan of Consolidation be submitted to a vote at the 1961 annual convention of the synod or each of the synods whose members have the voting rights of each such respective party:

Name of Corporation	Date of Board of Directors Meeting
Augustana Theological Seminary	May 26, 1961
The Theological Seminary of the Evangelical Lutheran Church at Chicago, Illinois	April 26, 1961
Suomi Lutheran Theological Seminary	April 12, 1961

ARTICLE SIX

As to each corporation, the said Plan of Consolidation was then presented to the 1961 annual conventions of the synod or synods having the voting rights thereof, and as to each corporation, the Plan of Consolidation was adopted by the affirmative vote of at least two-thirds of the total number of delegates to such convention of the Suomi Synod (said delegates being the persons having voting rights in Suomi Lutheran Theological Seminary), and by the affirmative vote of at least two-thirds of the votes entitled to be cast by members present or represented by proxy at each of such conventions of each of the other synods having voting rights as to each of the other corporations who are parties to these Articles of Consolidation. The name of each Synod whose delegates or members have voting rights for each corporation party to this Consolidation, and the date of the meeting of each such Synod are set forth below. There was a quorum present at each such convention.

Name of Synod	Date of Meeting
As to Augustana Theological Seminary:	
Augustana Evangelical Lutheran Church	June 13, 1961
As to The Theological Seminary of the	
Evangelical Lutheran Church at Chicago,	
Illinois:	
Illinois Synod	May 15, 1961
Wartburg Synod	May 17, 1961
Michigan Synod	May 16, 1961
Indiana Synod	May 8, 1961
Pittsburgh Synod	June 6, 1961
As to Suomi Lutheran Theological	
Seminary:	
Finnish Evangelical Lutheran Church	
of America--Suomi Synod	June 26, 1961.

ARTICLE SEVEN

All provisions of the laws of the State of Illinois and the State of Michigan applicable to the proposed consolidation have been complied with.

ARTICLE EIGHT

The purpose or purposes for which this Corporation is organized are to establish and maintain a theological seminary in the State of Illinois.

ARTICLE NINE

The period of duration of the Corporation is: Perpetual

ARTICLE TEN

The first Board of Directors shall be eighteen in number, their names and addresses being as follows:

    Rev. Dr. Richard B. Pearson,
      235 Weston Street, Waltham 54, Massachusetts

    Rev. Dr. Malvin H. Lundeen,
      2445 Park Avenue, Minneapolis 4, Minnesota

    Rev. Dr. O. V. Anderson,
      327 South LaSalle Street, Chicago 4, Illinois

    Rev. Harold Skillrud,
      1617 E. Emerson Street, Bloomington, Illinois

Dr. Kermit Almos,
4137 Forest Avenue, Western Springs, Illinois

Rev. Philip Nelson,
309 S. Catherine Street, Bay City, Michigan

Dr. Gustaf A. Peterson,
5201 Pepin Place, Madison, Wisconsin

Mr. Harold H. Jordan,
100 East Chicago Avenue, Elgin, Illinois

Mr. Carl L. Bergendoff,
DuPage Trust Company, Glen Ellyn, Illinois

The Rev. Luther C. Mueller, D.D.,
Box 187, Harvard, Illinois

The Rev. Frank P. Madsen, D.D.,
20954 Grand River Avenue, Detroit 19, Michigan

The Rev. A. Howard Weeg, D.D.,
105 West Adams Street, Chicago 2, Illinois

The Rev. Walter M. Wick, D.D.,
445 N. Pennsylvania Street, Indianapolis 4, Indiana

Mr. Fred Drinhaus,
1540 Eastwood Avenue, Highland Park, Illinois

Pastor Thomas Asuma,
Marquette, Michigan

Mr. V. Richard Hietikko
DeKalb, Illinois

Mr. Harry S. Andersen,
8500 Maryland Avenue, Chicago 19, Illinois

Mr. Harry Gjelsteen,
218 First Avenue, Menominee, Michigan.

ARTICLE ELEVEN

That the said Directors hereinabove named as the first Board

of Directors were elected as required by the Plan of Consolidation,

as follows:

By the Board of Directors of Augustana Seminary:

Rev. Dr. Richard B. Pearson,
Rev. Dr. Malvin H. Lundeen,
Rev. Dr. O. V. Anderson,
Rev. Harold Skillrud,
Dr. Kermit Almos,
Rev. Philip Nelson,
Dr. Gustaf A. Peterson,

Articles of Consolidation

By the Board of Directors of Maywood Seminary:

    Mr. Harold H. Jordan,
    Mr. Carl L. Bergendoff,
    The Rev. Luther C. Mueller, D.D.,
    The Rev. Frank P. Madsen, D.D.,
    The Rev. A. Howard Weeg, D.D.,
    The Rev. Walter M. Wick, D.D.,
    Mr. Fred Drinhaus,

By the Board of Directors of Suomi Synod:

    Pastor Thomas Asuma,
    Mr. V. Richard Hietikko,

By the Board of Directors of Grand View College and
Grand View Seminary:

    Mr. Harry S. Andersen,
    Mr. Harry Gjelsteen.

ARTICLE TWELVE

The address of the initial REGISTERED OFFICE is: 105 West
Adams Street in the City of Chicago, County of Cook; and the name
of its initial REGISTERED AGENT at said address is: A. HOWARD WEEG.

ARTICLE THIRTEEN

The voting rights of the members of the new Corporation shall
be established, determined and regularized by the constitution of
the new Corporation.

IN WITNESS WHEREOF, AUGUSTANA THEOLOGICAL SEMINARY has caused
its corporate seal to be hereunto affixed and these presents to be
signed by the Chairman of its Board of Directors and attested by
the Secretary of said Board, and THE THEOLOGICAL SEMINARY OF THE
EVANGELICAL LUTHERAN CHURCH AT CHICAGO, ILLINOIS, has caused its
corporate seal to be hereunto affixed and these presents to be
signed by the Chairman of its Board of Directors and attested by
the Secretary of said Board, and SUOMI LUTHERAN THEOLOGICAL SEMINARY
has caused its corporate seal to be hereunto affixed and these presents to be signed by the majority of its Board of Directors and by
the Chairman of its Board of Directors and attested by the Secretary
of said Board, all on the _____9th_____ day of _____July_____, 1962.

Articles of Consolidation

AUGUSTANA THEOLOGICAL SEMINARY

Affix

Corporate Seal

Here

By _[signature]_
Chairman of the Board of Directors

ATTEST:
[signature]
Secretary of the Board of Directors

THE THEOLOGICAL SEMINARY OF THE EVAN-
GELICAL LUTHERAN CHURCH AT CHICAGO,
ILLINOIS

Affix
Corporate Seal
Here

By _[signature]_
Chairman of the Board of Directors

ATTEST:
[signature]
Secretary of the Board of Directors

SUOMI LUTHERAN THEOLOGICAL SEMINARY

By _[signatures]_

A Majority of the Directors of
the Board of Directors

[signature]
Chairman of the Board of Directors

Affix
Corporate Seal
Here

ATTEST:
[signature]
Secretary of the Board of Directors

209

Articles of Consolidation

I, _Lloyd E. Anthony_ , a Notary Public, do hereby certify that on the _9th_ day of _July_ , A.D. 1962, personally appeared before me _Richard B. Pearson_ , who declares that he is the Chairman of the Board of Directors of Augustana Theological Seminary, one of the corporations executing the foregoing documents, and being first duly sworn, acknowledged that he signed the foregoing Articles of Consolidation in the capacity therein set forth and declared that the statements therein contained are true.

IN WITNESS WHEREOF, I have hereunto set my hand and seal the day and year before written.

Affix
Notarial Seal
Here

_____
Notary Public

My Commission expires: _8-2-65_

210

Articles of Consolidation

STATE OF____ILLINOIS____)
) SS:
COUNTY OF __K A N E_____)

    I, ____Esther A. Palm_____, a Notary Public, do
hereby certify that on the ____12th__ day of ____July____,A.D.
1962, personally appeared before me ____HAROLD H. JORDAN____,
who declares that he is the Chairman of the Board of Directors
of The Theological Seminary of the Evangelical Lutheran Church
at Chicago, Illinois, one of the corporations executing the foregoing documents, and being first duly sworn, acknowledged that
he signed the foregoing Articles of Consolidation in the capacity
therein set forth and declared that the statements therein contained are true.

    IN WITNESS WHEREOF, I have hereunto set my hand and seal
the day and year before written.

    Affix
Notarial Seal
    Here
                        Notary Public

    My Commission Expires: __February 14, 1965__

Articles of Consolidation

   I, <u>   Bernice K. Johnson   </u>, a Notary Public, do
hereby certify that on the <u> 15th </u> day of <u>   August   </u>, A. D.
1962, personally appeared before me <u>Martin F. Saarinen   </u>
who declares that he is the Chairman of the Board of Directors
of Suomi Lutheran Theological Seminary, one of the corporations
executing the foregoing documents, and being first duly sworn,
acknowledges that he signed the foregoing Articles of Consolidation
in the capacity therein set forth, and declared that the statements
therein contained are true, and that the foregoing signatures by
Directors of Suomi Lutheran Theological Seminary constitute the
signatures of a majority of the Directors of the Board of Directors of Suomi Lutheran Theological Seminary.

   IN WITNESS WHEREOF, I have hereunto set my hand and seal the
day and year before written.

      Affix
   Notarial Seal   _Bernice K. Johnson_
      Here   Notary Public
                                      Bernice K. Johnson
                      My Commission Expires: <u>Dec. 23, 1963</u>

212

Appendix III

INTER-SEMINARY COMMITTEE

Inter-Seminary Committee	Term Began	Term Expired	No. of Meetings Attended				
			1958	1959	1960	1961	1962

I Augustana Theological Seminary
  Representatives
  A. Regular Members

	Term Began	Term Expired	1958	1959	1960	1961	1962
1. the Rev. Dr. G. E. Arden	1961	1962				1	2
2. the Rev. Dr. Arthur O. Arnold	1958	1962	4	4	3	5	2
3. the Rev. Dr. Oscar A. Benson	1959	1962		1	1	0	0
4. the Rev. Dr. O. O. Gustafson	1958	1958	1				
5. the Rev. Clarence Hall	1959	1962		3	4	4	2
6. the Rev. Dr. Arthur O. Hjelm	1958	1958	1				
7. Mr. Tage Joranson	1960	1960			2		
8. the Rev. Ralph Lindquist	1960	1962			4	4	2
9. the Rev. Dr. Malvin H. Lundeen	1960	1962			1	3	1
10. the Rev. Dr. Karl E. Mattson	1958	1962	4	5	4	5	2
11. the Rev. Dr. Richard B. Pearson	1960	1962			3	4	2
12. Mr. Lloyd A. Schwiebert	1958	1959	4	2			
13. the Rev. Dr. D. Verner Swanson	1958	1959	3	1			
14. the Rev. Dr. Eric H. Wahlstrom	1958	1961	2	4	2	3	
15. the Rev. Dr. Granger Westberg	1958	1961	2	5	3	4	

  B. Alternate Members

	Term Began	Term Expired	1958	1959	1960	1961	1962
1. the Rev. Dr. Arnold E. Carlson (for Dr. Arthur O. Arnold)	1959	1959		1			
2. the Rev. Dr. A. D. Mattson (for Dr. Robert Mortvedt)	1958	1958	1				
3. Mr. O. W. Olson (for Dr. Arthur O. Hjelm)	1958	1958	1				
4. the Rev. Dr. Richard B. Pearson for Mr. Lloyd Schwiebert)	1959	1959		1			

  C. Advisory Members

	Term Began	Term Expired	1958	1959	1960	1961	1962
1. the Rev. Dr. O. V. Anderson	1959	1962		3	4	4	2
2. the Rev. Dr. P. O. Bersell	1959	1959		1			
3. Mr. Tage Joranson	1960	1962			0	0	0

  D. Board of Christian Higher
     Education—Augustana Lutheran
     Church (1960f. also ULCA)

	Term Began	Term Expired	1958	1959	1960	1961	1962
1. Dr. Robert Mortvedt	1958	1962	3	4	4	5	2

  E. Augustana Lutheran Church
     Representatives on Initial
     LSTC Board of Directors

	Term Began	Term Expired	1958	1959	1960	1961	1962
1. Dr. Kermit Almos	1961	1962				1	1
2. the Rev. Dr. O. V. Anderson	1961	1962				1	2
3. Mr. Paul Kotila	1961	1962				0	0

Inter-Seminary Committee	Term Began	Term Expired	No. of Meetings Attended				
			1958	1959	1960	1961	1962
4. the Rev. Dr. Malvin H. Lundeen	1961	1962				0	1
5. the Rev. Philip A. Nelson	1961	1962				1	2
6. the Rev. Dr. Richard B. Pearson	1961	1962				0	2
7. the Rev. Harold C. Skillrud	1961	1962				1	2
II Grand View Theological Seminary Representatives							
A. Regular Members							
1. the Rev. Dr. A. E. Farstrup	1961	1962				4	1
2. the Rev. Dr. Alfred Jensen	1958	1958	2				
3. the Rev. Axel Kildegaard	1958	1962	3	0	4	5	2
B. American Evangelical Lutheran Church Representatives on Initial LSTC Board of Directors							
1. the Rev. Harry Anderson	1961	1962				0	2
2. Mr. Harry Gjelsteen	1961	1962				0	1
III Suomi Lutheran Theological Seminary Representatives							
A. Regular Members							
1. the Rev. Karlo J. Keljo	1958	1961	2	3	1	1	
2. the Rev. Dr. Walter Kukkonen	1958	1962	1	3	4	4	2
3. the Rev. Dr. Raymond Wargelin	1960	1962			1	3	0
B. Advisory Members							
1. the Rev. Thomas V. Asuma	1961	1961				1	
2. the Rev. Evert E. Torkko	1961	1961				1	
C. Finnish Evangelical Lutheran Church of America Representatives on Initial LSTC Board of Directors							
1. the Rev. Thomas V. Asuma	1961	1962				1	0
2. Mr. V. Richard Hietikko	1961	1962				1	0
IV Theological Seminary of the Ev. Lutheran Church at Chicago, Ill. Representatives							
A. Regular Members							
1. the Rev. Dr. R. R. Belter	1958	1962	1	0	0	0	0
2. the Rev. Lyman Grimes	1958	1960	4	5	1		
3. the Rev. Dr. Donald Heiges	1960	1962			2	5	1
4. Mr. Harold Jordan	1960	1962			1	3	1
5. the Rev. Dr. Johannes Knudsen	1958	1960	4	5	2		
6. the Rev. Dr. Frank P. Madsen	1958	1962	3	5	4	4	1
7. the Rev. Dr. Luther Mueller	1960	1962			2	4	2
8. the Rev. Alfred Stone	1958	1959	3	2			

Inter-Seminary Committee	Term Began	Term Expired	No. of Meetings Attended 1958	1959	1960	1961	1962
9. the Rev. Dr. A. Howard Weeg	1958	1962	3	3	4	5	2
10. the Rev. Dr. Armin G. Weng	1958	1962	3	5	4	5	0
11. the Rev. Dr. Walter Wick	1958	1962	3	4	3	3	2
B. Alternate Members							
1. the Rev. Dr. Johannes Knudsen	1962	1962					1
(for Dr. Donald Heiges)							
2. Mr. Alfred J. Pfenner	1962	1962					1
(for Dr. Armin G. Weng)							
3. the Rev. Alden L. Salstrom	1960	1962			3	4	1
(Permanent Alternate)							
4. the Rev. Andrew Swasko	1961	1961				1	
(for Dr. R. R. Belter)							
C. Graduate School							
1. the Rev. Dr. Johannes Knudsen	1962	1962					1
D. School of Missions							
1. the Rev. Dr. James A. Scherer	1960	1962			1	1	1
E. School of Missions—Alternate							
1. the Rev. Donald Flatt	1962	1962					1
F. Board of World Missions ULCA							
1. the Rev. Dr. Earl S. Erb	1962	1962					1
2. the Rev. Dr. Arthur L. Ruths	1961	1961				1	
G. Board of Christian Higher Education—ULCA							
1. the Rev. Dr. Gould Wickey	1958	1959	4	3			
H. Associate Secretary for Theological Education—ULCA							
1. the Rev. Dr. E. Theodore Bachmann	1961	1962				2	2
I. United Lutheran Church in America Representatives on Initial LSTC Board of Directors							
1. Mr. Carl Bergendoff	1961	1962				0	2
2. Mr. Fred Drinhaus	1961	1962				0	2
3. Mr. Harold Jordan	1961	1962				1	1
4. the Rev. Dr. Frank P. Madsen	1961	1962				1	1
5. the Rev. Dr. Luther Mueller	1961	1962				1	2
6. the Rev. Dr. A. Howard Weeg	1961	1962				1	2
7. the Rev. Dr. Walter M. Wick	1961	1962				0	2

V Special Consultants
  A. Joint Commission on Lutheran Unity
    1. the Rev. Dr. Malvin H. Lundeen, Chairman — 1

Inter-Seminary Committee	Term Began	Term Expired	No. of Meetings Attended 1958	1959	1960	1961	1962
B. JCLU Committee on Seminaries							
1. the Rev. Dr. Oscar Benson, Chairman 1956-1960 (Augustana)				1	1		
2. the Rev. Dr. P. O. Bersell, Chairman 1961-1962 (Augustana)						2	1
3. the Rev. Dr. Franklin Clark Fry (ULCA)				1		1	
4. the Rev. Dr. Ralph Jalkanen (Suomi)							
5. the Rev. Ronald Jespersen (AELC)				2			
C. Hamma Divinity School							
1. the Rev. Dr. Donald Elder				3			
D. Northwestern Theological Seminary							
1. the Rev. Ingoll B. Kindem					1		
2. the Rev. Dr. C. H. Zeidler					1		
E. Northwest Synod—ULCA							
1. the Rev. Dr. Charles A. Puls						1	
F. Proposed Wisconsin-Upper Michigan Synod—LCA							
1. the Rev. Robert B. Anderson							1
2. the Rev. D. C. Kalweit							1
G. Inter-Seminary Committee's Committee on Special Programs— Consultants							
1. the Rev. Giles Ekola							1
2. the Rev. Dr. Walter Kloetzli							1

Appendix IV

LSTC OFFICIAL DOCUMENTS

OFFICIAL DOCUMENTS

of the

LUTHERAN SCHOOL

OF THEOLOGY

at

Chicago

Summary of Agreements

The Constitution

The Plan of Consolidation

Necessary Actions by boards, churches and synods

Consolidation of Seminaries

I.

SUMMARY OF AGREEMENTS

Following is a summary of agreements prepared by the Inter-Seminary Committee of Augustana Theological Seminary, Grand View Theological Seminary, Suomi Lutheran Theological Seminary and the Theological Seminary of the Evangelical Lutheran Church at Chicago, Illinois, presented to the boards of the various seminaries and the supporting churches or synods for adoption.

PREAMBLE

Merger negotiations in the Joint Commission on Lutheran Unity have been in progress since December, 1956, with the following churches participating: The Augustana Evangelical Lutheran Church, The American Evangelical Lutheran Church, The Finnish Evangelical Lutheran Church of America, and The United Lutheran Church in America. These negotiations, God willing, will result in the formation of the Lutheran Church in America, which will begin corporate existence in June, 1962.

According to the table of provisional alignments of synods and seminaries for the first biennium of the new church to be submitted for approval to the constituting convention of the Lutheran Church in America, the four seminaries here represented, located in the same geographical area, will be owned and operated by the same assigned synods of the new church. This fact prompted the Board of Directors of Chicago Lutheran Theological Seminary to invite Augustana Theological Seminary, as well as Grand View Theological Seminary and Suomi Lutheran Theological Seminary, to enter into discussions looking toward the consolidation of these and other interested seminaries of the new church into a new seminary in the general Chicagoland area. These discussions have been carried on since September, 1958, and have developed to the point where the boards of directors of all four seminaries have authority to prepare plans for consolidation for presentation to the churches or synods owning or controlling the seminaries.

Augustana Theological Seminary was established in 1860 in Chicago, was moved in 1863 to Paxton, Illinois, and in 1875 to Rock Island, Illinois, where it has occupied its present complex of buildings since 1923. Founded by Swedish Lutheran immigrants, the institution has as its purpose "to train young men for the holy ministry in the Lutheran Church, especially for congregations within the Augustana Synod," as the original charter stated. The seminary embraced two departments, a preparatory and a theological. In 1869 a new constitution was adopted, giving the institution the name of Augustana College and Theological Seminary. As such it continued until September 1, 1948, when, as a result of final action at the 1948 convention of the Augustana Lutheran Church, the college and the seminary became separate corporations. The government of the seminary is vested in a Board of Directors of twelve elected members, eight pastors and four laymen, elected by the church, with the president of the church serving as an ex-officio member and the president and treasurer of the seminary as advisory members.

The Chicago Lutheran Theological Seminary, as the institution is commonly called, was founded in 1891 on the north side of Chicago. In 1910 this campus was sold and property for a new campus was purchased in Maywood, Illinois. That same year most of the buildings which now constitute the present seminary plant were erected. The school was established by the General Council of the Evangelical Lutheran Church for the purpose of preparing English-speaking ministers for the Lutheran Church. The seminary has continued to pioneer in several other areas. A division of graduate studies with a year-round program was established as a vital part of the total program of the seminary; a program for the reorientation of chaplains returning to parish service was begun at the close of World War II; and in the summer of 1948 a program for lay men and women, particularly those contemplating or engaged in full-time Christian service, was initiated. In 1955 the seminary was selected as the location for the newly established School of Missions of the United Lutheran Church in America, which school was opened in September, 1957. The Augustana Lutheran Church has co-operated in this program since 1960. Since the formation of the United Lutheran Church in America in 1918, ownership and control of the seminary has been vested in a Board of Directors elected by synods of the church which grant regular financial support to the seminary. At present these synods are: Illinois, Indiana, Wartburg, Michigan and Pittsburgh. The total membership of the board is sixteen, with the president of the seminary and the presidents of the supporting synods serving as ex-officio members.

Grand View Seminary was founded in northwestern Wisconsin in 1886 by the Danish Evangelical Lutheran Church in America. Doctrinal differences soon divided the seminary and eventually the church. In 1896 that part known as the Danish Lutheran Church (now American Evangelical Lutheran Church), which drew its inspiration from the Church of Denmark and particularly from the insights of Bishop N. F. S. Grundtvig, established Grand View College and Seminary in Des Moines, Iowa. In 1952 the college and seminary were given a separate corporate existence. At its convention in 1959 the American Evangelical Lutheran Church voted to affiliate the seminary with the Chicago Lutheran Theological Seminary in Maywood, effective September 1, 1960. The government of Grand View Seminary is vested in the Board of Directors of Grand View College and Grand View Seminary, which numbers ten members with the president of the church serving as an *ex-officio* member and the president of the college and the liaison professor of the seminary as advisory members.

Suomi College and Theological Seminary was organized in 1896 in Hancock, Michigan, by the Finnish Evangelical Lutheran Church. The first seminary class graduated in 1906. At its 1957 convention the Suomi Synod voted to continue merger discussions in the Joint Commission on Lutheran Unity. At the same convention the Synod also decided to separate the college and the seminary and instructed the Consistory of the church to appoint a special committee to make plans for the affiliation of the seminary with some larger Lutheran seminary of one of the churches represented in the Joint Commission on Lutheran Unity. The Consistory reported to the 1958 convention, recommending that the seminary be affiliated with Chicago Lutheran Theological Seminary in Maywood, Illinois. The proposal was adopted and the seminary began operations on the Maywood campus on September 1, 1958. The Seminary was incorporated as a Michigan

Corporation immediately prior to this affiliation. The Board of Directors has six elected members, with the president of the Church serving *ex-officio* and the liaison professor serving as an advisor.

Although the immediate occasion for the seminary merger discussion was the imminent church merger, it early became apparent to the members of the Inter-Seminary Committee that a unique opportunity for creative action in the field of theological education had been granted the church. The area of the four seminaries is the only area within the Lutheran Church in America where all four of the merging churches have a seminary. Only in this area is it possible for the Lutheran Church in America to bring together four seminaries representing distinct heritages in American Lutheranism. This new seminary of the Lutheran Church in America thus becomes a significant visible symbol of the new unity in the Lutheran Church in America.

In connection with the discussion of a new site for the united seminary, since it was deemed undesirable to locate the seminary on either of the present sites in Rock Island or Maywood, the matter of proximity to a university was seriously considered. At this point also it appeared that a unique opportunity for creative action had been granted the church.

Throughout the discussions in the Inter-Seminary Committee, emphasis was placed not only on the strongest possible basic curriculum of theological studies leading to the B.D. degree, but also on the need of establishing a program of graduate studies in theology that would meet the needs of the church as effectively as possible. Also envisaged was a program of missionary education that would serve the expanding needs of the Lutheran Church in America, as well as a program of theology for laymen preparing for or engaged in part-or full-time work in the church.

Confident that God is leading His Church in our midst into a new day of opportunity and responsibility in the preaching of His Word, and grateful that discussions have successfully reached this point, the Inter-Seminary Committee of Augustana Theological Seminary, Chicago Lutheran Theological Seminary, Grand View Seminary and Suomi Lutheran Theological Seminary hereby presents the following summary of agreements, together with a constitution and plan of consolidation, to their respective boards and churches or synods for approval or disapproval.

The Board of Directors

The initial Board of Directors of this seminary shall be elected by the boards of directors of the seminaries uniting to form the new seminary. The Board of Grand View College and Grand View Theological Seminary shall elect two (2) members, the Board of Augustana Theological Seminary shall elect seven (7) members, the Board of the Theological Seminary of the Evangelical Lutheran Church at Chicago, Illinois, shall elect seven (7) members, and the Board of Suomi Lutheran Theological Seminary shall elect two (2) members.

The names of the initial Board of Directors shall be given in the articles of consolidation. These directors shall serve until their successors are elected at the conventions of the supporting synods in 1963 and have qualified. As soon as is feasible after the filing of the articles of consolidation at some time between September 1, 1962, and January 1, 1963, and approval has been given by the Secretary of State of the State of Illinois, the directors shall meet to organize

224

and assume the operation of the new seminary. The convener of the first meeting of the initial board shall be designated by the Board of Directors of Suomi Lutheran Theological Seminary.

The first election of a Board of Directors by the supporting synods shall be held at the convention of the synods in 1963. Board members shall be elected in accordance with the stipulations of the constitution. In addition thereto it is provided that the members to be nominated and elected by the supporting synods shall be allocated as follows: 8 members from the Illinois Synod, 4 pastors and 4 laymen; 5 members from the Wisconsin-Upper Michigan Synod, 3 pastors and 2 laymen; 3 members from the Indiana-Kentucky Synod, 1 pastor and 2 laymen; and 2 members from the Michigan Synod, 1 pastor and 1 layman.

It is further provided that of the first members of the Board of Directors to be elected in 1963, church membership at the time of merger shall have been as follows: 7 in the Augustana Lutheran Church; 2 in the American Evangelical Lutheran Church; 2 in the Finnish Evangelical Lutheran Church; and 7 in the United Lutheran Church in America.

Allocations for the first elections are provided as follows:

Illinois Synod

Pastors	—One pastor formerly A. E. L. C.
	Two pastors formerly Augustana
	One pastor formerly U. L. C. A.
Laymen	—One member formerly Suomi
	Two members formerly U. L. C. A.
	One member formerly Augustana

Indiana-Kentucky Synod

Pastors	—One pastor formerly U. L. C. A.
Laymen	—One member formerly U. L. C. A.
	One member formerly Augustana

Michigan Synod

| Pastors | —One pastor formerly Augustana |
| Laymen | —One member formerly U. L. C. A. |

Wisconsin-Upper Michigan Synod

Pastors	—One pastor formerly U. L. C. A.
	One pastor formerly Augustana
	One pastor formerly Suomi
Laymen	—One member formerly A. E. L. C.
	One member formerly Augustana

For a period of four years thereafter, in elections the synods shall give consideration to proper representation of the groups uniting to form the consolidated seminary.

Members of the faculties of Augustana Theological Seminary, Grand View Theological Seminary, Suomi Theological Seminary and the Theological Seminary of the Evangelical Lutheran Church at Chicago shall be retained as members of the faculty of the Lutheran School of Theology at Chicago as follows:

1. Augustana Theological Seminary

   G. Everett Arden
   Arthur O. Arnold
   Arnold E. Carlson
   Theodore E. Conrad
   Hjalmar W. Johnson
   Paul M. Lindberg
   A. D. Mattson
   Karl E. Mattson

2. Chicago Lutheran Seminary

   Robert H. Fischer
   George W. Forell
   Donald R. Heiges
   Johannes Knudsen
   Robert J. Marshall
   Arthur Vööbus
   Armin George Weng
     School of Missions
     Donald C. Flatt
     James A. Scherer

3. Grand View Theological Seminary
   Axel C. Kildegaard

4. Suomi Theological Seminary
   Walter J. Kukkonen

Professorial rank previously granted shall be honored, but specific titles and positions must be subject to possible revision by the new administration and board.

The election of additional faculty members or changes in professorial rank or status prior to the time the new board assumes operation of the seminary or seminaries shall take place only after consultation by the Boards of Directors of Augustana Theological Seminary and Chicago Lutheran Theological Seminary.

MEMORIALS AND HISTORIC TRADITIONS

Certain names have been memorialized in the lives and traditions of the four schools contemplating consolidation. The Board of Directors shall honor all commitments, and, when it is desirable, perpetuate names. The curriculum shall also be designed to prepare men to recognize these historic traditions as need may be. Appropriate courses shall be included on an elective basis considering the historic roots of the four traditions and seminaries involved in this consolidation. Attention shall also be given to the preservation and growth of library collections involving these traditions and the historic roots out of which the seminaries and churches have emerged. On the basis of authority granted by the president of this seminary, members of the faculty who represent such historic traditions may hold meetings and arrange for participation in special interest conferences authorized by the Executive Council of the Church.

PENSIONERS

The Board of Directors of the new seminary shall, in accordance with the legal provisions of consolidation, honor all institutional pension commitments made by the uniting seminaries.

LIBRARIES

The libraries of the seminaries consolidating to form the Lutheran School of Theology at Chicago shall become the property of the new seminary and shall be integrated into one library. The librarian shall be given faculty rank and status.

MOVING PROCEDURES AND COSTS

All movable properties which are suitable for use and needed in the new seminary shall be transported to the new site and location. The cost of such transportation, as well as van and travel costs of the faculty, shall be assumed by the new corporation.

TIME OF UNION

The initial Board of Directors shall be designated in the plan of consolidation. The legal plan of consolidation shall be filed with the Secretary of State of the State of Illinois at some time between September 1, 1962, and January 1, 1963. Until such time as the Board of Directors is prepared to begin the operation of the new seminary at a new site, Augustana Theological Seminary and the Theological Seminary of the Evangelical Lutheran Church at Chicago, Illinois, shall be maintained in their present locations with their present administrations. Each unit will also retain its own assets and funds until such time as the Board begins the operation of the new seminary at the new site.

INTERIM COMMITTEE ON LIAISON AND ADMINISTRATION

Until such time as the Board of Directors of the new seminary assumes its legal responsibility, a Committee on Liaison and Administration shall maintain the cooperation between the seminaries, referring any necessary decisions to the respective Boards of Directors. The Committee on Liaison and Administration shall consist of six members, three elected by the Board of the Augustana Theological Seminary, and three elected by the Board of the Chicago Lutheran Theological Seminary.

ESTIMATE OF ASSETS AND LIABILITIES

I. Augustana Theological Seminary
II. The Theological Seminary of the Evangelical Lutheran Church at Chicago, Illinois
III. Grand View Seminary
IV. Suomi Lutheran Theological Seminary

	I	II	III	IV	Total
Assets					
Cash	$ 41,311.99	$ 17,683.48	$ 15,000.00	$ 1,251.78	$ 75,247.25
Accounts and Notes Payable	5,054.32	4,261.52		2,050.00	11,365.84
Investments (Cost)	428,544.61	393,676.80		34,000.00	856,221.41
Plant Assets					
Campus	31,745.85	244,640.98			276,386.83
Buildings	933,521.87	941,431.26			1,874,953.13
Equipment and Books	124,861.73	89,095.17		150.00	214,106.90
	$1,565,040.37	$1,690,789.21	$ 15,000.00	$ 37,451.78	$ 3,308,281.36
Liabilities					
Accounts and Notes Payable	$ 7,022.44	$ 148,398.75	$	$	$ 155,421.20
Student Room Deposit	490.00				490.00
Mortgages	47,517.11	158,945.19		21,707.74	228,170.04
Surplus Current Fund	487.17	2,488.71		5,023.46	7,025.00
Endowment Funds	450,251.26	244,720.52		10,720.58	705,692.36
Loan Fund	4,624.93	4,454.11			90,790.04
Students' Assistance	1,982.26				1,982.26
Plant Fund Unexpended Funds	2,246.13	6,321.43			8,567.56
Plant	1,042,612.34	1,116,222.22			2,158,834.56
Agency Fund	8,781.07	1,750.68	15,000.00		25,531.75
Deferred Taxes		4,205.09			4,205.09
Deferred Insurance		3,282.50			3,282.50
	$1,565,040.37	$1,690,789.21	$ 15,000.00	$ 37,451.78	$ 3,308,281.36
Date of Audit	8-31-60	6-30-60		3-31-61	

Prepared 3-21-61

II.

CONSTITUTION

LUTHERAN SCHOOL OF THEOLOGY AT CHICAGO

ARTICLE I

NAME, SUCCESSION AND OBJECT

Section 1. The name and corporate title of this seminary shall be Lutheran School of Theology at Chicago, hereinafter referred to as this seminary.

Section 2. This seminary is the legal and historic successor of Augustana Theological Seminary formerly of Rock Island, Illinois; Grand View Theological Seminary formerly Grand View College and Grand View Seminary of Des Moines, Iowa; Suomi Lutheran Theological Seminary formerly of Hancock, Michigan; and the Theological Seminary of the Evangelical Lutheran Church at Chicago, Illinois, formerly of Maywood, Illinois.

Section 3. The objects of this seminary shall be:

    a. To prepare men for the Gospel ministry, especially in the Lutheran church;

    b. To equip men and women for missionary service;

    c. To prepare men and women for leadership in Christian education, parish service and such other areas as may be required by the church;

    d. To provide instruction in theology for laymen;

    e. To encourage and assist in the in-service training of pastors; and

    f. To establish and maintain a program of graduate study in theology.

ARTICLE II

DOCTRINAL BASIS

The program of this seminary shall be in harmony with the Confession of Faith of the Lutheran Church in America, which is as follows:

Section 1. This church confesses Jesus Christ as Lord of the Church. The Holy Spirit creates and sustains the Church through the Gospel and thereby unites believers with their Lord and with one another in the fellowship of faith.

Section 2. This church holds that the Gospel is the revelation of God's sovereign will and saving grace in Jesus Christ. In Him, the Word Incarnate, God imparts himself to men.

Section 3. This church acknowledges the Holy Scriptures as the norm for the faith and life of the Church. The Holy Scriptures are the divinely inspired record of God's redemptive act in Christ, for which the Old Testament prepared the way and which the New Testament proclaims. In the continuation of this proclamation in the Church, God still speaks through the Holy Scriptures and realizes His redemptive purpose generation after generation.

Section 4. This church accepts the Apostles', the Nicene, and the Athanasian creeds as true declarations of the faith of the Church.

Section 5. This church accepts the unaltered Augsburg Confession and Luther's Small Catechism as true witnesses to the Gospel, and acknowledges as one with it in faith and doctrine all churches that likewise accept the teachings of these symbols.

Section 6. This church accepts the other symbolical books of the evangelical Lutheran church, the Apology of the Augsburg Confession, the Smalcald Articles, Luther's Large Catechism, and the Formula of Concord as further valid interpretations of the confession of the church.

Section 7. This church affirms that the Gospel transmitted by the Holy Scriptures, to which the creeds and confessions bear witness, is the true treasure of the church, the substance of its proclamation, and the basis of its unity and continuity. The Holy Spirit uses the proclamation of the Gospel and the administration of the Sacraments to create and sustain Christian faith and fellowship. As this occurs, the Church fulfills its divine mission and purpose.

ARTICLE III

The Board of Directors

Section 1. a. The government of this seminary shall be vested in a Board of Directors. Eighteen (18) directors shall be elected by the synods supporting this seminary. Six (6) additional directors shall be nominated by the Board of Theological Education of the Lutheran Church in America and elected by the supporting synods. The presidents of the synods of the Lutheran Church in America supporting this seminary shall be *ex-officio* members of the Board. The elected membership of the Board of Directors shall include an equal number of pastors and laymen.

b. The president, the academic dean or deans, and the treasurer of this seminary shall be advisory members with seat and voice. The Executive Secretary of the Board of Theological Education of the Lutheran Church in America and the executive Secretary of the Board of World Missions of the Lutheran Church in America shall be consultative members.

c. Presidents of synods shall not serve as officers of the Board or of its Executive Committee.

Section 2. The term of office of a director shall be three (3) years except as otherwise provided in this constitution, and except that the terms of office of the first Board of Directors elected by the synods shall be such as to give effect to the requirements of paragraph a. of this section. A director shall serve until his successor is elected and qualified. If a member of the Board of Directors absents himself from three consecutive meetings without excuse, his office shall be declared vacant by action of the Board.

a. Directors shall be elected in such a manner that the term of office of one-third (⅓) of them shall expire each year.

b. The number of directors allocated to each supporting synod shall be determined by the Board of Directors in proportion to the total number of confirmed members in good standing of the supporting constituency.

c. No elected member of the Board may succeed himself for a third consecutive full term.

d. Vacancies in the Board of Directors shall be filled until the next convention of the synod by the Executive Committee of the supporting synod involved, when necessary upon nomination by the Board of Theological Education of the Lutheran Church in America.

e. Directors of this seminary shall be members in good standing of a congregation of the Lutheran Church in America.

Section 3. The duties and powers of the Board of Directors shall be:

a. To govern this seminary in accordance with the instructions of the suporting synods and the counsel of the Board of Theological Education of the Lutheran Church in America and as prescribed in the articles of consolidation and constitution of this seminary;

b. To manage the financial affairs of this seminary;

c. To have charge of all funds and other property;

d. To purchase, acquire, sell and convey, mortgage, pledge and otherwise dispose of real estate and all other property of whatsoever nature;

e. To receive and disburse funds;

f. To elect, after consultation with the faculty, a president, faculty members and administrative officers;

g. To elect a vice-president, who shall act in the absence of the president, and perform the duties assigned to him by the president or the Board;

h. To elect a treasurer who need not be a member of the Board;

i. To determine the salaries of all officers and faculty members;

j. To establish in consultation with the faculty a regular program of sabbatical leaves, to grant leaves of absence to members of the faculty for such time as it is deemed proper, and to provide for faculty participation in learned and professional societies;

k. To discipline, suspend or discharge incompetent or unworthy officers or faculty members as hereinafter prescribed;

l. To approve the granting of degrees as recommended by the faculty;

m. To adopt and enforce such by-laws, rules and regulations as are necessary for the operation of this seminary;

n. To approve courses of study as recommended by the faculty, and to determine the teaching load of the faculty;

o. To fix the tuition and fees to be paid by students;

p. To establish scholarships and aid funds;

q. To meet periodically with the faculty or its official representatives;

r. To authorize an annual audit of the finances and operation of the corporation;

s. To decide on time and place for holding regular and special meetings; and

t. To submit to the supporting synods and the Board of Theological Education of the Lutheran Church in America an annual report on the state of the seminary.

ARTICLE IV

Officers and Committees of the Board

Section 1. The officers of the Board shall be a chairman, a vice-chairman, a secretary and a treasurer, whose terms of office shall be for one year or until their successors are elected and qualified.

Section 2. The duties of the Chairman of the Board shall be:

a. To preside at meetings of the Board;

b. To call special meetings when requested to do so by at least one-fourth ($\frac{1}{4}$) of the members of the Board and at such other times as are necessary;

c. To exercise such disciplinary power as is hereinafter prescribed; and

d. To present a written annual report to the Board for approval and submission to the supporting synods and to the Board of Theological Education of the Lutheran Church in America.

Section 3. The duties of the secretary shall be those that usually pertain to that office.

Section 4. The duties of the treasurer shall be:

a. To give corporate, surety and fidelity bond in such amount as shall be fixed by the Board;

b. To receive and have charge of all funds belonging to the corporation and to invest and disburse the same according to such regulations as the Board may establish;

c. To keep full and systematic accounts of all finances of the corporation;

d. To assist the president in the preparation of the annual budget; and

e. To present to the Board at the end of each fiscal year, and when otherwise requested by the Board, a full statement of the financial condition of the corporation.

Section 5. The Executive Committee of the Board shall consist of the chairman, vice-chairman, and secretary of the Board of Directors, the presidents of the supporting synods, and the chairmen of standing committees of the Board. The president and treasurer of this seminary shall be advisory members.

Section 6. Between meetings of the Board, the Executive Committee shall act for and on behalf of the Board in all matters referred to it by the Board.

Section 7. At the annual meeting of the Board the following standing committees shall be appointed by the chairman: Policy and Personnel, Building and Grounds, Publicity and Promotion, and Finance and Investment.

ARTICLE V

MEETINGS

Section 1. The Board of Directors shall hold at least two regular meetings each year and such other meetings as may be determined by the Board. Written notice of all regular and special meetings shall be mailed to all Board members not less than ten days before the meeting.

Section 2. The annual meeting of the Board shall be the first meeting following the annual conventions of the supporting synods. At this meeting the Board shall elect its officers.

Section 3. A majority of the elected and ex-officio members of the Board shall constitute a quorum.

232

ARTICLE VI

Section 1. The president shall be a pastor of the Lutheran Church in America. He shall be elected by ballot by the Board. A two thirds (⅔) vote shall be necessary for election. Following his election he shall be duly installed in his office at which time he shall subscribe to the doctrinal basis of this seminary. The tenure of office of the president of this seminary shall automatically terminate at the close of the academic year during which he attains the age of sixty-eight (68) years.

Section 2. The duties of the president shall be:

a. To serve as executive officer of this seminary;

b. To serve as chairman of the faculty;

c. To promote the objects of this seminary and its ideals of scholarship;

d. To encourage Christian fellowship and concord in the seminary community;

e. To foster living relationships between this seminary, its supporting synods, the Lutheran Church in America, and its Board of Theological Education;

f. To give attention to the devotional and worship life of the faculty and students;

g. To exercise such disciplinary power as is hereinafter prescribed;

h. To appoint the members of the standing committees of the faculty; and

i. To present to the Board an annual written report on the state of this seminary.

Section 3. a. If definite charges of inefficiency or neglect of duty, be preferred against the president and be presented in writing to the Chairman of the Board by two or three responsible persons, he shall bring a copy of the charges to the President privately. If the Chairman shall deem the charges sufficiently serious, he shall bring the charges to the Board. The Board may cite the President to appear, and after reasonable notice has been given him in writing, proceed to hear evidence upon the preferred charges in his presence. If the President shall refuse to appear, or unnecessarily delay his appearance the Board may hear evidence and come to a decision. A two-thirds (⅔) affirmative vote shall be necessary to sustain the charges. In case the charges are sustained, the Board of Directors shall have the power to suspend or dismiss the President upon a two-thirds (⅔) affirmative vote.

b. If the charges involve false doctrine or un-Christian conduct the matter shall be referred to the synod of which the President is a member for disciplinary action in accordance with the provisions of Section II, item 13 of the By-laws of the Lutheran Church in America.

Section 4. a. The Board shall elect an academic dean or deans as the program of this seminary may require. Deans shall have faculty rank and status. Provisions for the election and dismissal of faculty members shall apply.

b. The duties of the academic dean or deans shall be:

1. To arrange, in cooperation with the faculty, courses of study and class schedules;

2. To supervise academic relationships within the faculty and between the faculty and students;

233

3. To enforce academic rules adopted by the faculty and Board of Directors; and

4. To exercise general supervision over the academic program assigned.

Section 5. The Board may elect such other administrative officers as are necessary. The area of assigned service and authority shall in each case be specifically defined.

ARTICLE VII

FACULTY

Section 1. The faculty shall determine the time, place and manner of holding its meetings, elect its own secretary and keep proper records. A majority shall constitute a quorum.

Section 2. In addition to its teaching responsibilities, the duties and powers of the faculty shall be:

a. To adopt aims and policies of instruction;

b. To recommend courses of study to the Board of Directors;

c. To determine and maintain academic standards and grading policies, and to establish the time and manner of examinations;

d. To recommend candidates for degrees;

e. To recommend to the President the suspension or dismissal of students for cause; and

f. To recommend the length of the academic year for approval by the Board of Directors.

Section 3. a. The Board of Directors shall elect members of the faculty and determine their academic rank and status after consultation with the faculty in joint session. The initial election shall normally be for a period of three years. Election shall be by ballot and a two-thirds (⅔) affirmative vote shall be required for election.

b. Permanent tenure shall be reserved for members of the faculty who achieve the rank of associate professor or professor. Election to permanent tenure or promotion in academic rank shall take place after consultation with the faculty in joint session and shall be by ballot. A two-thirds (⅔) affirmative vote shall be required for election or promotion.

c. The following academic ranks shall be established: instructor, assistant professor, associate professor and professor.

1. The rank of instructor shall usually be given to persons who serve as members of the faculty temporarily.

2. The rank of assistant professor shall usually be given to persons as they begin their career in the seminary when it is clearly the intention of the Board of Directors that they may later achieve permanent tenure.

3. The rank of associate professor shall usually be given to persons who have completed three years of satisfactory work as assistant professors.

4. The rank of professor shall usually be given to persons who have completed three years of satisfactory work as associate professors, who have earned a doctor's degree or its equivalent, or who serve as head of a department or area of study.

d. Members of the faculty on leave from other educational institutions or service in the church shall usually be appointed as visiting professors or lecturers.

Section 4. a. An associate professor or professor shall be a pastor of the Lutheran Church.

b. Associate professors or professors shall be installed in their office, at which time they shall subscribe to the doctrinal basis of this seminary.

Section 5. a. If definite charges of inefficiency or neglect of duty be preferred against any ordained member of the faculty or if definite charges of inefficiency, neglect of duty, false doctrine or un-Christian conduct be preferred against any unordained member of the faculty and if these charges are presented in writing to the president of this seminary by two or more responsible persons, he shall bring a copy of the charges to the person concerned privately. If the President shall deem the charges sufficiently serious, he shall bring the charges to the Chairman of the Board. If these officials cannot adjudicate the matter, they shall have authority to suspend the professor or instructor, referring the matter to the Board for final decision. The Board may cite the person in question to appear after reasonable notice has been given him in writing, and proceed to hear evidence upon the preferred charges in his presence. If the said person shall refuse to appear or unnecessarily delay his appearance, the Board may proceed to hear the evidence and come to a decision. A two-thirds ($\frac{2}{3}$) affirmative vote shall be necessary to sustain the charges. In case the charges are sustained the Board of Directors shall have the power to suspend or dismiss the professor or instructor upon a two-thirds ($\frac{2}{3}$) affirmative vote.

b. If the charges involve false doctrine or un-Christian conduct by an ordained member of the faculty, the matter shall be referred to the synod of which he is a member for disciplinary action in accordance with the provisions of Section II, item 13 of the By-laws of the Lutheran Church in America.

Section 6. The tenure of office of a member of the faculty shall automatically terminate at the close of the academic year in which he attains the age of sixty-eight (68) years.

ARTICLE VIII
STUDENTS

Section 1. This seminary shall be open to such students as meet the established qualifications for entrance and agree to the regulations of this seminary.

Section 2. Admission of students to this seminary shall be controlled by faculty committees on admissions which shall administer policies established by the faculty and Board of Directors.

Section 3. A student may be suspended or dismissed:

a. For persistent idleness, negligence or insubordination, after just and proper means have been taken by the faculty to correct the fault.

b. For any conduct showing his character is such that he is unworthy to remain in this seminary.

c. For failure to maintain the required minimum scholastic standing.

Section 4. A student who is suspended or dismissed may make written appeal to the Board of Directors whose decision shall be final.

ARTICLE IX

AMENDMENTS

This constitution, with the exception of Article II, may be amended at a regular meeting of the Board of Directors by a two-thirds (⅔) affirmative vote of the members of the Board, provided that the proposed amendment has first been submitted in writing to the Board at a previous meeting, and has received preliminary approval by a majority vote of the members of the Board, as well as approval by a majority vote of each of the synods supporting this seminary, said synodical approval in combination to represent not less than two-thirds of the total confirmed members in good standing of the supporting constituency. Article II may not be amended except by Board decision as prescribed in this article and with the consent of the Lutheran Church in America.

III.

PLAN OF CONSOLIDATION

The Parties of this Plan of Consolidation are:

Augustana Theological Seminary, an Illinois Corporation and herein sometimes referred to as "Augustana Seminary";

The Theological Seminary of the Evangelical Lutheran Church at Chicago, Illinois, an Illinois Corporation and herein sometimes referred to as "Maywood Seminary"; and

Suomi Lutheran Theological Seminary, a Michigan Corporation and herein sometimes referred to as "Suomi Seminary,"

WITNESSETH:

1—Whereas, each of the parties hereto is a non-profit corporation incorporated for the purpose of educating persons for the Christian ministry and other specific Christian service, and owns and is possessed of a theological seminary and of assets, real and personal; and

2—Whereas, each of the parties hereto is supported by one or more synods as follows:

a—Augustana Seminary by Augustana Evangelical Lutheran Church, a Minnesota Corporation, formerly known as Augustana Synod, and herein sometimes referred to as "Augustana Synod;"

b—Maywood Seminary by the Illinois Synod of the United Lutheran Church in America, an Illinois Corporation and herein sometimes referred to as "Illinois Synod," the Wartburg Synod of the United Lutheran Church in America, an Illinois Corporation and herein sometimes referred to as "Wartburg Synod," the Michigan Synod of the United Lutheran Church in America, a Michigan Corporation and herein sometimes referred to as "Michigan Synod," the Indiana Synod of the United Lutheran Church in America, an Indiana Corporation and herein sometimes referred to as "Indiana Synod," and the Pittsburgh Synod of the Evangelical Lutheran Church, a Pennsylvania Corporation and herein sometimes referred to as the "Pittsburgh Synod;"

c—Suomi Seminary by the Finnish Evangelical Lutheran Church of America—Suomi Synod, a Michigan Corporation and herein sometimes referred to as the "Suomi Synod;"

The delegates from time to time to the respective synod or synods aforementioned supporting each party hereto, constitute the members having voting rights of each such party, as that term is used in the Illinois statute hereinafter mentioned.

3—Whereas, the American Evangelical Lutheran Church, an Iowa Corporation and herein sometimes referred to as "A.E.L.C.," The United Lutheran Church in America, a New York Corporation and herein sometimes referred to as "U.L.C.A." and the aforementioned Augustana Synod and Suomi Synod, are now engaged in consolidation proceedings under the laws of the State of Minnesota for the purpose of consolidating said four corporations into a new corporation as a Minnesota Corporation under the name of Lutheran Church in America; and the aforementioned Illinois Synod, Wartburg Synod, Michigan Synod, Indiana Synod and Pittsburgh Synod are synods within the said U.L.C.A., which is a national church body; and

237

4—Whereas, it is the desire of the parties hereto that they be consolidated into a new non-profit corporation under and in accordance with the General Not for Profit Corporation Act of the State of Illinois and as may be permitted by the statutes of the State of Michigan in such case made and provided.

5—THE PARTIES HERETO HEREBY AGREE to consolidate into a new corporation under and in accordance with the General Not for Profit Corporation Act of the State of Illinois, upon the following terms, conditions and provisions, namely:

6—The name of the new Corporation is LUTHERAN SCHOOL OF THEOLOGY AT CHICAGO.

7—The period of duration of the New Corporation is perpetual.

8—The address of the Initial Registered Office of the New Corporation in the State of Illinois is: 105 West Adams Street, in the City of Chicago, County of Cook, and the name of its initial Registered Agent at said address is: A. HOWARD WEEG.

9—The purpose or purposes for which the new Corporation is organized are to establish and maintain a theological seminary in the State of Illinois.

10—The new Corporation shall not permanently establish or maintain its theological seminary, or any part thereof, on or near any site now owned or used by any of the parties hereto as and for a seminary, except that on a temporary basis only the new Corporation may conduct its operation on the present sites of Augustana Seminary and Maywood Seminary until it has established a seminary elsewhere.

11—The voting rights of the members of the new Corporation shall be established, determined and regularized by the constitution of the new Corporation.

12—The number, election, terms of office and qualifications of the directors of the new Corporation shall be fixed by the constitution of the new Corporation, except that the number of directors of the initial board of directors shall be eighteen and they shall be elected prior to the execution of the Articles of Consolidation, in the following manner:

A) Seven by the board of directors of Augustana Seminary,
   Seven by the board of directors of Maywood Seminary,
   Two by the board of directors of Suomi Seminary, and
   Two by the board of directors of Grand View College and Grand View Seminary, an Iowa Corporation.

B) The directors so elected shall be named in said Articles of Consolidation as constituting the initial board of directors of the new Corporation.

13—This Plan of Consolidation shall be adopted in the following manner: The board of directors of each of the parties hereto shall adopt a resolution approving this Plan of Consolidation and directing that it be submitted to a vote at the 1961 annual convention of the synod or each of the synods whose members have the voting rights of such respective party. Such synod or synods are named in Paragraph 2 hereof. Each such convention shall be called and notice thereof shall be given to each delegate entitled to vote at each such meeting within the time and in the manner provided in the statutes of Illinois or Michigan in such case made and provided. This Plan of Consolidation shall be and constitute the plan adopted for the corporate consolidation of Augustana Seminary, Maywood Seminary and Suomi Seminary, upon receiving at the 1961 annual conventions aforementioned, the affirmative vote of at least two-thirds (a) of the total number of delegates to such convention of the Suomi Synod and (b) of the votes entitled to be cast by members present or represented by proxy at each such convention of the other six synods named in paragraph 2 hereof.

14—When the Consolidation has been effected, the new Corporation by virtue of the statutes of Illinois and Michigan in such case made and provided, succeeds to all the property and liabilities of the Consolidating Corporations by operation of law or otherwise. Grand View College and Grand View Seminary, an Iowa Corporation, shall be deemed to have approved and accepted the provisions of this Plan of Consolidation when with the authorization therefore by A.E.L.C., it has transferred and conveyed to the new Corporation, all property, real and personal, which it holds for the use and benefit of the Grand View Seminary. The property acquired by the new Corporation by virtue of the consolidation and as herein provided, shall be devoted by the new Corporation for the establishment and maintenance of a new seminary in accordance with this Plan of Consolidation and provisions of the Articles of Consolidation.

15—The procedure for consolidation hereunder shall be so timed that the consolidation shall become effective on September 1, 1962 or as soon thereafter as shall be reasonably possible.

16—The new Corporation shall consolidate institutionally into one new united seminary the four institutions commonly known as:

        a) Augustana Seminary
           of Rock Island, Illinois

        b) Maywood Seminary
           of Maywood, Illinois

        c) Suomi Seminary
           now affiliated with the said
           Maywood Seminary

        d) Grand View Seminary
           now affiliated with the said
           Maywood Seminary

In Witness Whereof, Augustana Theological Seminary has caused its corporate seal to be hereunto affixed and these presents to be signed by the Chairman of its board of directors and attested by the Secretary of said board, and The Theological Seminary of the Evangelical Lutheran Church at Chicago, Illinois, has caused its corporate seal to be hereunto affixed and these presents to be signed by the Chairman of its board of directors and attested by the Secretary of said board, and Suomi Lutheran Theological Seminary has caused its corporate seal to be hereunto affixed and these presents to be signed by the majority of its board of directors and attested by the Secretary of said board, all on the

day of _____ 1961.

Augustana Theological Seminary

By _____

(Seal)   Chairman of the Board of Directors

Attest:

_____

Secretary of the Board of Directors

The Theological Seminary of the Evangelical Lutheran Church at Chicago, Illinois

By _____

(Seal)   Chairman of the Board of Directors

Attest:

_____

Secretary of the Board of Directors

Suomi Lutheran Theological Seminary

By _____

_____

_____

_____

_____

(Seal)   _____

A Majority of the Directors of the Board of Directors

Attest:

_____

Secretary of the Board of Directors

240

IV.

ACTION BY BOARDS OF DIRECTORS

AUGUSTANA

RESOLVED by the Board of Directors of AUGUSTANA THEOLOGICAL SEMINARY, an Illinois corporation, (1) that the Plan of Consolidation between Augustana Theological Seminary, The Theological Seminary of the Evangelical Lutheran Church at Chicago, Illinois, an Illinois corporation, and Suomi Lutheran Theological Seminary, a Michigan corporation, in the form hereto appended, be and is hereby approved; (2) that the said Plan of Consolidation be submitted to a vote at the 1961 annual convention of the Augustana Evangelical Lutheran Church, a Minnesota corporation, pursuant to written or printed notice, setting forth the said Plan of Consolidation or a summary thereof and stating the place, day and hour of such convention or meeting, to be delivered not less than five days nor more than forty days before the date of such convention or meeting, either personally or by mail, by or at the direction of the president or the secretary of the said Augustana Evangelical Lutheran Church, to each delegate entitled to vote at such convention, which notice if mailed shall be addressed to the delegate at his or her address as it appears on the records of the said Augustana Evangelical Lutheran Church, with postage prepaid, and deposited in the United States mail; and (3) that the said Plan of Consolidation shall be and constitute the Plan adopted for the corporate consolidation of the above named three seminary corporations, upon receiving at the 1961 annual conventions of the synods hereinafter referred to, the affirmative vote of at least two-thirds (a) of the total number of delegates to such meeting of the Suomi Synod and (b) of the votes entitled to be cast by members present or represented by proxy at each such meeting of the other six synods named in Paragraph 2 of said Plan of Consolidation.

MAYWOOD

RESOLVED by the Board of Directors of THE THEOLOGICAL SEMINARY OF THE EVANGELICAL LUTHERAN CHURCH AT CHICAGO, ILLINOIS, an Illinois corporation, (a) that the Plan of Consolidation between The Theological Seminary of the Evangelical Lutheran Church at Chicago, Illinois, Augustana Theological Seminary, an Illinois corporation, and Suomi Lutheran Theological Seminary, a Michigan corporation, in the form hereto appended, be and is hereby approved; (b) that, pursuant to Illinois statute in such case made and provided, the said Plan of Consolidation be submitted to a vote at the 1961 annual convention or meeting of each of the following five synods:

1) Illinois Synod of the United Lutheran Church in America,
   an Illinois corporation;
2) Wartburg Synod of the United Lutheran Church in America,
   an Illinois corporation;
3) Michigan Synod of the United Lutheran Church in America,
   a Michigan corporation;
4) Indiana Synod of the United Lutheran Church in America,
   an Indiana corporation; and
5) Pittsburgh Synod of the United Lutheran Church in America,
   a Pennsylvania corporation;

each pursuant to written or printed notice setting forth said Plan of Consolidation or a summary thereof and stating the place, day and hour of such respective convention or meeting, to be delivered not less than five days nor more than forty days before the date of such respective convention or meeting, either personally or by mail, by or at the direction of the president or the secretary of such respective synod to each delegate entitled to vote at such synod's convention, which notice, if mailed, shall be addressed to the delegate at his or her address as it appears on the records of such respective synod, with postage prepaid, and deposited in the United States mail; and (c) that said Plan of Consolidation shall be and constitute the plan adopted for the corporate consolidation of the above named three seminary corporations, upon receiving at the 1961 annual conventions of the synods, hereinafter referred to, the affirmative vote of at least two-thirds (a) of the total number of delegates to such meeting of the Suomi Synod and (b) of the votes entitled to be cast by members present or represented by proxy at such meeting of the other six synods named in Paragraph 2 of said Plan of Consolidation.

SUOMI

RESOLVED by the Board of Directors of the SUOMI LUTHERAN THEOLOG-ICAL SEMINARY, a Michigan corporation, (1) that the Plan of Consolidation between the Suomi Lutheran Theological Seminary, Augustana Theological Seminary, an Illinois corporation, and The Theological Seminary of the Evangelical Lutheran Church at Chicago, Illinois, an Illinois corporation, in the form hereto appended, be and is hereby approved; (2) that said Plan of Consolidation be submitted to a vote by ballot at the 1961 annual convention or meeting of the Finnish Evangelical Lutheran Church in America-Suomi Synod, a Michigan corporation, called separately for the purpose of taking the said Plan of Consolidation into consideration, pursuant to due notice stating the time, place and object of such convention or meeting, which notice shall be given by publication at least once a week for three successive weeks next preceding the date of said convention or meeting in a newspaper published in the county wherein said Suomi Synod has its registered office, and which notice shall also be mailed to the known post office address of each delegate entitled to vote at such convention, at least twenty days prior to the date of such convention or meeting; (3) that at said convention or meeting the said Plan of Consolidation shall be considered and a vote by ballot, in person or by proxy, shall be taken for the adoption or rejection of the same; and (4) that said Plan of Consolidation shall be and constitute the plan adopted for the corporate consolidation of the above named three seminary corporations, upon receiving at the 1961 annual conventions of the synods hereinafter referred to, the affirmative vote of at least two-thirds (a) of the total number of delegates to such meeting of the Suomi Synod and (b) of the votes entitled to be cast by delegates present or represented by proxy at each such meeting of the other six synods named in Paragraph 2 of said Plan of Consolidation.

V.

ACTION BY CHURCHES AND SYNODS

RESOLVED by (here insert name of Synod) that the Plan of Consolidation between Augustana Theological Seminary, an Illinois corporation, The Theological Seminary of the Evangelical Lutheran Church at Chicago, Illinois, an Illinois corporation, and Suomi Lutheran Theological Seminary, a Michigan corporation, in the form hereto appended, be and the same is hereby approved and adopted, and that in the event said Plan of Consolidation shall be adopted in accordance with the provisions of Paragraph 13 of said Plan of Consolidation, the Articles of Consolidation therefore be and are hereby authorized and directed to be executed, verified, acknowledged and filed, and affidavit of compliance be executed and filed, all in the manner provided by the statutes of Illinois and Michigan in such case made and provided.

ACTION BY A.E.L.C.

The Plan of Consolidation hereto appended be and is hereby approved and accepted, and in accordance with the provisions of this Plan of Consolidation, the Board of Directors of Grand View College and Grand View Seminary is hereby authorized and instructed to transfer and convey to the new corporation, all property, real and personal, which is held for the use and benefit of Grand View Seminary.

ACTION BY BOARDS AND SYNODS OR CHURCHES

The summary of agreements presented by the Inter-Seminary Committee and hereto appended be and is hereby approved.

ACTION BY BOARDS AND SYNODS OR CHURCHES

The constitution of the new seminary presented by the Inter-Seminary Committee and hereto appended be and is hereby recommended for adoption by the Board of Directors of the new corporation.

Appendix V

REPORT OF ADVISORY COMMITTEE
to the
COMMITTEE ON SITE OF THE INTERSEMINARY COMMITTEE

Dear Brethren:

We have appreciated very much the opportunity to consult with you regarding the all-important question of the location of the new theological seminary of the Lutheran Church in America, which is to represent the combined strength of the present Augustana Theological Seminary, Chicago Lutheran Theological Seminary, Grand View Seminary, Suomi Lutheran Theological Seminary, and the School of Missions, plus intangible but very real assets resulting from this new symbol of Lutheran unity and forward-looking acceptance of responsibility.

In our study of this question we have been guided by the considerations set forth in the Memorandum of December 28, 1960, prepared for us by Dean Donald R. Heiges, as interpreted and amplified by your Committee in our two conferences with you on January 12th and 14th. Between these two meetings we personally visited Northwestern University and the University of Chicago, and three of the theological institutions adjacent to them. We conferred with Dean Brauer of the Divinity School of the University of Chicago, President Schomer of the Chicago Theological Seminary, Vice-Chancellor Philbey of the University of Chicago, President Loder of Garrett Biblical Institute, President Miller of Northwestern University and Mr. Kerr, Business Manager of the University. We also had a most helpful conference with Mr. Julian Levi, a specialist in urban renewal who is intimately involved in the whole movement to develop the area adjacent to the University of Chicago. At the Chicago Theological Seminary we were invited to share in a "family night dinner" after which we heard a student discussion of the program of the seminary which was interesting and helpful.

Following our second conference with your Committee we conferred together and agreed on the report which we now present to you. The sequence of topics in the report, proceeding from general background considerations to the specific question of location, is designed to cover in logical order the various aspects of the problem which we understand you desire us to review.

I. A UNIVERSITY ENVIRONMENT

We are in hearty agreement with the thinking that has led you hitherto to investigate the possibility of a site for the new seminary within easy walking distance of a university. On theological grounds we believe that the student preparing for the ministry should not only be thoroughly at home in the Christian Gospel and the history of the Church, but should also be prepared to follow the Lord whom we preach into the world to which He came and to the people whose predicament He addressed. Therefore, it behooves us to know the world in which we live, to speak a language intelligible to it, and to profit by the studies which may reveal to us the depths and complexities of man's plight.

Bluntly, the sociological and psychological sciences are important for the ministry. Moreover, the universities which teach these sciences are representative of the total secular order, into which we believe the theological students should be plunged long before the time after graduation when they will encounter, often traumatically, the realities of modern life to which they should earlier have been exposed.

The university informs; it presents facts with which a live theology must constantly deal. If ministers are to present the "more excellent way," they must know accurately what way it is that they are combatting or criticizing, with a degree of knowledge and precision that commands respect. Although proximity to a university does not necessarily mean that a seminary will be receptive to its opportunities, over the years the danger of intellectual sterility is diminished. High standards next door will tend to shame sentimentality, complacency and narrow isolation. Where there is an attitude of eager receptivity, the teaching program of the seminary can be enriched and supplemented in a multitude of ways.

There are other advantages also. How can the graduates of a seminary be expected to speak with power to the millions of their educated brethren through the years of their ministry if they have not been able to make themselves intelligible—and intellectually respectable—to these same brethren in their student days? Again, the extras which a university provides, such as lectures by men of world renown, a lively response to the currents of modern life as reflected in literature and art, social concern, international awareness—these and many more help to create an intellectually stimulating climate. All of this leads us to confirm the judgment you have already expressed, that the seminary should be near a university. Despite the attractions of green grass and of an intimate, self-contained, semi-monastic company of scholars, neither universities nor their graduates are likely long to pay serious attention to those who ignore the involvements which university life represents. The Church has a duty, and the denominational seminary shares this responsibility, to witness at the heart of university life. We are all convinced of the importance of a close-knit seminary community, but we are equally sure that this community, to be most constructive, must be found in the midst of pressures such as the theological student will feel after graduation rather than in retreat from them.

This philosophy of involvement seems to us most important. It has its dangers, of course. Some may fear that it will tend to a secular intellectualism inconsistent with the spiritual objectives of a seminary. But a faith that could be defended only by isolating it from the currents of modern thought is hardly likely to seem relevant to the needs of our times. A competent theological faculty can surely be expected to hold its own in a dialogue with scholars of other disciplines. We see this as greatly strengthening rather than weakening the distinctive character of theological education.

II. THE CITY

Proximity to a university also means close involvement in the life of the city. Again, we heartily concur in your judgment that, if theological students are to minister effectively upon ordination to the urban and suburban areas in which so many Lutheran churches are located, they should learn the problems of these churches while yet students. Further, we live in a culture which, whether we like it or not, is increasingly urban-dominated.

As teachers we acknowledge our propensity to create a little fenced-in world of our own, and to beget intellectual children after our own kind who too often need the corrective to pride of learning which costly involvement— controlled and graded according to the students' maturity and capacity— supplies. In other words, here in the city are widely-varied opportunities for supervised field work, in both churches and social agencies, which are not present in a remote or semi-remote rural setting. We consider this carefully-regulated and well directed field work a highly important part of theological education.

At the same time, direct involvement in urban life does not preclude a broad emphasis on other aspects of contemporary culture, both in the class room and in field contacts, as the present experience of other seminaries and universities clearly demonstrates. It can be equally true of the Lutheran seminary we are envisioning. A city locale need not mean an exclusively urban emphasis, but it is a recognition of the dominant urban influence in the life of our time.

III. CHICAGO

A seminary of perhaps 500 students will need access to many churches and agencies in order that the best of them, to which the seminary can look with high esteem and confidence, may assist its program. Again, we recommend the thinking which has led you to choose Chicago as the best place for a Lutheran center of theological learning and practical training. Our own homes are in three other regions of this country. But we recognize that Chicago is at once both the most complex core of American culture and a focal point of Lutheran strength. For the new seminary to locate in Texas or on the Pacific Coast or even in a city a few hundred miles away would seem to us the abandonment of a divinely appointed duty to the Lutheran Church in America in this particular area and its central city. From no other point does it seem to us possible for a seminary to have contact with and to influence so great an area which is so characteristic of the varied aspects of American culture as well as of the ethnic and social influences which have had significance for Lutheran development.

IV. THE TWO UNIVERSITY LOCATIONS

Your commission to us was to retrace and comment upon the path of decisions you have already made and to assist you, if we can, in the perplexing problem of where you should settle in Chicago. You asked us to consider primarily the academic aspects of this problem, but we were all aware from the beginning that these were necessarily closely related to sociological, practical and financial considerations. For example, if a site could be obtained no closer than two miles from a university, the assumed academic advantages of proximity might be difficult to utilize. At least the value of association with a university would diminish with increasing distance. On the other hand, if proximity meant that the seminary, which should cultivate an intimate company of scholars, was set in an area in which its professors would refuse to live, this sociological factor would seriously affect academic performance. Recognizing this interaction of academic and other factors, we nevertheless believe that the thinking which has led you to this point is sound and that the importance of a university location in Chicago should be recognized. We therefore turn to a consideration of the relative advantages of Evanston and Hyde Park.

Let us at once pay tribute to the spirit of hospitality toward a new Lutheran seminary manifested at both Northwestern University and the University of Chicago. Each would welcome the new school and would value the mutual enrichment that would follow proximity. In each place there are friendly accredited seminaries which are eager for the coming of a strong sister school. Each location has valuable facilities, including large university libraries and excellent smaller theological libraries, now at hand. Each would provide an intellectual climate favorable to theological study and preparation for the type of ministry which this report is presupposing. However, each has certain advantages and disadvantages peculiar to its own situation.

Academic Considerations

A. **Evanston and Northwestern University**
The following are some of the academic advantages of a site in Evanston adjacent to Northwestern University:
1. Two theological seminaries are already established in this area:
    a. Garrett Biblical Institute, with a faculty of approximately 37 members, has long enjoyed an excellent working arrangement with the university. In addition to other advantages of a practical sort, this gives B.D. students access to appropriate courses in the university and provides opportunity for work for advanced degrees.

In addition to a strong general program of undergraduate and graduate studies, Garrett has a strong emphasis on practical training for both urban church and rural church work.

    b.   Seabury-Western Theological Seminary adds its resources to the pool of theological competence here.

2.   The Ecumenical Institute, although new, is attracting noted scholars—for example, in 1960-61, Dr. Theodore O. Wedel and Bishop Nygren—and has great potential significance.

3.   Among the special features of the university's program which would have significance for theological education are its strong Schools of African Studies, Speech, Music, Journalism, and Education. The African Studies would be of particular interest to students of the School of Missions.

4.   For the B.D. students at the Lutheran Seminary, courses would be open at the University as well as at Garrett and Seabury-Western.

5.   For graduate students, the University would give the Master's and Doctor's degrees. Garrett professors now share in the preparation of students for these degrees and a similar arrangement could probably be made for professors of the Lutheran Seminary.

6.   For students of the School of Missions, in addition to the School of African Studies, the University's strength in anthropology and the presence of the Ecumenical Institute should have great value.

7.   The University is prepared to offer to the Lutheran Seminary students ancillary advantages similar to those enjoyed by the students of schools within the University, as health insurance, gymnasium privileges, etc.

B.   **Hyde Park and the University of Chicago**

The following are among the academic advantages of a site adjacent to the University of Chicago:

1.   Here also is an intellectual climate highly favorable to the reception of a Lutheran Seminary. The University has a long history of interest in theology and respect for it. In addition to the fact that a Divinity School is part of the academic structure of the University and in the past has furnished two presidents of the University, this concern is reflected in the close working relations between the Divinity School

and other branches of the University; in the character of the libraries and in the bearing of theology on other professional emphases.

2.   The presence here of the Divinity School and of the Chicago Theological Seminary provides rich resources of theological scholarship, including opportunities for vocational specializations of various sorts, as in institutional chaplaincy, religious social work and social research. The Divinity School, in particular, has an unusual emphasis on graduate study. Several eminent Lutheran scholars are now members of these faculties.

3.   The University now includes many students who take courses for credit in other institutions of learning, including the theological schools, and its courses are open to the students of such institutions. It would be easy for students of a Lutheran Seminary to glean a rich harvest of university offerings.

4.   Among the aspects of the University program which would have special bearing on theological education the following should be mentioned:

   a.   In all phases of the social sciences the University is adequately, even superbly equipped. The anthropology department is one of the country's best.

   b.   There are rich resources for the study of philosophy, the classics, history and languages. The close relation between the Divinity School and the history department, for example, is shown by the practice of having all students of church history take a course in historical methods given by the University.

   c.   In studies of Religion and Personality and in the Sociology of Religion there is little that is comparable in our land. The Department of the History of Religions also deserves special mention.

   d.   Cooperative Studies in Education offer a depth and range of opportunity that are unusual and attractive to high-grade work. We believe the graduate school in this field has high potential value for theological students.

5.   The Far East Studies and South East Asian programs are, perhaps, unique in this country. The Oriental Institute is world-famed. These are among the features that would be particularly attractive to students of the School of Missions.

251

6. The opportunities for graduate studies leading to higher degrees to be given by the University are of great variety and of the highest quality. The University now has about 110 divinity students preparing for the Ph.D. degree, of whom 45 are Lutherans.

Other Considerations

A. Evanston

Evanston is a socially privileged, highly restricted, beautiful residential community, offering excellent living conditions and educational facilities. However, it would be, from every point of view, an expensive place in which to locate the new seminary. Its entire area is almost completely built up. Land sells at $350,000 an acre and there are virtually no acres for sale. Northwestern, to meet its expansion needs, is forced to reclaim land from Lake Michigan on which to build. We are advised that no good available property of a size to accommodate the Lutheran Seminary seems to be in sight short of a distance of about ten miles from the University. A restriction of the height of buildings to 45 feet would prevent the seminary from going upward on a small plot, even if this type of seminary skyscraper seemed advisable. Living quarters near at hand for faculty and students would be almost prohibitively expensive.

B. Hyde Park

We have been led to believe that it would probably be possible to secure a suitable site, conveniently near the University, at a reasonable cost. However, the great disadvantage of a location here is the blighted neighborhood. This has long been one of the least desirable living areas in Chicago. On the other hand, a broad gauge program of renewal and improvement is now firmly established. Substantial funds are available from Federal, city and private sources. The University is active in extending and developing its holdings. Plans for superior elementary school and high school facilities and for expanded park areas are well under way. It is confidently asserted that within ten years the most serious blight in the immediate neighborhood of the University will be overcome. The area is attracting an unusual galaxy of educational, cultural, and service institutions, which add to its advantages as a site for a seminary.

V. WEIGHING THE ADVANTAGES

1. It is obvious that each location has certain advantages and certain disadvantages. Before attempting to weigh these we would mention some considerations which are applicable to both.

    a. In either location the new Lutheran Seminary would be an independent institution, responsible to its own Church.

Whatever cooperative relationships it established with a university or with other seminaries would not limit its control over its own program or require any modification of its doctrinal position.

b. Specifically, the B.D. course, the School of Missions, and the present Th.M. program would continue under the control of the Seminary with only such modifications as might be desired in order to utilize the teaching, research and library facilities of other institutions.

c. In either case the adjacent university could be looked to to provide the facilities for doctoral work. This we understand to be your desire.

d. In each location the presence of other competent theological faculties would be intellectually stimulating and would permit such advantages as more frequent sabbatical leaves, less duplication and more variety in courses, and greater cross-fertilization for all.

2. Academically, the scales seem to us to be weighted in favor of a relationship with the University of Chicago. This is so for several reasons:

a. For the B.D. student, who is the man we have chiefly in mind, we believe the professionally oriented setting of the University of Chicago offers a more suitable mental climate than does Northwestern which is primarily an undergraduate institution, increasingly interested in engineering. There is now considerable dialogue on the South Side among the faculties of theology, law, medicine and business to the enrichment of each and the profit of their pupils.

b. If you are right—as we think you are—in your emphases and your presuppositions of theological education, the strength of Chicago in the social sciences meets your need, but is balanced by corresponding excellence in philosophy, history and classical studies.

c. It is when we contemplate advanced theological studies that the manifold advantages of the University of Chicago are clearest. As we earlier noted, it already has about 110 divinity students working for the Ph.D. degree, of whom 45 are Lutherans. There is an atmosphere of mental excitement and mutual stimulation at this advanced level, a flexibility and applicability of doctoral programs born of long competence together with great resources representing every field of scholarship which has importance for theological education. Moreover, for a strong Lutheran seminary to be in a position to maintain direct contact with this considerable number of Lutheran doctoral candidates should have great value both for them and for the Lutheran Church. This is a situation ready-made for your advantage.

d. For the students of the School of Missions, it seems plain that the resources of the University of Chicago in languages, education, comparative religions, anthropology, history and related fields will more than adequately meet their interests and needs.

e. There seems to us to be a sharper focus here than at Northwestern on various specialized aspects and needs of the ministry and a greater opportunity for technical training when desired (as in the chaplaincy, social work, research, etc.). This is facilitated by the significant emphasis in the University on research and on a close working relationship among all faculties. Further, from this location there is easy access to many institutions for clinical and field work experiences.

Thus, the more the new seminary becomes, on the one hand, a center of practical preparation for the Lutheran ministry and world mission and, on the other, the focal point of advanced studies for the Lutherans of America, the more advantageous proximity to the University of Chicago appears to be. This is not to imply that this would be the only suitable location for your new Seminary, but that, in relation to the factors which you asked us to consider, this appears to us to be the best solution of your problem.

Incidentally we mention that the dissolution of the Federated Faculty does not seem to us to weaken the resources that we have listed, and may, in fact, provide a more favorable situation for the reception of a Lutheran Seminary than before. Both the Divinity School and the Chicago Theological Seminary would rejoice if the Lutheran Seminary should be located here.

3. On other than academic grounds, also, we feel that the weight of the evidence is on the side of a site adjacent to the University of

254

Chicago. This is primarily for practical reasons but is said with the hope and expectation that the present sociological disadvantage of such a site will be gradually overcome and that substantial improvement may be anticipated within a reasonably short period.

We wish that circumstances had permitted us to make a more thorough study, but we have no reason to feel that this would have led us to any different conclusion.

We are grateful for the privilege of working with you and wish you the fullest measure of success in your most important undertaking. If we can be of further assistance we are at your call.

Respectfully submitted,

Charles L. Taylor
Oren H. Baker
Hermann N. Morse

February 2, 1961

Appendix VI

BOARD OF DIRECTORS

1963 - 1968

BOARD OF DIRECTORS, 1963-1964

Officers of the Board

Chairman — Rev. Harold C. Skillrud
Vice-Chairman — Rev. Robert B. Anderson
Secretary — Rev. Dr. Harold R. Lohr
Treasurer — Mr. Fred W. Soderberg, Jr.

Members of the Board

I. Elected by Synods

Illinois Synod Representatives

Dr. Kermit O. Almos
Rev. Harry S. Andersen
Mr. Fred Drinhaus
Mr. V. Richard Hietikko
Rev. Dr. Harold R. Lohr
Rev. Dr. George L. Lundquist
Rev. Dr. Luther C. Mueller
Rev. Harold C. Skillrud
Mr. Jack Sundine
Mr. Albert H. Wohlers

Indiana-Kentucky Synod Representatives

Rev. Dr. William G. Arbaugh
Dr. Robert F. Borkenstein
Mr. Arnold L. Johnson
Rev. Dr. Paul H. Krauss

Michigan Synod Representatives

Rev. Kenneth Granquist
Dr. George E. Mendenhall
Dr. Stephen J. Turille

Wisconsin-Upper Michigan Synod Representatives

Rev. Dr. O. V. Anderson
Rev. Robert B. Anderson
Rev. Thomas Asuma
Rev. Charles F. Burmeister
Mr. Edwin S. Pedersen
Dr. Gustof A. Peterson
Mr. Edward J. Seiy

II. Ex-officio Members

Rev. Dr. Frank P. Madsen, President, Michigan Synod
Rev. Dr. Robert J. Marshall, President, Illinois Synod
Rev. Dr. Theodore E. Matson, President, Wisconsin-Upper Michigan Synod
Rev. Dr. Walter M. Wick, President, Indiana-Kentucky Synod

III. Consultative Members

Rev. Dr. Conrad Bergendoff, Executive Secretary, Board of Theological Education, LCA

Rev. Dr. Earl S. Erb, Executive Secretary, Board of World Missions, LCA

IV. Advisory Members

President
Rev. Dr. Stewart Herman

Administrative Vice-Presidents
Maywood Campus: Rev. Dr. Armin G. Weng
Rock Island Campus: Rev. Dr. Karl E. Mattson

Deans
Acting Dean-Maywood: Rev. J. Stephen Bremer
Graduate School-Maywood: Rev. Dr. Johannes Knudsen
School of Missions-Maywood: Rev. James A. Scherer
Rock Island Campus: Rev. Dr. Arthur O. Arnold

Treasurer
Mr. Fred W. Soderberg

Associate Treasurers
Maywood: Mr. Carl Bergendoff
Rock Island: Mr. William Peterson

V. Consultant
Mr. C. H. Anderson

BOARD OF DIRECTORS, 1964-1965
Officers of the Board

Chairman — Rev. Harold C. Skillrud
Vice-Chairman — Rev. Robert B. Anderson
Secretary — Rev. Dr. Harold R. Lohr
Treasurer — Mr. Fred W. Soderberg, Jr.

Members of the Board

I. Elected by Synods

Illinois Synod Representatives

Dr. Kermit O. Almos
Rev. Harry S. Andersen
Mr. Fred Drinhaus
Mr. V. Richard Hietikko
Rev. Dr. Harold R. Lohr
Rev. Dr. George L. Lundquist
Rev. Dr. Luther C. Mueller
Rev. Harold C. Skillrud
Mr. Jack Sundine
Mr. Albert H. Wohlers

Indiana-Kentucky Synod Representatives

Rev. Dr. William G. Arbaugh
Dr. Robert F. Borkenstein
Mr. Arnold L. Johnson
Rev. Dr. Paul H. Krauss

Michigan Synod Representatives

Rev. Kenneth Granquist
Dr. George E. Mendenhall
Mr. Philip Wargelin

Wisconsin-Upper Michigan Synod Representatives

Rev. Dr. O. V. Anderson
Rev. Robert B. Anderson
Rev. Thomas Asuma
Rev. Charles F. Burmeister
Mr. Harry Gjelsteen
Mr. Edwin S. Pedersen
Mr. Edward J. Seiy

260

II. Ex-officio Members

Rev. Dr. Robert J. Marshall, President, Illinois Synod
Rev. Dr. Walter M. Wick, President, Indiana-Kentucky Synod
Rev. Dr. Frank P. Madsen, President, Michigan Synod
Rev. Dr. Theodore E. Matson, President, Wisconsin-Upper Michigan Synod

III. Consultative Members

Rev. Dr. E. Theodore Bachmann, Executive Secretary, Board of Theological Education of the Lutheran Church in America

Rev. Dr. Earl S. Erb, Executive Secretary, Board of World Missions of the Lutheran Church in America

IV. Advisory Members

President

Rev. Dr. Stewart W. Herman

Administrative Vice-Presidents

Maywood Campus: Rev. Dr. Armin George Weng
Rock Island Campus: Rev. Dr. Arthur O. Arnold

Deans

Dean of Faculty: Rev. Dr. L. Dale Lund
Dean of Students, Maywood: Rev. J. Stephen Bremer
Dean of Graduate School, Maywood: Rev. Dr. Johannes Knudsen
Dean of School of Missions, Maywood: Rev. James A. Scherer

BOARD OF DIRECTORS, 1965-1966

Officers of the Board

Chairman — Rev. Harold C. Skillrud
Vice-Chairman — Rev. Robert B. Anderson
Secretary — Rev. Dr. Harold R. Lohr
Treasurer — Mr. Fred W. Soderberg, Jr.

Members of the Board

I. Elected by Synods

Illinois Synod Representatives

Dr. Kermit O. Almos
Rev. Harry S. Andersen
Mr. Fred Drinhaus
Mr. V. Richard Hietikko
Rev. Samuel W. Jensen
Rev. Dr. Harold R. Lohr
Rev. Dr. George L. Lundquist
Rev. Harold C. Skillrud
Mr. Jack Sundine
Mr. Albert H. Wohlers

Indiana-Kentucky Synod Representatives

Rev. Dr. William G. Arbaugh
Dr. Robert F. Borkenstein
Mr. Arnold L. Johnson
Rev. Dr. Paul H. Krauss

Michigan Synod Representatives

Rev. Kenneth Granquist
Dr. George E. Mendenhall
Mr. Philip Wargelin

Wisconsin-Upper Michigan Synod Representatives

Mr. A. Roy Anderson
Rev. Dr. O. V. Anderson
Rev. Robert B. Anderson
Rev. Thomas Asuma
Rev. Charles F. Burmeister
Mr. Edwin S. Pedersen
Mr. Edward J. Seiy

II. Ex-officio Members

Rev. Dr. Robert J. Marshall, President, Illinois Synod
Rev. Dr. Walter M. Wick, President, Indiana-Kentucky Synod
Rev. Dr. Frank P. Madsen, President, Michigan Synod
Rev. Dr. Theodore E. Matson, President, Wisconsin-Upper Michigan
Synod

III. Consultative Members

> Rev. Dr. E. Theodore Bachmann, Executive Secretary, Board of Theological Education of the Lutheran Church in America
>
> Rev. Dr. Earl S. Erb, Executive Secretary, Board of World Missions of the Lutheran Church in America

IV. Advisory Members

President

> Rev. Dr. Stewart W. Herman

Administrators

> Maywood Campus: Rev. Dr. Armin George Weng
> Rev. Dr. Johannes Knudsen
> Rock Island Campus: Rev. Dr. Arthur O. Arnold

Deans

> Dean of Faculty: Rev. Dr. L. Dale Lund
> Dean of Graduate School, Maywood: Rev. Dr. Johannes Knudsen
> Dean of School of Missions, Maywood: Rev. James A. Scherer

BOARD OF DIRECTORS, 1966-1967

Officers of the Board

> Chairman — Rev. Harold C. Skillrud
> Vice-Chairman — Rev. Robert B. Anderson
> Secretary — Rev. Dr. Harold R. Lohr
> Treasurer — Mr. Fred W. Soderberg, Jr.

Members of the Board

I. Elected by Synods

Illinois Synod Representatives

> Dr. Kermit O. Almos
> Rev. Harry S. Anderson
> Mr. Fred Drinhaus
> Mr. V. Richard Hietikko
> Rev. Samuel W. Jensen

263

Mr. Lorentz A. Johanson
Rev. Dr. Harold R. Lohr
Rev. Dr. George L. Lundquist
Rev. Harold C. Skillrud
Mr. Albert H. Wohlers

Indiana-Kentucky Synod Representatives

Dr. Robert F. Borkenstein
Rev. Dr. Paul H. Krauss
Rev. Ronald Lavin
Mr. Eldon A. Swanson

Michigan Synod Representatives

Rev. Kenneth Granquist
Dr. George E. Mendenhall
Mr. Phillip Wargelin

Wisconsin-Upper Michigan Synod Representatives

Mr. Alan Anderson
Mr. A. Roy Anderson
Rev. Dr. O. V. Anderson
Rev. Robert B. Anderson
Rev. Thomas Asuma
Rev. Charles F. Burmeister
Mr. Edward J. Seiy

II. Ex-officio Members

Rev. Dr. Robert J. Marshall, President, Illinois Synod
Rev. Dr. Walter M. Wick, President, Indiana-Kentucky Synod
Rev. Dr. Frank P. Madsen, President, Michigan Synod
Rev. Dr. Theodore E. Matson, President, Wisconsin-Upper Michigan
Synod

III. Consultative Members

Rev. Dr. E. Theodore Bachmann, Executive Secretary, Board of
Theological Education of the Lutheran Church in America

Rev. Dr. Earl S. Erb, Executive Secretary, Board of World Missions
of the Lutheran Church in America

IV. Advisory Members

President

Rev. Dr. Stewart W. Herman

Administrators

Maywood Campus: Rev. Dr. Johannes Knudsen
Rock Island Campus: Rev. Dr. Arthur O. Arnold

Deans

Dean of Faculty: Rev. Dr. L. Dale Lund
Dean of School of Missions: Rev. James A. Scherer

BOARD OF DIRECTORS, 1967-1968

Officers of the Board

Chairman — Rev. Harold C. Skillrud
Vice-Chairman — Rev. Russell J. Olson
Secretary — Mr. Howard L. Peterson
Treasurer — Mr. Fred W. Soderberg, Jr.

Members of the Board

I. Elected by Synods

Central States Synod Representatives

Rev. Vernon F. Jacobs
Dr. Dean F. Werner

Illinois Synod Representatives

Dr. Kermit O. Almos
Dr. James N. BeMiller
Mr. Fred Drinhaus
Dr. Kenneth H. Eckhert
Mr. V. Richard Hietikko
Rev. Samuel W. Jensen
Rev. Dr. Harold R. Lohr
Rev. Dr. George L. Lundquist
Rev. Harold C. Skillrud

Indiana-Kentucky Synod Representatives

    Dr. Robert F. Borkenstein
    Rev. Dr. Paul H. Krauss
    Mr. Eldon A. Swanson
    Rev. Albert R. Swasko

Iowa Synod Representatives

    Rev. Dr. David R. Belgum
    Mr. Richard T. Grau
    Mr. Leonard C. Larsen
    Rev. Russell J. Olson

Michigan Synod Representatives

    Rev. Godfrey E. Alberti
    Rev. Sidney W. Jones
    Dr. George E. Mendenhall
    Mr. Philip J. Wargelin

Nebraska Synod Representatives
    Rev. Lawrence H. Beck
    Dr. Emory Lindquist
    Mr. Howard L. Peterson
    Rev. Walter E. Rowoldt

Rocky Mountain Synod Representatives

    Rev. Dr. John F. Futchs
    Dr. Paul Hultquist

Texas-Louisiana Synod Representatives

    Dr. Gordon Anderson
    Rev. Vance M. Daniel

Wisconsin-Upper Michigan Synod Representatives

    Mr. Alan R. Anderson
    Mr. A. Roy Anderson
    Rev. Dr. O. V. Anderson
    Rev. Robert B. Anderson
    Rev. William R. Sarvela
    Mr. Edward J. Seiy

II. Ex-officio Members

Rev. Dr. N. Everett Hedeen, President, Central States Synod
Rev. Dr. Robert J. Marshall, President, Illinois Synod
Rev. Dr. Walter M. Wick, President, Indiana-Kentucky Synod
Rev. Dr. Raynold J. Lingwall, President, Iowa Synod
Rev. Dr. Frank P. Madsen, President, Michigan Synod
Rev. Dr. Reuben T. Swanson, President, Nebraska Synod
Rev. Dr. Leeland C. Soker, President, Rocky Mountain Synod
Rev. Dr. Philip L. Wahlberg, Jr., President, Texas-Louisiana Synod
Rev. Dr. Theodore E. Matson, President, Wisconsin-Upper Michigan Synod

III. Consultative Members

Rev. Dr. E. Theodore Bachmann, Executive Secretary, Board of Theological Education of the Lutheran Church in America

Rev. Dr. Arne B. Sovik, Executive Secretary, Board of World Missions of the Lutheran Church in America

IV. Advisory Members

President
Rev. Dr. Stewart W. Herman

Dean of Faculty
Rev. Dr. L. Dale Lund

BOARD OF DIRECTORS, 1968-1969

Officers of the Board

Chairman — Rev. Harold C. Skillrud
Vice-Chairman — Rev. Russell J. Olson
Secretary — Mr. Harry Gjelsteen
Treasurer — Mr. Fred W. Soderberg, Jr.

Rocky Mountain Synod Representatives

> Rev. Dr. John F. Futchs
> Dr. Paul Hultquist

Texas-Louisiana Synod Representatives

> Dr. Gordon Anderson
> Rev. Dr. F. Leslie Conrad, Jr.

Wisconsin-Upper Michigan Synod Representatives

> Mr. Alan R. Anderson
> Rev. Dr. O. V. Anderson
> Mr. Harry Gjelsteen
> Rev. Dr. Eric J. Gustavson
> Mr. Earl Jacobson
> Rev. William R. Sarvela

II. Ex-officio Members

> Rev. Dr. N. Everett Hedeen, President, Central States Synod
> Rev. Dr. Gerald K. Johnson, President, Illinois Synod
> Rev. Dr. Walter M. Wick, President, Indiana-Kentucky Synod
> Rev. Dr. Raynold J. Lingwall, President, Iowa Synod
> Rev. Dr. Frank P. Madsen, President, Michigan Synod
> Rev. Dr. Reuben T. Swanson, President, Nebraska Synod
> Rev. Dr. Leeland C. Soker, President, Rocky Mountain Synod
> Rev. Dr. Philip L. Wahlberg, Jr., President, Texas-Louisiana Synod
> Rev. Dr. Theodore E. Matson, President, Wisconsin-Upper Michigan Synod

III. Consultative Members

> Rev. Dr. E. Theodore Bachmann, Executive Secretary, Board of Theological Education of the Lutheran Church in America
>
> Rev. Dr. Arne B. Sovik, Executive Secretary, Board of World Missions of the Lutheran Church in America

IV. Advisory Members

President

> Rev. Dr. Stewart W. Herman

Dean of Faculty

> Rev. Dr. Wesley Fuerst

Appendix VII

NEW SEMINARY FLOOR PLAN

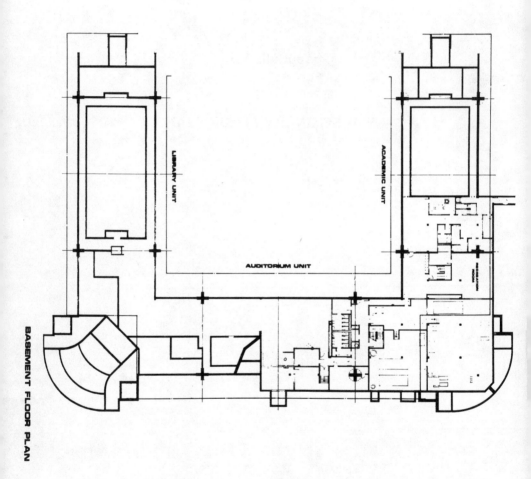

BASEMENT FLOOR PLAN

LIBRARY UNIT

ACADEMIC UNIT

RECREATION ROOM

AUDITORIUM UNIT

272

PLAZA FLOOR PLAN

LIBRARY UNIT

ACADEMIC UNIT

AUDITORIUM UNIT

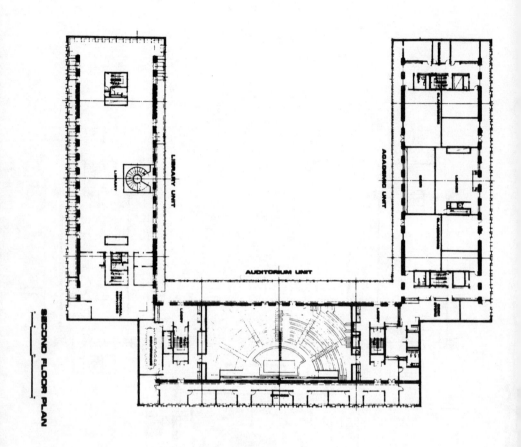

SECOND FLOOR PLAN

LIBRARY UNIT

AUDITORIUM UNIT

ACADEMIC UNIT

THIRD FLOOR PLAN

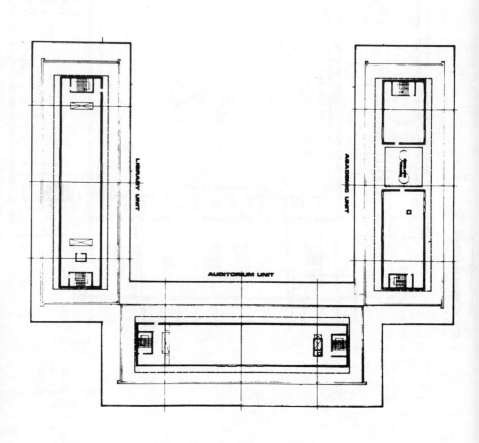

PENTHOUSE FLOOR PLAN

276

Appendix VIII

ORDER FOR GROUNDBREAKING

OCTOBER 6, 1965

ORDER FOR GROUNDBREAKING

for the new

LUTHERAN SCHOOL OF THEOLOGY AT CHICAGO

55th Street between University
and Greenwood Avenues

1:30 in the afternoon
October 6, 1965

ORDER OF GROUNDBREAKING

55th Street between University and Greenwood Avenues
Lutheran School of Theology at Chicago
October 6, 1965, 1:30 p.m.

In the Name of the Father, and of the Son, and of the Holy Ghost.

AMEN.

O Lord, open thou my lips.
R. And my mouth shall show forth thy praise.
Make haste, O God, to deliver me.
R. Make haste to help me, O Lord.
Except the Lord build the house:
R. They labor in vain that built it.
Glory be to the Father, and to the Son, and to the Holy Ghost:
R. As it was in the beginning, is now, and ever shall be, world
without end. Amen.

Psalm 122 (Read responsively)

I was glad when they said unto me: Let us go into the house of
the Lord.
Our feet shall stand within thy gates: O Jerusalem.
Jerusalem is builded as a city: that is compact together;
Whither the tribes go up, the tribes of the Lord: unto the testimony
of Israel, to give thanks unto the Name of the Lord.
For there are set thrones of judgment: the thrones of the house of
David.
Pray for the peace of Jerusalem: they shall prosper that love thee.
Peace be within thy walls: and prosperity within thy palaces.
For my brethren and companions' sakes: I will now say, Peace be
within thee.
Because of the house of the Lord our God: I will seek thy good.

Glory be to the Father, and to the Son, and to the Holy Ghost:
as it was in the beginning, is now, and ever shall be, world without end. Amen.

The Lessons: Ex. 3:1-6

Luke 8:4-8

280

Meditation

Lord, have mercy upon us.
    R.   Lord, have mercy upon us.
Christ, have mercy upon us.
    R.   Christ, have mercy upon us.
Lord, have mercy upon us.
    R.   Lord, have mercy upon us.

Our Father, who are in heaven, . . .

The Lord be with you.
    R.   And with thy spirit.

Let us pray.

Accept, O Lord, this place and let thy blessing descend upon it as the dew from heaven, that hence may arise adoration, thanksgiving and praise of thy holy Name; that here thy Word may be proclaimed and thy way revealed; that this may be thy House and the Place where thine honor dwelleth. Let thy gracious benediction ever abide here and upon all who shall gather here to worship and serve thee; through Jesus Christ, our Lord. AMEN.

Let the beauty of the Lord our God be upon us, and establish thou the work of our hands upon us; that as, in thy Name, we undertake the building of a House to thy glory, we may of thee be blessed in its beginning, prospered in its continuance, and established in its completion; through Jesus Christ, our Lord. AMEN.

The Groundbreaking

In the faith of Jesus Christ this work is begun and this ground is broken: In the Name of the Father, and of the Son, and of the Holy Ghost. May true faith, the fear of God and the love of the brethren flourish here; and may this place be set apart for the invocation and adoration of the Name of our Lord Jesus Christ, who with the Father and the Holy Ghost, liveth and reigneth, one God, world without end. Amen.

O God, in whom every good thing has its beginning, and by whom it increases and advances to greater worth: Grant us, thy servants, that what we have this day undertaken to the glory of thy Name, may, by the aid of thy fatherly wisdom, be successfully completed; through Jesus Christ, our Lord. AMEN.

Bless be the Lord.
    R.   Thanks be to God.

The Blessing of Almighty God, the Father, the Son, and the Holy Ghost be with you all. AMEN.

This ceremony is being performed at the southern boundary of the block which will be used in its entirety for the academic building. Here will be housed a chapel-auditorium with a seating capacity of 500, a dozen classrooms with total student stations exceeding 600, the commons area where as many as 200 persons may be accommodated, a library with a 250,000 book capacity, and the offices for faculty and administrative personnel.

In the blocks immediately north and northeast of this site the Lutheran School of Theology at Chicago owns buildings containing nearly 200 apartments which will be devoted to the housing of both single and married students. Longer range plans include the erection of a single men's domitory.

Across 55th Street to the south is the campus of the University of Chicago. The building at the corner of University Avenue and 55th Street in Pierce Tower and its commons area, newest men's residence hall of the University.

Participants:

Chairman of the Board of Directors:
    The Reverend Harold C. Skillrud (Liturgist)

Synod Presidents:
    Dr. Frank P. Madsen, Michigan Synod
    Dr. Robert J. Marshall, Illinois Synod
    Dr. Theodore E. Matson, Wisconsin-Upper Michigan Synod
    Dr. Walter M. Wick, Indiana-Kentucky Synod (Preacher)

Board of Theological Education of LCA:
    Dr. E. Theodore Bachmann, Executive Secretary

President of the Lutheran School of Theology at Chicago:
    Dr. Stewart W. Herman

Appendix IX

FOUNDATION FESTIVAL

APRIL 24, 1966

The Lutheran School of Theology
at Chicago

Chicago's Place in LSTC History

1860 Augustana Seminary founded in Chicago at Immanuel Lutheran Church "to train young men for the holy ministry," moved to Paxton, Illinois, in 1863 where it became both college and seminary in 1869.

1872 The General Council (subsequently a part of the United Lutheran Church in America) invites Augustana Synod to join in the establishment of a theological seminary in Chicago, but the Synod felt unable to sever the theological department from Augustana College which was on the point of moving to Rock Island.

1874 Dr. W. A. Passavant presents a two-acre site in Lake View (now Wrigley Field) for seminary use but Chicago fire and successive financial crises postponed beginning of school.

1886 *Grand View Seminary established in northwestern Wisconsin by Danish Evangelical Lutheran Church.*

1891 Chicago Lutheran Theological Seminary opened in St. Mary's Chapel (German) near the Lake View site under the auspices of the General Council but without its "pecuniary" support.

1893 Cornerstone-laying for Eliza Hall, first dormitory and classroom building of CLTS was scheduled on February 6 but had to be postponed for two days when a "blinding, furious snowstorm claimed the day for its own." The ceremony was again postponed for two days after the temperature dropped to 8 below zero in 24 hours. It was not until February 10 that a small, shivering company of people came cautiously over ice-covered roads to witness the historic event.

1896 *Suomi College and Theological Seminary organized in Hancock, Michigan by the Finnish Evangelical Lutheran Church.*

Continued on page 291

Foundation Festival of Praise, Hyde Park Campus

April 24, 1966   4:00 P.M.

Royal Fanfare

*Processional Hymn.....................................(*The Assembly stands)

Praise to the Lord, the Almighty, the King of creation;
O my soul, praise him for he is they health and salvation:
> All ye who hear, Now to his temple draw near
> Joining in glad adoration.

Praise to the Lord, who o'er all things so wondrously reigneth,
Shelters thee under his wings, yea, so gently sustaineth:
> Hast thou not seen? All that is needful hath been
> Granted in what he ordaineth.

Praise to the Lord, who doth prosper thy work and defend thee;
Surely his goodness and mercy here daily attend thee.
> Ponder anew What the Almighty can do,
> If with his love he befriend thee!

Praise to the Lord, O let all that is in me adore him;
All that hath life and breath, come now with praises before him!
> Let the Amen sound from his people again;
> Gladly for aye we adore him.   Amen.

*The Invocation....................................The Rev. Harold C. Skillrud,
Chairman of the Board

The Psalm #48.....................................Maywood Campus Choir

The Lessons: I Chronicles 29:10-18........Mr. Daniel Erlander, Rock Island, Lector
I Peter 2:1-7...............Mr. Bruce Welander, Maywood, Lector

*The Apostles' Creed

Introduction of Speaker.............................Dr. Stewart W. Herman

The Address . . . "The Throne and the Faculties"........Dr. Conrad J. I. Bergendoff

The Hymn—Anthem . . . "The Lord Our God Alone is Strong".Maywood Campus Choir

*The Prayer   V. The Lord be with you
R. And with thy spirit.
Let us pray.

*The Litany of Thanksgiving

> O Lord, open Thou our lips
> And our mouths shall show forth Thy praise.

Almighty God, our Heavenly Father, from whom comes every good and perfect gift, we recall Thy loving kindness and Thy tender mercies, and with grateful hearts we lift to Thee the voice of our thanksgiving:

For the glory with which Thou dost invest the things of the earth,
For the mystery of the creative process, and the wonder of design,
For the eye that beholds, and the mind that conceives and delights,
For the hands that draw blueprints, and the hands that weld steel,
For the materials of concrete, steel and glass, and the labor of men who build with them,

> R. We praise Thee, O God.

For the streams of religious tradition merged in the building of this school,
For the Suomi tradition of intimate, personal comradeship with the living Christ,
For the Danish tradition of awareness that we are living stones of God's house,
For the Augustana tradition of faith in the Heavenly Father whose children we are,
For the United Lutheran tradition of ecumenical concern and Lutheran unity,

> R. We praise Thee, O God.

For the University of Chicago, and all the neighboring schools of this community,
For education, and all the privileges we enjoy through literature, science and art,
For all true knowledge of Thee and Thy love which we are permitted to learn and to teach,
For every opportunity this new school will have of serving our generation in its concern for social justice, human dignity and international peace,
For every occasion this school will have of manifesting the love of Christ to men in our city and in all the world,

> R. We praise Thee, O God.

God of all grace and love, we have praised Thee with our lips; Grant that we may not fail to hear Thee in the cry of human need. Help us to see Thee in the hunger and distress of Thy people. May we serve Thee by serving them in consecrated and faithful lives, to Thy honor and glory, through Jesus Christ our Lord.

> R. Amen.

*The Collect for Divine Blessing...........................Dr. Robert J. Marshall,
Chairman, Building and Site Committee

O Lord Jesus Christ, Son of the Living God, who art the one Foundation, and the
Chief Cornerstone of the Holy Church: Bless what we do now in sealing this stone
in Thy Name, and be Thou, we beseech Thee, the beginning, the increase, and the
consumation of this our work, which is undertaken to Thy glory; who with the
Father and the Holy Ghost lives and reigns, one God, world without end.

> R. Amen

A copper box containing a copy of the Holy Scriptures is then inserted in the cornerstone by President Stewart W. Herman and the bronze plaque lifted into place.

Sealing the Cornerstone...................................Dr. Robert J. Marshall

> In the faith of Jesus Christ I do now seal the Cornerstone of this house of
> prayer and study, to be known as the Lutheran School of Theology at Chicago.

Declaration of Purpose.................................Dr. Theodore E. Matson

> Here may true faith, and the fear of God, and brotherly love ever abide; and
> let this place be set apart for the teaching of the Word, the preparation of men
> for the ministry of the Gospel to the world, and the invocation and praise of
> the Name of our Lord Jesus Christ, who with the Father and the Holy Ghost
> lives and reigns, one God, world without end.

> R. Amen

*The Collect for Divine Renewal...........................Dr. Frank P. Madsen

> O Lord God, who makest the assembly of Thy saints an everlasting dwelling-
> place for Thy Majesty: Bless and prosper the building of this edifice, and grant
> that in like manner we also, as living stones, may be built up into a spiritual
> house and an abiding temple of Thy glory; through Jesus Christ our Lord.

> R. Amen

*The Lord's Prayer

*The Benediction...Dr. Paul H. Krauss

*The Hymn

Built on a rock the church doth stand, even when steeples are falling;
Crumbled have spires in every land, bells still are chiming and calling;
Calling the young and old to rest, calling the souls of men distressed,
Longing for life ever-lasting.

Not in our temples made with hands God, the almighty, is dwelling;
High in the heavens his temple stands, all earthly temples excelling;
Yet he who dwells in heaven above deigns to abide with us in love,
Making our bodies his temple.

We are God's house of living stones, built for his own habitation;
He fills our hearts, his humble thrones, granting us life and salvation;
Were two or three to seek his face, he in their midst would show his grace,
Blessings upon them bestowing.   Amen.

The Litany of Thanksgiving was written by Professor Morris Niedenthal

*Royal Fanfare by Brass Quartet—Trumpets . . . Randy and Jordan Sandke;
French Horn . . . Hans Sittler; Trombone . . . Suzanne Eigen.*

1962 The Lutheran School of Theology at Chicago was formally established on September 4, as a result of the merger of four institutions: Augustana Theological Seminary at Rock Island, Illinois and Chicago Lutheran Theological Seminary at Maywood, Illinois, with which both Grand View Seminary at Des Moines, Iowa and Suomi Theological Seminary at Hancock, Michigan had already been affiliated since 1960.

The new school serves the Lutheran Church in America and is governed by a Board of Directors elected by the four synods which in addition to bearing the major share of regular operating costs, are contributing over $5,000,000 for the construction of the future campus. These synods are Illinois, Indiana-Kentucky, Michigan and Wisconsin-Upper Michigan. LSTC is also receiving substantial support from the church's Board of Theological Education and the Board of World Missions.

1964-

65 The exact site of the new $4,000,000 academic unit fronting on 55th Street between University and Greenwood Avenues was selected in mid-summer 1964. Purchase of the entire block was completed in May 1965. Demolition of existing buildings began the following September and there was a ground-breaking ceremony on October 6. The large building, which was designed by Perkins & Will and is being erected by James McHugh Company, is expected to be ready for use in September 1967. The new campus, including the adjacent dormitory block, comprises about six acres.

The cornerstone is located at the southwest entry between the library and the chapel-auditorium. A "timeless capsule" contains the Holy Bible and a copy of today's program. All other pertinent documents and mementos of the occasion will be preserved in the archives of the school.

> "For the pillars of the earth are the Lord's,
> And he has set the world upon them."
> Song of Hannah

Appendix X

CENTRAL-LSTC ARTICLES OF MERGER

STATE OF NEBRASKA

Department of State

Frank Marsh, Secretary of State of the
State of Nebraska does hereby certify that
the attached is a true and correct copy of the
Articles of Merger of Central Lutheran Theological
Seminary, a Nebraska corporation, merging with and
into LUTHERAN SCHOOL OF THEOLOGY AT CHICAGO, an
Illinois corporation authorized to conduct affairs
in the State of Nebraska as a non-profit corporation,
as filed and recorded in this office on June 30,
1967.

In Testimony Whereof, I have hereunto set my hand and
affixed the Great Seal of the State
of Nebraska.

Done at Lincoln this

_____thirtieth_____

day of _____June_____
in the year of our Lord, one thousand nine hundred and sixty-seven.

SECRETARY OF STATE

_____
DEPUTY

294

Filing Fee _____

Date Paid _____

Clerk _____

TO: Frank Marsh, Secretary of·State, State of Nebraska

The undersigned corporations, pursuant to Section 21-1937 of the Nebraska Non-Profit Corporation Act hereby execute the following Articles of Merger:

ARTICLE ONE

The names of the corporations proposing to merge and the names of the States under the laws·of which such corporations are organized, are as follows:

Name of Corporation	State of Incorporation
Lutheran School of Theology at Chicago	Illinois
Central Lutheran Theological Seminary	Nebraska

ARTICLE TWO

The laws of Illinois, the State under which such foreign corporation is organized, permits such merger.

ARTICLE THREE

The surviving corporation shall be LUTHERAN SCHOOL OF THEOLOGY AT CHICAGO, and it shall be governed by the laws of the State of Illinois.

ARTICLE FOUR

The plan of merger is as follows:

PLAN OF MERGER

The Parties to this Plan of Merger are:

Lutheran School of Theology at Chicago, an Illinois not-for-profit corporation, herein sometimes referred to as "Lutheran School"; and

Central Lutheran Theological Seminary, a Nebraska non-profit corporation, herein sometimes referred to as "Central Lutheran", WITNESSETH:

1. WHEREAS, each of the parties hereto is a not-for-profit corporation incorporated for the purpose of educating persons for the Christian ministry and other specific Christian service, and owns and is possessed of a theological seminary and of assets, real and personal; and

2. WHEREAS, the Voting Members of Central Lutheran are the Board of Directors of Central Lutheran, constituting twenty-one members; and

3. WHEREAS, the Voting Members of Lutheran School are the members of the Board of Directors of Lutheran School, constituting twenty-seven members; and

4. WHEREAS, it is the desire of the parties hereto that Central Lutheran be merged with and into Lutheran School, under and in accordance with the General Not For Profit Corporation Act of the State of Illinois, and as such merger is permitted by the applicable statutes of the State of Nebraska and the State of Illinois.

5. THE PARTIES HERETO AGREE that Central Lutheran shall merge with and into Lutheran School upon the following terms, conditions and provisions, namely:

6. The name of the surviving corporation shall be: LUTHERAN SCHOOL OF THEOLOGY AT CHICAGO (hereinafter referred to as the "surviving corporation").

7. The Articles of Incorporation of the surviving corporation shall be deemed to be amended to the extent, if any, that changes in its Articles are stated in the Articles of Merger.

8. The Constitution and By-Laws of the surviving corporation as constituted and existing on the effective date of said merger shall be and constitute the Constitution and By-Laws of the surviving corporation until amended or repealed.

9. The voting rights of the members of the surviving corporation shall be established, determined and regularized by the By-Laws of the surviving corporation.

10. The number, election date, terms of office and qualifications of the officers of the surviving corporation shall be fixed by the Constitution and By-Laws of the surviving corporation.

11. In that the members of the Board of Directors of each of the respective parties to the Plan of Merger are the voting members of the respective corporations, the Board of Directors of each corporation, by a two-thirds majority vote, shall pass a resolution adopting the said Plan of Merger at a meeting of the Board of Directors of each constituent corporation where a quorum of the members entitled to vote thereon shall be present or by a consent in writing signed by all members entitled to vote with respect thereto.

12. When the Articles of Merger filed pursuant to the Plan of Merger become effective, the parties hereto shall be a single corporation which shall be that corporation designated in the Plan of Merger as the surviving corporation.

13. The separate existence of all parties to the Plan of Merger, except the surviving corporation, shall cease.

14. Such surviving corporation shall have all the rights, privileges, immunities, and powers and shall be subject to all the duties and liabilities of a corporation organized under the Illinois "General Not For Profit Corporation Act".

15. Such surviving corporation shall thereupon and thereafter possess all the rights, privileges, immunities and franchises of each of the merging corporations; and all property, real, personal and mixed, and all debts due on whatever account, and all other choses in action, and all and every other interest, of or belonging to or due to each of the corporations so merged, shall be taken and deemed to be transferred to and vested in such single corporation without further act or deed; and the title to any real estate, or any interest therein, vested in any of such corporations shall not revert or be in any way impaired by reason of such merger.

16. Such surviving corporation shall thenceforth be responsible and liable for all the liabilities and obligations of each of the corporations so merged; and any claim existing or action or proceeding pending by or against any of such corporations may be prosecuted to judgment as if such merger had not taken place, or such surviving corporation may be substituted in its place. Neither the rights of creditors nor any liens upon the property of any such corporations shall be impaired by such merger.

17. The procedure for merger hereunder shall be so timed that the merger shall become effective on June 30, 1967, or as soon thereafter as shall be reasonably possible.

18. For the convenience of the parties hereto and to facilitate the filing and recording of the Plan of Merger, any number of countersigned parts may be executed and, if executed, counterpart shall be deemed to be an original instrument.

ARTICLE FIVE

The members of the Board of Directors of Lutheran
School of Theology at Chicago and Central Lutheran Theological
Seminary are the voting members of the respective corporations.
As to each corporation, the voting members, by two-thirds majority vote, passed a resolution adopting the aforesaid Plan of
Merger at a meeting of the members of Lutheran School of Theology
at Chicago held on January 25, 1967, and Central Lutheran Theological Seminary held on February 17, 1967. A quorum of the members
entitled to vote thereon of such corporations respectively was
present at each such meeting; and such Plan of Merger received
at least two-thirds of the votes entitled to be cast by members
present or represented by proxy at each such meeting.

ARTICLE SIX

All provisions of the laws of the State of Illinois and
the State of Nebraska applicable to the proposed merger have been
complied with.

ARTICLE SEVEN

No change in the Articles of Incorporation of Lutheran
School of Theology at Chicago shall be deemed to have been effected
by these Articles of Merger.

ARTICLE EIGHT

Under a Certificate of Authority dated January 27, 1967,
and recorded on Film Roll No. 22, Misc. Inc. at Page 943, the
Secretary of State of Nebraska has authorized Lutheran School of
Theology at Chicago to conduct affairs in the State of Nebraska
as a non-profit corporation. In addition to its qualifying as a

foreign non-profit corporation, Lutheran School of Theology at Chicago expressly agrees:

 (a) that it may be served with process in the State of Nebraska in any proceeding for the enforcement of any obligation of any domestic corporation which is a party to the merger herein set forth; and

 (b) that the Secretary of State of the State of Nebraska is irrevocably appointed as its agent to accept service of process in any such proceeding.

 IN WITNESS WHEREOF each of the undersigned corporations has caused these Articles of Merger to be executed in its name by its _____president and by its _____ secretary on this _____17th_____day of _____February_____, 1967.

<table>
<tr><td></td><td>LUTHERAN SCHOOL OF THEOLOGY
AT CHICAGO
(Exact Corporate Title)</td></tr>
<tr><td>Place
(CORPORATE SEAL)
Here</td><td>By__Harold C. Hilbul__
  Its _____President</td></tr>
<tr><td></td><td>By__Harold R 2hr__
  Its _____Secretary</td></tr>
<tr><td></td><td>CENTRAL LUTHERAN
THEOLOGICAL SEMINARY
(Exact Corporate Title)</td></tr>
<tr><td>Place
(CORPORATE SEAL)
Here</td><td>By_____
  Its _____President</td></tr>
<tr><td></td><td>By__Walter E Roosvelt__
  Its _____Secretary</td></tr>
</table>

VERIFICATION:

 It is hereby certified by the undersigned president and secretary that the Articles of Merger as set out hereinabove were submitted to the Corporation's Board of Directors, also known as

Board of Trustees, on the 25th day of January, 1967. Said meeting was called pursuant to and in compliance with the Corporation's Articles of Incorporation, Constitution and By-Laws and the laws of the State of Illinois and that said Board of Directors, with a quorum present, adopted a resolution setting forth the Plan of Merger and directed that it be submitted to a vote at the meeting of the members having voting rights.

Harold C. Skillrud
President

Attest:

Harold R John
Secretary

VERIFICATION:

It is hereby certified by the undersigned president and secretary that the Articles of Merger as set out hereinabove were submitted to the Corporation's Board of Directors, also known as Board of Trustees, on the 17th day of February, 1967. Said meeting was called pursuant to and in compliance with the Corporation's Articles of Incorporation, Constitution and By-Laws and the laws of the State of Nebraska and that said Board of Directors, with a quorum present, adopted a resolution setting forth the Plan of Merger and directed that it be submitted to a vote at the meeting of the members having voting rights.

Russell James Olson
President

Attest:

Walter G. Rexroat
Secretary

STATE OF NEBRASKA) ss
COUNTY OF DODGE   )

I, Bernard T. Schafersman, a Notary Public, do hereby certify that on February 17, 1967, Harold C. Skillrud, President of Lutheran School of Theology at Chicago, and Russell James Olson, President of Central Lutheran Theological Seminary, personally appeared before me, and after being sworn on their oaths, both acknowledged that they signed the foregoing articles as Presidents of said corporations and declared the statements therein contained are true.

IN WITNESS WHEREOF, I have set my hand and seal the day above written.

Bernard T. Schafersman
Notary Public

My Commission Expires
October 1, 1971.

STATE OF NEBRASKA)
)   AFFIDAVIT
COUNTY OF DODGE)

     BERNARD T. SCHAFERSMAN, being duly sworn on oath, deposes and says that as attorney for Central Lutheran Theological Seminary, he attended a meeting of the Board of Directors on February 17, 1967 in Fremont, Dodge County, Nebraska, at which time the Articles of Merger of said corporation with the Lutheran School of Theology at Chicago were duly presented and passed, and the name and address of each member of the Board of Directors, also known as Board of Trustees, is as follows:

NAME	ADDRESS
Dr. N. Everett Hedeen	3527 Broadway, Suite 501 Kansas City, Missouri 64111
Mr. Laurence Anderson	2020 South Erie Wichita, Kansas 67211
Mr. Herman Langholz	438 West Wichita Avenue Russell, Kansas 67665
Mr. G. O. Lindgren	3812 West 51st Shawnee Mission, Kansas 66205
The Rev. Norman Ullestad	316 South Seventh Street Salina, Kansas 67401
The Rev. Raynold J. Lingwall, D.D.	4931 Douglas Avenue Des Moines, Iowa 50310
The Rev. Russell J. Olson, Pastor Trinity Lutheran Church	12th and Jackson Sioux City, Iowa 51105
Mr. Fridolph Hanson Iowa Lutheran Hospital	Seventh and Parnell Des Moines, Iowa 50316
Mr. Leonard C. Larsen	1822 Primrose Street Cedar Falls, Iowa 50313
The Rev. Wilbur E. Wicklund	215 South Seventh Street Council Bluffs, Iowa 50613
Mr. Tom Irwin	9004 Urbandale Avenue Des Moines, Iowa 50322
The Rev. David Belgum	104 Sunset Drive Iowa City, Iowa 52241

NAME	ADDRESS
The Rev. Reuben T. Swanson,D.D	124 South 24th St., Suite 204 Omaha, Nebraska 68102
Mr. William Hasebroock	West Point, Nebraska 68788
The Rev. Walter E. Rowoldt	1031 Sunset Trail Omaha, Nebraska 68132
The Rev. Lawrence H. Beck	6340 North 30th Street Omaha, Nebraska 68111
The Rev. Theodore Johnson,D.D.	501 North Burlington Avenue Hastings, Nebraska 68901
Mr. Marius Christensen	P.O. Box 73 Sidney, Nebraska 69162
Dr. Thomas Miller	1710 West B Street North Platte, Nebraska 69101
The Rev. Leeland C. Soker,D.D.	105 Fillmore Street, Suite 201 Denver, Colorado 80206
The Rev. Richard C. Wolf, Ph.D.	The Divinity School Vanderbilt University Nashville, Tennessee 37203
The Rev. Ray Tiemeyer	2390 North Road Los Alamos, New Mexico 87544
Mr. Roger Larson	6185 South Columbine Way Littleton, Colorado 80120
The Rev. Philip L. Wahlberg, Jr. D.D.	P.O. Box 4367 Austin, Texas 78751
Dr. Gordon Anderson	2508 Calewood Pl. Austin, Texas 78703
The Rev. Vance M. Daniel	7719 De Moss Houston, Texas 77036

Bernard T. Schafersman

SUBSCRIBED and sworn to before me this 26th day of
June, 1967.

Lila A. Greunke
Notary Public

Appendix XI

INAUGURATION OF PRESIDENT HERMAN

May 3, 1964

THE INAUGURATION OF

THE REVEREND STEWART WINFIELD HERMAN

AS PRESIDENT OF

THE LUTHERAN SCHOOL OF THEOLOGY AT CHICAGO

LUTHERAN CHURCH IN AMERICA

ROCKEFELLER MEMORIAL CHAPEL

FIVE-THIRTY O'CLOCK

MAY THIRD + NINETEEN HUNDRED SIXTY-FOUR

THE INAUGURATION SERVICE

ORGAN PRELUDE: Chorale Prelude in A Minor .... Cesar Franck
Chorale Prelude, "Come Holy Ghost" .... Dietrich Buxtehude
Toccata and Adagio in C .... J. S. Bach

PROCESSIONAL
(The Congregation will stand during the Procession and remain standing until after the Psalm)

THE PROCESSION

The Marshal

The Delegates from Colleges, Universities, Seminaries, and Learned Societies

The Representatives of the Church

The Faculty of the Lutheran School of Theology

The Board of Directors

The Representatives of the Board of World Missions of the Lutheran Church in America

The Representatives of the Board of Theological Education of the Lutheran Church in America

The Administrative Vice Presidents

The President and Secretary of the Board of Directors

The President of the Lutheran Church in America and the President of the Lutheran School of Theology at Chicago

VESPERS

The Reverend Dr. Harold R. Lohr, *Officiant*
Secretary, Board of Directors

THE HYMN "O Holy Spirit, enter in" .... *Wie Schoen Leuchtet*

O Holy Spirit, enter in
Among these hearts thy work begin,
 Thy temple deign to make us;
Sun of the soul, thou light divine,
Around and in us brightly shine,
 To strength and gladness wake us.
  Where thou shinest,
Life from heaven there is given;
 We before thee
For that precious gift implore thee.

O mighty Rock, O Source of life!
Let thy dear word, 'mid doubt and strife,
 Be so within us burning,
That we be faithful unto death
In thy pure love and holy faith,
 From thee true wisdom learning.
  Lord, thy graces
On us shower; by thy power
 Christ confessing,
Let us win his grace and blessing. Amen.

THE PSALM 67, *Deus misereatur nostri* (Said responsively)

God be merciful unto us, and bless us: and cause his face to shine upon us.

That thy way may be known upon earth: thy saving health among all nations.

Let the people praise thee, O God: let all the people praise thee.

O let the nations be glad and sing for joy: for thou shalt judge the people righteously and govern the nations upon earth.

Let the people praise thee, O God: let all the people praise thee.

Then shall the earth yeild her increase: and God, even our own God shall bless us

God shall bless us: and all the ends of the earth shall fear him.

Glory be to the Father, and to the Son, and to the Holy Ghost: As it was in the beginning, is now, and ever shall be, world without end. Amen.

307

THE FIRST LESSON: Isaiah 55: 6-11
The Reverend Dr. Karl E. Mattson, Vice President, Rock Island Campus

O Lord, have mercy upon us.
R̸. Thanks be to God.

ANTHEM: "The Heavens are Telling" .... Beethoven (arr. Saar.)

THE SECOND LESSON: John 16: 23-30
The Reverend Dr. Armin G. Weng, Vice President, Maywood Campus

O Lord, have mercy upon us.
R̸. Thanks be to God.

THE VERSICLE AND CANTICLE: The Magnificat (Congregation standing)

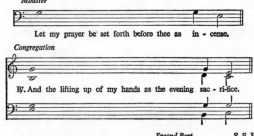

My soul doth ' magni - fy the ' Lord,
   * and my spirit hath re ' joiced in ' God my ' Saviour.
For ' he hath re ' garded
   * the ' low es ' tate of his ' handmaiden.
For be ' hold from ' henceforth
   * all gener ' ations shall ' call me ' blessed.
For he that is mighty hath done to me ' great ' things;
   * and ' holy ' is his ' Name.
Repeat second part of Chant for following verse only:
And his mercy is on ' them that ' fear him
   * from gener ' ation to ' gener ' ation.
He hath   shewed ' strength · with his ' arm;
   * He hath scattered the proud in the imagi ' nation of ' their ' hearts.
He hath put down the ' mighty · from their ' seats,
   * and exalted ' them of ' low de ' gree.
He hath filled the hungry with ' good ' things;
   * and the rich he hath ' sent ' empty a ' way.
He hath holpen his servant Israel, in re ' membrance · of his ' mercy;
   * as he spake to our fathers, to ' Abraham and · to his ' seed for ' ever.
GLORY ' be to the ' Father:
   * and to the ' Son · and to the ' Holy ' Ghost;
As it ' was in · the be ' ginning,
   * is now and ever shall be ' world without ' end. A ' men.

THE PRAYER

¶ *The Minister shall sing or say:*

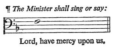

Lord, have mercy upon us,

R̸. Lord, have mer - cy up - on us. Christ, have mer - cy up - on us.

Lord, have mer - cy up - on us.

OUR FATHER, who art in heaven, Hallowed be thy Name, Thy kingdom come, Thy will be done, on earth as it is in heaven. Give us this day our daily bread; And forgive us our trespasses, as we forgive those who trespass against us; And lead us not into temptation, But deliver us from evil. For thine is the kingdom, and the power, and the glory, for ever and ever. Amen.

The Lord be with you. R̸. And with thy spirit.

The Collect for Rogate Sunday

O God, from whom all good things do come: Grant to us thy humble servants, that by thy holy inspiration we may think those things that be right, and by thy merciful guiding may perform the same; through thy Son, Jesus Christ our Lord, who liveth and reigneth with thee and the Holy Ghost, one God, world without end. R̸. *Amen.*

The Collect for Theological Seminaries

O God, who through thy Holy Spirit dost illuminate the minds and sanctify the lives of those whom thou dost call to the work of pastors and teachers: Look with thy favor upon all seminaries for the instruction and discipline of those who are to serve in the sacred Ministry of thy Church; bless those who teach and those who learn, that they may apply themselves with such diligence to the knowledge which is able to make men wise unto salvation, and submit themselves with such ready obedience to the law of thy Son, our Saviour, that they may fulfill their ministry with joy; through the same Jesus Christ, our Lord. R̸. *Amen.*

The Collect for Peace

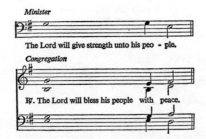

Minister

The Lord will give strength unto his peo - ple.

Congregation

℟. The Lord will bless his people with peace.

O God, from whom all holy desires, all good counsels, and all just works do proceed: Give unto thy servants that peace which the world cannot give; that our hearts may be set to obey thy commandments, and also that by thee, we, being defended from the fear of our enemies, may pass our time in rest and quietness; through the merits of Jesus Christ our Saviour, who liveth and reigneth with thee and the Holy Ghost, one God, world without end. ℟. *Amen.*

BENEDICAMUS:

Minister   *Congregation*

Bless we the Lord.   ℟. Thanks be to God.

HYMN: "Lord keep us steadfast in thy word" .... *Erhalt Uns, Herr*

Lord keep us steadfast in thy word,	Lord, Jesus Christ, thy power make known	O Comforter of priceless worth,
Curb those who fain by craft or sword	For thou art Lord of lords alone;	Send peace and unity on earth;
Would wrest the kingdom from thy Son,	Defend thy Christendom, that we	Support us in our final strife,
And set at naught all he hath done.	May evermore sing praise to thee.	And lead us out of death to life. Amen.

THE ADDRESS: The Reverend Dr. Franklin Clark Fry
President, Lutheran Church in America

THE INDUCTION OF THE PRESIDENT
The Reverend Harold C. Skillrud, Chairman of the Board of Directors

ANTHEM: "Gloria in Excelsis" from *Missa Brevis* .... Healy Willan

THE INAUGURAL ADDRESS The Reverend Dr. Stewart Winfield Herman, President

THE PRAYER AND BENEDICTION President Fry

The Lord be with you.
℟. And with thy spirit.

O Most Holy Spirit of God, from whom alone floweth the fulness of wisdom and life: Come in thine everlasting power and glory, we beseech thee, upon thy Church and into the hearts of men; to bring to the world a new birth of holiness, new interpretations of truth and new unity in love; through Jesus Christ our Lord, who with the Father and thee liveth and reigneth, one God, world without end. ℟. *Amen.*

The Grace of our Lord Jesus Christ, and the Love of God, and the Communion of the Holy Ghost, be with you all. ℟. *Amen.*

HYMN: "Lead on, O King eternal" .... *Lancashire*

Lead on, O King eternal,	Lead on, O King eternal,	Lead on, O King eternal:
The day of march has come;	Till sin's fierce war shall cease,	We follow, not with fears,
Henceforth in fields of conquest	And holiness shall whisper	For gladness breaks like morning
Thy tents shall be our home;	The sweet Amen of peace;	Where'er thy face appears:
Through days of preparation	For not with swords loud clashing,	Thy Cross is lifted o'er us;
Thy grace has made us strong,	Nor roll of stirring drums,	We journey in its light;
And now, O King eternal,	But deeds of love and mercy,	The crown awaits the conquest;
We lift our battle song.	Thy heavenly kingdom comes.	Lead on, O God of might. Amen.

THE RECESSIONAL: Chaconne in G Minor .... Louis Couperin
(The Congregation remains standing during the Recession)

✠

J. Stephen Bremer, *Marshal*
Dean of Students, Maywood Campus

Edward Mondello, *Organist*
Rockefeller Memorial Chapel

Choirs, Lutheran School of Theology
Dr. Henry Veld, *Director*
William Montgomery, *Organist*

Ushers: Seminarians, Rock Island Campus

Acolytes: Seminarians, Maywood Campus

311

THE DELEGATES FROM COLLEGES, UNIVERSITIES, AND SEMINARIES

DATE OF FOUNDING	INSTITUTION	INDIVIDUAL
1861	Luther College	President E. D. Farwell
1869	Luther Theological Seminary	President Alvin N. Rogness
1829	McCormick Theological Seminary	President Arthur R. McKay
1844	Meadville Theological School	President Malcolm R. Sutherland, Jr.
1945	Mennonite Biblical Seminary	President Erland Waltner
1887	Midland Lutheran College	Mr. Robert Benne
1848	Muhlenberg College	The Reverend Eugene C. Kreider, Jr.
1856	Newberry College	The Reverend John C. Cooper
1784	New Brunswick Theological Seminary	The Reverend R. J. Coert Rylaarsdam
1850	North American Baptist Seminary	The Reverend Dr. Frank H. Woyke
1913	Northern Baptist Theological Seminary	The Reverend Dr. Edwin E. Steward
1891	North Park Theological Seminary	Dr. Earl C. Dahlstrom
1920	Northwestern Lutheran Theological Seminary	President C. H. Zeidler
1833	Oberlin College, Graduate School of Theology	The Reverend Dr. Richard C. Wolf
1952	Pacific Lutheran Theological Seminary	The Reverend Walter Stuhr, Jr.
1794	Pittsburgh Theological Seminary	The Reverend Thomas N. Stark
1842	Roanoke College	Dr. Samuel L. Keller, Jr.
1858	Seabury-Western Theological Seminary	President Charles Upchurch Harris
1874	St. Olaf College	President Sidney A. Rand
1866	Thiel College	The Reverend Dr. Richard H. Gerberding
1812	Union Theological Seminary (Virginia)	The Reverend Leighton M. McCuthen, Jr.
1836	Union Theological Seminary (New York)	The Reverend Dr. John W. Bachman
1960	United Theological Seminary of the Twin Cities	The Reverend William Siemers
1893	Upsala College	The Reverend Dr. O. V. Anderson
1859	Valparaiso University	President O. P. Kretzmann
1883	Wagner College	The Reverend Dr. Joseph Sittler
1852	Wartburg College	President C. H. Becker
1854	Wartburg Seminary	President Alfred Ewald
1911	Waterloo Lutheran University	The Reverend Eric R. Weber

Appendix XII

REV. DR. KARL E. MATTSON

REV. DR. ARMIN G. WENG

Dr. Mattson

Dr. Karl E. Mattson had been the only president of Augustana Seminary in Rock Island, since the separation from the college took place in 1948. His sudden and unexpected death at the age of 59 on November 16, 1964, removed one of the influential figures in the negotiations which had brought about the merger and relocation plans. His significant contributions to theological education in the Lutheran Church were summarized in a tribute by President Herman:

> Dr. Karl Mattson's contribution to the steady improvement of pastoral education in our church and in our time was historic.
>
> From the date of its independence in 1948, he fostered the growth of the former Augustana Theological Seminary, and subsequently devoted himself just as vigorously to the shaping of a larger plan calling for the merger of four seminaries in the Lutheran School of Theology.
>
> Its constitution is primarily his handiwork. No one was more concerned with the need for higher standards in the preparation of Christian ministers.
>
> To this end, he dedicated himself with the utmost devotion of his enormous energy and splendid talents.
>
> A gaping hole has been torn in the fabric of our fellowship, but the memory of a noble spirit and a warm personal friend sustains us, who had the great privilege of working with him.[1]

Funeral services for Dr. Mattson were held in First Lutheran Church, Moline, Illinois, November 19, 1964. Dr. Herman and Dr. Malvin H. Lundeen, Secretary of LCA, gave expressions of gratitude from the seminary and the Church, and Dr. Arthur O. Arnold, who became successor to Dr. Mattson as Administrative Vice-President for the Rock Island campus, delivered the sermon.

By action of the Board of Directors of LSTC a *Karl E. Mattson Memorial Fund* was established, the earnings from which were designated for the provision of lectures by distinguished theologians and churchmen in the areas of ecumenics and the mission of the church, both special interests of Dr. Mattson.[2] In addition, the board unanimously passed the following resolution:

> In recognition of the able, vigorous, and dedicated service of Dr. Karl E. Mattson to the former Augustana Lutheran Church as President of the Augustana Theological Seminary, Rock Island, Illinois, from 1948 to September, 1962, when the Lutheran School of Theology came into being; his major contribution, as a member of the Inter-Seminary Committee, in the preparation of the Articles of Consolidation of the Lutheran School of Theology at Chicago; his cooperation with and service to the Interim Board and the Board of

[1]*The Illinois Lutheran*, December, 1964, p. 3.
[2]LSTC Board of Directors, *Minutes*, January 27-28, 1965, p. 80.

Directors of LSTC; and his leadership as Vice President of LSTC, Rock Island Campus

Be it Resolved, That we thank God for the life and ministry of Karl Mattson

And that we assure Mrs. Mattson and family of our continued concern and affection

And that this memorial be spread on the Minutes of the Board of Directors of LSTC.[3]

"His free-ranging imagination foresaw the Seminary we hope to have."[4]

Dr. Weng

Dr. Armin G. Weng's name had been associated with the Maywood campus for over thirty years—first as President of the Illinois Synod-ULCA, then as the school's Acting President 1941-42 and 1947-48, and finally as President 1948-62. When the merger occured in 1962, he was designated Administrative Vice-President of the Lutheran School of Theology at Chicago—Maywood Campus.

Under his leadership the seminary grew in enrollment from a low of nineteen students his first year, to a regular enrollment of over 100, in one decade. Likewise the faculty rolls were strengthened, buildings were renovated, the seminary brought under Church control, a new Library was built, a School of Missions added, and the Graduate Program enlarged. Though he had a deep loyalty to the seminary at Maywood, he was among the first to recognize that merger was a necessity in the light of the pending LCA merger, and composed the letter which precipitated the initial conversations leading to the new LSTC.[5]

Dr. Weng retired as Administrative Vice-President and Professor of Functional Theology on February 28, 1966, and the next day began a one year terminal furlough to compensate for the sabbatical leave he had not completed earlier because of administrative demands on the campus. Dr. Johannes Knudsen succeeded him as Administrative Vice-President for the final year on the Maywood campus. At the time of retirement Dr. Weng was granted the title of Administrative Vice-President Emeritus, and was "requested—in collaboration with the President—to continue such services as he may wish to render, especially in the area of relations between LSTC and the congregations of the supporting synods."[6] Honored affectionately at a farewell party at the time of retirement by faculty, administration, students, and board,[7] he also received the

[3]*Ibid.*, p. 69.
[4]*LSTC Epistle*, January, 1965, p. 2.
[5]*Supra*, p. 51.
[6]LSTC Board of Directors, *Minutes*, June 17, 1965, p. 1.
[7]The dinner was held February 18, 1966, in Oak Park. Papa Weng, as he was known to the students, was honored by several greetings and then presented a tape recorder and a volume of 240 personal letters.

official thanks of the Church in the following resolution adopted by the Board of Administration:

Whereas, The Reverend Doctor Armin George Weng has served as the Pastor of three congregations of the Church—First English Lutheran Church, Bridgeport, Connecticut, 1922-27; Immanuel Lutheran Church, Philadelphia, Pennsylvania, 1927-30; and Holy Trinity Lutheran Church, Elgin, Illinois, 1930-39; and

Whereas, He has guided the Illinois Synod, United Lutheran Church in America, as its President, 1937-48; and

Whereas, He has been both Acting President and President of the Chicago Lutheran Theological Seminary, Maywood, Illinois, 1941-42 and 1947-62; and

Whereas, He has served as Administrative Vice-President of the Lutheran School of Theology at Chicago—Maywood Campus, 1962-66; and

Whereas, He has given of his time and ability in dedicated service to the Church-at-large as Secretary, National Lutheran Council, 1941-45, 1948-51; Chairman, Student Service Division, National Lutheran Council, 1944-52; Secretary, Lutheran Service Commission, 1939-47; Board of Education, United Lutheran Church, 1940-48; Board of Publication, United Lutheran Church, 1948-60; Lutheran Service Commission, 1949-58; Bureau of Service to Military Personnel, 1949-58; and Board of Ministers Life and Casualty Union, Minneapolis, Minnesota, 1950 to the present (serving as Chairman of the Board, 1961 to the present); therefore,

Be it Resolved, That the Board of Directors, Lutheran School of Theology at Chicago,

(1) Commend Dr. Weng for his many years of faithful stewardship to his Lord and to his Church;

(2) Express heartfelt gratitude and appreciation to Dr. Weng for the devoted leadership he has given to Chicago Lutheran Theological Seminary and to the Lutheran School of Theology at Chicago—Maywood Campus; and

(3) Pray that Almighty God will richly bless Dr. Weng in his future years as he continues to present himself to God "as one approved, a workman who has no need to be ashamed, rightly handling the word of truth" (II Timothy 2:15).[8]

The veteran leader of theological education closed out his career by addressing the graduates of both campuses at the 1966 commencements.

A few months after the completion of his terminal furlough, Dr. Weng died suddenly at the age of 69 on August 29, 1967, just one month before the new campus opened for the first school year. At a simple funeral service, in

---

[8]LSTC Board of Directors, *Minutes*, April 24-26, 1966, pp. 119-20.

keeping with his preferences, in his home congregation, St. Luke's Evangelical Lutheran Church of Park Ridge, Illinois, on August 31, 1967, Dr. Weng's colleagues, former students, and many friends gathered to worship God and express gratitude for a life of service and devotion. Dr. Robert J. Marshall, President of the Illinois Synod, preached the sermon. The Board of Directors subsequently adopted the following resolution:

BE IT RESOLVED THAT, noting the death of the Rev. Armin George Weng, Ph.D., D.D., the Board of Directors of LSTC expresses its gratitude for his service to the school as parish pastor, as synod president, as president of Chicago Lutheran Theological Seminary and as vice president of the Maywood Campus of LSTC, particularly for his vision of a school marked by church control and academic excellence, for seeking a capable faculty, developing an administrative staff, supporting a creditable library, promoting building programs, encouraging students, favoring new programs of study, contributing to merger of seminaries and adapting to change. The board mourns the loss to his family and to the church, but rejoices in the Gospel promise that God provides for the departed in the church triumphant and for those who remain in the church militant.[9]

[9]*Ibid.*, October 11-12, 1967, p. 173.

Appendix XIII

1967-68 FACULTY ROSTER

Professors

Gothard Everett Arden
  Professor of Church History
    A.B., University of Denver; B.D., Augustana Theological Seminary;
    Ph.D., University of Chicago. Graduate Study: Uppsala University.

Arthur O. Arnold
  Professor of Functional Theology
  Dean of Students
    A.B., Gustavus Adolphus College; B.D., Augustana Theological
    Seminary; M.A., Northwestern University; D.D., Pacific Lutheran
    College. Graduate Study: University of Minnesota; University of
    Chicago.

Carl E. Braaten
  Professor of Systematic Theology
    A.B., St. Olaf College; B.Th., Luther Theological Seminary; Th.D.,
    Harvard University. Graduate Study: Fulbright Scholar at the
    University of Paris (Sorbonne); Kent Fellow of the National Council
    of Religion in Higher Education; Sinclair Kennedy Traveling Fellow
    at the University of Heidelberg.

Theodore Emanuel Conrad
  Professor of New Testament Language and Literature
  Director of Admissions, Registrar
    A.B., Gustavus Adolphus College; B.D., Augustana Theological
    Seminary; Ph.D., University of Chicago. Graduate Study: University
    of Minnesota; State University of Iowa.

Robert Harley Fischer
  Professor of Church History
    A.B., Gettysburg College; B.D., Lutheran Theological Seminary,
    Gettysburg; Ph.D., Yale University.

Donald C. Flatt
  Professor of Anthropology and Africa Studies in the School of Missions
    A.B., M.A., Oxford University (Honors); B.D., Augustana
    Theological Seminary. Graduate Study: Oxford University; Kennedy
    School of Missions; University of Chicago.

Axel C. Kildegaard
  Professor of Functional Theology

Director of Internship
    A.B., State University of Iowa; Cand. Theol., Grand View Seminary; S.T.M., Yale University.

Johannes Knudsen
    Professor of Church History and New Testament
    Dean of Graduate Studies
        Cand. Mag., University of Copenhagen; S.T.M., Ph.D., Hartford Seminary Foundation.

Walter J. Kukkonen
    Professor of Systematic Theology
        Study at Concordia Theological Seminary, Springfield; Suomi Theological Seminary. B.S., Northern Illinois University; B.D., S.T.M., S.T.D., Chicago Lutheran Theological Seminary. Graduate Study: University of Helsinki.

Wilhelm C. Linss
    Professor of New Testament
        B.D. (equiv.), Erlangen University; Th.D., Boston University School of Theology. Graduate Study: Muenster University.

Lowell Dale Lund
    Professor of Systematic Theology
    Dean of Faculty
        A.B., Gustavus Adolphus College; S.M., Augustana Theological Seminary; Ph.D., Drew University.

James A. Scherer
    Professor of Missions
    Dean of School of Missions
        A.B., Yale University; B.D., Union Theological Seminary, New York. Study at Chicago Lutheran Theological Seminary. Graduate Study: Union Theological Seminary; Columbia University; International Christian University, Japan; Oxford University; Ph. D., Union Theological Seminary.

Richard R. Syre
    Professor of Old Testament
        A.B., University of Vienna; S.T.B., New York Theological Seminary; S.T.M., Lutheran Theological Seminary, Gettysburg. Graduate Study: Princeton Theological Seminary. Ph.D., University of Nebraska; Litt.D., Midland Lutheran College.

Arthur Vööbus
    Professor of New Testament and Church History
        Cand. Theol., Mag. Theol., Dr. Theol., University of Tartu, Estonia.

Associate Professors

Wesley J. Fuerst
>Associate Professor of Old Testament
>>A.B., Midland Lutheran College; B.D., Central Lutheran Theological Seminary. Graduate Study: Erlangen University. Th.D., Princeton Theological Seminary.

David M. Granskou
>Associate Professor of New Testament
>>A.B., St. Olaf College; B.D., Luther Theological Seminary; Th.D., Princeton University.

George F. Hall
>Associate Professor of Biblical Theology in the School of Missions
>>A.B., Augustana College; B.D., Augustana Theological Seminary; Ph.D., University of Chicago. Graduate Study: Union Theological Seminary; Columbia University; University of Minnesota.

Philip James Hefner
>Associate Professor of Systematic Theology
>>A.B., Midland Lutheran College. Graduate Study: Fulbright Scholar at the University of Tuebingen. B.D., Chicago Lutheran Theological Seminary; M.A., Ph.D., University of Chicago.

Horace Hummel
>Associate Professor of Old Testament
>>A.B., B.D., S.T.M., Concordia Theological Seminary, St. Louis; Ph.D., Johns Hopkins University. Graduate Study: University of Heidelberg; Archeological Expedition, Shechem, Jordan; Hebrew University and the Hebrew Union College, Jerusalem.

David Lloyd Lindberg
>Associate Professor of Missions and World Religions
>>A.B., Gustavus Adolphus College; B.D., Augustana Theological Seminary. Graduate Study: University of Chicago.

Morris James Niedenthal
>Associate Professor of Functional Theology
>>B.D., Northwestern University; B.D., Chicago Lutheran Theological Seminary. Graduate Study: Fulbright Scholar at Manchester University, England; Ph.D., Union Theological Seminary.

Nels Leroy Norquist
>Associate Professor of New Testament

A.B., Augustana College; B.D., Augustana Theological Seminary; S.T.M., Wittenberg University; Ph.D., Hartford Seminary Foundation.

Franklin Eugene Sherman
Associate Professor of Christian Ethics
A.B., Muhlenberg College; B.D., Chicago Lutheran Theological Seminary; M.A., Oxford University; A.M., Ph.D., University of Chicago.

Paul Reginald Swanson
Associate Professor of Pastoral Care
A.B., Augustana College; B.D., Augustana Theological Seminary; S.T.M., Andover Newton Theological School; Ph.D., Boston University.

Theodore Norman Swanson
Associate Professor of Old Testament
A.B., Augustana College; B.D., Augustana Theological Seminary; S.T.M., Andover Newton Theological School. Graduate Study: University of Chicago.

Robert Ira Tobias
Associate Professor of Ecumenics
Director of Continuing Education
A.B., Phillips University; M.A., Graduate School of Theology, Phillips University; B.D., Union Theological Seminary; Th.D., University of Geneva and Graduate School of Ecumenical Studies.

Assistant Professors

John Arthur
Assistant Professor of Liturgics
Chaplain
A.B., B.Mus., Gustavus Adolphus College. Study at Wartburg Theological Seminary. B.D., Augustana Theological Seminary; M.Th., Western Theological Seminary. Study at Pacific Lutheran Theological Seminary; Stanford University.

Robert Benne
Assistant Professor of Church and Society
A.B., Midland Lutheran College; M.A., University of Chicago. Graduate Study: Erlangen University. University of Chicago.

Ralph Walter Holmin
Assistant Professor of Religious Education
A.B., Upsala College; B.D., Augustana Theological Seminary. Study at Union Theological Seminary. M.A., Columbia University. Graduate Study: New York University.

Instructors

Harold J. Hinrichs
Instructor in Pastoral Care
A.B., Wartburg College; B.D., Wartburg Theological Seminary; S.T.M., Andover Newton Theological School.

Daniel H. Sandstedt
Instructor in Pastoral Care
A.B., Gustavus Adolphus College; B.D., Augustana Theological Seminary. Graduate Study: University of Chicago.

Allen W. Townsend
Visiting Lecturer in Speech
A.B., St. Olaf College; Diploma, McCormick Theological Seminary. Graduate Study: Northwestern Seminary.

Director of Library

Joel Waldemar Lundeen
Director of Library
A.B., Augustana College; B.D., Augustana Theological Seminary. M.A., University of Chicago.

Emeriti
(Dates indicate years of service at the Lutheran School of Theology at Chicago and its predecessor institutions.)

Henry Grady Davis, B.D., D.D., 1937-1966
Professor of Functional Theology

Gerhard Gieschen, B.D., D.D., 1953-67
Acting President of Central Lutheran Theological Seminary, Professor of Systematic Theology

Hjalmar Wilhelm Johnson, B.D., Ph.D., 1944-64
Professor of History and Philosophy of Religion

E. Bryan Keisler, B.D., A.M., S.T.M., S.T.D., D.D., 1947-64
  President of Central Lutheran Theological Seminary, Professor of Practical Theology

Alvin Daniel Mattson, B.D., S.T.M., S.T.D., 1931-1964
  Professor of Christian Ethics and Sociology

Thomas D. Rinde, B.D.,D.D., 1934-1964
  Dean of Central Lutheran Theological Seminary, Professor of Historical Theology

Eric Herbert Wahlstrom, B.D., D.D., Th.D., 1931-1961
  Professor of New Testament Language and Literature